A HISTORY OF THE SISTERHOOD OF THE HOLY NATIVITY

A History of the Sisterhood of the Holy Nativity

Advancing the Anglo-Catholic Movement in the Episcopal Church

SHERYL A. KUJAWA-HOLBROOK

Foreword by Matthew Gunter

☙PICKWICK *Publications* · Eugene, Oregon

A HISTORY OF THE SISTERHOOD OF THE HOLY NATIVITY
Advancing the Anglo-Catholic Movement in the Episcopal Church

Copyright © 2024 Sheryl A. Kujawa-Holbrook. All rights reserved. Except for brief quotations in critical publications or reviews, no part of this book may be reproduced in any manner without prior written permission from the publisher. Write: Permissions, Wipf and Stock Publishers, 199 W. 8th Ave., Suite 3, Eugene, OR 97401.

Pickwick Publications
An Imprint of Wipf and Stock Publishers
199 W. 8th Ave., Suite 3
Eugene, OR 97401

www.wipfandstock.com

PAPERBACK ISBN: 979-8-3852-0536-3
HARDCOVER ISBN: 979-8-3852-0537-0
EBOOK ISBN: 979-8-3852-0538-7

Cataloguing-in-Publication data:

Names: Kujawa-Holbrook, Sheryl A., author. | Gunter, Matthew, foreword.

Title: A history of the sisterhood of the holy nativity : advancing the anglo-catholic movement in the episcopal church / Sheryl A. Kujawa-Holbrook ; foreword by Matthew Gunter.

Description: Eugene, OR : Pickwick Publications, 2024 | Includes bibliographical references.

Identifiers: ISBN 979-8-3852-0536-3 (paperback) | ISBN 979-8-3852-0537-0 (hardcover) | ISBN 979-8-3852-0538-7 (ebook)

Subjects: LCSH: Episcopal Church—History. | Episcopal Church—Parties and movements. | Anglo-Catholicism.

Classification: BX5917.C8 .K85 2024 (paperback) | BX5917.C8 .K85 (ebook)

12/30/24

For the Sisterhood of the Holy Nativity (SHN)

"To make known the Faith and to win souls for Christ."
Constitutions and Rule of the Sisters of the Holy Nativity,
Whitsunday, 1889

Contents

List of Illustrations | ix

Foreword by Matthew Gunter | xi

Acknowledgements | xiii

Introduction | 1

1 A Hidden Way of Holiness | 16

2 Rest and Devotion in Bethlehem | 43

3 Advancing the Catholic Faith in Wisconsin—Serving with Indigenous Peoples | 77

4 Missionary Spirit | 108

5 Soul Work | 138

6 Navigating Change—Hoping for Renewal | 165

Appendix A: The Sisterhood of the Holy Nativity (SHN)—Life Professed Sisters | 191

Appendix B: Convents, Mission Houses, and Retreat Houses—Sisterhood of the Holy Nativity | 211

Appendix C: Significant Dates in the History of the Sisterhood of the Holy Nativity (SHN) | 213

Appendix D: Interviews for this Book | 221

Appendix E: Illustrations | 224

Bibliography | 245

About the Author | 264

List of Illustrations

1. Charles Chapman Grafton (1830–1912), "Father Founder" | 224
2. Mother Ruth Margaret, SHN (1826–1910), "Mother Foundress," Superior 1884–1908 | 225
3. Cornerstone, Convent of the Holy Nativity, Fond du Lac | 225
4. The Heart of Christmas— Christmas Altar, Convent of the Holy Nativity, Fond du Lac | 226
5. Music Class. Hobart Mission Day School, Oneida | 226
6. Oneida Lace-Makers | 227
7. Mother Katherine Edith, SHN, Superior 1908–1919 | 227
8. Mother Matilda, SHN, Superior 1919–1942 | 228
9. Novitiate Class | 228
10. Sister Sylvia, SHN, in the Margaret Peabody Lending Library | 229
11. Recorder Class | 229
12. Sewing Wimples | 230
13. The Altar Bread Department | 230
14. The Embroidery Department | 231
15. Sample Embroidery—Lamb of God (Agnus Dei) | 231
16. The Picture Department | 232
17. The Sacristy | 232
18. The Divine Office | 233
19. Intercessory Prayer | 233
20. Sister of Holy Nativity Participates in a Baptism, the Church of St. Mary the Virgin | 234

LIST OF ILLUSTRATIONS

21. Mother Ruth Mary, SHN, Superior 1942–1961 | 234
22. Mother Alicia Theresa, SHN, Superior 1961–1972 | 235
23. Garden in Baltimore | 235
24. Sisters at Recreation | 236
25. Sisters in the Garden, Holy Nativity Retreat Center, Bay Shore, Long Island | 237
26. On Retreat | 237
27. Mother Boniface, SHN, Superior 1973–1996, 2007–2011 | 237
28. St. Matthias Church School, Los Angeles | 238
29. Sister Paula, SHN, Recognized by the Diocese of Los Angeles | 238
30. Nursey School Worship, All Saints Episcopal School, San Diego | 239
31. Christmas at Bethlehem Chapel, Santa Barbara | 239
32. Sister Julia Elizabeth, SHN, and the Morris Award Winner —Best Household Pet | 240
33. Centenary Celebration 1982 | 240
34. Mother Maria, SHN, Superior 1996–2007 | 241
35. Sister Ruth Angela's 100th Birthday Celebration | 241
36. August 2007 Grafton Commemoration, Bethlehem-by-the-Lake | 242
37. Sister Abigail, SHN, Life Profession, Mother Superior 2012–2023 | 242
38. Sister Charis and Saint, St. Peter's, Ripon | 243

Foreword

I AM GRATEFUL TO Sheryl Kujawa-Holbrook for writing this history of the Sisterhood of the Holy Nativity. For over 100 years, the Sisters of the Holy Nativity have been integral in the Diocese of Fond du Lac in northeast Wisconsin and active across the United States from Providence, Rhode Island, to Santa Barbara, California. The sisters cultivate personal sanctification and a missionary spirit grounded in the monastic rhythm of prayer and worship, solitude and community, enclosure and mission. Committed primarily to teaching, they served as teachers, Sunday School teachers, retreat leaders, summer camp counselors, etc. More than that, their presence has been a sacramental reminder that all Christians are called to deny themselves, take up the cross, and follow Jesus in self-sacrificial love. Dedicated to a life set apart from this world's usual commitments and distractions, they have been a reminder that we are all called to a degree of detachment and attention to eternal things.

This is good to remember. All things in this world are transitory. That includes our lives. It includes institutions of the Church. It sometimes includes religious communities. And so, it is with the Sisterhood of the Holy Nativity which has been moving toward the final chapter of its rich history. You now hold an account of that history in your hands. May it be a reminder of the eternal things to which the sisters dedicated themselves. The order might come to a close, but the faithful witness of the Sisterhood endures. In God's economy, nothing is finally lost. The lives of the sisters, past and present, are held in the loving gaze of God.

Charles Grafton (1830–1912), the co-founder of the Sisterhood of the Holy Nativity and 2nd Bishop of the Episcopal Diocese of Fond du Lac wrote a handbook of *Meditations and Instructions* given to each member of the order. In it, he wrote this, which one hopes each sister took to heart and which we might also hold in ours,

Rest in the smile of Jesus, be detached from self, even from your own growth in grace. Don't be worried if you are not getting on; try, but do not worry. It hinders His work, be patient, leave self to God, and pray Him to make you what He would have you to be. He has His plan for each soul, and so, we can have no plan of saintliness: be willing to be like one of the 'queer things' in the medley among beautiful pictures and statues, one of His odd works of grace, different, singular, peculiar, hard to make, but having its own place in the owner's heart.

The Rt Rev. Matthew Gunter
VIII Bishop of Fond du Lac
Feast of the Presentation 2024

Acknowledgments

THIS BOOK RESULTS FROM the legacy of love surrounding the Sisterhood of the Holy Nativity. Learning about the sisterhood by engaging their many friends around the Church has been a joy. Thanks, too, to Sister Abigail, SHN, and Sister Charis, SHN, who agreed that the story of their community should be shared, and Matthew Gunter, bishop of the Diocese of Fond du Lac, and the many friends of the sisterhood who supported the project.

Historians will understand that three years is not such a long time for a book originating from primary sources. The project's success owes a great deal to the behind-the-scenes organization accomplished by Matthew Payne, the archivist and historiographer of the Episcopal Diocese of Fond du Lac. Matthew's work organizing the sources, assisted by Lisa Baltes and Emily Gilbert, was indispensable to this researcher's access and progress, as was his knowledge of diocesan and Wisconsin Episcopal history. Matthew and Maggie Payne also provided lavish hospitality during my trips to Appleton for research. The research for this book was further enhanced through the efforts of earlier historians who worked on portions of the history of the Sisterhood of the Holy Nativity, including Kathleen Reeves, the late Steven Peay, and the late Sister Julia Elizabeth, SHN. The staff of the Frances Donaldson Library, Nashotah House, David Sherwood, Bramwell Richards, and Carolina Johnson were incredibly generous with their time and resources. Richard Mammana, the founder of Project Canterbury, resident of Philadelphia, and discoverer of many sources related to Episcopal sisterhoods, graciously answered my queries and sent sources I did not know I needed until they arrived in my inbox! Lynn Biese-Carroll and John Magerus of the DeKoven Center and Archives in Racine provided warm hospitality and stimulating conversations on the importance of documenting Episcopal sisterhoods. The Sisterhood of the Holy Nativity Collection has found a safe and responsive home there.

ACKNOWLEDGMENTS

The history of the Sisterhood of Holy Nativity is connected to the history of other religious orders, many of whom took the time to consult their archives and share their stories and perspectives. Thanks to Sister Adele Marie, SSM, Mother Miriam, CSM, Sister Ellen Stephen, OSH, Brother Robert Leo Sevensky, OHC, Brother James Koester, SSJE, Brother Todd Blackman, SSJE, Sister Ana Clara, OSA, Sister Barbara Jean, AF, Sister Julian Wilson, AF, Brother Samuel Timothy, AF, Brother Scott Borden, OHC, Sister Greta Ronningen, CDL, Sister Madeline Mary, CSM, Sister Monica Clare, CSBJ, Sister Pamela, CSJB, Sister Elizabeth Rolfe-Thomas, SSJD, Sister Constance Joanna Geffert, SSJD, Sister Elizabeth Ann Eckert, SSJD, and Father David Brinton, OGS (CAROA).

Of course, religious history involves making many connections, and the research for this book was deepened by the network of Episcopal archivists, administrators, clergy, and SHN Associates and friends who graciously shared their archives, stories, photographs, and artifacts. (In alphabetical order.) Keith Ackerman, John Alexander, Patty Allen, Paul Aparicio, Mollie Bailey, Valerie Bailey, David Baumann, Bill Bippus, Norman and Zulette Catir, Regina Christianson, Jamie Coats, Michael Corrigan, Rebecca Dinovo, Elizabeth Estey, Stephen Gerth, Anthony Guillén, Frank Tracy Griswold, Lada Hardwick, Dorsey Henderson, Barbara Henry, Jane Herbst, Anna Jacqua, Russ and Jerrie Jacobus, Michael Kaehr, Wayne Kempton, John King, Mary Klein, Marianna Garthwaite Klaiman, David Klutterman, Carol Knox, Nancy Kuhn, Donald Langlois, Louise Lawson, Jeffrey Lee, Anita van Leeuwen, Carol Maddux, Max Manuel, Jeffrey Mello, Ted McConnell, Mary Ann Mello, Andrew Nardone, Daphne Noyes, Todd Ousley, Rodger Patience, Ezgi Saribay Perkins, Phoebe Pettingell, Carol Hanson Pollnac, Neff and Dorothy Powell, Will Quekett, Bill Radant, Sue von Rautenkrantz, Mary Robison, Susan Ross, Jolene Rueden Schatzinger, Karl Schaffenburg, Lynn Shaw, Steve Sims, Ed Smith, Alistair So-Schoos, Richard Valantasis, Anna Wager, Edgar Wallace, Michele Whitford, Keith and Suzanne Whitmore, Kathy Whitt, Bob Williams, Clare Woodbridge. In addition, the many friends and colleagues of the sisterhood who consented to interviews gave me a rich background on the sisters beyond the printed sources. Most of the sisters and Bishop Grafton live now in God's embrace. Still, the love that never dies remains, and I feel that through the generosity of their friends, I got to know and love them, too. Special thanks to the *Anglican Digest* and *The Historiographer* for publicizing the book project and my query for sources. Megan Anderson's copy-editing skills were instrumental in improving the manuscript.

I undertook this research to tell the story of a sisterhood that gave so much to the Church and to inspire further research on the history of

Anglican and Episcopal religious orders. My love of God and neighbors has been expanded through learning about the courageous and dedicated Sisterhood of the Holy Nativity and sharing their joys and frustrations. Their consecrated lives and compassionate presence have contributed to the spiritual legacy of the Episcopal Church and responded to the most profound human needs. It has been an honor to serve them and to make this portion of their story known.

The Rev. Dr. Sheryl A. Kujawa-Holbrook, EdD, PhD
Feast of the Presentation 2024

Introduction

THE SISTERHOOD OF THE HOLY NATIVITY (SHN) was founded in 1882 during the catholic revival of sisterhoods within Anglicanism. The renewal of the religious life for women in Anglicanism is considered one of the most significant achievements of the nineteenth-century catholic revival, also known as the Oxford Movement.[1] The first formal Anglican sisterhoods for women since the sixteenth century were founded in the mid-nineteenth century by Tractarian clergymen and included women associated with these clergy and the Oxford Movement.[2] The richness of the Anglo-Catholicism

  1. Herringer, "The Revival of the Religious Life," 387–88. The standard abbreviation for the Sisterhood of the Holy Nativity, SHN, is used throughout this book.
  2. "Tractarian" refers to clergymen in sympathy with the Tractarian Movement of the 1830s, also known as the Oxford Movement. The movement began when three clergymen of the Church of England, Edward Bouverie Pusey, John Henry Newman, and John Keble. The three, along with others, authored the *Tracts for the Times*, which called upon the Church of England to return to the ancient church in doctrine, devotional practices, and sacramental life. The writers of the tracts and their supporters became known as Tractarians. Some vehemently attacked them as papists, but they also found support as the movement became a force in the Church of England. The Oxford Movement had supporters in the Episcopal Church. Tractarian parishes were founded throughout the United States, particularly in the Midwest. A second generation of clergy was known as the Ritualists. While the early Oxford Movement emphasized the recovery of catholic doctrine and practice, the second generation advocated enriching ceremonial in public worship. It brought a sacramental social vision to impoverished urban areas. The term "Anglo-Catholic" is a fusion of these first two movements. (There was a third movement, catholic socialism, that originated in England in the 1870s with Stuart Headlam (1847–1924.) The Tractarians and the Ritualists brought renewal and controversy to the Church of England and the Episcopal Church. The term "High Church" is also used, at times incorrectly, related to the Oxford Movement. The high church tradition preceded the Oxford Movement and began in the seventeenth century in opposition to the Puritan wing of the Church of England. In the Episcopal Church, the high church party began in Connecticut; after the American Revolution, high church leadership was centered in John Henry Hobart (1775–1830). The high church movement was not concerned with ritual or ceremonial, as were the later Tractarians and Ritualists. Instead, the high church movement stressed the importance of

that birthed the Sisterhood of the Holy Nativity and other sisterhoods emphasized eucharistic worship, sacramental confession, and personal holiness. The theological vision of the tradition stressed the spiritual roots of ancient Christianity in conversation with the needs of contemporary society. Anglo-Catholic theology emphasized the Church as the Body of Christ and the Eucharist as the symbol of the sacramental transformation of the world. At the center of Anglo-Catholic spirituality was the doctrine of the Incarnation, "the Word became flesh,"[3] which supported the movement in humanitarian service. Just as Jesus Christ became human, so was the image of God revealed in all people and, by extension, the material world. The Anglo-Catholic social vision that infused the founders of the Sisterhood of the Holy Nativity held an optimistic view of human potential and the power of grace to transcend human limitations. In many places, the Anglo-Catholic Movement interrupted the association of Anglicans with the establishment, instead developing a closer affinity with working people and the poor, particularly in urban areas. The transformation of the Church at the parish level was critical to the Anglo-Catholic social vision, wherein the liturgy was a foretaste of the Kingdom of God. Like other leaders in the Anglo-Catholic Movement, the founders of the Sisterhood of the Holy Nativity realized that for their social vision to succeed, they needed the local church as a contextual base to address the people's spiritual and material struggles.[4]

Convents were an accepted part of the religious landscape in medieval Britain and Ireland. Many flourished until the Dissolution of the monasteries by Henry VIII between 1536 and 1541. For the next three hundred years, Anglican women did not have the option of living a vowed religious life unless they joined Roman Catholic sisterhoods on the Continent, despite the traces of the monastic life that remained within the English tradition.[5] Societal and spiritual trends supported the revival of Anglican sisterhoods in the nineteenth century. The need for devout unmarried women to find socially acceptable ways to channel their energies into charity and service, combined with growing societal concerns regarding the plight of the poor, provided the context. The Victorian tendency to establish benevolent organizations laid the groundwork for communal responses to social problems. Spiritually, the emphasis of the catholic revival on the importance of prayer

---

the apostolic succession, the threefold order of ministry as found in the New Testament—bishops, priests, and deacons, the sacraments of Baptism and Eucharist, and adherence to the *Book of Common Prayer*.

3. John 1:14.

4. Leech, "The Radical Anglo-Catholic Social Vision," 3–5, 8, 10; Interview, Frank Tracy Griswold, February 24, 2022.

5. Allchin, *The Silent Rebellion*, 15–35.

and the sacraments inspired lay people to aspire to greater holiness. The simplified version of the Divine Office preserved in the *Book of Common Prayer* after the Reformation, along with a growing tradition of choral worship, supported the ideal of monastic prayer as a part of daily life in Anglicanism and thus easily adapted to the formation of new religious communities.[6]

Influential seventeenth-century churchmen such as Matthew Parker (1505–1575), Lancelot Andrews (1555–1626), and Jeremy Taylor (1613–1667) valued celibacy.[7] They emphasized the advantages of virginity for those who wished to cultivate their spirituality and live consecrated lives, though these beliefs were controversial. Pious Anglican households in the seventeenth and eighteenth centuries, such as Kings Cliffe in Northamptonshire, directed by William Law (1686–1761), or Ledston in North Yorkshire, founded by Elizabeth Hastings (1707–1791), were centers for philanthropy and women's education that continued monastic values past the Dissolution. The disciplined spiritual practice cultivated at Little Gidding (1626–1657) by the Ferrar family in the seventeenth century is often cited as an example of the continuity of the religious life in England between the Reformation and the Oxford Movement.[8] By the beginning of the eighteenth century, educational models such as Mary Astell's (1666–1731) "Protestant Nunnery" were advocated by women intellectuals, emphasizing the need for environments where women could be free from the gendered expectations of society to cultivate their gifts fully.[9]

By the 1840s, over one hundred Anglican sisterhoods were established; some early experiments closed or were absorbed into other religious communities. The interest in Anglican sisterhoods grew in popularity on both sides of the Atlantic by the 1880s. By 1900, there were several thousand sisters and an estimated sixty sisterhoods in the Church of England alone. Between 1845 and 1900, approximately 10,000 women tried their vocations in an Anglican sisterhood.[10] The revival of Anglican sisterhoods in England and the United States was part of an expansive revival of European women's religious communities, resulting in new Roman Catholic orders in France,

---

6. Herringer, "The Revival of the Religious Life," 387; Anson, *The Call of the Cloister*, 3.

7. Allchin, *The Silent Rebellion*, 26–28; Herringer, "The Revival of the Religious Life," 387.

8. Allchin, *The Silent Rebellion*, 18–25.

9. Allchin, *The Silent Rebellion*, 26–28; Herringer, "The Revival of the Religious Life," 387.

10. Herringer, "The Revival of the Religious Life," 388.

Belgium, and Ireland. Many of these new Roman Catholic communities founded sister houses in the United States and England after 1829.[11]

THE FIRST ANGLICAN SISTERHOODS

Considered "un-Anglican" by more Protestant church members on both sides of the Atlantic, sisterhoods, through lives of prayer and sacrificial service, sought to be agents "of bringing the world into the realm of God."[12] A spiritually attractive option to many women and innovative in their work, Anglican sisterhoods were considered controversial on several accounts. Religiously, they were controversial due to their association with Roman Catholic practice. Culturally, they were controversial because they expanded the parameters of acceptable gender roles for women beyond the traditional home and family. Some clergy were suspicious of women living in all-female spaces devoid of paternal authority.[13] One scholar argues that sisterhoods "appeared chimerical to British Protestant culture and Victorian gender ideology which idealized home and family as the heart of woman's mission."[14] Rather than focusing their mission on traditional women's roles in the home and family, the first Anglican sisterhoods embraced the same values of self-sacrifice and spiritual devotion through a monastic model and broader philanthropic works such as nursing, the care of orphans, teaching, and service to the poor.

The first Anglican sisterhood, the Sisterhood of the Holy Cross, was founded in 1845 in London by Jane Ellacombe, Mary Bruce, and Sarah Anne Terrot, with Edward Bouverie Pusey (1800–1882), a leading figure of the Oxford Movement, along with other Tractarian clergymen. By 1841, Pusey had already received the private vows of Marian Hughes, who otherwise could not join a sisterhood because of family obligations. Pusey's daughter Lucy was also keen to join a sisterhood.[15] The Puseys researched existing sisterhoods; Lucy visited Roman Catholic convents in France, and Edward visited convents in Ireland.[16]

11. Herringer, "The Revival of the Religious Life," 388.

12. Kujawa-Holbrook, "Conclusions," 279; Ellen Stephen, "Apart and Together," 13–25.

13. Anderson-Faithful and Holloway, *Women and the Anglican Church Congress 1861–1938*, 186.

14. Eleanor Joy Frith, "Pseudonuns," ii; Anson, *The Call of the Cloister*, 1–27.

15. Herringer, "The Revival of the Religious Life," 389. Hughes founded the Society of the Holy and Undivided Trinity in Oxford when her family circumstances changed in 1849.

16. Herringer, "The Revival of the Religious Life," 389

Other leading figures of the Oxford Movement, such as John Keble (1792–1866) and John Henry Newman (1801–1890), also supported religious orders for women and men within Anglicanism. Clergy associated with the Oxford Movement believed the Church of England had abandoned its historical catholic and apostolic heritage. They emphasized the need to reclaim Anglicanism as part of the one, holy, catholic, and apostolic church before the Reformation. The term "Anglo-Catholic" was first used by some leaders of the Oxford Movement to denote the historical continuity of Anglicanism with catholic Christianity. Though the conversion of John Henry Newman and other prominent clergy to Roman Catholicism brought a crisis, the Oxford Movement continued in Anglicanism due to the work of Pusey, Keble, and a second generation of priests who worked among the urban poor, known as the Ritualists. In addition to the revival of religious orders within Anglicanism, the influence of the Oxford Movement brought a renewed emphasis on the sacraments, particularly the centrality of the Eucharist and the apostolic succession, as well as a recovery of ancient doctrine, ceremonial, and devotional practices.[17]

The first Anglican sisterhood, the Sisterhood of the Holy Cross, courageously nursed immigrants from Ireland during the famine, as well as soldiers during the Crimean War. However, the internal dynamics of the sisterhood suffered due to inexperience in religious life among the sisters and the clergy who supported them. Under Pusey's guidance, some of the sisters practiced asceticism to such a degree that they were left unable to work. Some sisters and their spiritual directors converted to Roman Catholicism. While nursing in Crimea, the sisterhood was placed under the leadership of Priscilla Lydia Sellon (1821–1876), who created the Congregation of the Religious of the Society of the Most Holy Trinity. Sellon eventually formed three separate sisterhoods. In addition to sisters who worked among the poor, she founded a contemplative community and a sisterhood that started a school in Hawaii. Pusey considered Sellon "the restorer, after three centuries, of the Religious Life in England."[18] Cited as the most controversial of the early founders of Anglican Sisterhoods, Sellon had vision and administrative skills. She was also considered self-righteous and domineering.[19] However, given that religious authority was the bastion of male clergy, it would have been unlikely for Sellon to accomplish what she did without

17. Gilley, "Keble, Froude, Newman, and Pusey," in Brown, Nockles, Pereiro, *The Oxford Handbook of the Oxford Movement*, 82, 97–110.

18. Anson, *Call of the Cloister*, 259–260; Reeves, "Hidden in Christ," n.d., The Sisterhood of the Holy Nativity Collection, hereafter, SHNC, 7; The names of Sellon's sisterhoods vary, see Williams, "The Beginnings of Anglican Sisterhoods," 353–55.

19. Herringer, "The Revival of the Religious Life," 390–92.

much persistence, a strong personality, and a deep commitment to the importance of sisterhoods.

Another early Anglican sisterhood was founded by clergy widow Harriet Monsell (1811–1833) and Thomas Thellusson Carter (1808–1901), rector of Clewer in England. Their work among abused and destitute women was started in 1849 by another clergy widow, Mariquita Tennant, who was unable to attract additional helpers. By 1852, Mother Harriet was professed as the first superior of the Community of St John Baptist by Samuel Wilberforce (1805–1873), bishop of Oxford. With the support of Wilberforce and relatively free of controversy, the order continued its work, training impoverished women to work as servants. The Community of St. John Baptist flourished, eventually establishing houses throughout England, the United States, and India. By 1884, the Community of St John Baptist numbered over two hundred sisters; by 1900, there were three hundred sisters at Clewer alone.[20]

An early Anglican sisterhood with deep connections to the Sisterhood of the Holy Nativity was the Society of St. Margaret, East Grinstead. Founded by Ritualist priest John Mason Neale (1818–1866), the first sisters provided nursing care to the rural poor in their homes. At the time, nursing was considered an occupation only for those women "who were too old, too weak, too drunken, too dirty, too stolid, or too bad to do anything else."[21] In 1850, there was a dire need for skilled nurses in the rural deanery Neale served, and he believed that trained single women were valuable as nurses. Most women became familiar with the rudiments of nursing by caring for family members at home. Given his prominence as a clergyman, Neale was approached by three women interested in exploring religious vocations. He visited the sisterhood at Clewer and obtained funding from his associates. Soon after Britain entered the Crimean War in 1854, public opinion shifted regarding accepting nursing as a socially acceptable profession for women. Under Neale's guidance, the first sisters entered Sackville College Almshouse to begin formation and nursing training.[22]

Officially founded in 1855, the Society of St. Margaret proliferated during its first two decades. In addition to nursing, the sisters worked in orphanages and conducted parish visits. They received medical training at Westminster Hospital (later known as the Children's Hospital at Great Ormond Street in London), and Neale took great care to support the sisters'

---

20. Bonham, *A Place in Life*, 93–96, 117, 133; Anson, *The Call of the Cloister*, 313–316; Herringer, "The Revival of the Religious Life," 292.

21. Ferry, *The Old Convent*, 23.

22. Ferry, *The Old Convent*, 23–25.

spiritual formation. Neale preached three weekly sermons for the sisters and encouraged their scripture and doctrine study. He believed sisters needed to be theologically literate to provide spiritual guidance in nursing care. He also introduced catholic liturgical practices to the sisterhood. In 1856, the Society of St. Margaret was the first religious community in the Church of England to have a daily celebration of the Eucharist, and a year later, they were likely the first to practice the Reservation of the Blessed Sacrament. Though the ability to make the sacrament readily available to the sick and the dying was the rationale behind the Reservation of the Blessed Sacrament, anti-catholic fervor was such that the practice was kept secret from those outside the sisterhood.[23]

Neale aspired to establish a missionary sisterhood open to the world. The Society of St. Margaret eventually expanded to London, throughout Britain, to North America, Ceylon, and South Africa. His experience with the sisters at Clewer reinforced Neale's belief that selecting the right woman as the first superior was critical. Mother Ann, born Sarah Ann Gream (1808–1881), was the daughter and sister of clergymen and nursed her father during his final illness. Mother Ann chose the patronal saint for the sisterhood, St. Margaret of Antioch, one of the most venerated medieval saints. Mother Ann's sister became Mother Katherine of the Community of St. Mary's in Brighton in 1858.[24] After establishing houses in Aberdeen and London, the Society of St. Margaret was invited in 1871 by Charles Chapman Grafton to take charge of the Children's Hospital in Boston, and it was through this connection that the Sisterhood of the Holy Nativity was founded in 1882.[25]

In addition to these early Anglican sisterhoods, additional communities were founded in Tractarian parishes throughout the 1850s, mainly focused on nursing, education, parish visiting, orphanages, and work with impoverished women. Although half of the early sisterhoods worked with destitute women, orders founded after 1870 were more likely to focus on the poor and children. By 1860, approximately one hundred women were living in fourteen different sisterhoods. The number of Anglican sisterhoods expanded rapidly over the next generation; by 1890, several thousand sisters were living in fifty-four different sisterhoods.[26]

Because few sources reveal personal data about individual members of Anglican sisterhoods — except for the founders— we have limited

---

23. Sister Catherine Louise, SSM, *The Planting of the Lord*, 9.
24. Ferry, *The Old Convent*, 25, 29.
25. Sister Catherine Louise, SSM, *The Planting of the Lord*, 18–19.
26. Herringer, "The Revival of the Religious Life," 393.

information regarding the demographics and motivations of these early pioneers in religious life. What is known, though, is that nineteenth-century women's religious vocations were motivated by both spiritual and practical concerns. For some women, the desire to have meaningful work and to remain single or widowed combined with their spiritual motivations. Many women were from the middle classes and lived in market towns or rural areas. Some sisterhoods divided orders by social class; those of higher social status were choir sisters, while women from working-class backgrounds became lay sisters. Across Anglican sisterhoods, most of the leadership roles went to women with higher family status.[27] Approximately half the women who entered the novitiate left before taking vows; those who lasted through their novitiate had a greater chance of remaining in the sisterhood for life.[28]

Though initially ridiculed by the secular press, Anglican sisterhoods gained respect after the early decades through their courageous work and the depth of their devotion. Many bishops in the Church of England were initially suspicious of sisterhoods due to their limited formal governance structures and because their existence challenged traditional gender roles and marriage and family values. Though the sisterhoods eventually proved otherwise, some churchmen did not believe that women had the administrative capacity to manage their affairs. Even otherwise sympathetic bishops objected to taking life vows— a deep desire for many sisters— due to the Roman Catholic overtones of the practice. Women attracted to sisterhoods did not experience the vowed life as restrictive but as the most complete spiritual commitment possible while utilizing their skills in meaningful work. However, the taking of vows presented bishops with theological and political complications. If women were allowed to take vows privately, they would not be under the authority of bishops. But if religious vows were considered like marriage vows, indissoluble, then canons would need to be developed to govern them. Thus, taking vows was a significant church issue beyond individual religious communities.[29]

By the 1870s and through the 1880s, the relationship between sisterhoods and the episcopacy improved as bishops acknowledged the value of sisterhoods in their dioceses and even began to form local religious orders. The taking of vows was granted in the Church of England in 1891. In 1897, the Lambeth Congress approved the revival of Anglican sisterhoods and

---

27. Bonham, *A Place in Life*, 124–28; Herringer, "The Revival of the Religious Life," 393; Mumm, *Stolen Daughters, Virgin Mothers*, 13–16, 40.

28. Mumm, *Stolen Daughters, Virgin Mothers*, 28–29.

29. Dunstan, "The Revival of the Religious Life in the Church of England," 6–7.

brotherhoods.[30] The example set by early Anglican sisterhoods improved nineteenth-century church and society and paved the way for women's professional participation in education, nursing, and social work.[31]

EPISCOPAL SISTERHOODS

The formation of sisterhoods within the Episcopal Church reflected many of the same motivations and values as Anglican sisterhoods in Britain. Most Episcopal sisterhoods were founded soon after the Civil War. The social impact of the war and the deaths of millions, including an estimated 650,000–850,000 soldiers, meant that many women would remain single and financially insecure for life. These social changes and the theological perspectives brought by the Oxford Movement provided a climate whereby the accepted gender roles within the Protestant tradition regarding the primacy of marriage and family could be challenged. By the mid-nineteenth century, parallel to the formation of the first sisterhoods in England, Episcopal women in the United States, motivated by concern for the poor and drawn to a life of service within the confines of the Church, looked to the possibility of founding sisterhoods. Given the standards of propriety of the era, it was more allowable for a group of women to undertake work outside of the home under the auspices of the Church. As in England, the influence of the Oxford Movement in the Episcopal Church contributed to the development of sisterhoods amid some controversy. However, unlike the Church of England, the Episcopal Church is not an established national church. Due to the size of the United States and diocesan diversity, the catholic revival in the Episcopal Church had strength in particular dioceses or individual parishes within dioceses. As one sister commented, "There were many little movements, scattered, sporadic, tending in the same direction and destined in the end to approach one another, and yet relatively independent and isolated." [32]

Anne Ayres (1816–1896) was the first woman to be professed in the Episcopal Church in 1845 at the Church of the Holy Communion in New

---

30. Anderson-Faithful and Holloway, *Women and the Anglican Church Congress 1861–1938*, 187.

31. Mumm, *Stolen Daughters, Virgin Mothers*, x, xxi, 9–10, 74–75, 79–95, 115–18, 125–28; Herringer, "The Revival of the Religious Life," 384–96; Allchin, *The Silent Rebellion*, 175.

32. Sister Hilary, CSM, "The Revival of Monasticism,"199; Donovan, *A Different Call*, 29–31. For Civil War mortality rates, see Bob Zeller, "How Many Died in the Civil War, "*History Newsletter*, January 6, 2022, www.history.com/news/amwrican-civil-war-deaths. Accessed February 20, 2022.

York City by William Augustus Muhlenberg (1796–1877). A convert to the Episcopal Church from Lutheranism, Muhlenberg's Church of the Holy Communion became the first in New York City to celebrate Holy Communion weekly. Muhlenberg's vision inspired a church without pew rents that provided spiritual care through the sacraments and humanitarian aid for the poor. He proclaimed himself an "evangelical catholic" as a compromise between church parties. Anne Ayres was in her late twenties when she met Muhlenberg and was employed as a teacher for affluent girls, including his niece. Muhlenberg's sermon on Jephthah's daughter so moved Anne Ayres that she was compelled to dedicate her life to God. After her profession, Ayres worked in the parish. Muhlenberg founded St. Luke's Hospital in New York in 1850; Anne and several other women served as nurses and formed the Sisterhood of the Holy Communion in 1852.[33]

The Sisterhood of the Holy Communion was united by a commitment to charity rather than traditional religious vows. Aware of the hostility of some Episcopal Church members toward religious orders, Ayres and Muhlenberg were careful to disassociate the Sisterhood of the Holy Communion from Roman Catholic religious orders, instead referring to it as a thoroughly Protestant "evangelical sisterhood." Inspired by nursing deaconesses in Germany, rather than sisterhoods in England, women who joined the sisterhood made a three-year commitment instead of lifetime vows. They were allowed to leave the community by notifying Muhlenberg of their intent to depart. Rather than formal habits, the sisters wore simple attire. Though each sister was expected to participate in communal worship, Bible reading, and personal devotions, the center of community life revolved around charitable works. Though the sisters had no formal nursing training, they gained expertise through practical experience and were among the first pioneers of the nursing profession in the United States. The sisterhood grew slowly; the first formal professions were Meta Brevoort (1853), Sister Catherine (1854), and Sister Harriet (1857).[34]

Beyond St. Luke's Hospital, Ayres and Muhlenberg collaborated on various innovative ministries until he died in 1877. The legacies of these ministries continue in the Episcopal Church today. They instituted a weekly offering for the poor, Fresh Air Fund, Thanksgiving food drive, employment society, parish day school, and Sunday schools. Ayres also served as the principal of a secondary school for girls established in the church building. In addition to the hospital, they opened a seventeen-bed infirmary, outpatient

---

33. Anson, *The Call of the Cloister*, 554–55; Donovan, *A Different Call*, 31–33.
34. Anson, *The Call of the Cloister*, 555–56; Donovan, *A Different Call*, 31–33.

clinic, and dispensary. The sisters served as visiting nurses, dispensing food, clothing, and medication.[35]

Anne Ayres' expansive vision of vocational options for women came when unmarried devout women of the Church considered various roles, including "ministering sisters, deaconesses, lady-nurses, or whatever else they may call themselves . . ."[36] She wrote,

> And here I cannot help wishing that our bishops and pastors would speak more directly to us women, on these points than they do," she wrote. 'It is customary to urge men to the work of ministry, missions, etc., and should not holy arguments be sometimes addressed to us, also, to stir us up into something in the Christian life more distinct and impressive than that now common to us? Yet when do we hear a word from the pulpit to this effect? We women have a little faith, we have warm affections and our impulses, we have heads and hands; why not show us that we are not living up to our vocation, not turning to good account the powers we are imbued with, that communicants though we may be, we are frittering away our lives . . . at the best, allowing ourselves to be dwarfed and cramped into the niches of custom and worldly conformity, when we might be developing by healthful exercise in pure Christian air, toward perfect stature in Christ?[37]

Anne Ayres resigned from her "First Sister" role in 1863, and the sisterhood was dissolved. The remaining members were urged to form a "Company of Ladies" to continue at the hospital, with Ayres as matron. Harriet Starr Cannon (1823–1896) and four other women, Mary Heartt, Jane Haight, Amelia Asten, and Sarah Bridge, returned to their families but later formed the Community of St. Mary. Cannon and her associates grew discontented with the leadership of Ayres and Muhlenberg. Seeking a more formal sisterhood, they oversaw a "House of Mercy" for "fallen" women and girls. Cannon eventually obtained the support of Horatio Potter, the bishop of the Episcopal Diocese of New York, for a new sisterhood. The Community of St. Mary held their first chapter in 1865. The Sisterhood of the Holy Communion was temporarily revived in 1871 under Sister Catherine, who continued the work at St. Luke's Hospital and founded a home for aged women, a convalescent home, and a home for working girls and women.

---

35. Anson, *The Call of the Cloister*, 555–56; Donovan, *A Different Call*, 33–34.
36. Ayres, "Practical Thoughts on Sisterhoods," iii.
37. Ayres, 'Practical thoughts on Sisterhoods," 63–64.

This first "sisterhood" in the Episcopal Church continued until the death of the last members in 1934.[38]

The influence of the Oxford Movement on the Episcopal Church was most evident in urban centers where the Church was numerically the strongest, and the same pattern applied to sisterhoods. Early Episcopal sisterhoods included the Sisterhood of the Good Shepherd in Baltimore (1863), the Community of St. Mary (1865), the Sisterhood of the Good Shepherd (1869) in New York, the Sisterhood of St. John the Evangelist (1872) in Brooklyn, and the Sisterhood of the Holy Child of Jesus (1872) in Albany. In addition, several English sisterhoods founded houses in the United States during the 1870s: the Society of All Saints' Sisters of the Poor in Baltimore, the Society of St. Margaret in Boston, and the Community of St. John Baptist in New York City.[39]

Traditional historical accounts of English sisterhoods commonly credit male clergy as the founders; however, among Episcopal sisterhoods, only the Sisterhood of the Holy Communion and the Sisterhood of the Holy Nativity were co-founded by prominent clergy. But clergy played an integral role in establishing sisterhoods, as it was unlikely that women would receive church approval without them. Clergymen like William Augustus Muhlenberg and Charles Chapman Grafton (in the case of the Sisterhood of the Holy Nativity) had a high regard for the contributions of women. They were inspired by a vision of the Church where religious orders played a central role. This said, traditional histories of Anglican and Episcopal sisterhoods generally undervalue the efforts of the women themselves in establishing sisterhoods. Their deep conviction and organizational effectiveness revealed their remarkable accomplishments when there were no formal roles for women within Anglicanism. Their persistence earned many of the women founders' reputations as difficult personalities. However, this persistence was essential to the success of early Episcopal sisterhoods, given the number of obstacles they faced.[40]

About twenty years after the first Anglican sisterhoods were founded, the deaconess movement gained momentum on both sides of the Atlantic. There was a fluidity between sisterhoods and deaconesses in the early years of both movements, with women shifting between the two vocational

---

38. Anson, *The Call of the Cloister*, 555–56; Sister Hilary, CSM, "The Revival of Monasticism," 203, 235–38. There is a dispute over the number of women from the Sisterhood of the Holy Communion that formed the Community of St. Mary. Sister Hilary, CSM, a member of the community, states that there were five, not four, including Harriet Starr Cannon; Anson, *The Call of the Cloister*, 536–38.

39. Donovan, *A Different Call*, 30.

40. For a related discussion, see Donovan, *A Different Call*, 30–31.

options; several members of the Sisterhood of the Holy Nativity previously served as deaconesses, worked with deaconesses, or were trained at deaconess training schools.[41] Deaconess Florence Isabel Ormerod ministered in the Missionary District of Nevada during the 1930s among Indigenous peoples in the Dakotas. Ormerod eventually entered the Sisterhood of the Holy Nativity and was professed in 1950 as Sister Isabel. Sister Esther Beulah was a former deaconess who also served in Nevada with Sister Hilary, a medical doctor and former missionary to Puerto Rico.[42] Another former deaconess in the sisterhood was Sister Veronica. Although Sister Mary Angela was not formally set apart as a deaconess, she received training in social work from St. Margaret's House, the deaconess training school in Berkeley, California.[43]

The deaconess movement began with the establishment of Kaiserswerther (Kaiserwerth) Diakonie in 1837, a hospital and training center in Germany. In the Church of England and the Episcopal Church, the deaconess movement was supported by evangelical low church clergy who considered it a more acceptable alternative to sisterhoods.[44] Both deaconesses and sisterhoods dressed distinctively and performed similar roles in parishes and institutions. The two differed in that deaconesses frequently lived alone and were "set apart" rather than taking life vows, a practice of sisterhoods considered "too catholic" by many Protestants. European and American deaconesses considered themselves the restorers of an apostolic order with a biblical precedent that originated in the early Christian church, identifying with the deaconess Phoebe in the New Testament rather than with ordained male transitional deacons.[45]

Almost 500 Episcopal women were set apart as deaconesses in the United States between 1885–1970. In 1889, the Episcopal Church passed

---

41. Herringer, "The Revival of the Religious Life," 387–388; Legath, *Sanctified Sisters*, Prelinger, "The Female Diaconate in the Anglican Church," 161–92.

42. Chase, *The Episcopal Church in Nevada, 1860–1959* (Carson City, Nevada, 2000), 172–74.

43. See Appendix, Life Professed Sisters.

44. The term "low church" originated in the eighteenth-century Church of England. Then, the term was synonymous with "latitudinarianism," a position that emphasized royal supremacy and minimized the authority of the episcopate. The low church movement also privileged preaching over the sacraments. In the nineteenth century, the low church supporters of John and Charles Wesley, who remained in the Church of England, became known as the evangelicals. By this time, the low church party became associated with an emphasis on the authority of scripture, evangelistic preaching, personal religious experience, conversion by the Holy Spirit, and a dislike of ritual.

45. Legath, *Sanctified Sisters*, 13; Sue Anderson-Faithful and Catherine Holloway, *Women and the Anglican Church Congresses, 1861–1938*, 54–55.

a deaconess canon, officially sanctioning the order, establishing guidelines, and founding training schools. At the time, the vocation of deaconess was considered less controversial than the vowed religious life of sisterhoods. Even so, the deaconess movement was not as numerically successful as sisterhoods in either the Church of England or the Episcopal Church. Competition from organizations such as the Salvation Army, the more solitary lifestyle, and less clergy support than sisterhoods are reasons for this disparity in the number of vocations between deaconesses and sisterhoods.[46]

Episcopal Church history suggests that all significant efforts to enlarge vocational options for women— from sisterhoods to deaconesses, missionaries, lay professionals, the diaconate, priesthood, and the episcopate— were initially resisted and considered controversial by the larger Church. A similar pattern informs the history of women's roles in other churches in the Anglican Communion and other denominations. Despite the resistance, women made great sacrifices to challenge the limited roles open to them within the Church and eventually earned respect for their effectiveness and dedication. The sacrificial spirit of the first generations of women who served the Church, including sisterhoods, also reinforced the belief that women's role is to serve but not to exercise institutional authority through direct governance. While women hold some of the highest offices in the Episcopal Church today, gender disparities continue to challenge the leadership and authority of women despite constituting most of church membership.[47]

The legacies of Anglican and Episcopal sisterhoods are their vision, persistence, and innovative ministries. For all the attempts to diminish them, sisterhoods profoundly affected those around them through the depth of their commitment to their faith and service to the marginalized. That they influenced so many parishes and dioceses and established such vibrant ministries with limited resources and institutional support is a testament to their indomitable spirits. The history of the Sisterhood of the Holy Nativity is an example of sacrificial commitment and missionary spirit. Not only did they teach and offer spiritual guidance to thousands of people over 140 years, but their efforts also contributed to the Episcopal Church's vitality. While clergy furthered the theological and liturgical tradition of

---

46. Herringer, "The Revival of the Religious Life," 387; Prelinger, "The Female Diaconate in the Anglican Church," 161–192; Legath, *Sanctified Sisters*, 10–13.

47. For data on the current role of women in the Episcopal Church and gender disparities, see Sheryl A. Kujawa-Holbrook, "Women and the Episcopacy," 82–103. For an analysis of the historical trends throughout Episcopal women's ministries, see Heather Ann Huyck, "To Celebrate A Whole Priesthood."

the Oxford Movement, advancing the catholic faith among the laity was central to the work of sisterhoods. This history of the Sisterhood of the Holy Nativity investigates how they advanced the catholic faith in the Episcopal Church. Their dedication transformed local churches and dioceses as their missionary spirit expanded the spiritual vitality of the laity and responded to humanitarian needs.

I

A Hidden Way of Holiness

For generations, the spirituality of the Sisterhood of the Holy Nativity evoked the ideal of the "hidden way" of holiness found in the life of Jesus. His three years of public ministry rested upon thirty years of "hiddenness" or spiritual preparation from which he gained power and strength. So, too, the Mystical Body of Christ, the Church, draws its power and strength from its hidden way of prayer and solitude. For the Sisterhood of the Holy Nativity, the hidden way was found in the cloister and their vocation of prayer, "believing that the closer they are to God, the more real help they bring to the world. . . .For Love calls no soul to stop at diligence in work, since every soul is made for Love, and is called on throughout all our duties to our Lord, who is Love himself."[1]

This legacy of the Sisterhood of the Holy Nativity contributed to advancing religious vocations for women and expanding the Oxford Movement in the Episcopal Church. The emphasis on the "hidden way" meant that sisters did not seek recognition or advertise their accomplishments—a challenge for historians seeking to uncover their history today. The fact that sisterhoods were comprised of lay women significantly factored into how traditional historical narratives valued their leadership and contributions to the Church. In some dioceses and parishes, the Sisterhood of the Holy Nativity worked for generations, teaching thousands of students, preparing adults and children for the sacraments, tending the altars, and visiting the sick, with scant recognition in official institutional histories. In some

---

1. Sister Mary Kathleen, "The Interior Life," 3, 8. Thanks to Kathleen Reeves for her reflections on the "hidden way." Interview, Kathleen Reeves, October 7, 2021.

contexts where they ministered, their contributions are historically invisible and only revealed through considerable research.

A confluence of events created the Sisterhood of the Holy Nativity in November 1882. Most historical narratives cite Charles Chapman Grafton (1830–1912), a former member of the Society of St. John the Evangelist (SSJE) and eventual bishop of the Episcopal Diocese of Fond du Lac in Wisconsin, as the founder of the Sisterhood of the Holy Nativity. There is no question that Grafton's missionary vision and commitment to religious life were integral to the foundation and continuation of the sisterhood. Grafton's commitment to advancing the catholic faith of the Oxford Movement in the Episcopal Church provided the framework for his ministry and the sisterhood, encapsulated in the phrase, "Press on, the Kingdom."[2] Self-described as both evangelical and catholic, he strove to put the Church's needs above ecclesiastical politics. In addition to his spiritual leadership, Grafton significantly leveraged his ecclesiastical position, extensive social network, and personal fortune to support the sisterhood. Early sources of the Sisterhood of the Holy Nativity refer to Grafton as "our Father and founder." The narrative of his ministry is intertwined with the narrative of the sisterhood's progress.[3]

Notably, Charles Grafton did not claim to be the sole founder of the Sisterhood of the Holy Nativity. He considered Mother Foundress Ruth Margaret Vose (1826–1910) a co-founder, and correspondence reveals a working partnership in all matters related to the sisterhood. Vose came to the religious life in her fifties, having delayed her vocation for the sake of her aging parents. She was a mature woman and a spiritual force in her own right, and while she had a deep respect for the clergy, she also had her perspectives on religious life. Grafton attributed much of the "character" of the Sisterhood of the Holy Nativity to the "great practical wisdom" and "great spirit of devotion" of Mother Foundress Ruth Margaret Vose: "Her Community is the noblest monument to her saintly memory," he wrote at the time of her death.[4]

While there are fewer sources related to Vose's personal history than Grafton's, evidence suggests she was a persistent force in the foundation of the Sisterhood of the Holy Nativity. Vose inspired deep devotion among her

---

2. Pendleton, *Press On, The Kingdom*, 118. The abbreviation for the Society of St. John the Evangelist used throughout this book is SSJE, also known as the "Cowley Fathers."

3. Sister Katherine, SHN, Sister Rebecca, SHN, Sister Agnes, SHN "A Letter Concerning the Founding of Our Sisterhood," SHNC, 1. Privately bound extended narrative letter to the SHN novitiate by the three living founding sisters.

4. *Journal of the Thirty-Sixth Annual Council of the Diocese of Fond du Lac*, 1910, 41.

sisters, which was significant given that interpersonal turmoil challenged other sisterhoods. Her leadership figures prominently in the narrative of the first six sisters of the Sisterhood of the Holy Nativity, who consciously claimed their role as first-generation "Lady Founders." In addition to Mother Ruth Margaret, Sister Mary Margaret, Sister Hannah Margaret, Sister Katharine, Sister Rebecca, Sister Agnes, and laywomen Associates from the Church of the Advent in Boston all played integral roles in establishing the Sisterhood of the Holy Nativity. They believed preserving their first-hand account of the foundation of the sisterhood for future generations of sisters was critical.[5]

On a spiritual level, the founders of the Sisterhood of the Holy Nativity believed that beyond human agency, Christ himself brought them together: "We are not like a Society planned out by some one, but as *a Society* we came into being, through the stress of circumstances," . . . wrote Grafton at the dedication of the first sisters. "He [Christ] took us and then gradually unfolded His purpose for us. And our joy is, that we know it is not a human work, or a personal or individual work, but the work of Christ."[6]

CHARLES CHAPMAN GRAFTON —EARLY FORMATION

Charles Chapman Grafton was born in Boston in 1830. As a child, he lived with an aunt and uncle, both strict Congregationalists. There, he attended Sunday school and adult services. When bribed with pie, he notably memorized the entire Westminster Catechism. His father and brothers served in the armed forces. Grafton's early years followed the pattern of many young men of established Boston families. A gifted student, Grafton was educated at Boston Latin School and Phillips Andover Academy. He entered Harvard Law School and received his degree in 1953. As a promising law student, Grafton grappled with the era's significant social and moral issues. He was drawn to the abolitionist movement and believed that, as a lawyer, he could support eradicating slavery. In the 1850s, Boston was deeply embroiled in the national debates on slavery, having stakeholders on all sides of the issue. While in law school, Grafton witnessed the impact of the Fugitive Slave Law and wrote a pamphlet opposing slavery that impressed his law professor, notable abolitionist Wendell Phillips. Grafton was convinced of the

---

5. Sister Katherine, SHN, et al., "A Letter Concerning the Founding of Our Sisterhood," 26–27.

6. Sister Katherine, SHN, et al., "A Letter Concerning the Founding of Our Sisterhood," 1–2.

rightness of the abolitionist position through his study of the legal aspects of slavery under Phillips' tutelage.[7]

At the time of his awakening to the abolitionist movement, Grafton was also in a vocational crisis. At seventeen, he began attending the Church of the Advent, a controversial center of the Oxford Movement in low church Boston. Grafton's lifetime spanned the early years of the Oxford Movement and the later growth and institutionalization of the movement in the Episcopal Church. He was drawn to the Church of the Advent for its liturgical splendor and concern for the poor. From its founding in 1844, the Church of the Advent attracted worshipers drawn to the beautiful liturgies, the cultivation of personal piety, and access to frequent Holy Communion. The church was also noteworthy for the absence of pew rents—it was supported through free will offerings—making worship there accessible to people from all walks of life.[8] The founders of the Church of the Advent were conscious that it was a decade since the beginning of the Oxford Movement in Anglicanism in the 1830s, and thus, it was time to establish such a parish in Massachusetts. "The time seemed to have come to throw off the shackles that had bound her for so many years to the Puritan tradition, and to reaffirm, by a more distinctive teaching and ritual, the catholic doctrines always held by the Anglican Church."[9]

Grafton's sister and closest sibling, [Maria] Josephine Grafton Minot, and her family were also members of the Church of the Advent. (Later, Minot would prove instrumental in founding the Sisterhood of the Holy Nativity.) "I was of a worldly disposition and pleasure loving, and I went somewhat into society," wrote Grafton of his youthful years. "I was thought to be a good dancer and I remember leading the cotillion in Boston. On discovering my own weakness and that one must make a decision; I was led to turn to Christ and finally confirmed."[10]

The low church bishop of the Diocese of Massachusetts, Manton Eastburn (1801–1872), aggressively opposed the presence of the Church of the Advent in his diocese and refused to attend services there. The fact that thousands of impoverished Irish immigrants were settling in Boston heightened anti-catholic sentiments throughout the city. Yet despite Eastburn's hostility and the fact that the most influential churches in Boston were Congregationalist or Unitarian, the Church of the Advent gained a

---

7. Pendleton, *Press On, The Kingdom*, 3–6; Alexander," Grafton and the Religious Life," 2–3, 9.

8. Morris, *A History of the Church of the Advent*, 7.

9. Goodrich, *The Parish of the Advent in the City of Boston*, 10–11.

10. Grafton, *A Journey Godward*, 57.

positive reputation. At the Church of the Advent, Grafton met curate Oliver Sherman Prescott (1824–1903). Prescott arrived in Boston after participating in a short-lived monastic community for men in North Carolina, the Brotherhood of the Holy Cross. Prescott tutored Grafton in catholic teachings and nurtured his nascent religious vocation.[11]

In law school, Grafton struggled with his life direction. Was his true vocation in politics or the Church? The realization that it was in the Church came to him as "a poor soul stumbled toward God."[12] Grafton held nothing back and pledged the rest of his life to Christ's service. "I therefore determined to live for him and for him alone; to forgo marriage and family; to consecrate whatever I might have in means or ability to his service; and to live upon such as amount as alone would be necessary to cover the expenses of food, raiment and shelter."[13]

Feeling unworthy to pursue the priesthood, Grafton briefly practiced law. Most of his family, particularly his eldest brother, who invested in his legal education, were not pleased and declined to support his theological education. As Grafton discerned his vocation, the position of the Church of the Advent did not improve with the diocesan bishop. Oliver Prescott battled with Manton Eastburn; he endured three inconclusive heresy trials before seeking refuge in the Diocese of Maryland with William Rollinson Whittingham (1805–1879), a bishop in sympathy with the tenets of the Oxford Movement.[14] Whittingham was also sympathetic to the religious life and ordained Grafton a deacon in 1855 and a priest in 1858.[15]

Grafton's ten years in Maryland were marked by poverty and struggle. While preparing for ordination, Grafton assisted Prescott in mission work near Baltimore. As a deacon, Grafton worked among the poor in Baltimore in both white and African American communities. The mission house, perhaps the first settlement house in the Episcopal Church, provided humanitarian aid. After his ordination to the priesthood, Grafton was considered ineligible for a parish post, given his sympathies with the Union in the Civil War.[16]

While in Baltimore, Grafton worked closely with deaconesses under the leadership of Adeline Blanchard Tyler (1805–1875), a Boston widow

11. Pendleton, *Press On, The Kingdom*, 6–9; Alexander, "Grafton and the Religious Life," 2–3.
12. Charles Chapman Grafton, *A Journey Godward*, 29, 55.
13. Charles Chapman Grafton, *A Journey Godward*, 29.
14. Pendleton, *Press On, The Kingdom*, 6–13; Alexander, "Grafton and the Religious Life," 3–4.
15. Alexander, "Grafton and the Religious Life," 4.
16. Pendleton, *Press On, The Kingdom*, 12–14.

who was a Church of the Advent member.[17] After her husband died in 1853, Tyler was set apart as a deaconess in 1856.[18] Three years later, Tyler accepted the invitation to lead a deaconess community and infirmary in Baltimore. Grafton became chaplain to this community of deaconesses. Tyler eventually resigned her post at the infirmary in Baltimore after a man was put in charge instead. She later worked in military hospitals during the Civil War, drawing controversy by treating the wounded regardless of their loyalty to the Union. When illness prevented Tyler from continuing at Children's Hospital in Boston, she suggested to Grafton that he request support from a sisterhood in England, the Society of St. Margaret. They responded positively and, in 1871, sent a trained nurse, Sister Teresa, and two additional sisters in 1873. Grafton served as the sisters' chaplain, and Tyler became an associate of the Society of St. Margaret in 1875.[19]

Charles Grafton's interest in sisterhoods was connected to his vocation to religious life. He believed the Holy Spirit inspired a revival of the catholic faith within the Anglican Communion.[20] Critical of Roman Catholicism, he was attracted to the non-papal catholicity of Eastern Christianity.[21] His desire for monastic formation brought him to England in 1865, where he met Edward Bouverie Pusey, a leading figure in the Oxford Movement who introduced him to catholic clergy. Grafton was also introduced to Priscilla Lydia Sellon, the founder of the Society of the Most Holy Trinity. Pusey and Grafton assisted the sisters in caring for the sick; Grafton drove a cholera wagon through the streets to carry patients to the sisters' hospital.[22]

Grafton's years in England provided a link between the Episcopal Church and Anglican sisterhoods. As English sisterhoods founded houses in the United States, they attracted a primarily American membership. Among other clergy involved with sisterhoods that Grafton met in England was John Mason Neale (1818–1866), the founder of the Society of St. Margaret. He also met Upton Richards (1811–1873), who supported Harriet Brownlow Byron (1818–1887) in founding the Society of All Saints Sisters of the Poor, and Thomas Thelluson Carter (1808–1901), the founder of the

---

17. Daphne B. Noyes, "Adeline Blanchard Tyler: The First Episcopal Deaconess," https://www.youtube.com/watch?v=L_JyvKDMQuU; *also*, www.episcopaldeacons.org.

18. Fox, "Telling the Story of Our First Deaconesses."

19. Alexander, "Grafton and the Religious Life," 5–6; Anson, *Call of the Cloister*, 561–562; Sister Catherine Louise, SSM, *The House of My Pilgrimage*, 21–39.

20. Morris, *A History of the Church of the Advent*, 70.

21. Ramsey, "Charles C. Grafton, Bishop and Theologian, 5, 7.

22. Kathleen Reeves, "Hidden in Christ," 7.

Confraternity of the Blessed Sacrament and chaplain to the Community of St. John Baptist at Clewer.[23]

In England, Grafton met another priest interested in the religious life for men, Simeon Wilberforce O'Neill (1837–1882). Together, they met with Richard Meux Benson (1824–1915) about starting a religious order for men with the intention of an affiliated house in the United States. Benson agreed with the condition that Grafton remain in England before returning to the United States. In 1865, Benson became superior of the new Society of St. John the Evangelist, known colloquially as the "Cowley Fathers," the first men's religious community in the Anglican Communion since the English Reformation. The name is derived from the English town of Cowley, near Oxford, where Benson served as vicar. The agreement with Benson was that once the society reached twelve professed priests, a Rule, and a Constitution would be instituted, along with a branch in the United States with Grafton in charge.[24]

Given that men had more vocational options in the Church than women, it was difficult for men's religious communities to gain momentum. Ordination was open to men, and the types of work open to sisterhoods, like nursing and caring for poor women and children, were considered inappropriate for them. Fortunately, Grafton found a few like-minded priests who shared the vision of a religious community for men. Impressed with the work of sisterhoods among the poor, they were committed to supporting women to navigate ecclesiastical structures. Grafton served as spiritual director for several women's communities in England, including the Society of St. Margaret and the Society of All Saints Sisters of the Poor.[25]

Grafton and his clergy contemporaries were mainly focused on domestic missions with the unchurched urban poor rather than overseas missions. They viewed the local parish as a sacramental mission center focused on evangelizing the lapsed rather than converting those from other religious traditions. Sisterhoods were integral to this vision as they were entrusted with religious education and pastoral care. Anglican historian Rowan Strong argues that Anglo-Catholic parishes "believed that dramatic and ritualistic services centered around the eucharist, drew the labouring poor and the working classes to church, because it offered them an appealing contrast to the drabness of their everyday lives." The devotion of the priests and sisters, along with more acceptance of working-class culture than evangelicals and

23. Williams, "The Beginnings of Anglican Sisterhoods," 368–69; Reeves, "Hidden in Christ," 6–7.

24. Sister Katherine, SHN, et al., "A Letter Concerning the Founding of Our Sisterhood," 2–4.

25. Reeves, "Hidden in Christ," 10.

non-conformists, contributed to the success of these catholic urban missionaries.[26]

Richard Meux Benson, founder of the Society of St. John the Evangelist, was instrumental in early Anglo-Catholic missions. For Benson, Grafton, and other catholic clergy, the missions undertaken by Anglican religious orders were entirely new. Their success was due to their ability to compromise regarding ritualistic practices when necessary. Where overseas missions were founded, such as the Society of St. John the Evangelist's mission in India, Benson rejected the "civilizing" agenda prevalent among missionaries. Instead, he believed that Christianity should be responsive to the Indian context and, therefore, different than in England or the United States. "It is a very difficult thing for any people to receive the message of heaven from their earthly social superiors. This difficulty one finds in England; it is the difficulty of modern mission work."[27]

During the early years of the Cowley Fathers, Grafton and his colleagues advanced evangelization across society, particularly among the poor, many of whom did not have the benefits of the Church. To respond to this deep need, mission priests instituted short-term preaching missions in parish churches to advance the catholic faith. The compelling preaching of the Cowley Fathers attracted followers throughout England. In London alone, 60,000 people from 140 churches participated in one week-long preaching mission. Through these preaching missions, the Oxford Movement moved from academic settings into local dioceses and parishes. Upon his return to the United States, Grafton instituted preaching missions in the Episcopal Church. Support for preaching missions through religious education and preparation for the sacraments became a vital role for the Sisterhood of the Holy Nativity in the evangelization process in local churches. Before a preaching mission, sisters would visit a local church "to awaken the interest of the people in the coming Mission" by offering religious instruction and preparation for the sacraments and assisting the clergy during the mission.[28]

In Boston, the Church of the Advent found itself without a rector in 1870. The church corporation asked the Cowley Fathers to oversee the church in the interim. In response, Benson sent over two English priests, much to the dismay of the bishop of the Diocese of Massachusetts, who was wary about allowing priests in his diocese not under his ecclesiastical authority. The bishop finally agreed to accept Grafton and Prescott; though

---

26. Strong, "Origins of Anglo-Catholic Missions," 91–92.

27. Strong, "Origins of Anglo-Catholic Missions," 94–95, 103.

28. "The Sisterhood of the Holy Nativity," 1928, SHNC, 4–5; Reeves, "Hidden in Christ," 10.

he found their churchmanship disturbing, he allowed it because they were Americans and not "foreign emissaries."[29] Grafton was eventually called as rector of the Church of the Advent in 1872. Benson permitted Grafton to accept the call, and he left for Boston intending to form a religious community of mission priests in a house near the church. High on Grafton's agenda was to have a sisterhood work with him to advance the catholic faith in Boston. Grafton approached three different English sisterhoods about coming to Boston. When the Society of St. Margaret responded positively, Grafton hoped to attract enough sisters to start a branch house in the United States. He also actively supported the Society of the All Saints Sisters of the Poor as they began their work in Baltimore in 1872.[30]

RUTH TUFTS VOSE—EARLY FORMATION

Women affiliated with the Church of the Advent were interested in religious life, and some became Associates of the Society of St. Margaret. One of those first Associates was Ruth Tufts Vose. Vose was born in Boston in 1826 into a wealthy Unitarian family. Her brother, Henry Vose, was a judge in Boston, and an uncle, James Walker, was a president of Harvard College, a Unitarian minister, and a founder of the American Unitarian Association. Ruth Vose was received into the Episcopal Church by James Otis Sargent Huntington (1854–1935), the rector at Emmanuel Church in Boston. (In 1884, Huntington established the Order of the Holy Cross, an Anglican Benedictine men's monastic community of the Episcopal Church.) Vose was close enough to the Society of St. Margaret to travel to England with a novice for her profession. While there, Sister Louisa Mary was elected superior of the new house in Boston, near the Children's Hospital. As the number of sisters at St. Margaret's House in Boston grew, the community moved several times. In 1881, St. Margaret's established a convent in Louisburg Square in Boston, where they remained until the end of the twentieth century.[31]

Though deeply attracted to the religious life, Ruth Vose was responsible for caring for her aging parents. She eventually entered the Society of St Margaret in 1878 at fifty-two. Although two friends entered the Community of St. John the Baptist at Clewer in England, Vose decided to stay in Boston. That Grafton was St. Margaret's chaplain was a factor in her decision to

---

29. Reeves, "Hidden in Christ," 12.

30. Sister Katherine, SHN, et al., "A Letter Concerning the Founding of Our Sisterhood," 4–5; Sister Catherine Louise, SSM, *The Planting of the Lord*, 18.

31. Sister Katherine, SHN, et al., "A Letter Concerning the Founding of Our Sisterhood," 5–6.

stay in the United States. Upon entering the novitiate in 1879, Sister Ruth Margaret sailed to England with another novice for formation; Grafton accompanied them, as did Rebecca Vose, a niece of Sister Ruth Margaret and an associate of St. Margaret's. Rebecca Vose entered St. Margaret's as a postulant in the same year. Upon her return to Boston in 1880, Sister Ruth Margaret was put in charge of a girls' boarding school.[32]

THE SOCIETY OF ST MARGARET (SSM)

The Society of St. Margaret was the primary source of religious formation for the first generation of the Sisterhood of the Holy Nativity. Shortly after arriving in Boston, the Society of St. Margaret gained a positive reputation in the Church of the Advent and the wider Boston community. They were known for their work at the Children's Hospital, St. Mary's Orphanage in Lowell, and St. Margaret's School for Girls in Boston. The sisters supported the Church of the Advent, serving as parish visitors, teachers, and relief workers. Noted internationally for their skill in ecclesiastical embroidery, the sisters made vestments and altar linens for use in Anglo-Catholic parishes, which also served as a source of income for the sisterhood. Within a few years after arriving in Boston, the order grew to twenty-five sisters; they also sponsored a group of women's guilds that supported their work.[33]

The first sign of the conflict, which eventually led to the creation of the Sisterhood of the Holy Nativity, did not originate between the sisters but arose between the Cowley Fathers in the United States and England. A polity dispute occurred between Benson, who asserted that as superior, he had authority over members of the society in the United States, and bishops in the Episcopal Church, who were reluctant to allow priests to function in dioceses not under their ecclesiastical authority. This conflict put the American Cowley Fathers in a difficult situation within the Episcopal Church. Although the sisterhoods were growing, it was difficult for the Cowley Fathers to attract new members within the Episcopal Church because few priests were willing to go against their bishops to do so. Grafton despaired of any significant growth in the United States unless the society was autonomous from the English branch and conformed to the polity of the Episcopal Church. "This we Americans felt to be necessary because the two Churches [the Church of England and the Episcopal Church] were distinct bodies,

---

32. Sister Katherine, SHN, et al., "A Letter Concerning the Founding of Our Sisterhood," 6–7.
33. Pendleton, *Press On, The Kingdom*, 62.

and any other arrangement would involve us in an entanglement in respect to our ordination vows," stated Grafton.[34]

Moreover, as the number of priests in the Society of Saint John the Evangelist surpassed twelve professed members and the time came to start an American house with a Rule and Constitution, Benson resisted. Grafton contended that no official society existed until the Chapter of the Society of St. John the Evangelist adopted a formal Rule and Constitution. Benson refused to comply with the original agreement, arguing that none of the Americans had true vocations and that Grafton was mentally ill. In 1882, American members Grafton, Prescott, and Walter R. Gardner requested a release from the English house (but not from their vows) to form an American society. Two years later, Benson gave his blessing to this request.[35]

Charles Grafton's release from the Cowley Fathers in August 1882 caused him great personal sorrow. Though secure in his job as rector of the Church of the Advent, his release from the Cowley Fathers affected his role as chaplain for the Society of St. Margaret. Friends informed Grafton that some English fathers encouraged the Society of St. Margaret to request his resignation as chaplain. It was unusual because the chaplain was ordinarily considered a life office; there was no provision in their Constitution for this situation. Mother Louisa Mary called a Chapter to take a vote on the matter with the chaplain. Two weeks before the vote, Sister Ruth Margaret and Sister Margaret Mary met with Mother Louisa Mary. They asked if it would be possible to form an American house of the Society of St. Margaret with Grafton as the chaplain. Mother Louisa Mary said the option was untenable, but "they could withdraw and form an entirely new Sisterhood and have Fr. Grafton for their Chaplain."[36] She suggested they take along Sister Rebecca (Sister Ruth Margaret's niece, then a novice) and consider moving into a vacant house near the Church of the Advent.[37]

The controversy surrounding Grafton's status as chaplain caused considerable turmoil for the sisters. Grafton was responsible for bringing the Society of St. Margaret to the United States and was a devoted chaplain and advocate. The sisters on Grafton's side felt that the request for his resignation

---

34. Quoted in Sister Katherine, SHN, et al., "A Letter Concerning the Founding of Our Sisterhood," 10–11.

35. Charles Chapman Grafton, "A Letter Addressed to the Members of the Society of S. John the Evangelist," Boston, November 1883, printed not published; Sister Katherine, SHN, et al., "A Letter Concerning the Founding of Our Sisterhood," 7–10.

36. Sister Katherine, SHN, et al. "A Letter Concerning the Founding of Our Sisterhood," 9–13; Kinney, *Grafton of Fond du Lac*, 148–54.

37. Sister Katherine, SHN, et al. "A Letter Concerning the Founding of Our Sisterhood," 13.

was unjust. For a short time, they hoped that a compromise might be possible whereby those sisters loyal to Grafton could form a branch house of the Society of St. Margaret.[38] They were also profoundly attached to Mother Louisa Mary and the other sisters in the community. It was difficult for the sisters sympathetic to Grafton to consider separating from their religious community entirely. Their formation in religious life was due to the Society of St. Margaret. The matter was further complicated in that Grafton and Sister Ruth Margaret had just donated a substantial share of their personal wealth to purchase the new buildings the Society of St. Margaret inhabited in Louisburg Square. Moreover, while the sisters requested Grafton's resignation because he left the Cowley Fathers, those allied with him contended there was nothing in the Rule or Constitution to force such a resignation; the chaplain's office was a life office.[39]

The anxiety over the status of Grafton's chaplaincy continued as the Chapter was postponed several times. Questions about the legitimacy of the Chapter arose as sisters felt pressured to divulge their votes in advance. The postponement continued until enough votes accumulated against Grafton to ask for his resignation. One source argues that the sisters were coerced to vote against Grafton and asked to make "this sacrifice which God was asking of them."[40] Yet technically, the Rule "left the Sisters free to vote always in accordance with their convictions, and always without being asked to *declare* their vote before the Chapter was held, so that the result could not be foreseen."[41]

When the Chapter finally convened, the Society of St. Margaret requested Charles Grafton's resignation as chaplain. The professed sisters who disapproved of this action then withdrew from the Society of St. Margaret. At the same time, Mother Louisa Mary unsuccessfully attempted to rescind her permission for the withdrawn sisters to start a new sisterhood. Shortly afterward, she was recalled to the Motherhouse in England and informed that she had exceeded her authority and was not authorized to call the Chapter or to make a change in chaplain. The sisters in England were more sympathetic to Grafton and understood the procedural issues more clearly. The sisters who withdrew noted: "It cannot be truly claimed that

---

38. Pendleton, *Press On, The Kingdom.* 85.

39. Sister Katherine, SHN, et al. "A Letter Concerning the Founding of Our Sisterhood," 14–16.

40. Sister Katherine, SHN, et al. "A Letter Concerning the Founding of Our Sisterhood," 17.

41. Sister Katherine, SHN, et al. "A Letter Concerning the Founding of Our Sisterhood," 16–18.

a manipulated Chapter is the action of the Holy Spirit: on the contrary, it comes down to the level of any ordinary political campaign."[42]

FOUNDATION OF A NEW SISTERHOOD

In anticipation of Graton's departure as chaplain, arrangements were underway to start a new sisterhood. Women from the Church of the Advent, including Catherine Codman, Susan Bertram, Josephine Minot (Grafton's sister), Elizabeth Cobb, Eliza Davis, Emma Andrews, and Grace Minot, provided much of the material support needed to launch the fledging sisterhood. Susan Bertram and Elizabeth Cobb were considered so foundational that they were later included among the photos of the founding members of the Sisterhood of the Holy Nativity.[43] They all withdrew as Associates of the Society of St. Margaret. Catherine Codman gave the sisters temporary shelter; Susan Bertram rented a house near the Church of the Advent on Brimmer Street for the sisters and commissioned the first sign, "Sisterhood of the Holy Nativity." Other women from the parish furnished the house and purchased the fabric for new habits.[44]

One of the first tasks for the new sisterhood was to outfit a chapel as the symbol of community life. In addition to its central role in the sisterhood's devotional life, the Sisterhood of the Holy Nativity chapel also served a missional purpose as it was opened to women Associates and other "devout-minded" people for private prayer and retreat. As the number of sisters in the house allowed, the chapel was the site for twenty-four-hour intercessory prayer "for the making known of the Faith and the conversion of souls to Christ."[45] Through this "hidden way" the sisters made the light of Christ known to the world. Throughout the sisterhood's history, each mission house was outfitted with a chapel as soon as possible upon arrival. "[Christ's] was a personal and individual work, and ours is, not like great institutions working for bodies, but souls, preparing children for the Sacraments, the poor, giving people help and teaching truth," Grafton wrote.

---

42. Sister Katherine, SHN, et al. "A Letter Concerning the Founding of Our Sisterhood," 18.

43. Record Book of Associates, Vol 1, February 1883-February 1921; SHNC. For photos of the founders, see the SHN Collection. Grafton formally received the first Associates on February 22, 1883, in the SHN Chapel.

44. Sister Katherine, SHN, et al. "A Letter Concerning the Founding of Our Sisterhood," 18–24; Pendleton, *Press On, The Kingdom*, 86.

45. *Constitutions and Rule of the Sisters of the Holy Nativity*, Whitsunday 1889, 3.

"We are carrying on [Christ's] personal, individual ministry with souls. It is hidden work, but so dear."[46]

The Sisterhood of the Holy Nativity Constitution states that the sisters' works of mercy spring from their mystical union with Christ. As they are "sacramentally incorporated into Him, they may, by the transforming power of the indwelling Spirit, become so one with Him that, in the words of their dedication, the "Spirit of Prayer, Charity, Humility, and the Missionary Spirit of Christ himself "should reign in them. Devotion to Jesus, work for Jesus, love toward one another in Jesus; or, in other words, 'Self-hidden in Jesus,' 'Jesus hidden in us,' all 'One in Jesus,' [became] the spirit of the Sisterhood."[47] The sisters viewed their work as an extension of Christ, their Lord and Spouse. "They are to keep house for Him. They will go out to seek him in the homes of the poor. They will wait upon and relieve the sick as if attending upon Him. They will care for the Altar and make vestments, as the Blessed Mother made garments for Him, or as the holy women prepared the spices for the embalming of His Blessed Body." [48]

During those first months of the Sisterhood of the Holy Nativity, the sisters began sponsoring retreats, primarily for women. The integral role of women Associates in the life and work of the Sisterhood of the Holy Nativity was evident when, within months of the foundation, a litany and prayers for Associates were written, and crosses were ordered for them from the Holy Land.[49] The first retreat was hosted in February 1883 and attended chiefly by working women. It was one of the first retreats for laywomen in the Episcopal Church. In the same year, an Associate provided a home in Rindge, New Hampshire, as a retreat house. Frequent retreats were integral to the Sisterhood of the Holy Nativity from its inception. "Some of the most treasured meditations and instructions by Fr. Grafton were given there. Large portions of our Holy Rule are the result of the hours spent on his knees in front of the Blessed Sacrament."[50]

Sister Ruth Margaret was reluctant to attend her final Chapter meeting as a Society of St. Margaret member. She went instead to rest in New Hampshire with Catherine Codman and sent her vote directly to Mother Louisa Mary. She never returned to St. Margaret's Convent. Sister Rebecca left about the same time and stayed at her sister Charlotte Manning's home. Manning hired a seamstress to make three habits: one each for Sister Rebecca, Sister

---

46. Grafton, *Meditations and Instructions*, 70.
47. *Constitutions and Rule of the Sisters of the Holy Nativity*, Whitsunday 1889, 3. 9.
48. *Constitutions and Rule of the Sisters of the Holy Nativity*, Whitsunday 1889, 14.
49. Reeves, "Hidden in Christ," 17–18, 22.
50. Reeves, "Hidden in Christ," 19–20.

Mary Margaret, and Sister Ruth Margaret. Sister Mary Margaret attended her last chapter at St. Margaret's, knowing the Associates would deliver a new habit and a carriage to take her to the Codman house after the meeting. In all the excitement, the package with the habit got misplaced. Sister Mary Margaret left the Society of St. Margaret in her bathrobe; she later found the package with the habit by the door and took it with her. Eventually, the first professed sisters of the Sisterhood of the Holy Nativity were joined by seven novices. All but one woman bid a tearful goodbye to Mother Louisa Mary. The last novice was a minor and feared being forbidden to leave, so she went to the Codman house alone. Grafton insisted that she receive permission from her father, a priest outside Boston, to join the new community. Permission was denied, and the young woman returned to her parent's home.[51]

One of the professed sisters who intended to join the new sisterhood, Sister Hannah Margaret, oversaw an orphanage and was delayed in joining the others. After that, a Chapter was called with the three professed sisters and Grafton as the chaplain. Sister Hannah Margaret was provisionally elected superior for one year. On the Feast of the Nativity 1882, the professed sisters began the tradition of signing the profession book of their new sisterhood, dedicating themselves "to the service of God in a life of chastity, poverty, and obedience, to which by the authority of the Church [they were] set apart," and pledging to live in obedience to their Rule."[52]

Of the original six novices who formed the Sisterhood of the Holy Nativity, four were elected for profession in 1884: Sister Katherine, Sister Faith, Sister Rebecca, and Sister Agnes. (In 1887, Sister Faith was received into the Community of Saint Mary in New York.) Also, in 1884, Sister Ruth Margaret was elected superior at fifty-eight. When other women might consider slowing down, Mother Ruth Margaret took on the leadership of a new sisterhood. Recognized for her spiritual depth, Mother Ruth Margaret was an exemplary religious and role model for those seeking mystical union with Christ. She believed that the love of Christ should animate the whole community. "It [the Sisterhood of the Holy Nativity] is full of the happiness, brightness, and joy of a united Christian fellowship, and animated with a glowing zeal for souls," commented Grafton about the early years with Mother Ruth Margaret.[53]

The founding members of the Sisterhood of the Holy Nativity shared in the ministry of the Church of the Advent. They advanced the catholic

51. Reeves, "Hidden in Christ," 17–18,
52. Life Profession Book, Sisterhood of the Holy Nativity, 1, SHNC
53. *Journal of the Thirty-Sixth Annual Council of the Diocese of Fond du Lac*, 1910, 41.

faith through religious education, parish visiting, preparing people for the sacraments, and serving in the sacristy. Grafton continued as rector there and advocated that religious teaching should be provided for all who requested it, regardless of age, gender, social class, or race. A new church was built in 1883 (funded by Grafton) to accommodate the rapidly growing congregation. The congregation all attended Sunday school together; it took instructors of great skill to teach in a multigenerational environment. The work in Boston also contributed to forming the congregation of St. Augustine and St. Martin in Boston, considered the region's first African American Episcopal mission.[54]

The early work of the Sisterhood of the Holy Nativity in Boston set a pattern later replicated in mission houses across the country. The sisters brought food and clothing to recent immigrants living in Boston's North End. They visited the sick and cared for women and children in crisis. Because of the growing numbers of the unchurched seeking membership at the Church of the Advent, the Sisterhood of the Holy Nativity worked assiduously to provide instruction for Baptism and Confirmation. By the time the Sisterhood of the Holy Nativity moved to Providence in 1888, more adults and children were baptized and confirmed in the Church of the Advent than in all the other eighteen Episcopal Churches in Boston combined.[55]

Soon, invitations to the Sisterhood came from parishes and dioceses across the Episcopal Church. Throughout its history, the number of invitations issued to the Sisterhood of the Holy Nativity far outnumbered the available sisters. Episcopal parishes in Providence, New York, Philadelphia, and Baltimore wrote to request their assistance in advancing the catholic faith. Bishops from "out West" in Wisconsin, Illinois, and Kansas were eager for the sisters to establish themselves in their dioceses. The newly formed Diocese of Fond du Lac requested sisters to work among the Oneida. Though the new sisterhood remained committed to parish work, numerous requests were received from church institutions, primarily schools and orphanages. Two sisters were sent to an orphanage in Providence for two years. Their experience confirmed parish work rather than serving in institutions was the primary mission of the Sisterhood of the Holy Nativity. In 1889, two sisters from the Sisterhood of the Holy Name of Jesus, founded in Boston in 1884, joined the Sisterhood of the Holy Nativity. One of these sisters was Sister Katherine Edith, the former superior of the Sisterhood of the Holy Name of Jesus, and "A woman of great intellectual ability . . . a precious gift

---

54. Goodrich, *The Parish of the Advent in the City of Boston*, 72–73.
55. Pendleton, *Press On, The Kingdom*, 88–89; Reeves, "Hidden in Christ," 22–23.

of God to the community," according to Mother Ruth Margaret.⁵⁶ Sister Katherine Edith guided the Sisterhood of the Holy Nativity through Mother Ruth Margaret's final years and was elected superior in 1908. Sister Alice also came to the community from the Sisterhood of the Holy Name and remained until she died in 1929.⁵⁷

Among the founding sisters of the Sisterhood of the Holy Nativity, Sister Mary Margaret was appointed the first Novice Mistress; in 1884, she volunteered to do parish work in Kansas City with the possibility of opening a house there. After her year as provisional superior, Sister Hannah Margaret served in Providence and Fond du Lac. Sister Katherine spent many years serving among the Wisconsin Oneida and in Portland, Maine, and Philadelphia. Sister Rebecca was the last surviving sister from the original foundation at the time of her death in 1937. An avid supporter of Charles Grafton and her aunt, Mother Ruth Margaret, Sister Rebecca was active in Rhode Island after the motherhouse moved to Providence. She also served as Sister-in-Charge of the mission house in Fond du Lac before the sisterhood moved there in 1905. In Fond du Lac, Sister Rebecca became Charles Grafton's administrative assistant. The last of the founding sisters, Sister Agnes, served in Providence and Fond du Lac. These "Lady Founders" were active when the relationship between sisterhoods was the most fluid. In the future, professed sisters could not move to another community without the consent of their sisterhood.⁵⁸

THE FIRST YEARS—BOSTON, 1882–1888

The formative years of the Sisterhood of the Holy Nativity were marked by discernment and prayer. Convinced of the importance of a written Rule and Constitution after his experience with the Cowley Fathers, Grafton drafted both for the Sisterhood of the Holy Nativity beginning in 1883. Adapted and revisited over the history of the order, the core values articulated by Grafton –charity, humility, prayer, and missionary spirit—are central to the

---

56. Reeves, "Hidden in Christ," 23; Letter, Mother Ruth Margaret to Charles Chapman Grafton, 1889, SHNC.

57. Anson, *The Call of the Cloister*, 595.

58. Sister Katherine, SHN, et al. "A Letter Concerning the Founding of Our Sisterhood," 24–27; Pendleton's book confuses the names of some of the first members of the Sisterhood of the Holy Nativity. The first provisional superior (1882–1884) was Sister Hannah Margaret, not Harriet Margaret as noted on page 87. Moreover, the photo on the same page is of the Mother Foundress, Sister Ruth Margaret, SHN (Ruth Tufts Vose), who became superior in 1884. There was no Sister Hattie or Harriet in the first generation of the SHN.

Constitution and Rule of the Sisterhood of the Holy Nativity today. Grafton believed the Rule's purpose was to bind the community together. "The Sisterhood is not an aggregation of units, each member leading her own individual Christian life, but forms one body, leading a common life and animated by one spirit. The creation of this body is the work of God."[59]

The Constitution and Rule of the Sisterhood of the Holy Nativity emerged from meditations on vocation that Grafton shared during the early years of the sisterhood. Grafton and the sisters considered their formation in the Society of St. Margaret and the Society of St. John the Evangelist to be the spiritual inheritance of the Sisterhood of the Holy Nativity. "This work did not begin from when we went out from another organization, but we are to see through the whole course of our lives He [Christ] was disciplining us for this one object, for this we are subjected to His schooling and disciplining, overruling all for His glory."[60]

The mission statement of the Sisterhood of the Holy Nativity figures prominently at the beginning of the Constitutions and Rule published in 1889 and remained a touchstone guiding the corporate life and spirituality of the community throughout its history:

> *Called by Divine Providence, in the midst of much suffering, to the rest and devotion of Bethlehem, the Sisters of the Holy Nativity, drawn by the Love of Jesus, into the charity, humility, spirit of prayer, and missionary spirit of his interior life, receive their Constitution and Rule as the gift from their dear Lord and Spouse.*[61]

Pastoral and practical in tone, the Constitutions and the Rule were designed to provide a framework for the governance of the sisterhood. Divided into three parts and based on the Pauline metaphor of the Body of Christ, the first part focuses on the body of the sisterhood, including how it is governed and how persons are admitted into it. The second part relates to the body's functions, such as the lines of authority and the duties of the sisters. "It explains the duties of the Sisterhood under two aspects, namely, towards God and for Him: first prayer and personal sanctification; and, secondly, the winning of souls to Him."[62] The third part relates to the spiritual life, the sisterhood's "own school of Christian perfection," its spirit and calling, and its devotional tradition and training methods.[63]

---

59. *Constitutions and Rule of the Sisters of the Holy Nativity*, Whitsunday 1889, 15.
60. Grafton, *Meditations and Instructions*, 94.
61. *Constitutions and Rule of the Sisters of the Holy Nativity*, Whitsunday 1889, 1.
62. *Constitutions and Rule of the Sisters of the Holy Nativity*, Whitsunday 1889, 1.
63. *Constitutions and Rule of the Sisters of the Holy Nativity*, Whitsunday 1889, 1.

Unlike historians who date the origins of monasticism with the desert fathers and mothers of the third and fourth centuries, or even from Benedict in the sixth century, Charles Grafton believed that the foundation of the religious life was established by Jesus Christ and embodied through his own life lived in poverty, chastity, and obedience.[64] All baptized Christians have a vocation; the religious are also called by virtue of their baptism.[65] The unique charism of religious life is the embodiment of the Incarnation. Through the Incarnation, all Christians participate in the life of Christ and bring forth a new creation. By his Incarnation, Christ makes possible the restoration of the fallen world and the participation of all creation in divine life. Grafton's theology of the Incarnation was reminiscent of his teachers, Pusey, Benson, and Henry Parry Liddon (1989–1890). At first, he thought that the "Sisterhood of the Incarnation" might be a suitable name for the new community. The eventual dedication of the Sisterhood to the Holy Nativity drew inspiration from the doctrine of the Incarnation.[66] Grafton believed that the Church was a palpable expression of the Incarnation on earth and that the Eucharist was the practical means for communicating divine life within the Body of Christ. "Thus, as the virtues of Christ pass into each individual soul, the whole body of the faithful as the Bride of Christ will reflect the beauty of the Lord. The Church herself thus becomes the extension of the Incarnation."[67]

According to Grafton, all Christians are called to poverty, chastity, and obedience as appropriate to their vocation. Those called to the religious life are icons of a more complete union with Christ and the embodiment of his love in the world. Thus, the founders of the Sisterhood of the Holy Nativity stressed the cultivation of the interior life as integral to their call as religious. For the Sisterhood of the Holy Nativity, daily Holy Communion and the adoration of the Blessed Sacrament were at the center of their spiritual practice. Through this grounding in Christ, the sisters undertook their works of mercy. "As a soul grows closer to Christ, so does the recognition that all creatures are made in the image and likeness of God. This recognition leads to participation in Christ's ministry to all in need."[68]

---

64. Grafton, *Vocation*, 96; Grafton, *A Journey Godward*, 88–100; Alexander, "Grafton and the Religious Life," 14–16.

65. *Constitutions and Rule of the Sisters of the Holy Nativity*, 1889, 2.

66. Grafton, *Christian and Catholic*, 69–70; Ramsey, "Charles C. Grafton, Bishop and Theologian," 5.

67. Grafton, *A Journey Godward*, 112, 147–149; Alexander, "Grafton and the Religious Life," 16; Pendleton, *Press On, The Kingdom*, 88.

68. Grafton, *Vocation*, 96, 101–03, 112–13.

Commitment to the teachings of the catholic faith and the prominence of the doctrine of the Incarnation inform both the name of the Sisterhood of the Holy Nativity and the community's charism. Grafton's formation in Ignatian discernment was the basis of the Sisterhood of the Holy Nativity's formation; they were taught how to pray the Gospel and to guide the prayer of others. Concern for each soul, including their own, was the central focus of the Sisterhood of the Holy Nativity. For this purpose, they dedicated their lives to providing the resources needed by the laity in local churches to bring them closer to Christ. "This they do by house-to-house visiting, finding out and reporting cases of spiritual destitution, and where desired, giving to such persons the necessary instruction and preparing them for Sacraments."[69]

The founders of the Sisterhood of the Holy Nativity perceived the need for a unique religious order focused on parish ministry and working with societies of religious priests. Dedicated to "Make Known the Christian Faith and Win Souls For Christ," the new sisterhood was envisioned as a missionary order of women focused on advancing the catholic faith in local parishes and dioceses under the ecclesiastical jurisdiction of the Episcopal Church. The Constitution of the Sisterhood of the Holy Nativity bonded the sisters to the doctrine, discipline, and worship of the Episcopal Church. It forbade the sisterhood from working in any diocese without the bishop's permission.[70]

To undertake their mission, the Sisterhood of the Holy Nativity needed rigorous training in scripture, the *Book of Common Prayer,* and sacramental theology. Given their zeal to care for individual souls, the sisters were called to enrich the prayer lives of the laity through spiritual direction, retreats, quiet days, and preparation for the sacraments. The sisters' devotion to the Church's liturgical life was reflected in their commitment to support catholic worship through care of the sacristy and altar guild training. The sisters provided spiritual care, food, clothing, shelter, medical care, childcare, and financial assistance as parish visitors.[71] "There is a vast amount of benevolence among the masses that only women can do," wrote Grafton.[72]

Grafton's historical inspiration for the Sisterhood of the Holy Nativity were the women who worked with the apostles, consecrated widows, virgins, and deaconesses of the early church. Movements to oppose women's ministries for "too long kept the Church in apathy and quenched the spirit

---

69. "The Sisterhood of the Holy Nativity," 1928, SHNC, 141.
70. *Constitutions and Rule of the Sisters of the Holy Nativity*, Whitsunday 1889, 3.
71. Pendleton, *Press On, The Kingdom*, 86.
72. Grafton, *Vocation*, 34–35.

which has been poured out upon her daughters yearning to consecrate themselves, as did the Phoebes and Priscillas of Apostolic times, to the labours to which the love of Christ constrained them," he wrote.[73] Grafton considered the ministries of the sisterhood an extension of the priesthood, just as the women of the early church extended the ministry of the apostles. He believed that all Christian women were called to church work. The most practical way for women to be effective in ministry full-time was to live together in a community and be freed from family responsibilities. "It is into this splendid heritage of self-sacrificing labor that our Church, by the revival of Sisterhoods, has entered in our day."[74]

The structure and governance of the Sisterhood of the Holy Nativity was inspired by their call to make known the catholic faith. One of the limitations of the first Anglican and Episcopal sisterhoods was the tendency to take on too much, given the overwhelming needs, and then become overburdened with commitments.[75] Given the dedication of the women who formed the first sisterhoods, it is easy to see how these situations developed. Indeed, the legitimacy of sisterhoods was argued by citing the importance of giving women opportunities to be "useful" through Christian service. The Sisterhood of the Holy Nativity founders had experience with other sisterhoods and consciously decided on a different focus. "When, therefore, I was called by divine providence to found a community, I limited the scope of its work," wrote Grafton. "We needed, I believed, in our Church, a community in which there would be large room for the cultivation of the spiritual life, and which would especially be given to aid the parochial clergy and have as a chief object the winning of souls."[76] Except for emergencies such as epidemics or war, when it might become necessary to take charge of institutions, the Constitution of the Sisterhood of the Holy Nativity forbade them to do so, even when requested. "The importunities of good men in the seeming needs and emergencies of the Church must not lead the Sisters in the future to depart from the Spirit of the Sisterhood."[77]

The Rule, devised by Charles Grafton with Mother Ruth Margaret, was Augustinian in tradition like other Anglican sisterhoods at the time and devotional and practical in tenor.[78] The sisterhood prides itself on the fact

---

73. Grafton, *Vocation*, 34.
74. Grafton, *Vocation*, 45, 53–56; Pendleton, *Press On, The Kingdom*, 86–87.
75. Grafton, *Vocation*, 53–56.
76. Grafton, *A Journey Godward*, 103–4.
77. Grafton, *Vocation*, 45–46; Constitutions and Rule of the Sisters of the Holy Nativity, Whitsunday 1889, 3.
78. Williams, "The Influence of S. Augustine," 245–47.

that the first Rule was spiritually and psychologically advanced for its era and, thus, needed to be revised sparingly over the first hundred years of its existence. The Rule focused on providing the sisters a path toward union with Christ. The founders felt that having too many regulations hindered rather than cultivated spiritual maturity. The founders of the Sisterhood of the Holy Nativity also departed from the rigorous ascetical practices of other Anglican sisterhoods, instead advocating for a moderate and balanced lifestyle.[79] The labor required of sisters made it impractical to follow ascetical practices that weakened the body to a state where they could not accomplish their work. Grafton once wore a spiked belt and hairshirt, kept frequent fasts, and sometimes slept on the floor. Finding that severe asceticism made him irritable to others, he later abandoned the practices. The sisterhood believed that the highest form of discipline was to love and that it is harder to practice love and kindness to all community members than to practice rigorous asceticism. The Rule of the Sisterhood of the Holy Nativity states that the superior "must see that no sister injures her health by fasting or over-fatigue" and ensure an appropriate diet, "for it is far better to have a moderate Rule observed than the appearance of keeping a severe one which must be broken."[80] Ideally, relationships between the sisters were to mirror "the loving union of the Holy Family in Jesus by the cultivation of a divine charity towards its members."[81]

RECONCILIATION WITH THE SOCIETY OF SAINT MARGARET

Relations between the Society of St. Margaret and the Sisterhood of the Holy Nativity remained conflicted until 1888. That year, the Sisterhood of the Holy Nativity decided to move their motherhouse to Providence.[82] The joy of the new sisterhood was dampened by the feelings resulting from the

---

79. Grafton, *Vocation*, 45–46; Constitutions and Rule of the Sisters of the Holy Nativity, Whitsunday 1889, 3.

80. *Constitutions and Rule of the Sisters of the Holy Nativity*, Whitsunday 1889, 19, 37.

81. *Constitutions and Rule of the Sisters of the Holy Nativity*, Whitsunday 1889, 2.

82. "Letters Concerning the Separation of the Sisters Who Left the Society of S. Margaret in Order to Found the Sisterhood of the Holy Nativity, 1882 (1888), SHNC. In addition to the original manuscripts, these letters exist in several formats in the SHN archives. The SHN believed that their reputation was at stake, and thus, they needed to make clear that their foundation was legitimate and that the life professed sisters did not break their vows. Thus, they ensured that the original letters were copied and available for prosperity.

circumstances of their departure from the Society of St. Margaret. The loss to the Society of Saint Margaret of three professed sisters and seven novices—roughly half the community—plus several close Associates was a setback. In addition to the financial support the sisters and Associates involved brought to the Society of St. Margaret, there was also the need to cover their workloads. With Grafton's departure as chaplain, the Society of St. Margaret was forced to find another priest to celebrate the sacraments and minister with the Associates. Grafton's departure further predicated a break with the Church of the Advent and Society of St. John The Evangelist. When the English members of the Cowley Fathers decided to remain in Boston, they opted to form a separate mission congregation. Thus, the Society of St. Margaret worked at the Church of St. John the Evangelist on Bowdoin Street, and the Sisterhood of the Holy Nativity affiliated with the Church of the Advent only blocks away on Brimmer Street.[83] Despite the difficulties, the Society of St. Margaret met the challenges and flourished.[84]

The movement toward possible reconciliation with the Society of St. Margaret was initiated in early 1888 by Sr. Virginia Margaret, Assistant Superior at the motherhouse in England, who wrote the Sisterhood of Holy Nativity a letter of "love and peace." Though there was no official communication with the Society of St. Margaret in Boston, the relationship began to mend. Mother Louisa Mary accepted visits from the Sisterhood of the Holy Nativity, which facilitated future reconciliation.[85]

When the professed sisters departed from the Society of St. Margaret, Mother Louisa Mary verbally permitted them to form a new sisterhood (novices were always free to leave on their own accord), reasoning that the presence of unhappy sisters would destabilize the community. At the time, Grafton, as chaplain, believed that the Constitution of the Society of Saint Margaret allowed the superior to make this decision in unusual circumstances without a vote from the Chapter. When the sisters parted, those who formed the Sisterhood of the Holy Nativity believed that the verbal permission of the superior was adequate and binding; they had no intention of breaking their vows. However, after the novices moved out of the Convent, the three professed sisters who left to establish the Sisterhood of the Holy Nativity, Sister Ruth Margaret, Sister Hannah, and Sister Mary,

---

83. Pendleton, *Press On, The Kingdom*, 85. The original sequence of events from the perspective of the Society of St. Margaret is found in the Superiors' Diary, 1882, found in the Archives of the Episcopal Church in Austin, Texas, and at the time of this writing, inaccessible. Pendleton reproduces a portion of this record on pages 84–85 of his book.

84. Sister Catherine Louise, SSM, *The House of My Pilgrimage*, 39.

85. Reeves, "Hidden in Christ, 24.

heard hurtful accusations that they had broken their vows because they did not receive permission to depart by Chapter vote.[86]

The conflict between the two sisterhoods ignited a scandal that tarnished the reputation of the Sisterhood of the Holy Nativity. On the one hand, Mother Louisa Mary referred to the departed professed sisters as "renegade sisters." On the other hand, the newly formed Sisterhood of the Holy Nativity was anxious to clarify that no sister broke her vows and that they were a legitimate foundation. Moreover, there was the practical consideration that the two sisterhoods would often encounter each other on the street, given their geographic proximity, making the lack of clarity awkward. Grafton and Arthur Hall (1847–1930), a former curate at the Church of the Advent and the new chaplain for the Society of St. Margaret, believed that reconciliation between the two sisterhoods without a third-party mediator would be discreet and advantageous. When the conflict between Grafton and the Cowley Fathers erupted, Hall remained in the English congregation.[87] (Correspondence reveals that Mother Ruth Margaret would have preferred a third-party arbitrator.) By the time the two sisterhoods were ready to negotiate a reconciliation, it was 1888, six years after the events of 1882, that founded the Sisterhood of the Holy Nativity.

Initial correspondence from Arthur Hall to Grafton suggests that he believed a prompt reconciliation would be affected as soon as the three sisters of the Sisterhood of the Holy Nativity repented of their disobedience.[88] Under some pressure from her superior in England, Mother Louisa Mary stressed the imperative of a Chapter vote before any professed sister leaves the community, and the lack of recognition of this fact on the part of the Sisterhood of the Holy Nativity impeded any potential reconciliation. Grafton showed the letter to the three sisters in question and informed Hall that they rejected its contents. Mother Ruth Margaret, speaking as one of the three professed sisters involved, took the lead in the reconciliation process. Grafton did not question her reasoning and sent the entirety of her response to Hall without comment. She made the argument that if vows were broken, then it was the responsibility of the Society of St. Margaret to prove that they were broken. Otherwise, they needed to rescind the accusation and apologize.[89] "Before making an acknowledgement that we have done wrong, we

---

86. Sister Catherine Louise, SSM, *The House of My Pilgrimage*, 39.

87. Goodrich, *The Parish of the Advent in the City of Boston*, 68–72.

88. "Letters Concerning the Separation of the Sisters Who Left the Society of S. Margaret in Order to Found the Sisterhood of the Holy Nativity, 1882 (1888); Arthur Hall to Charles Chapman Grafton, St. Paul's School, Concord, New Hampshire, June 5, 1888, SHNC.

89. Charles Chapman Grafton to Arthur Hall, Boston, June 1888, SHNC.

ought to know definitely what the wrong doing was," wrote Mother Ruth Margaret. After citing the Society of St. Margaret's Constitution, Mother Ruth Margaret acknowledged the scandal's cost, stating that "for five years we have been condemned and cast out of the company of all Religious with this charge. The alienation and scandal caused by this re-iterated and widespread accusation has been dishonoring to our Church, to the cause of Holy Religion, and an occasion of separation and division among those otherwise united in the maintenance and extension of the Catholic Faith."[90]

Hall was more inclined than Grafton to comment on the letters of Mother Ruth Margaret and Mother Louisa Mary. In his response, Hall stated that he found the sisters' actions to be both "irregular and schismatical" and held Grafton responsible for the situation because of the conflict over his role as chaplain, thus, he gave the sisters questionable advice.[91] Grafton resisted coming to his own defense, instead urging reconciliation for the sake of the Church.[92] Hall then wrote to Mother Ruth Margaret directly, stating that he did not believe she had read all the correspondences on the issue from the perspective of the Society of St. Margaret. Her five-page response stated that she read every correspondence and felt compelled to answer his charges, though the issue of broken vows remained the most serious. She wrote: "We were allowed to go without warning that we were violating our vows or acting in any other than a regular and lawful manner. It seems therefore unjust and contrary to the law of Divine Charity that we should be accused of breaking our vows. At such a time of pain and excitement mistakes must have been made and we are willing to express our regret for them or for anything which may have cause pain for those we loved then and still love."[93]

After receiving Mother Ruth Margaret's reply, Hall responded that diverse recollections of the conflict make it impossible to pursue any reconciliation. She disagreed and refused to be chastised for speaking up: "Conflicting recollections of the past ought not to hinder that it might be forgotten, and peace restored . . . We kept silence and would only defend ourselves on one point—till you forced us to speak and then negotiations

---

90. Mother Ruth Margaret, SHN to Charles Chapman Grafton, n.d. (June 1888), SHNC.

91. Arthur Hall to Charles Chapman Grafton, Mission House of S. John, Boston, July 7, 1888, SHNC.

92. Charles Chapman to Arthur Hall, Boston, July 1999, SHNC.

93. Mother Ruth Mary, SHN to Arthur Hall, Rindge, New Hampshire, August 1888; Mother Louisa Mary, SSM to Arthur Hall, St. Margaret's House, Boston, August 1, 1888; Arthur Hall to Mother Ruth Margaret, SHN, August 4, 1888, SHNC.

are broken off on our having spoken."[94] Grafton then wrote to Mother Louisa Mary to assure her that she acted out of wisdom and compassion. He also took responsibility for the lack of a Chapter vote, expressing that his reading of the Constitution did not require it. Thus, he advised the sisters accordingly. "I will not enter into any controversy either as defending myself by what I believe as inaccurate reflections, or by saying anything aught anyone," he wrote. "I shall always remember your more than considerate care and sympathy in time of trouble . . . Let me in the interests of peace be the scapegoat."[95]

Conflating several issues, Hall then wrote to Grafton asking him to return library books that belonged to the Society of St. John the Evangelist, urging him to resign as a building trustee for the church occupied by them in Boston, and further encouraging the resignation of the three sisters of the Holy Nativity serving as property trustees for the Society of St. Margaret.[96] At this point, Grafton argued that the issues around broken vows and property were distinct and that all the books in his possession were his own.[97] The two sisterhoods stayed on course and exchanged statements of regret and reconciliation in late 1888: Mother Ruth Margaret, Sister Mary Margaret, and Sister Hannah Margaret of the Sisterhood of the Holy Nativity "protesting" that they had no intention of violating their vows, yet apologizing for any actions that were "irregular or calculated to do harm." "I will always cherish the remembrance of the tenderness from which you parted from me and have dreamed that perhaps some day I might have it again," wrote Mother Ruth Margaret to Mother Louisa Mary."[98]

94. Mother Ruth Mary to Arthur Hall, Rindge, New Hampshire, August 29, 1888; Mother Louisa Mary, SSM to Arthur Hall, St. Margaret's House, Boston, September 6, 1888, SHNC.

95. Charles Chapman Grafton to Mother Louisa Mary, SSM, Rindge, New Hampshire, September 21, 1888, SHNC.

96. Details surrounding the conflicts over the ownership and occupation of church buildings in Boston is found in Charles Chapman Grafton, "A Letter Addressed to the Society of S. John the Evangelist," Boston, November 1883," printed not published, SHNC.

97. Author Hall to Charles Chapman Grafton, North Conway, New Hampshire, September 20, 1888; Charles Chapman Grafton to Arthur Hall, Providence, October 23, 1888, both in the SHNC. Property concerns regarding St. Margaret's Convent in Louisburg Square, Boston, were related to the cost of the building, $29,000, paid by Grafton and Mother Ruth Margaret before both left the Society of St. Margaret. Neither were interested in disturbing the sisters who lived there. Similarly, Grafton used his personal funds to support both the Church of the Advent and the Society of St. John the Evangelist while he was rector, SHNC.

98. Mother Ruth Mary to Mother Louisa Mary, Providence, October 28, 1888; draft statement by Arthur Hall as amended by the Sisters of the Holy Nativity, SHNC.

In response to the olive branch, Mother Louisa Mary responded with joy that the two communities might be united in friendship once again. Two months later, the Chapter of the Society of St. Margaret accepted the apology but was more circumspect than their superior. Stating that they "deplored the action of its Sisters in leaving the Society," they welcomed the expression of regret, recognized the Sisterhood of the Holy Nativity, and buried "all past breaches of charity."[99]

Predictably, the records of the two sisterhoods suggest that each community experienced the separation events differently. It is also the case that during the early years of Anglican and Episcopal sisterhoods, it was not uncommon for new communities to regularly diverge from older ones. Many sisterhoods lasted only a few years or for one generation.[100] Significantly, the Society of St Margaret and the Sisterhood of the Holy Nativity flourished for over a century; the Society of St. Margaret is active in many mission partnerships and continues to receive vocations today.[101]

In addition to reconciliation with the Society of St. Margaret, September 1888 signaled a move to Providence, Rhode Island, for the Sisterhood of the Holy Nativity. Having resigned as rector of the Church of the Advent, Grafton was elected bishop of the Diocese of Fond du Lac in Wisconsin. Although his dream of starting a religious community of mission priests never materialized, Grafton was considered the leading Anglo-Catholic voice of the Episcopal Church for the last twenty years of his life. He confirmed that the Sisterhood of the Holy Nativity significantly contributed to the growth of the Diocese of Fond du Lac and beyond during his episcopate.[102] Grafton and Mother Ruth Margaret worked cooperatively to ensure the future of the Sisterhood of the Holy Nativity; she resigned as superior due to ill health in 1908 and died in 1910; he died two years later. The spiritual legacy of the founders and the first generation of the Sisterhood of the Holy Nativity was integral to advancing the Anglo-Catholic Movement in the Episcopal Church to the present day.

---

99. Mother Louisa Mary, SSM to Charles Chapman Grafton, Boston, October 4, 1888; Mother Louisa Mary to Mother Ruth Margaret, St. Margaret's House, Boston, October 1888; statement forwarded from Mother Louisa Mary to Mother Ruth Margaret, St. Margaret's House, Boston, December 5, 1888, SHNC.

100. An early list of extinct women's communities, Anson, *The Call of the Cloister*, 595-97.

101. For information on the Society of St. Margaret today, see www.societyofstmargaret.org.

102. Pendleton, *Press On, The Kingdom*, 118-19.

2

Rest and Devotion in Bethlehem

MOTHERHOUSE AND MISSION HOUSES IN RHODE ISLAND

The Sisterhood of the Holy Nativity served the Episcopal Diocese of Rhode Island for almost one hundred years (1888–1983). Starting with their "first real Convent" in Providence, the sisterhood advanced the catholic faith in at least twenty separate churches, orphanages, state hospitals, a woman's prison, reformatories, and at their Convent, mission, and retreat houses. Though closely associated with parishes and the diocese, the sisters administered the work of the Sisterhood of the Holy Nativity in Rhode Island. Like other short-term and long-term missions established by the sisterhood throughout their history, they were the decision-makers and managers. The sisters worked closely with diocesan bishops and local clergy on the spiritual side of their endeavors. They were supported by growing numbers of dedicated Associates who followed a Rule of life and gave their time, treasure, and talent to the Sisterhood of the Holy Nativity.

Mother Foundress, Mother Ruth Margaret, wrote detailed instructions on the role and management of the sisterhood's mission houses. Aware of religious orders that maintained autonomous branch houses, each with its own elected superior, she intentionally devised a structure of "mission houses" under the same Mother Superior, each with a Sister-in-Charge deputized to maintain the Rule and the work in a specific location. Mother Ruth Margaret believed a centralized structure was nimbler and more responsive to change than autonomous branch houses. Generally, two to seven sisters were resident at a mission house at one time, all engaged in multiple ministries at several locations. The structure of mission houses allowed sisters to be assigned and houses to be open and closed more quickly, supporting the missionary spirit of the sisterhood.[1]

Despite the arduous schedules and prodigious output of every able-bodied woman in the sisterhood, there were only enough sisters to satisfy a fraction of the requests for help. The sisters worked *in* many dioceses and parishes but belonged to the Sisterhood of the Holy Nativity. They were ultimately accountable to their Mother Superior, who made the decisions about personnel and assets, often (but not always) in consultation with the sisters' Council. Local bishops and clergy had spiritual authority in the churches and institutions served by the sisters. The sisterhood negotiated the ministry they undertook; when conflicts arose, the course of action was ultimately the Mother Superiors' decision. This direct authority allowed the sisterhood to place sisters where they were most needed and where the work was aligned with the Rule and move them when necessary.

The most extensive association for the Sisterhood of the Holy Nativity in Rhode Island, St. Stephen's Church in Providence, resulted from a connection between Charles Grafton and the rector, George McClellan Fiske (1850–1923). Fiske was a friend of Grafton and the rector of St. Stephen's since 1884. By 1888, Fiske corresponded with Grafton about needs in Providence. He highly regarded Mother Ruth Margaret as "keen in intelligence, wide in reading, and a sterling character."[2] In the same year, Grafton resigned as rector at the Church of the Advent, Boston, and decided to move with the sisters to Providence. In June 1888, when it was still possible for a diocese to elect a bishop without consulting him in advance, Fiske was notified that he was elected bishop of the Diocese of Fond du Lac. The people of St. Stephen's implored him to stay. Fiske committed the decision to prayer and declined the election to remain in Providence. The Diocese of Fond du Lac next elected Charles Grafton to be their bishop, which he accepted and prepared to move to Wisconsin after the election was ratified. Fond du Lac could not accommodate the sisters then, so they decided to remain in Providence. With Grafton's departure for Wisconsin, Fiske agreed to serve as the sisters' chaplain. Grafton continued to visit St. Stephen's Church during his episcopate: His preaching and teaching enriched the parish, and they generously supported the sisterhood and the Diocese of Fond du Lac. Grafton

---

1. Mother Foundress, *Mission Houses of the Sisterhood of the Holy Nativity*, 4–5.
2. Pettingell, "Bethlehem in Providence," 8, SHNC.

used the mission house in Providence as a home base when traveling to the East Coast for fundraising and to recruit clergy for his diocese.[3]

Although the sisterhood was active throughout the Diocese of Rhode Island, they shared a special relationship with St. Stephen's Church. The church was founded in 1839 on the east side of Providence near Brown University. The Tractarian movement influenced the first clergy. In 1850, when an African American parish, Christ Church, Providence, was forced to close, members joined St. Stephen's, making it one of the first racially integrated congregations in the country. During their shared history, some of the clergy at St. Stephen's worked more closely with the sisters than others, and the funding for their support varied. During the early years of the partnership, the Sisterhood of the Holy Nativity was instrumental in working with St. Stephen's to establish new churches in the diocese.[4]

The charter for the Sisterhood of the Holy Nativity was approved by the General Assembly of the State of Rhode Island in January 1890 and lists the following sisters: Sister Ruth Margaret, Mother Superior, Sister Mary, Sister Hannah, Sister Katharine, Sister Rebecca, Sister Agnes, Sister Augustine, and Sister Margaret.[5] The sisterhood grew rapidly in Rhode Island. By 1893, eleven years after its founding, the Sisterhood of the Holy Nativity reached twenty-five members.[6] The sisterhood's first residence in Providence was an old mansion at 385 Benefit Street, where the "sweet chapel bell rang its seven times daily call to prayers." The house was chosen for its size and location, "standing apart from the city's confusion, among its lofty sheltering trees," while being accessible to the work and the needed ambiance for a religious residence and retreat house.[7] The motherhouse included a library and workshops for making vestments, altar linens, and altar breads.[8]

The people of St. Stephen's had a deep affection for the Sisterhood of the Holy Nativity, and the missionary spirit there established a pattern later reflected in other locations where the sisters were called. There, the sisters taught the catholic faith to all ages and trained the altar guild, acolyte guild, and other groups connected with women and children. Women from the

---

3. Catir, *Saint Stephen's Church in Providence*, 73–74; Pettingell, "Bethlehem in Providence," 14,21.

4. John D. Alexander to Sheryl A. Kujawa-Holbrook, email correspondence, February 28, 2022.

5. "An Act to Incorporate the Sisterhood of the Holy Nativity in the City of Providence, State of Rhode Island, In General Assembly, January Session, A.D. 1890," SHNC.

6. *The Churchman* (April 19, 1893) 12.

7. *The Churchman* (April 19, 1893) 5; Catir, *St. Stephen's Church in Providence*, 74.

8. Yearbook 1900, Providence, 108, SHNC.

parish were trained to embroider vestments and make altar linens to support the rich catholic ceremonial of the parish. The sisters organized Bible studies, prepared all ages for the sacraments, and made home and hospital visits. Fiske's liturgical ideal focused on "six points" of Anglo-Catholicism: altar lights (candles); eucharistic vestments; wafer bread (not soft bread); the mixed chalice (water and wine); East-facing celebrations (the priest facing the altar); and incense. St. Stephen's was one of the rare Episcopal churches of the era to include all six practices in its liturgy. It was also the site of the Holy Nativity ward of the Confraternity of the Blessed Sacrament, a devotional society transferred by Charles Grafton to the United States from England in 1867. The House of the Nativity in Providence was possibly the first Episcopal religious house to reserve the Blessed Sacrament in its chapel. The sisters instituted the practice when Mother Ruth Margaret's health prevented her from attending the daily Eucharist.[9]

The sisters visited colleges and universities in Providence, such as Brown University. Sister Katherine and Sister Faith were heavily involved in caring for children at St. Mary's orphanage for two years until the demands forced them to take on a more limited role.[10] Aware of the desperate needs of people confined to state institutions, the Sisterhood of the Holy Nativity served as volunteer chaplains, visiting and teaching at the women's prison, reformatories for girls and boys, mental health institutions, and homes for the aged.[11]

Through their work in state hospitals, the sisters became acquainted with some English mill operatives from Thornton, Rhode Island. They were offered the use of a barn in Thornton and hastily outfitted it as a temporary chapel operated as a mission of St. Stephen's. During these years of establishing congregations, St. Stephen's spent more on mission activities than its operating budget.[12] The first service in the Thornton mission was held on the Feast of the Epiphany in 1891. The sisters also contributed to the mission financially and lived in the barn until living space was obtained. A permanent chapel and Sunday school room were built through gifts from the sisters, their Associates, and the Church of the Messiah. It was known as the Mission of the Holy Nativity and was founded at Christmastide in a stable.[13] Each week, the sisters staffed the Sunday school of 160 pupils. "The

9. Pettingell, "Bethlehem in Providence," 17.

10. Bridge and Reinken, "Saint Mary's Episcopal Church," 8, SHNC.

11. Lee, "Remembering Our Sisters: The Rhode Island Herstory Project," n.d. 52, SHNC.

12. Pettingell, "Bethlehem in Providence," 18. Interview, Zulette and Norman Catir, April 20, 2022.

13. *The Churchman* (April 19, 1893) 5; Catir, *St. Stephen's Church in Providence*, 79–80.

unusual prosperity of the Mission is due, under God, to the Rev. S. B. Blunt and the Sisters of the Holy Nativity. Scarcely another parish or mission can be found in our diocese wherein the entire number of registered communicants are *actual* communicants."[14]

The Sisterhood of the Holy Nativity served churches across Providence, teaching and visiting homes. For example, in 1900, the sisters made 1759 visits: 462 for St. Stephens, 822 in East Providence, and 275 in Thornton. In the same year, the sisters prepared 18 persons for the sacraments at St. Stephen's, 20 in East Providence, and 70 at the mission in Thornton.[15] They also assisted at other parishes in the Providence area, including the Church of the Epiphany, Christ Church, Church of the Redeemer, and Church of the Savior. The sisterhood assisted with the library at the diocesan cathedral and taught at St. Mary's, East Providence. In Olneyville, "a large, earnest Bible-class and guild of factory girls are [were] in the Sisters' care."[16]

In 1915, the five sisters in Providence made 1655 visits and received 1208 visitors and retreatants at the mission house. In addition, they taught 154 classes, offered private instruction to 123, managed 174 guild meetings, made 60 hospital visits, and facilitated 34 baptisms. During the 1920s, the sisters offered additional classes and teacher training in response to the state offering time off for public school children to receive religious instruction. During monthly meetings with the Associates, it was not uncommon for a sister to give an address. By 1929, with four sisters in residence, the number of visits increased to 2421, with 1087 visitors and retreatants staying at the house. Ten years later, the sisters were making 2436 visits, and the number of guild meetings (324), classes (433), and private instruction for the sacraments (109) continued to grow. Private instruction for the lapsed returning to the Church was part of the teaching. When sisters with musical talents were assigned to the house in Providence, they played the organ at St. Stephen's and conducted a children's choir. Except for summer programs, the sisters closed mission houses over the summer months to accommodate their rest periods, community time, and annual retreats.[17]

---

14. George McClellan Fiske, "Church of the Holy Nativity, Thornton," *Convention Journal* 1901 [Episcopal Diocese of Rhode Island] 145; *The Churchman* (April 19, 1893), 9, SHNC.

15. Yearbook 1900, Providence, 90, SHNC.

16. *The Churchman* (April 19, 1893) 9

17. Yearbook, 1915-1918, 1919-1920, Providence, 20-21, SHNC; Yearbook 1920-1931, Providence, 233-35. SHNC; Annual Reports of Convent and Mission Houses, 1940-1943, Providence, 7-8, SHNC.

The Sisterhood of the Holy Nativity worked in churches throughout the Diocese of Rhode Island: Church of the Ascension, Cranston, St. Bartholomew's, Cranston, Grace Church, Phillpsdale, St. James, Woonsocket, St. Mark's, West Warwick, St. George's, Central Falls, St. Paul's, Wickford, and St. Michael's, Bristol, to name a few. They started two homes for "rest and recreation" in eastern Rhode Island: one in Tiverton for teachers, nurses, and other working women of limited means, and one in Barrington for working girls and poor families. The building for the House of Rest on the seashore in Tiverton was donated by an Associate from Boston in 1891 to provide women with a place of "spiritual as well as physical refreshment" beyond a parish environment.[18] The House of Rest in Tiverton resulted in the establishment of a church in the village. During the summer, St. Helena's Rest in Barrington offered similar opportunities for working women and poor families."[19]

After the Sisterhood of the Holy Nativity relocated the motherhouse to Fond du Lac in 1905, the Associates in Rhode Island secured funding for two sisters to remain in a house at 63 John Street in Providence. In July 1907, 117 and 119 George Street, across from St. Stephen's, were purchased as a Convent, which the sisters occupied until 1946 when the block was cleared for Brown University use. The new house had enough room for visiting Associates and a "House of Rest for Ladies" that needed light nursing care. The larger space also accommodated the library.[20] Associates provided financial support through various activities, most visibly through an annual retreat before the sisters left Providence each summer.[21]

During the years 1947–1956, the Providence mission house was located at 27 Cabot Street. The Cabot Street house was intentionally designed to accommodate more retreatants. "The new house will be particularly adapted for individual and small group retreats, [that] the church women in the city may learn to generally values and use the opportunity to get away, . . . from the over-activity and strain of modern living."[22] The final mission house in Providence was located at 134 Power Street and opened on Christmas in 1957.[23] From 1953 until 1962, Sister Veronica was Sister-in-Charge of the Providence mission house, guiding all with "quiet wit and deep devotion."[24]

18. Yearbook, 1915–1918, SHNC.
19. Yearbook, 1915–1918, SHNC.
20. Pettingell, "Bethlehem in Providence," 20.
21. Pettingell, "Bethlehem in Providence," 20.
22. *St. Stephen's Magazine*, [ca. December 1946] n.p.
23. Catir, *St. Stephen's Church in Providence*, 94.
24. Catir, *St. Stephen's Church in Providence*, 182.

"The contribution made by the Sisters of the Holy Nativity to the church school, the Acolytes Guild, to the Altar and Women's Guilds, and in a host of ways to the pastoral life of Saint Stephen's cannot be overestimated," writes Norman J. Catir, a former curate.[25]

The rich religious diversity of Rhode Island—from the time of settlement, one of the most religiously diverse regions on the Atlantic coast—provided opportunities for the Sisterhood of the Holy Nativity to foster ecumenical and interfaith relationships early in their history, with the enthusiastic support of the founders, Bishop Grafton, and Mother Ruth Margaret. One of the legacies of the Sisterhood of the Holy Nativity is their historic commitment to ecumenism and church unity. The sisters interacted socially and shared spiritual talks with the Roman Catholic Convent of the Sacred Heart, the Sisters of Notre Dame, and the Sisters of Mercy of St. Joseph. In the twentieth century, these relationships grew to include Jewish-Christian events. Later in their history, the sisterhood participated in ecumenical retreats and programs beyond Providence in Fond du Lac and Bay Shore. [26]

MISSION HOUSE IN NEWPORT

Newport, Rhode Island, was the site of the second long-term mission house of the Sisterhood of the Holy Nativity. In 1914, Sarah Morris Fish Webster, the wife of Sidney Webster, private secretary to President Franklin Pierce, pledged the use of a house in Newport for the sisters and endowed it with a legacy after she died in 1925.[27] From there, the sisters taught at St. Michael's School, Emmanuel Church, and the Zabriskie Memorial Church of St. John the Evangelist. St. John's was the site of the mission house from 1914 to 1953, almost forty years. During their first year, the three sisters in Newport made 2225 visits, received 1318 guests and retreatants, held 188 guild meetings, hosted 199 altar guild meetings, gave 128 classes, and prepared 118 for the sacraments privately.[28]

In Newport, the Sisterhood of the Holy Nativity in Newport worked primarily with women and children, taught the catholic faith to all ages, and extensively visited homes and hospitals. During the years of World War I,

---

25. Catir, *St. Stephen's Church in Providence*, 182.

26. Scotti, "The Sacrifice Gives Strength," 14; 'From Seder to Last Supper," *The Providence Journal* (March 16, 1962), n.p. SHNC.

27. One of the Sisters, "The Sisterhood of the Holy Nativity," *Holy Cross Magazine* (September 1935) 235, SHNC. Also, see the New York Historical Society on Sarah Morris Fish (1838-1925), nyhistory.org.

28. Yearbook, 1915-1918, 1919-1920, Newport, 34-35, SHNC.

the guilds they organized divided their time between parish work, missionary projects, and war relief. "They have contributed $135 for the Belgian and Armenian children, 'adopted' a prisoner of war, made a large number of flannel shirts, pajamas, socks, scarves, and wristlets, and have helped considerably with surgical dressings and bandages."[29] Given Newport's connection with the United States Navy, the mission house was heavily engaged in Red Cross work throughout the war, with the sisters supervising "much of the cutting out, finishing, packaging, etc." of medical supplies.[30] The sisters worked valiantly, "nursing and carrying nourishment" during the Spanish flu epidemic in 1918. Two sisters caught the flu simultaneously, leaving a novice to press on until she, too, caught the flu: "[H]er services were greatly appreciated, particularly by two Jewish families and some Portuguese Roman Catholics."[31]

At St. John's, the Sisterhood of the Holy Nativity was involved in the arts and assisted with the annual summer festival, vacation Bible school, plays, and pageants. Newport is known for its seasonal festivals, and the sisters enthusiastically supported Christmas festivities. "At Christmas, Sister Grace trained the children for the Mystery Play, which was most successful," notes the house record for January 1921.[32] Sr. Bernadine was a puppeteer and offered puppet shows at the children's shelter, and Sister Hildegarde wrote children's plays.[33] Though the sisterhood closed the house in Newport in 1953, local lore suggests their ghosts continue to inhabit 55 Washington Street. "While lying on the sofa reading one evening at dusk, I experienced a ghostly vision," shared a recent owner of the house. "Three nuns passed through the chapel and entered a small side room to the right filled with bookshelves. It was very non-threatening, almost peaceful, and has always stayed with me."[34]

BETHLEHEM IN FOND DU LAC

The Diocese of Fond du Lac became a spiritual center for the Sisterhood of the Holy Nativity when Charles Grafton was elected bishop in 1888. The sisterhood began missionary work there in 1889 and established a mission house after two experimental years. At the time, the sisterhood was only

29. Yearbook, 1915–1918, 1919–1920, Newport, 69, SHNC.
30. Yearbook, 1915–1918, 1919–1920, Newport, 145, SHNC.
31. Yearbook, 1915–1918, 1919–1920, Newport, 146, SHNC.
32. Yearbook 1920–1931, Newport, 42–43, SHNC.
33. Yearbook 1920–1931, Newport, 67, SHNC
34. Stuart, "Nuns on the Point," 9.

eight years old but already recognized for its contributions to parish preaching missions.[35] "Founded only eight years since, the Sisterhood has grown in the respect and esteem of the general Church, and we should be grateful as a Diocese that it now has a permanent home in our midst."[36]

In 1905, the sisterhood established a new Convent in downtown Fond du Lac, having moved there from their former motherhouse in Providence, Rhode Island. From the Convent of the Holy Nativity on Division Street, the sisters contributed immeasurably to the spread of catholic teaching and practice throughout the diocese, Wisconsin, and, over time, through as many as seven mission and retreat houses throughout the country. Here, too, the sisters lived out their first vocation as religious through the Divine Office, offering prayers of intercession, the adoration of the Blessed Sacrament, daily Mass, and community life.[37] The Convent and motherhouse in Fond du Lac was also the headquarters for the "missionary enterprises" of the sisterhood and a center for the ecclesiastical arts by producing altar bread, vestments and altar linens, devotional cards, and publishing educational resources. The library continued offering resources to clergy, seminary students, teachers, and interested laity and was replicated in some mission houses. The Convent also operated as a retreat center for women, and later for clergy, throughout the Diocese of Fond du Lac and the state of Wisconsin. Hundreds of Associates of the sisterhood from across the country considered the Convent of the Nativity in Fond du Lac a spiritual home, their "Bethlehem," and continue to live by the Associates' Rule today.[38]

From the Convent of the Holy Nativity in Fond du Lac, the Sisterhood of the Holy Nativity were primary evangelists for the catholic faith. They worked as educators and catechists on preaching missions with priests from the Society of St. John the Evangelist and the Order of the Holy Cross. They also served in parish missions in the Diocese of Fond du Lac with their bishop. In addition to temporary missions across the state of Wisconsin, much of the Sisterhood of the Holy Nativity's work in the city of Fond du Lac centered around St. Paul's Cathedral, St. Michael's Church in North Fond du Lac, and Grafton Hall School for girls. "They [The Sisterhood of the Holy Nativity] are regular attendants at the services and workers among the poor of the parish. Their work and prayers are of much influence," states

---

35. *Journal. Diocese of Fond du Lac. Sixteenth Annual Council,* 1890, 42, 55–56.

36. *Journal. Diocese of Fond du Lac. Sixteenth Annual Council,* 1890, 42.

37. *The Proper Offices for the Sisterhood of the Holy Nativity* (Providence: Snow and Farnham, n.d. [ca. 1900]).

38. Interview, Phoebe Pettingell, February 24, 2022.

the diocesan history.[39] One of the earliest missions of the Sisterhood of the Holy Nativity was on the Oneida Reservation, where two or three sisters worked with the Indigenous community. The sisterhood later extended its work in Wisconsin with a mission house at All Saints' Cathedral in the Episcopal Diocese of Milwaukee in 1909.[40]

CONVENT LIFE

In 1905, it took two days for the Sisterhood of the Holy Nativity to travel by train from Providence, Rhode Island, to their new Convent in Fond du Lac, Wisconsin. On the day of their arrival, the Fond du Lac River, which runs next to the Cathedral, overflowed its banks, and the bishop had to be rowed to safety. The house obtained for the sisters' convent and bishop's residence was a red brick, four-story mansion known as the Amory House. The Amory House was purchased in 1894 by Robert Codman of the Church of the Advent in Boston, the widower of Catherine Codman, one of the first Associates of the sisterhood. "Everything in the Convent proper is thoroughly church-like like but the simple and impressive beauty of all pleases the visitor," wrote one Milwaukee guest.[41] It stood on the northeast corner of East Division and Amory Streets and was enlarged and renovated for $30,000. A suite of rooms for Bishop Grafton on the first floor was later enlarged to accommodate his library. A second-floor chapel was added above the library and a three-story brick addition with frontage on Amory Street. Catherine Codman donated the chapel in memory of her mother, who was instrumental in founding the Sisterhood of the Holy Nativity in 1882.[42] German woodcutters, the Lang family of Oberammergau, Germany, and Manitowoc, Wisconsin, transformed the interior paneling, carvings, statues, and doors. Antiques inherited from the Grafton family were given to furnish the house.[43] The house was blessed and formally dedicated as the motherhouse of the Sisterhood of the Holy Nativity in September 1905 by Bishop Grafton.[44] Once consecrated, the motherhouse in Fond du Lac was

39. Curtiss, *History of the Diocese of Fond du Lac and Its Several Congregations*, 34, 37.

40. Curtiss, *History of the Diocese of Fond du Lac and Its Several Congregations*, 37.

41. "Dedication of the Convent of the Sisterhood of the Holy Nativity," Diocese of Milwaukee, 1905, SHNC.

42. "Holy Nativity Convent Dedicated," The Living Church (September 16, 1905) 672.

43. Kremer, "Convent of the Sisterhood of the Holy Nativity, *Fond du Lac Reporter* (July 8, 1967) n.p. SHNC.

44. Gores, "Motherhouse Moved to City by Bishop Grafton in 1905," 13; Karst, "Traditional Religious in a Secular World," 14.

the only Convent of the sisterhood; all other localities were considered mission houses. "Over all the Houses stands the Motherhouse in Fond du Lac as a very real mother, giving spiritual strength and succor to her daughters and sending out replacements to the mission houses: from it flows in a true sense the life of the Community."[45]

St. Michael's Church in North Fond du Lac was a mission to families in the railroad industry and a site the sisterhood used to train novices. The congregation's numbers ebbed and flowed according to where the railroad relocated families. At times, as many as three sisters were there each Sunday, teaching and playing the organ. The sisters also established an altar guild and a women's guild that were eventually assumed by the congregation. Through the efforts of the women's guild, the mission had fuel, light, and a paid vicar into the early 1920s.[46]

Despite the success of their missionary work, the Sisterhood of the Holy Nativity believed that their primary calling was religious life. "The object of the Community, next to the perfection of its members in the Religious Life, is the extension and establishment of the Catholic Faith," cites the sisterhood in a letter to associates.[47] Early descriptions of the order indicate it was directed to "ladies who feel called to a life of devotion and spiritual service," willing to provide "constant intercession for the conversion of sinners and the increase of Christ's kingdom."[48] The founders' vision for the Sisterhood of the Holy Nativity was based on the "mixed life" of the Augustinian Rule. A life of prayer combined with meaningful ministry and grounded in community life was attractive to women seeking vocations in the Church. The mixed life was also attractive to the broader church in an era of missionary expansion when large numbers of unpaid workers were needed, and cultural gender biases reinforced the importance of women being useful. "While the Sisterhood of the Holy Nativity is a mixed Order and its exterior works are what impress the world with its usefulness, in reality, it has from the first been dedicated to a life of intercession," noted one church periodical in 1919.[49]

---

45. *Sisterhood of the Holy Nativity,* 1882, pamphlet, n.d. [ca. 1960s] n.p [2], SHNC; Curtiss, *History of the Diocese of Fond du Lac and Its Several Congregations,* 39; "Sisterhood of the Holy Nativity, Formation: a Life Process," n.d, n.p. [ca. 1980s] SHNC.

46. Curtiss, *History of the Diocese of Fond du Lac and Its Several Congregations,* 66–67,

47. *For the Associates of the Holy Nativity,* the Sisterhood of the Holy Nativity, n.d. [ca. 1900] 6, SHNC.

48. *Journal. Diocese of Fond du Lac. Sixteenth Annual Council,* 1890, 83.

49. Barry, "Mission Work and Prayer," 337.

Anglo-Catholics were a minority in the Episcopal Church and in some dioceses contentious. Yet the social work accomplished by sisterhoods was highly valued, even by convicted Protestants who otherwise were suspicious of anything possibly considered "papist." Although the Sisterhood of the Holy Nativity valued both the contemplative and the active aspects of their vocation, the sisters strived to prioritize their roles as religious, even though it was a challenging balance.[50]

The daily routines of the Convent, replicated as closely as possible in the mission houses, valued routine, simplicity, and silence. The rhythm of the day was built on the Divine Office, daily Mass, and intercessory prayer. Through prayer and intercession, the Divine Office was the "sanctification of time" and the place for lifting the successes and failures of each day to God.[51]

Though the office was adapted to the community's needs, the liturgical heritage was the sevenfold Divine Office translated by John Mason Neale for the Society of St. Margaret. The day was divided into the offices of prime, terce, sext, none, vespers, compline, and lauds, in addition to daily Mass, with times for meals, meditation, housework, work in departments, study, tea, recreation, and free time.[52]

Throughout its history, the Sisterhood of the Holy Nativity enriched its catholic spirituality through liturgical life. Beginning on the feast of the Annunciation in 1930, the sisters prayed from *The American Missal*. The missal incorporated the complete *Book of Common Prayer* and devotional materials geared to Anglo-Catholic communities, including monastic offices, materials from the English missals, ceremonial manuals, and an expanded liturgical calendar with diverse patron saints. Well-received by Anglo-Catholics, the missal was never intended to replace the authorized *Book of Common Prayer* in the Episcopal Church, but to be used as a supplement. Mother Matilda noted that the book "fills a long-felt need" for the Sisterhood of the Holy Nativity.[53]

The Blessed Sacrament was reserved in the chapel, with each sister assigned a time for daily private prayer and intercession. "But the work on which we rely most is intercession; it is at the prayer-desk that we feel our best work is done for the Church and her needs."[54] The schedule varied

50. Mangion, "The 'Mixed Life," 165–79.

51. "The Divine Office," unidentified publication, SHNC, August 1983.

52. *Religious Communities in the American Episcopal Church and in the Anglican Church in Canada*, 1945, 96.

53. Yearbook 1920–1931, SHNC, 256. On the *Anglican Missal*, see American Missal, www.episcopalchurch.org.

54. For the Associates of the Holy Nativity, the Sisterhood of the Holy Nativity,

according to the number of sisters in the house, intending to grow the sisterhood to a size where ongoing perpetual adoration was possible. In times of crisis, the hours for prayer before the Blessed Sacrament were extended throughout the night. Given the sisterhood's commitment to ecumenism, the sisters lit a candle one day per week before the Blessed Sacrament to pray for Christian Unity. Each sister was remembered in prayer daily, especially those absent, ill, or engaged in extra challenging work. Prayer petitions came to the sisters from Associates and friends worldwide.[55] It was through intercessory prayer that the sisterhood's connection to world events was most evident. One journal entry in 1915 stated: "We had a Novena for the Allies—the American communities joining with those in England, at the request of the Superior General of SSJE."[56] A similar note, written by Mother Ruth Mary, was recorded during World War II: "As we begin this year of 1940, we find the world again plunged into war, and so the need of the real work of the Community—its prayers and intercessions—is again brought to the fore."[57]

The beauty of the Convent's liturgical life was enhanced through study and practice. Renowned musicologist Charles Winfred Douglas (1867–1944) was a canon residentiary of the Diocese of Fond du Lac and instructed the sisters in plainsong and organ for several years, starting in 1907. Douglas studied with the monks of Solesmes and was instrumental in bringing plainsong and the full choral service into general use in the Episcopal Church. He had a long relationship with the Community of St. Mary in Peekskill, New York, and Kenosha, Wisconsin. Douglas edited a plainsong psalter and monastic diurnal and contributed to *The New Hymnal* 1916 and *The Hymnal* 1940. One of Douglas' contributions to the liturgical life of the Sisterhood of the Holy Nativity was his arrangements of the Salve Regina and other hymns commemorating the Virgin Mary.[58]

The ministry of the Sisterhood of the Holy Nativity in the world flowed from a deep reservoir of divine love, nurtured through contemplation and silence. Meals were simple and usually taken in silence. The sisters met as a community for retreat, recreation, and renewal times. The Rule recognized the need for rest and recreation. Daily activities such as light reading, needlework, or walking in the garden were recommended. Long retreats for the

---

n.d. [ca. 1900] 9, SHNC; Curtiss, *History of the Diocese of Fond du Lac and Its Several Congregations*, 39; *Religious Communities in the American Episcopal Church and in the Anglican Church in Canada*, 1945, 96.

55. *For the Associates of the Holy Nativity*, 9–10, SHNC.
56. Yearbook 1915–1918, 1919–1920, SHNC, 15.
57. Annual Report of Convent and Mission Houses, 1940–1943, SHNC, 1.
58. Reeves, "Hidden in Christ," 2; Parker, "Full Choral Services," 13.

whole community and times of private retreats for individual sisters were a priority, as were the summer rest time and periodic family visits. The community rest time, held for almost 100 years at the sisters' property on Green Lake in Wisconsin, was an effort to build relationships when the sisters were dispersed in mission houses. "The sisterhood bought the land and first built their cottage there [on Green Lake] in 1923, purchasing a Ford Model T to make the commute."[59] "The Summer was a very happy one, some twenty Sisters coming home for their rest," wrote Mother Matilda in 1934. "The cottage has proved a great blessing in providing rest and refreshment for the Sisters and taking care of the overflow from the Convent."[60]

Convent life included joyful occasions, often celebrated within the liturgy. Professions, clothings, and anniversaries were celebrated, as were visits to mission and retreat houses. Christmas, the sisterhood's patronal festival, was particularly joyful, with special liturgies, music, prayer, meditation, decorations, and recreation. For over a week before the Feast of the Nativity, the sisters prepared the house for the coming of Jesus with festive decorations—trees, greens, pinecones, and ribbons. Pre-Christmas antiphons were sung daily in the chapel from December 16 until December 23.[61] A sister at Community of St. Mary the Virgin, the Anglican sisterhood in Wantage, England, made a creche for the Sisterhood of the Holy Nativity. The creche was organized before vespers, including every figure except the baby Jesus, who did not appear until midnight Mass. At the prayer of consecration during the Eucharist, the light was turned on in the creche. The altar was decorated with poinsettias from Associates and friends and flanked by two Christmas trees. The choir stalls and rood screen were festooned with greens and pinecones. A lighted creche also stood on the outside porch of the Convent to symbolize the Incarnation. Depending on the chaplain, the sisters sometimes celebrated three Masses for Christmas (midnight, dawn, and Christmas Day), after which they had breakfast and a "free day," except for the Divine Office. Some sisters decorated a tree in the Common Room. After vespers, carols were sung, and gifts opened. "The spirit of expectancy carried through the remaining festivals of the season."[62]

---

59. Yearbook 1920–1931, SHNC, 73.

60. Yearbook 1933–1934, SHNC 72.

61. "To our dear Associates, Christmas Day, 1950," SHNC; *The pre-Christmas Antiphons*, 1910, SHNC.

62. "To our dear Associates, Christmas Day, 1950," SHNC.

MEMBERSHIP IN THE SISTERHOOD

Traditionally, it took extensive training and years of prayer and discernment (on the part of the individual and the sisterhood) to become a life professed member of the Sisterhood of the Holy Nativity. The process typically started with a letter, or series of letters, from an applicant to the Mother Superior expressing her desires. Recommendations from clergy were received regarding the appropriateness of a candidate for religious life. A formal interview followed correspondence, and if deemed appropriate by the Mother Superior, an applicant was invited to formally visit the community as an aspirant for at least a month to get a feel for the religious life. During these visits, aspirants lived apart as guests yet participated in the rhythms of the community's life, getting to know the sisters and gaining a sense of the ministry.[63]

Technically, the Sisterhood of the Holy Nativity accepted applicants between the ages of eighteen and forty who were healthy, debt-free, and without family responsibilities. The sisters eventually admitted widowed or divorced women without dependents and unable to continue in their marriage vows.[64] Few sisters were life professed in their twenties. The sisterhood was known to take women over the age of forty if there were circumstances leading to a delayed vocation. Close to 75 percent of the Sisterhood of the Holy Nativity members were life professed in their thirties or forties. Out of eighty-seven sisters who remained in the community for life, only ten were life professed in their twenties. Thirteen sisters, or 15 percent, were life professed between the ages of fifty and sixty-five.[65] Given the focus of the Sisterhood of the Holy Nativity on teaching the catholic faith, the women who entered the community with a previous occupation were most often teachers, followed by nurses, artists, librarians, and musicians. The daughters or sisters of clergymen also joined the community, as did deaconesses and members of other sisterhoods. Also included in the sisterhood were two former parish secretaries, businesswomen, a medical doctor, an English professor, and two women with expertise in plumbing and hardware.[66]

---

63. *A Guide to Anglican Religious Communities in the United States and Canada*, 1965, 25.

Curtiss, *History of the Diocese of Fond du Lac and Its Several Congregations*, 39; "Sisterhood of the Holy Nativity, Formation: a Life Process," n.d, n.p.[ca. 1980s], SHNC.

64. Letter from Sister Patricia, SHN to the Mother Superior, SHN, n.d. [ca. 1930s], SHNC.

65. Calculations are based on a total of 87 sisters who were life professed and died while in the community or are currently living. Birthdates and life profession dates are available for all 87 sisters.

66. Family and occupational data for the Sisterhood of the Holy Nativity are

Although the requirements for admittance did not require a college degree, the Sisterhood of the Holy Nativity required applicants to have sufficient education to teach the catholic faith to all ages. Thus, many women who entered the sisterhood had formal education and professions before they entered religious life.[67] When the Sisterhood of the Holy Nativity was founded, approximately one-third to one-half of the applicants to women's orders were rejected. However, some were accepted upon later application or allowed to return after failed attempts. Failed attempts most often had to do with a candidate's inability to live successfully in the community rather than other issues.[68]

Typically, after a woman entered the sisterhood, she was a postulant for six months to a year to test her vocation. The number of years women were required to test their vocations before life profession varied over the history of the community. The novitiate was for two to three years; if a woman was elected to junior profession, that period of discernment was also for two to three years. Novices received a habit, veil, "religious" name, sometimes a version of their own name, or a more aspirational name after a saint. Junior professed sisters received training in the ministries of the community and could be sent to any of the mission houses at any time. After a period as a junior professed sister, a woman could be elected to life profession. Election to life vows, or any other stage in the formation process, was not automatic but an exercise in discernment between the community and the candidate. Life profession was not considered the end of formation but rather a sign of a life-long commitment to Christ. Some women were extended for periods before moving along in the process. In contrast, others discerned that they were not generally called to the religious life or to the Sisterhood of the Holy Nativity. During aspirancy, postulancy, and the novitiate, candidates received instruction in religious life, scripture, church history, theology, and the sacraments. Postulants and novices made renewable promises; the junior and life professed took vows. In addition to the traditional vows of poverty, chastity, and obedience, the Sisterhood of the Holy Nativity took a fourth vow—to live in charity in the community. This fourth vow, noted one sister, is "the most difficult to keep."[69]

---

included in the sisters' obituaries, entrance data, and correspondence. Biographical data confirmed on Ancestry.com for each sister listed in the Appendix of Life Professed Sisters.

67. *A Guide to Anglican Religious Communities in the United States and Canada*, 25; Ferry, *The Old Convent*, 110–13.

68. Ferry, *The Old Convent*, 112.

69. "Other Beloved I Have ... or Meet the Sisters of the Holy Nativity," by a Sister of St Agnes, n.d. [ca 1983] 4. SHNC; Curtiss, *History of the Diocese of Fond du Lac and Its*

The formation process for the Sisterhood of the Holy Nativity was long and demanding. It is easy in today's era of expanded opportunities for women in the Church to lose sight of the way sisterhoods expanded the choices and opportunities for women born in the nineteenth and early twentieth centuries when the Sisterhood of the Holy Nativity and other Anglican and Episcopal religious orders grew at a rapid rate. As one historian argues: "Such vows were understood to be demanding, hence the long training period. Yet the sisters were given far greater opportunities for reflection and release than the millions of Victorian women who made their marriage vows, also committing themselves for life, without any trial period or possibility of escape in an age when divorce was almost impossible."[70]

The "great pressure of work" among the sisters, in addition to the limitations of healthcare during the early years of the Sisterhood of the Holy Nativity, account for the frequent realities of illness and death.[71] Although the admissions criteria for the Sisterhood of the Holy Nativity stated that candidates needed "strength enough to keep the Rule," there were women with chronic illnesses, such as rheumatoid arthritis, migraines, scoliosis, epilepsy, or orthopedic braces who were admitted to the sisterhood, managed their conditions, and lived out their vocations.[72] The physicians who served the sisters seldom charged for their services but were limited to the treatments available at the time, with few available hospital beds. Sister Etheldreda, Sister-in-Charge of the Milwaukee mission house for many years, had severe glaucoma and underwent numerous surgeries to retain her eyesight.[73] Sister Adelaide's emergency appendectomy was performed on the refectory table at the Convent, and she survived. Lesser illnesses like colds and bronchitis kept sisters in bed for a week or two. The sisters noted that such conditions were minimized when they installed an oil burner in the Convent, "enabling us to keep a more even temperature."[74]

Each annual report from the Mother Superior included an overall health update, citing illnesses, accidents, surgeries, hospitalizations, and occasionally the need for a sister to receive long-term care. "The year has

---

Several Congregations, 39. Interview, Sister Barbara Jean, AF, with Stephen Peay, June 10, 2019.

70. Ferry, *The Old Convent*, 112.

71. For example, see the comments by Mother Matilda, Yearbook 1935–1936, 134, where she writes of her appreciation for the sisters' generosity despite the pressures of work.

72. *Religious Communities in the American Episcopal Church and in the Anglican Church in Canada*, 1945, 97.

73. Yearbook 1920–1931, SHNC, 194–95.

74. Yearbook 1920–1931, SHNC, 226

been one of widespread illness and death, in which God has honored us with a share," wrote Mother Matilda in 1929. In that year, three sisters had emergency surgeries; only one survived.[75] The detail provided in the report varied according to the superior who documented the cases, often with a minimal amount of commentary. Given the high value the sisters put on never complaining and their belief that enduring pain was a sign of holiness, it was not uncommon for severe illnesses to go undiagnosed.[76] For example, Sister Caroline returned to the Convent for rest "and ten days later informed the Mother that she had been suffering from cancer in the breast for several years, but did not wish to cause trouble by speaking of it."[77] Sister Caroline soon underwent surgery and fully recovered. Mother Katherine Edith, elected for an additional term as superior against her wishes, finally saw the Convent physician, who diagnosed her with terminal liver cancer. She died twelve days later; efficient until the end, she set into motion the process for the election of a new superior immediately upon returning from the doctor's office.[78] Sister Emily hid her abdominal cancer as fatigue until two months before her death.[79]

Documentation of mental illness is uneven throughout the records of the sisterhood and is often referred to as "nerves" or "fatigue" until the late twentieth century. In 1934, two sisters suffered from "nervous collapse" and took to their beds.[80] The records show that at least four sisters were committed to a state hospital; one sister returned to the Convent and, after that, permanently lived in the infirmary.[81] When a sister was institutionalized by necessity, she was regularly visited by her sisters and priests. Occasionally, a sister was unable to cope with "intense physical and mental strain" and left the community without warning, never to return.[82] Stress-related illnesses like migraines, heart conditions, and high blood pressure were common, with notes in the report about sisters who were so exhausted that they returned to the Convent from a mission house for an extended rest. Sister

---

75. Yearbook 1920–1931, SHNC, 194.

76. For an account of two sisters dying of undiagnosed conditions, see Yearbook 1931–1932, SHNC, 1.

77. Yearbook 1931–1932, SHNC 2.

78. Yearbook 1915–1918, 1919–1920, SHNC, 172.

79. Yearbook 1920–1931, SHNC, 167.

80. Yearbook 1933–1934, SHNC, 72.

81. Sister Edwina was also committed to the state hospital for severe epilepsy, Annual Report of Convent and Mission Houses, 1940–1943, SHNC, 27; Sister Anita was sent to a hospital in Missouri and, after treatment, returned to New York, see Yearbook 1931–1932, SHNC, 1,

82. Yearbook 1920–1931, SHNC, 25,

Adelaide and Sister Rebecca were among the sisters who were subject to frequent migraines.[83]

Before antibiotics, contagious diseases disproportionately affected the poor and those without adequate food, housing, sanitation, and healthcare. The sisters lived near each other, as well as with the vulnerable. Although the sisters received better food, housing, and medical care than the poor, the conditions in some mission houses were spartan. During the 1918 Spanish flu epidemic, sisters cared for their own while visiting the homes of the sick.[84] Pneumonia and tuberculosis were the most frequent causes of death for those sisters who died young; some of the sisters who survived had reoccurring bouts, leaving them with "weak lungs" or the need to have a lung removed. Sister Paula, Sister Hildegarde, and Sister Elsbeth were among the sisters who contracted tuberculosis and survived.[85] When the motherhouse was in Providence, Sister Hannah Margaret died of pneumonia shortly after the house physician diagnosed her on the road to recovery. Sister Margaret survived pneumonia at Oneida and had a lung removed. Sister Carlotta Mary died at the age of thirty-two due to peritonitis after surgery for fibroid tumors.[86]

The Convent contained an infirmary where sisters received temporary and end-of-life care. During the early years of the sisterhood, most women learned the rudiments of nursing care at home. Before modern medicine, the sisters were primarily treated at the Convent, though the community always provided professional care when needed. Sister Lillian had stomach problems for thirty years despite an operation for ulcers. One medical consultation revealed "she had an hourglass stomach and other trouble."[87] Starting in the 1940s, as the median age of the sisters began to rise, the number of those who needed extensive medical care grew to the extent that the sisterhood employed professional nurses. "At the Convent the year has been hard," wrote Mother Ruth Mary, "because our numbers have been few, and so many sisters are, at best, semi-invalids."[88] During the last thirty years, older sisters who needed nursing care, assisted living, or hospice were cared

83. Yearbook 1920–1931, SHNC, 255.

84. Yearbook 1915–1918, 1919–1920, SHNC, 146.

85. Yearbook 1920–1931, SHNC, 27.

86. Yearbook 1915–1918, 1919–1920, SHNC, 10, 136, 172. The State of Rhode Island provided information on Sister Carlota Mary's cause of death.

87. Health reports in yearbooks from 1912 until she died after breaking her hip in 1942 chart Sister Lillian's stomach ailments, for example, see Yearbook 1915–1918, 1919–1920, SHNC, 10, 136, 172.; Annual Report of Convent and Mission Houses, 1940–1943, SHNC.

88. Annual Reports of the Convent and Mission Houses, 1940–1943, 1.

for in medical facilities. Sisters living in the Convent infirmary continued to do what work they could, such as handwork, sewing hems, and always praying. Some sisters happily adjusted to life in the infirmary. Sister Harriet reportedly grew apricots in pots and was said to "hold court" there.[89]

At each mission house, the Sister-in-Charge received written instructions from the Mother Superior on what to do when a sister died, including directions for the undertaker and the train schedule to send the body to Fond du Lac. "When a Sister dies, the House or Parish has no further claim on her—she must be brought Home as promptly as possible."[90] Sisters who died when the motherhouse was in Providence are buried in the Swan Point Cemetery there. The rest of the community (with one exception) are buried in the Sisterhood of the Holy Nativity plot at the Rienzi Cemetery in Fond du Lac; individual crosses marking the graves were removed, though a community memorial still stands.[91]

Despite the health challenges facing the Sisterhood of the Holy Nativity, they were a resilient community of women overall. The average life expectancy of the community was 76.8 years. Out of the eighty-five life professed sisters who died, over 75 percent lived to reach the age of seventy, and over half (forty-six) lived to reach the age of eighty. Twenty percent of the Sisterhood of the Holy Nativity reached the age of ninety. Two sisters, Sister Mary Grace and Sister Ruth Angela, lived to reach 100 and 101, respectively. Only fourteen sisters died under the age of seventy. For some women, convent life, though challenging, brought relief from an abusive family or institution. Sister Mary Frances was an abandoned child who grew up in an orphanage. Sister Katrina was the physical education teacher at Grafton Hall before she entered the sisterhood under opposition from her mother, who lied about her daughter's health to get her rejected; Sister Katrina prevailed and died at ninety-one.[92]

---

89. For a general discussion of documentation on sisterhoods and illness, see Nadeau, "Uncovering the Date of Twentieth-Century Benedictine Sisters," 10–11, 20.

90. "Directions for the Sister-in-Charge of any House of our Community, in the event of a Sister dying there," n.d. [ca. 1930s], SHNC.

91. Swan Point Cemetery, Providence; Mother Ruth Margaret Vose, SHN (1826–1910), Find a Grave Memorial for Rienzi Cemetery, which includes photographs of the sisterhood's grave site.

92. These statistics are based on calculating the age at death for the 85 life professed members of the Sisterhood of the Holy Nativity who have died. The calculations do not include two living sisters and those life professed sisters who left the community.

GOVERNANCE OF THE SISTERHOOD

In the Sisterhood of the Holy Nativity, as in other Anglican and Episcopal women's orders, governance occurred through the Mother Superior, Chapter, and Council, depending on the decision to be made. In the second half of the nineteenth century, when many Anglican sisterhoods were founded, women had no equivalent role in the secular world. It was not until the late twentieth century that women more commonly exercised the level of authority that characterized the superiors of sisterhoods in the Church.[93] The Mother Superior exercised spiritual, pastoral, executive, and supervisory authority. She was elected for a four-year term; the number of terms was unlimited. She appointed the Assistant Superior, Novice Mistress, and local Sisters-in-Charge. The Mother Superior was assisted by a Council comprised of the officers and four elected professed sisters. The professed sisters comprised the community's annual Chapter, which proposed changes to the Rule and Constitution. By the late twentieth century, the Sisterhood of the Holy Nativity, like other women's orders, began to recast the role of Mother Superior and governance in general in more collaborative and democratic terms. Most of the superiors of the Sisterhood of the Holy Nativity served several terms, sometimes against their wishes. Sister Hannah Margaret was the first superior for a little over a year (from the end of 1882 until January 1884) when the sisterhood separated from the Society of Saint Margaret until Mother Foundress Ruth Margaret was elected (1884–1908). Future superiors included Mother Katherine Edith (1908–1919), Mother Matilda (1919–1942), Mother Ruth Mary (1942–1961), Mother Alicia Theresa (1961–1972), Mother Boniface (1973–1996; 2007–2011), Mother Maria (1996–2007), and Mother Abigail (2012–2023).[94]

The average term for superiors in the Sisterhood of the Holy Nativity, not counting interim superiors, was 16.5 years; four served for more than nineteen years out of eight superiors. In addition to the role of Mother Superior, the Assistant Superior and Novice Mistress exercised considerable authority; it was not uncommon for women elected as Mother Superior to have occupied a leadership role earlier. Beyond the Convent in Fond du Lac, there were Sisters-in-Charge of each mission house. While under the authority of the Mother Superior, they exercised local authority and a degree of independence. The Convent and mission houses also employed staff, including cooks, gardeners, cleaners, secretaries, and nurses, depending on

---

93. Ferry, *The Old Convent*, 113–14.

94. Those superiors marked with an asterisk * utilized both the title of "Mother" and "Sister" on different documents; also, see "The Sisterhood of the Holy Nativity, Formation— A Lifelong Process" pamphlet, n.d. [ca. 1980s], SHNC.

the needs of the location and the availability of workers. Sometimes, these roles were fulfilled by Associates familiar with the customs of a religious house and who lived nearby.

From its inception, the Sisterhood of the Holy Nativity worked closely with priests and bishops. The Bishop Visitors and Chaplain Generals had clearly defined spiritual, liturgical, and consultative roles within the sisterhood. It would have been impossible to have daily Mass or work within Episcopal churches and dioceses without the support of male clergy. The Chaplain General was a priest elected by the sisters to give spiritual counsel and oversee the liturgical life of the chapels.[95] In the 1930s, the sisters agreed to spiritual care by St. Paul's Cathedral clergy in Fond du Lac instead of hiring a resident chaplain.[96] The Bishop Visitor, the bishop of the Diocese of Fond du Lac, approved changes in the Rule and Constitution and was the community's link with the broader church. In the early years of the Sisterhood of the Holy Nativity, they were often closest to clergy in religious orders. Gradually, the sisters regarded other clergy and their families as extended family members.[97]

WEARING THE HABIT

For the Sisterhood of the Holy Nativity, as for other religious orders in the Episcopal Church, the wearing of habits related directly to a sisterhood's identity and mission. Throughout history, the Sisterhood of the Holy Nativity wore full-length black habits. Changing the habit was a source of conflict, and some sisters openly disparaged Roman Catholic orders that gave up wearing habits almost entirely after Vatican II. Initially, the Sisterhood of the Holy Nativity habit for life professed sisters consisted of a black tunic with long pointed sleeves, a long black veil, a white coif and wimple, and an ebony cross with monogram and silver edging. In the mid-twentieth century, the habit was modified, though still full-length, including a black tunic and scapular, with a white-rimmed veil and collar. Eventually, a summer-weight habit was adopted. Sisters professed in the original wimple and stiff veil were not required to wear the modified habits.[98]

---

95. The Sisterhood of the Holy Nativity, Formation— A Lifelong Process," SHNC.

96. Yearbook 1935–1936, 128, SHNC.

97. Interview, Russ Jacobus and Jerrie Jacobus, November 4, 2021; Interview, Ted McConnell, March 11, 2022: Interview, Keith and Suzanne Whitmore, October 22, 2021; Interview, Neff and Dorothy Powell, November 29, 2021.

98. *A Guide to Anglican Religious Communities in the United States and Canada*, 25; *Anglican Religious Orders and Communities. A Directory*, 1991, 91.

Consistently throughout its history, the Sisterhood of the Holy Nativity decided to continue wearing the habit as a symbol of their religious vows. In the Anglican world, religious orders are less than two hundred years old, and entire provinces are without resident religious communities. For most women in the Sisterhood of the Holy Nativity, the habit symbolized their catholic faith and was considered an evangelistic tool in the mission field. Although religious orders were known in Anglo-Catholic circles, that was not the case where the majority churchmanship was more Protestant. Habits served as a symbol of the sisters' consecrated lives and a witness to their vocational commitments. Other Episcopal sisterhoods eventually decided to relinquish wearing habits or to wear them only on specific occasions, believing that habits separate sisters from the people they serve. Interestingly, among Roman Catholic sisterhoods today, increasing numbers of women are joining or transferring to sisterhoods that wear the full habit as a symbol of their religious vows.[99]

THE ASSOCIATES

From its beginnings, the Sisterhood of the Holy Nativity cultivated a close relationship with a dedicated group of Associates. Their fervent desire to participate in the sisterhood's spiritual life and provide material support was characteristic of an era when devotional societies and guilds for Anglo-Catholic women were gaining popularity. At times during its history, the Sisterhood of the Holy Nativity Associates numbered over one thousand. The Associates were limited to lay women until 1906, when the sisterhood inducted the first clergy associates.[100]

The Associates of the Sisterhood of the Holy Nativity share in the spirituality and ministries of the order. As the unique charism of the Sisterhood of the Holy Nativity manifests distinctly in each sister, so, too, does each Associate manifest the charism in distinctive ways. "There has been a marked increase shown by the Associates and a deepening of their devotional lives," reflected Mother Matilda in 1923.[101] "The Sisters and the Associates together try to live out in their lives in the mystery of the Incarnation, of God's complete self-giving," wrote one of the sisters.[102] This included instruction

---

99. "Other Beloved I Have . . . or Meet the Sisters of the Holy Nativity," by a Sister of St Agnes, n.d. [ca 1983] 4. SHNC; Heath, *The Veil*, 84–85.

100. Reeves, "Hidden in Christ," 18–19.

101. Yearbook 1920–1931, SHNC, 73.

102. By a Sister, "The Sisterhood of the Holy Nativity," *Holy Cross Magazine*. LXXI, I (January 1960)14

on the foundations of the sisterhood as written by Mother Ruth Margaret and Bishop Grafton.[103] Much of the sisterhood's local mission and retreat work would have been impossible without the support of their Associates.

The Rule for Associates of the Sisterhood of the Holy Nativity cultivates catholic spirituality through parish involvement, liturgical participation, and local mission work. Spiritual discipline and commitment on the part of Associates were required beyond conventional church attendance. The Rule specified that Associates say daily morning and evening prayers, grace before and after meals, and the daily collects for sisters and Associates. It also specified that Associates receive Holy Communion on all Sundays and Holy Days; prepare for communion through self-examination and fasting; read scripture daily and spend at least five minutes in meditation; confess to a priest at least once a year; make a retreat at least once a year, preferably for three days; give alms; and participate in Associates' activities sponsored by the sisterhood.[104] Seventy to one hundred associates per year went on retreat at the Convent or one of the mission houses, staying from one night to a month and participating in monthly meetings and the annual Associates' liturgy.[105]

The Associates program expanded quickly alongside the growth of the sisterhood. At least one sister was tasked with maintaining relationships with the Associates. After a probationary period of testing the Rule, the Associates were admitted in a solemn ceremony. They were required to write and share something of their spiritual life and experience of the Rule at least once a year. Those who lived near one of the sisterhood's mission houses had the opportunity for regular retreats, quiet days, and monthly business meetings. The Associates elected officers who reported on the work of each chapter and shared the sisters' needs with them. At the Corporate Communion service held for Associates on the Feast of the Annunciation each year, all were asked to make a nominal donation—in 1920, the suggested donation was five dollars, although many gave more significant contributions. Those who committed to the Associates' Rule also shared in the sisterhood's work of intercessory prayer and were sent a list of petitions at regular intervals.[106]

---

103. For example, "A Centenary Collect for Sisters and Associates," n.d. [ca. 1982] SHNC.

104. *Manual of the Associates of the Sisterhood of the Holy Nativity,* n.d. [ca. 1920] "Examen. Based upon the Rule of an Associate of the Sisterhood of the Holy Nativity," SHNC, n.d.

105. For example, 85 guests stayed at the convent for retreats in 1923–1924: Yearbook 1920–1931, SHNC, 73.

106. *For the Associates of the Holy Nativity,* [ca. 1900] 1, 14, SHNC.

THE ECCLESIASTICAL ARTS

The vibrant liturgical life of the Oxford Movement contributed to the building of ornately decorated churches and the renewal of the ecclesiastical arts. This catholic revival was connected to vestments, altar linens, and other church appointments that stood for continuity and universality, as well as the centrality of the Eucharist. "Nevertheless, our devout needlewoman worked long hours in many places, and by this century the chasuble could be seen in over a thousand English parish churches."[107]

Traditional vestments survived the English Reformation, though local observance varied. Archbishop Thomas Cranmer (1489–1556) favored simplicity, while Elizabeth I favored traditional vestiture. After the Reformation, the usage of traditional vestments visibly declined but did not disappear entirely. Some vestments were hidden or worn a discreet distance from reformers. Edmund Grindal (1519–1583), the second Archbishop of Canterbury under Elizabeth I, actively discouraged the destruction of eucharistic accessories. Still, it was in the nineteenth century that the Oxford Movement revived the ecclesiastical arts, including creating elaborate vestments, altar frontals, paraments, and banners.[108]

Scholars date the revival of traditional vestments to the 1858 publication of the *Directorium Anglicanum*, a liturgical manual for celebrating Holy Communion and other rites of the Church of England.[109] The 1899 publication of Percy Dearmer's classic, *The Parson's Handbook*, contributed to the spread of adapted medieval ritual as "The English Use."[110] The return to Eucharistic vestments in the Episcopal Church was more varied. However, many seminaries and churches associated with the catholic revival in the Episcopal Church were also related to the Sisterhood of the Holy Nativity. For example, by 1871, chasubles were in use at Mount Calvary Church, Baltimore, which was later the site of a mission house of the Sisterhood of the Holy Nativity. The General Theological Seminary and Nashotah House were two seminaries that introduced vestments to students who then, as graduates, continued usage in their churches.[111]

---

107. Mayer-Thurman, 17–19.

108. Bailey, *Clerical Vestments*, 5–10.

109. Purchas and Lee, *Directorium Anglicanum; being a manual of directions for the right celebration of the Holy Communion, for the saying of matins and evensong, and for the performance of other rites and ceremonies of the Church, according to the ancient use of the Church of England*, 1858.

110. Dreamer, *The Parson's Handbook*; Mayer-Thurman, *Raiment for the Lord's Service*, 19.

111. Mayer-Thurman, *Raiment for the Lord's Service*, 19–20.

An interest in returning to the ceremony and splendor of the Middle Ages encouraged Anglo-Catholics to revive the industries which so richly contributed to the ascetics of the architecture and liturgy. Increased ceremonial in daily worship created a growing need for embroidered vestments, altar linens, and altar bread in Anglo-Catholic churches on both sides of the Atlantic and beyond. The earliest Anglican sisterhoods actively pursued the ecclesiastical arts to support mission work. Ecclesiastical embroidery flourished from the 1850s onward and closely connected local churches with sisterhoods. The fact that most well-bred women of the era were taught needlework and drawing at an early age contributed to the revival, which meant sisterhoods had the skills readily available. In 1854, John Mason Neale, a founder of the Society of Saint Margaret, was the first Anglican priest to wear vestments made for him by the sisters.[112]

Textile arts are a significant part of the history of women artists. In the Middle Ages, women donated, commissioned, and created textiles with intricate embroidery for religious use. Religious textiles forged a connection between women and worship and validated their contributions to the Church on a spiritual level. Gradually, during the religious reformation and economic change, the status and production of embroidery shifted to male-dominated professional guilds. By the seventeenth century, women's devotional arts, including embroidery, became centered in the home through the socially sanctioned activity of "sewing." The Anglo-Catholic spiritual revival of the nineteenth century reintegrated the arts and spirituality into the Church and created the means for women's participation. Making vestments and altar linens illuminated the artist's spirituality and through the creative process she became part of the art she produced. Religious textiles performed a mediative function by creating a sacred space between human bodies and the Divine. Within Eucharistic environments, religious textiles marked sites of privileged access; vestments, altar linens, and embroidered church appointments cover and honor the human body, as well as precious objects such as altars, liturgical vessels, baptismal fonts, relics, and pulpits. Just as those who participate in the Eucharist experience transcendence as they gaze upon ecclesiastical embroidery, so does the embroiderer experience transcendence as she works with a needle and thread. The embroiderer inserts her spirituality and devotion into her art, reflected in the liturgy's sacred sphere.[113] "What is more, the maker's essence is laid, stich by stich,

---

112. Ferry, *The Old Convent*, 130–132.

113. Gillian Huntley, "Stitching the Sacred," 26–27; Interview, Anna Wager, July 8, 2022.

into this liminal space of fabric that enables the wearer as well as the viewer to transcend, at least monetarily, from the human realm to the divine."[114]

The women of the Sisterhood of the Holy Nativity were not only artists in the technical sense; they were also ecclesiastical designers. Their artistic training and theological knowledge determined a piece visually and how it would interact with the environment and contribute to an overall liturgical aesthetic.[115] The Sisterhood of the Holy Nativity considered the ecclesiastical arts an extension of catholic spirituality and mission. Charles Grafton believed in the importance of beautiful vestments and altar linens to the liturgy. He thus hoped to make them available at a moderate cost to catholic parishes, based on each one's ability to pay. The sisterhood considered their "missionary enterprises" of ecclesiastical embroidery, altar bread, and devotional cards as an extension of their mandate to advance the catholic faith. Through these missionary enterprises, the sisterhood extended its Eucharistic spirituality by supporting the liturgical life of local churches. "In the instances where the need was very pressing, they have been given, and in all cases of Mission Stations and poor Churches, they have been furnished at the cost of materials. Many a letter has been received from grateful Priests, thanking the Sisters for thus helping them impress the catholic faith upon their people."[116] Custom vestments were also created as commissions for those who could pay the going rate.[117]

The Sisterhood of the Holy Nativity produced vestments, altar frontals and hangings, and altar linens for almost one hundred years, starting in Boston, then in Providence, and ultimately from the Convent of the Holy Nativity in Fond du Lac until 1988. The workrooms were organized according to levels of technical skill, from those sisters equipped to design and execute the most elaborate embroideries and who also taught and supervised others to those who did more straightforward sewing and finishing. Artistic skill in drawing and composition was needed as many of the finest designs were original. At the Fond du Lac Convent, Associates skilled in needlework were included in production.[118] The Sisterhood of the Holy Nativity first created vestments and altar appointments for their chapel, the Oneida mission, and the Cathedral in Fond du Lac. In many of the congregations they served, the sisters taught ecclesiastical embroidery to local altar guilds to equip them to enhance the beauty of their liturgies. The demand increased as their work

114. Huntley, "Stitching the Sacred," 28.
115. Huntley, "Stitching the Sacred," 7–11, 28–29.
116. Mayer-Thurman, *Raiment for the Lord's Service*, 19–20.
117. "The Sisterhood of the Holy Nativity," 1928, 5–6, SHNC.
118. Interview, September 13, 2021, Roger and Marie Funk.

became known through the mission house network. Elaborate commissions requiring intensive work from highly skilled artisans were produced along with more basic linens.[119]

The scope of vestments and altar linens created by the Sisterhood of the Holy Nativity is staggering. For example, in 1915, the sisters created eight altar cloths, seven antependia, thirty chasubles, twenty-four stoles and maniples, thirty-six eucharistic veils and burses, thirty-five office stoles, fifteen bookmarks, a dalmatic, one cincture, seventeen albs, twenty-three amices, thirteen girdles, ten surplices, nine fair linens, five credence table covers, nine corporals, five palls, ten, lawn veils, seventy-six purificators, thirty lavabos, four stoles' collars, and two linen covers.[120] Although the number of articles produced declined as churches became fully stocked, the sisterhood continued to create many more ornate articles with delicate embroidery. For example, in 1928, the sisters made twelve chasubles, thirty-six stoles, and copes and miters. The sisters also repaired existing garments.[121] As liturgical life adapted, so did the work of the sisters. The embroidery department diversified to produce altar pillows and large dossals.[122]

Perhaps the most notable artist and designer of the Sisterhood of the Holy Nativity was Sister Ruth Vera. Sister Ruth Vera, an artist skilled in ecclesiastical embroidery and theology, advanced the catholic faith through her designs. Sister Mary Constance, the daughter of a priest, was known for her skills as a seamstress; she made habits and vestments. Sister Ann Fidelia, once a student at the Art Institute of Chicago, worked with Sister Ruth Vera on vestment design. A generation before Sister Ruth Vera, Sister Hildegarde oversaw the embroidery department, followed by the capable Sister Regina. In the 1960s, just when it seemed the department would have to close, the work was revived by the artistry of Sister Margaretta, who designed an impressive banner for the Cathedral in Fond du Lac.

In addition to artistry, the Sisterhood of the Holy Nativity missionary enterprises required business acumen. The Sister-in-Charge of each department tracked and reported orders by income, expenses, and the type of goods sold or donated. Completing and shipping orders and corresponding with customers were included as part of the business, furthering the relationships between the sisterhood and local parishes and dioceses worldwide.

---

119. Curtiss, *History of the Diocese of Fond du Lac and Its Several Congregations*, 38–39.

120. Yearbook 1915–1918, 1919–1920, SHNC, 16; 88, 169, SHNC

121. Yearbook 1920–1931, SHNC, 200. 232, SHNC.

122. Annual Report of Convent and Mission Houses, 1940–1943, 60, SHNC.

The Sisterhood of the Holy Nativity's most extensive missionary enterprise involved the production of altar bread. An extension of Anglo-Catholic eucharistic theology, altar bread was an income stream for the sisterhood and an ecclesiastical art. "The Altar Bread department does its share in the extension of the Faith by preparing the 'earthly form' for the Sacramental Presence of our Lord on His Altars," states one of the order's publications.[123]

The Sisterhood of the Holy Nativity started baking altar bread in 1886, including the large priest's hosts and the smaller wafers for the people consecrated during the Eucharist. Altar bread was in high demand, as daily Mass, to the extent that a priest was available, was integral to the sisterhood and increasingly the practice in Anglo-Catholic parishes. For the Sisterhood of the Holy Nativity, daily Holy Communion reminded them of their commitment to the Incarnation. "The Holy Communion is a living witness of the Incarnation and Atonement," wrote one sister.[124] As with the production of vestments and altar linens, the sisters first supplied their chapel, the Oneida mission, and eventually the Cathedral in Fond du Lac and other mission houses. An ecumenical clientele purchased altar bread: Episcopalians, Lutherans, Roman Catholics, and Methodists from almost every state in the United States, Korea, Japan, Pakistan, the Bahamas, and other countries. The critical mass of the orders came from churches in Wisconsin, Illinois, Minnesota, and Michigan.[125]

The missionary enterprise of altar bread production expanded rapidly, and at its height, the Sisterhood of the Holy Nativity sent out over one million communion wafers annually. By 1894, when the motherhouse of the Sisterhood of the Holy Nativity was in Providence, the sisters baked over 4400 priest's hosts and over 47,700 communion wafers for their use, as well as St. Stephen's, Providence, and Church of the Advent, Boston. The total cost of production was $24.40.[126] The demand for altar bread steadily increased; in 1916, 19,139 priest's hosts and 211,464 communion wafers were distributed.[127] Over 500,000 communion wafers and almost 39,000 priest's hosts were baked and distributed by the Sisterhood of the Holy Nativity in 1921.[128] The eucharistic network, connected through altar bread, expanded throughout the early twentieth century to include all the mission houses of the Sisterhood, the Oneida mission, other Indigenous missions in South

---

123. By a Sister, "The Sisterhood of the Holy Nativity," 12, SHNC.
124. By a Sister, "The Drama of the Eucharist," n.d. SHNC.
125. Karst, "Traditional Religious in a Secular World," 14.
126. Yearbook 1894, "Report of Altar-Breads," SHNC, n.p.
127. Yearbook 1915–1918, 1919–1920, SHNC, 55.
128. Yearbook 1920–1931, SHNC, 199.

Dakota and Hawaii, campus ministries, and the Cathedral in Fond du Lac, averaging nearly 50,000 priest's hosts and 750,000 individual communion wafers annually. During World War II, the sisters sent altar bread to over twenty separate Army and Navy bases in the United States and abroad.[129] By 1971, the Sisterhood of the Holy Nativity and a staff of three women from Fond du Lac produced 1.8 million individual wafers and over 78,000 priest's hosts. The sisterhood provided altar bread free of charge to those who could not pay the fees.[130]

The Sisterhood of the Holy Nativity considered altar bread production an extension of the altar and, thus, resisted efforts to commercialize the operation. The wafers were baked, cut, stamped, and packed into rolls by hand for distribution. The wafers were embossed with eucharistic symbols like the Lamb of God. Rejected wafers were recycled as fish food. The baking was tricky as the wafers easily scorched. Standing over hot brick ovens while wearing wool serge habits took considerable spiritual discipline. The work typically required one sister full-time, assisted by several novices. Trusted Associates also worked in altar bread production. At the Fond du Lac Convent, youth groups, church school classes, and some adult groups were shown how the wafers were baked, stamped, and rolled for mailing. Sister Elizabeth ran the altar bread department for twenty-seven years until she developed tuberculosis in 1921; Sister Edwina was the next long-term sister-in-charge of the altar bread department, followed by Sister Jane Frances, and many novices took turns being trained in the art. "We deem it a great privilege to have our share in this work of preparing the 'earthly forms' for the Sacramental Presence of our Lord on His Altars," noted the sisterhood when describing what motivated them to produce altar bread.[131]

In addition to the ecclesiastical arts of making vestments, altar linens, and altar bread, the Sisterhood of the Holy Nativity advanced the catholic faith through two additional missionary enterprises: the picture department, and the lending library. The picture department furthered the catholic faith by distributing visual images, known as "holy pictures" or devotional cards, containing images and symbols of the Christian church. Art, architecture, and music were considered divinely inspired and essential to expressing catholic spirituality. The "picture department" was started as the "catechism department" in 1895 due to the urging of James Otis Sargent Huntington, OHC, the founder of the Order of the Holy Cross. The sisters worked closely

---

129. Annual Report of Convent and Mission Houses, 1940–1943, SHNC, for an example of the trend, see 58.

130. Karst, "Traditional Religious in a Secular World," 14.

131. By a Sister, "The Sisterhood of the Holy Nativity," 1928, 6.

with Huntington on his many preaching missions. Huntington desired a supplier of cards and pictures to use in Sunday schools and for teaching the catechism. The response was slow initially but grew in demand by 1897, especially during Christmas and Easter.[132] By 1917, the sisterhood sent out over 57,000 devotional cards; by 1919, that number had doubled to over 114,000.[133] The sisters stopped counting the number of individual cards in the 1920s.[134]

Like other forms of Christian visual art, the devotional cards distributed by the Sisterhood of the Holy Nativity were designed to tell the story of a particular feast or saint through color, symbols, and calligraphy that had spiritual significance. It was also an inexpensive way for people to afford religious art. Those who knew the tradition and could "read" the images could respond to devotional cards on a deeper level. The rich iconography of the catholic faith supported the use of images to guide prayer and spiritual reflection. Some of these images distributed through the Sisterhood of the Holy Nativity were imported from England, France, and Belgium, and others were created through the artistic talents of the sisters themselves. The artistic styles varied widely. Some were designed for use as bookmarks, used during commemorated events, or served as memorials. Others were actual religious holiday cards for Christmas and Easter in an era where people most often communicated through the post. Sometimes, the handmade cards served as gifts and mementos that triggered strong emotions. The sisters did not have personal funds to buy gifts for each other, so it was common for a sister to receive handmade cards from other sisters for her profession or an anniversary. Unlike other sacred art forms, devotional cards were intended to be distributed widely, tucked in prayer books, drawers, or displayed on a desk. The sisters carefully selected the images to ensure "they may be of real service and inspiration by correct teaching and devotional uplifting spirit."[135] The cards supported personal prayer and were evangelistic tools for teaching the catholic faith. The average church person of a century ago read more meaning into a picture than many could today.[136]

132. Yearbook 1898, "Report from the Catechism Department," SHNC, 33.
133. Yearbook 1915–1918, 1919–1920, SHNC, 53, 170.
134. For example, see Yearbook 1920–1931, SHNC, 198.
135. By a Sister, "The Sisterhood of the Holy Nativity," 1928, 6.
136. Calamari and DiPasqua, *Holy Cards*, 9–13.

THE MARGARET PEABODY LENDING LIBRARY

An accessible theological lending library to support teaching the catholic faith and make devotional literature available to clergy and laity was another lasting missionary enterprise of the Sisterhood of the Holy Nativity. An early Associate of the sisterhood asked the sisters to take over a library that her mother had created in 1884. The sisterhood did so, and in 1889, the Margaret Peabody Lending Library was born. The lending library was created when Episcopal Church agencies like the Church Periodical Club (1888) began publishing resources to facilitate Christian education and missionary work. Soon, diocesan chapters of the Episcopal Woman's Auxiliary founded lending libraries that made curricula and reference materials available to parishes. These initiatives made theological education accessible to both laity and clergy. Moreover, the lending libraries distributed curricula and devotional works written by the Sisterhood of the Holy Nativity throughout the Church.[137]

Under the administration of Sister Mary Margaret, the Margaret Peabody Lending Library gained momentum quickly. In the first year, the library sent 109 books to fifty-five patrons.[138] By 1902, the number of patrons almost tripled; most were laity.[139] By 1916, the library lent nearly one thousand books to 327 patrons.[140] The most significant circulation year was in 1932, with over 2500 books in circulation.[141] By the 1940s, the library regularly sent out two thousand books per year, and the volumes exceeded the Convent's space. The number of study groups utilizing the collection grew rapidly. The annual report for 1941 lists a geographically diverse set of patrons, including the New England Chapter of the Society of the Companions of the Holy Cross, guilds in North Dakota, the Daughters of the King in Kansas, the Episcopal Diocese of Eau Claire, the young people's group in the Diocese of California, a Lenten class of seventy women in Chicago, and a church in Washington, D.C. with war refugees. Notably, the list of patrons grew consistently among women's groups, young people, and laity

---

137. By a Sister, "The Sisterhood of the Holy Nativity," 1928, 7; Curtiss, *History of the Diocese of Fond du Lac and Its Several Congregations*, 38–39; *The Margaret Peabody Lending Library for the Distribution of Church Literature by Mail*, 1928, SHNC; The Margaret Peabody Lending Library," *Fond du Lac Clarion* (April 1983) n.p. SHNC; Donvan, *A Different Call*, 80.

138. Yearbook 1898, "Lending Library Report," SHNC, 29.

139. Yearbook 1902, "Margaret Peabody Lending Library," SHNC, 162.

140. Yearbook 1915–1918, 1919–1920, SHNC, 54; Yearbook 1920–1931, SHNC, 9.

141. Yearbook 1932, "Margaret Peabody Lending Library," SHNC.

in general, many of whom would otherwise not have access to theological education.[142]

During wartime, the Margaret Peabody Lending Library enlarged the scope of its work. In 1941, the library circulated 2402 books, the second-highest number in its history. Over 60 percent of the books were sent to American prisoners of war. Books were also sent for distribution by priest Associates serving as military chaplains to refugees from Shanghai and the American Church Institute for Negroes. "Among our readers are a young soldier in a training camp preparing for Confirmation; RAF corporal studying to take Orders after the war; two conscientious objectors in CPS camps; a little community in South Africa . . . ."[143]

Several women in the sisterhood were trained librarians, with Sister Edith Sylvia being the most associated with the Margaret Peabody Lending Library. The Margaret Peabody Lending Library made quality religious books available to all those who promised to return them. The collection focused on the Bible, church history, the prayer book, liturgy, devotional literature, sermons, religious biography, missions, religious life, and children's literature. Bishop Grafton donated his extensive library to the collection a year before his death. The Convent sent books annually to clergy, seminarians, teachers, students, and others who could not afford books or lived in remote areas. Individuals and parishes associated with the sisters depended on the library for Lenten studies and reading group materials until inexpensive paperback books were readily available. The cost of mailing and adding new titles was covered by Associates and others who believed in this vital work.[144]

In addition to providing access to a theological library, the Sisterhood of the Holy Nativity produced educational and devotional materials. As a religious order devoted to teaching, the Sisterhood of the Holy Nativity valued theological discourse and understood the need to publish works that supported their mission. Their writing emerged from the classroom and the sanctuary, focusing on the needs of the laity. The sisterhood distributed the works of Charles Grafton, including sermons and meditations. Though the sisters ordinarily did not publish under their names, several were known to be the authors of works published for distribution. Mother Katherine Edith wrote several texts used extensively in religious education, including *Our*

142. Annual Report of Convent and Mission Houses, 1940–1943, SHNC, 3; 30.

143. Annual Report of Convent and Mission Houses, 1940–1943, SHNC, 57.

144. By a Sister, "The Sisterhood of the Holy Nativity," 1928, 7.; Curtiss, *History of the Diocese of Fond du Lac and Its Several Congregations*, 38–39; *The Margaret Peabody Lending Library for the Distribution of Church Literature by Mail*, 1928), SHNC; "The Margaret Peabody Lending Library," *Fond du Lac Clarion* (April 1983) n.p. SHNC.

Family Ways, The New Creation, Holy Warfare, and *The King's Message: A Story of the Catacombs.*[145] Sister Emily Constance was the likely author of a famous address on "The Religious Life," given to the Society of the Companions of the Holy Cross in 1906.[146] Sister Patricia wrote and spoke widely on various theological topics, including *About Praying: A Series of Meditation,* published by the Sisterhood of the Holy Nativity on the fiftieth anniversary of her profession.[147] Mother Boniface taught and preached widely on behalf of the sisterhood, particularly on the sacraments and church history. The Associates also contributed to this literary output with devotional works such as a translation from the French of Abbé Grou's work on "Self-Consecration," commissioned by Bishop Grafton.[148] The sisterhood regularly published spiritual pamphlets to support retreats and contributed to a Bible study curriculum from the 1958 Lambeth Conference.[149]

From its inception, the Sisterhood of the Holy Nativity was focused on teaching the catholic faith, spiritual guidance and retreats, and a rich heritage in the ecclesiastical arts. Assisted by local clergy and Associates of the sisterhood, the sisters were spiritually nourished by a deep commitment to lives of prayer and service. The spiritual charism of the sisterhood, along with their missionary enterprises, deepened relationships to advance the catholic faith throughout the Episcopal Church.

---

145. The following are attributed to Sister Katherine Edith, SHN: *Our Family Ways; The New Creation; Holy Warfare; The King's Message.*

146. [Sister Katherine Edith], *The Religious Life,* August 1906, SHNC.

147. [Sister Patricia, SHN], *About Praying,* n.d. [ca. 1960] SHNC.

148. Abbé Grou, *Self-Consecration,* trans. An Associate of the Sisterhood of the Holy Nativity, 1887, SHNC.

149. By A Sister of the Holy Nativity, *The Early Days of the Christian Church,* [ca. 1959–1960]); Curtiss, *History of the Diocese of Fond du Lac and Its Several Congregations,* 38.

3

Advancing the Catholic Faith in Wisconsin—Serving with Indigenous Peoples

THE RULE OF THE SISTERHOOD of the Holy Nativity states that after the work of prayer, the order's charism is "to make known the Faith and to win souls for Christ." The Sisterhood of the Holy Nativity was at the center of the spiritual life of the Episcopal Diocese of Fond du Lac in northeast and north-central Wisconsin since Charles Grafton was elected bishop there in 1888. Then, the young sisterhood was recognized for its contributions "to build up and extend the Church."[1] Bishop Grafton and Mother Ruth Margaret agreed that the sisterhood would advance the catholic faith among people in local parishes across the state. They held few illusions about the challenges ahead. Wisconsin had the highest percentage of foreign-born immigrants in the Midwest, most of whom associated the Episcopal Church exclusively with English language and culture. The Roman Catholic Church was Wisconsin's most influential Christian denomination, followed by Lutheranism.[2]

The sisterhood established their first mission house at St. Paul's Church in Plymouth, Wisconsin. The priest there was Walter R. Gardner, a former member of the Society of St. John the Evangelist, invited by Bishop Grafton to serve as a local missionary. Gardner, later president of Nashotah House Seminary, instilled the catholic faith in the congregations he served. The

---

1. *Journal of the Sixteenth Annual Council of the Protestant Episcopal Church in the Diocese of Fond du Lac,* 1890, 42, 55–56.

2. Lauck, Whitney, and Hogan, eds., *Finding A New Midwest History,* 84–85, 196–98, 204.

sisters accompanied Gardner on a missionary trip to Belgian members of the Old Catholic Church in Door County, Wisconsin. During their first year in the Diocese of Fond du Lac, the Sisterhood of the Holy Nativity visited every parish and mission in the diocese at least once, teaching over one hundred classes and giving informal talks and addresses. They took charge of the Sunday schools at St. Paul's Cathedral and the Good Shepherd mission. They accomplished all this "two by two, in Apostolic fashion, accepting such hospitality as is offered."[3]

Although an Episcopal woman benefactor provided the sisters the house in Plymouth, there were more suitable long-term locations. The city of Fond du Lac was more central and had access to railroad connections across the state. Moreover, Bishop Grafton believed that locating the sisters in Fond du Lac would give them more contact with St. Paul's Cathedral. In 1890, he found the sisterhood a temporary house in Fond du Lac, naming it the House of the Visitation. The name was changed to the Mission House of the Holy Nativity by 1895. It was said of the sisterhood:

> They go on mission tours through northern Wisconsin among the lumbermen, and into many a wild, remote country place, visiting the people, teaching them, supplying books, holding informal meetings, opening Sunday schools, and giving talks to congregations gathered in some good woman's parlor, in the farmhouse kitchen or in the schoolhouse . . . Much cheer and instruction and gentle guidance is given to shut-in invalids and souls in the shadow of ignorance; long-lapsed Christians are often led back to the Faith . . . . The mission sisters live in the homes of the people.[4]

The new Convent in downtown Fond du Lac became the motherhouse of the Sisterhood of the Holy Nativity in 1905. The Convent in Fond du Lac also became the headquarters for the missionary enterprises of the sisters mentioned in the previous chapter, including the production of altar bread, vestments and altar linens, devotional cards, and the Margaret Peabody Lending Library. The Sisterhood of the Holy Nativity's work in Fond du Lac centered around the Cathedral Church of St. Paul, St. Michael's Church in North Fond du Lac, and Grafton Hall School for girls. The Convent also operated as a retreat center for women and later for clergy throughout the

---

3. *Journal of the. Sixteenth Annual Council of the Protestant Episcopal Church in the Diocese of Fond du Lac*, 1890, 55–56: Curtiss, *History of the Diocese of Fond du Lac and Its Several Congregations*, 17, 76–77; Reeves, "Hidden in Christ", 8–9, SHNC.

4. Quoted from *The Churchman* (April 1893) "Sisterhood of the Holy Nativity," *Conference on the Religious Life* (April 24–29, 2001) 13, SHNC.

Diocese of Fond du Lac and Wisconsin. "They [the Sisterhood of the Holy Nativity] are regular attendants at the services and workers among the poor of the parish. Their work and prayers are of much influence," states the diocesan history.[5]

During the first years of the Sisterhood of the Holy Nativity in Fond du Lac, the mission house was well-staffed: Sister Rebecca, the niece of Mother Ruth Margaret, was Sister-in-Charge and assisted Bishop Grafton. Sister Hannah, Sister Alice, Sister Dorothea, and Sister Emily Constance were also critical to the early success of the sisterhood. Sister Dorothea and Sister Emily Constance did home visits and parish missions around the diocese. During these early years, the sisters started guilds for women and girls, visited 2000 homes, and prepared over one hundred people for the sacraments. In addition, they oversaw the Sunday school at the Cathedral and taught embroidery. In introducing the art of ecclesiastical embroidery and in baking altar bread, the Sisterhood of the Holy Nativity supported catholic liturgy throughout the Diocese of Fond du Lac. "That decent, orderly, and reverent services may be insured, and as a means of making known the Catholic faith through object lessons, the Sisters agree to furnish these articles, at the lowest cost of material, to the Diocesan clergy."[6]

From the Convent in Fond du Lac, the Sisterhood of the Holy Nativity traveled extensively throughout the diocese. During 1895 alone, Sister Dorothea made eighty-five home visits and attended parish missions in the Wisconsin towns of Ahnapee (now Algoma), Berlin, Mosinee, Waupaca, Kewaunee, Wausau, Sheboygan, and Delafield. She undertook parish missions in Oshkosh, Ripon, Sheboygan, Sheboygan Falls, and Berlin the following year.[7] Sister Constance made 133 home visits and parish visits in Stevens Point and Centralia, in addition to working with the women of the Cathedral. Members of the sisterhood were regular visitors to the Children's Home, the Home for the Aged, the Home for the Friendless, the Industrial Home for Women, and a prison for non-violent offenders.[8] The sisters regularly instructed in preparation for the sacraments, taught in the choir school, gave lectures at the Cathedral, and started guilds for different groups. In addition, they hosted women and girls from Grafton Hall on retreat. Bishop Grafton also used the Convent as the retreat site for candidates

---

5. Curtiss, *History of the Diocese of Fond du Lac and Its Several Congregations*, 34, 37.

6. Yearbook, Mission House at Fond du Lac, 1891, 1892, n.p. SHNC; *Journal of the Sixteenth Annual Council of the Protestant Episcopal Church in the Diocese of Fond du Lac*, 1890, 56.

7. Yearbook, Mission House at Fond du Lac, 1896, n.p. SHNC

8. Yearbook 1933–1934, 75.

for the priesthood. Due to the sisters' efforts, "the missionary work in so many of the smaller towns [was] so successfully developed."[9] The sisters served as catechists on preaching missions with priests from the Society of St. John the Evangelist and the Order of the Holy Cross; they also coordinated parish missions in the Diocese of Fond du Lac with their bishop. In 1909, they extended their work in Wisconsin with a mission house at All Saints' Cathedral in the Episcopal Diocese of Milwaukee.[10]

THE EPISCOPAL CHURCH AND THE WISCONSIN ONEIDAS

The Episcopal Church came to what is now the state of Wisconsin through "the People of the Red Stone," known as the Oneidas. Soon after the founding of the Society for the Propagation of the Gospel in Foreign Parts (SPG) in 1701, an Anglican missionary priest working among the Mohawks reported that native peoples in upstate New York wanted to form a relationship. The sachems (tribal leaders or chiefs) of the Oneidas, one of the original five tribes of the great Iroquois League, including the Onondagas, Cayugas, Mohawks, and Senecas, were converted to Christianity. The first missionaries translated prayers and portions of the Bible into Mohawk. Missionaries reported that the people of the Iroquois League were receptive to Christianity because it resonated with their established values. "They think the Great Spirit made the earth and all that it contains for the common good of mankind . . . They would rather lie down themselves on an empty stomach than have it laid to their charge that they had neglected their duty by not satisfying the wants of the stranger, the sick or the needy," wrote one Moravian missionary.[11]

There was a strain of British "civilizing mission" within eighteenth-century Anglicanism and its colonial successors in the Americas. This worldview asserted that it was a moral duty for those of European descent to civilize "primitive" peoples by educating them about the benefits of white culture. As justification for colonialism, missionaries took on more than teaching the Gospel. Though missionaries affirmed the equality of all people before God, their practices included education for the "social betterment"

---

9. *Journal of the. Sixteenth Annual Council of the Protestant Episcopal Church in the Diocese of Fond du Lac*, 1890, 52.

10. Curtiss, *History of the Diocese of Fond du Lac and Its Several Congregations*, 37.

11. Holy Apostles Church, *Ta Luh Ya Wa Gu. Mission to the Oneidas (1822–1972)*, 3, SHNC; McLester, Hauptman, y Cornelius-Hawk, and House, *The Wisconsin Oneidas and the Episcopal Church*, 2–3, 169.

of colonized peoples through inculcating the language and culture of the English-speaking world. It was within settler colonies where Anglicanism was most implicated in the civilizing mission to establish the dominance of European culture over the Indigenous peoples who inhabited the land.[12]

The conversion of large numbers to Christianity, along with the social dislocation of the American Revolutionary War and subsequent threats to Indian lands in the 1780s, brought deep factionalism to the Oneidas.[13] Oneida lands were situated at transportation crossroads considered crucial to the economic growth of New York state. Despite the support that Chief Skenandoah (c.1706–1816) and the Iroquois League gave to white settlers and the Revolutionary War effort, the United States government caved to pressure and "transferred" the Oneida through a land grant to an old French trading post in Green Bay, Wisconsin. "It would seem that such fidelity [on the part of the Oneida] might have won the regard and consideration of the new American nation, and that the rights of the Indians in their ancestral home might have been respected," critiqued one missionary in 1811.[14]

After practicing Anglican Christianity for more than a century, the Oneida mission was recognized in 1816 by John Henry Hobart (1775–1830), bishop of the Diocese of New York, as the first "foreign" mission of the Episcopal Church.[15] Hobart hoped to expand the Church by moving westward and establishing a presence among other denominations already in the region.[16] The Oneida people differed in their response to the move West; some, having already experienced the influx of white settlers, opted to make the move, while others were reluctant to leave their ancestral lands. A portion of the tribe emigrated in 1822 and settled temporarily at Little Kakalin on the Fox River, and then permanently at Duck Creek, about ten miles from Green Bay. In 1825, the first Episcopal church in Wisconsin, a wooden structure called the "Log Church," was built. It was the first Protestant church in the Old Northwest Territory. "These first Oneidas who moved to Wisconsin in the 1820s and the 1830s were those who looked most favorably on white society, who were most under the influence of Christian missionaries, and who were the most willing to adopt white ways."[17]

12. Woods, *A Cultural Sociology of Anglican Mission and the Indian Residential Schools in Canada*, 1–3; Gladwin, "Mission and Colonialism," 287–89.

13. Campisi and Hauptman, eds., *The Oneida Indian Experience*, 66.

14. "The People of the Stone," *The Spirit of Missions*, 986; McLester III and Hauptman, eds. *A Nation within A Nation*, 51.

15. McLester et al., *The Wisconsin Oneidas and the Episcopal Church*, xviii.

16. McLester et al., *The Wisconsin Oneidas and the Episcopal Church*, 175.

17. Campisi and Hauptman, eds., *The Oneida Indian Experience*, 67; McLester et al., *The Wisconsin Oneidas and the Episcopal Church*, xix.

An enthusiastic supporter of the move from New York, Eleazer Williams (1788–1858) was an influential leader during the Oneida's early years in Wisconsin. Williams, a Dartmouth graduate of Mohawk and white parentage, was born a Roman Catholic. A great orator, Williams spoke both Mohawk and Oneida. In 1815, he became a member of the Episcopal Church. John Henry Hobart appointed him missionary to the Oneida in New York before the move to Wisconsin in 1817. Williams translated the *Book of Common Prayer* and some hymns into Mohawk and held the first Episcopal services for the Oneidas twelve years before the first white missionary bishop, Jackson Kemper (1789–1870), came to the region. Williams preached, instructed, wrote music and poetry, authored a spelling book for use in the Oneida parochial school, and baptized. He was ordained deacon by Bishop Hobart in 1824 and officially appointed a missionary in 1826. He was also the first non-Roman Catholic clergyman in the territory. Williams' influence in the Episcopal Church at Duck Creek continued until 1832, when the tribe disavowed him for failing to perform his duties and for some questionable financial dealings. However, the Episcopal Church in Oneida was not dependent on the efforts of the clergy alone. The laity exerted consistent leadership during and between missionaries. Chief Skenandoah and Chief Daniel Bread (1800–1873), both prominent Episcopal laymen, supported the church, hosted church events, and were known for their oratorical gifts. Oneida women, although not often recognized for their service, also significantly supported the work of the Episcopal Church at Oneida.[18]

By 1838, the Oneidas were considered the most vital congregation on the reservation and soon needed a larger church building to accommodate them. In the same year, the congregation officially became a parish of the Diocese of Fond du Lac in the Episcopal Church. It was the first non-Roman Catholic church consecrated in the Old Northwest Territory. In 1847, an Oneida delegate attended the first Episcopal Convention in Wisconsin. The Oneida became known for their rich choral and instrumental traditions.

18. Dibbert, *The Story of the First Anglicans in Wisconsin*, 1821, n.p; Curtiss, *History of the Diocese of Fond du Lac and Its Several Congregations*, 52, 70–71, 72; For background on Eleazar Williams, see the Wisconsin Historical Society, Williams, Eleazer 1788–1858, wisconsinhistory.org; Merrill, "Onon-get-go, A Priest of the Oneidas," *The Spirit of Missions*, 588–89; Henry Willmann from a Sermon by Fayette Derlin, "How Our Church Came to Wisconsin," *The Spirit of Missions*, 885–90; Holy Apostles Church, *Ta Luh Ya Wa Gu*, 4; "The History of the Oneida Indian Mission," *The People of the Red Stone*, 4, 9; "Wisconsin's 'King of France,'" *The Milwaukee Journal*, n.p., SHNC; Campisi and Hauptman, *The Oneida Indian Experience*, 66–71, 148–49; Cornelius, "Additional Notes on Eleazer Williams and the Origins of the Episcopal Tradition among the Oneidas," in Hauptman and McLester, *The Oneida Indian Journey. From New York to Wisconsin, 1784–1860*, 129–33; McLester et al., *The Wisconsin Oneidas and the Episcopal Church*, 8–9, Chapter 3.

Women and men sat on opposite sides of the aisle during church services; men wearing white garb and women in traditional dress.[19]

In 1842, Jackson Kemper succeeded in attracting James Lloyd Breck (1818–1876), William Adams (1813–1897), and John Henry Hobart Jr. (1837–1882) to settle at Nashotah.[20] Three young Oneida men attended Nashotah House for five years of education, including Cornelius Hill (1834–1907). Hill was made chief of the Bear Clan at the age of thirteen. A life-long Episcopalian, Hill was baptized by Jackson Kemper and served the Episcopal Church in many ways. He was chosen sachem (wise man) for several terms. As chief, Hill resisted attempts by the United States government to pressure the Oneidas in Wisconsin to sell their lands and move further west. "The whites claim to be civilized, and from them we must learn the arts and customs of civilized life," he said to the Council on Indian Affairs. "The civilization at which I and the greater part of my people aim is one of truth and honor; one that will raise us to a higher state of existence here on earth and fit us for a blessed one in the next world. For this civilization we intend to strive—right here where we are—being sure that we will find it no sooner in the wilds beyond the Mississippi."[21]

Under Jackson Kemper, the Episcopal Church in the Old Northwest Territory grew in communicants, churches, and dioceses.[22] At the outset, Kemper's mission field was not considered very conducive to the Episcopal Church, as "the Revolution was too recent for men to have forgotten that Bishops, Prayer Book and vestments belonged in the minds of most, to a time when King, Crown and taxes bore heavily on the minds of the people."[23] During his episcopacy, Kemper advocated for the Oneidas during the removal policies of President Andrew Jackson and considered it a priority to establish strong bonds between the Episcopal Church and the Oneida. Kemper respected Chief Daniel Bread and honored him at church Conventions. He frequently visited the Oneida mission to celebrate the sacraments and sponsored the education and training of Oneida clergy

19. Campisi and Hauptman, *The Oneida Indian Experience*, 71; Hauptman and McLester, *Chief Daniel Bread and the Oneida Nation of Indians of Wisconsin*, 8; McLester et al., *The Wisconsin Oneidas and the Episcopal Church*, xix.

20. For the early days of Nashota House, see Holcombe, *An Apostle of the Wilderness, James Lloyd Breck, D.D., His Missions and His Schools*; McLester et al., *The Wisconsin Oneidas and the Episcopal Church*, 79.

21. Holy Apostles Church, *Ta Luh Ya Wa Gu*, 4–8; McLester et al., *The Wisconsin Oneidas and the Episcopal Church*, 5; For the autobiography of Cornelius Hill, see Hauptman and McLester, *The Oneida Indians in the Age of Allotment, 1860–1920*, 101–04.

22. See Kemper's memoir, *An Apostle of the Western Church*.

23. Curtiss, *History of the Diocese of Fond du Lac and Its Several Congregations*, 5.

at Nashotah House. Kemper raised funds for the Oneida mission, urging Susan Fenimore Cooper (1813–1894), the daughter of writer James Fenimore Cooper, to write about them. When the Oneidas were threatened with removal from Wisconsin, Kemper used his political leverage to support the tribe.[24]

In his autobiography, Cornelius Hill credits missionary Ellen Saxon Greenough (1837–1870) with the idea of building a stone church.[25] The Hobart Church was struck by lightning in 1920 and restored as the Church of the Holy Apostles in 1922.[26] Fragments of the famous "Oneida Stone," located in Utica, New York, and the ancestral altar of the Oneida Nation, are preserved in the Church of the Holy Apostles. The Oneidas, known as "the keepers of the stone," refer to the Church of the Holy Apostles as the "Grandmother Church of the Diocese of Fond du Lac" and "the Cathedral for all Episcopal Indians."[27]

In 1903, Cornelius Hill, the last hereditary chief of the Oneida, was ordained to the priesthood at the age of sixty-nine by Charles Grafton after serving for twenty-five years as organist and interpreter.[28] Grafton and two hundred visitors arrived by train for the service, greeted by the Oneida brass band; ten clergy participated in the ordination. The service included thirty-seven confirmations; the *Gloria in Excelsis* and the *Te Deum* were sung in Oneida. With Hill's ordination to the priesthood, the Oneida would have the service of Holy Communion in their language. "The two days will forever stand out as red-letter days in the history of the people of the 'Red Stone' observed a participant."[29] Worship at the Oneida mission traditionally combined Anglo-Catholic liturgy with Oneida customs. The cultural adaptations in the liturgical life created a sense of agency among the Oneida within their Episcopal identity.[30]

24. McLester et al., *The Wisconsin Oneidas and the Episcopal Church*, 56–69, 175–77.

25. Hauptman and McLester, *The Oneida Indians in the Age of Allotment, 1860–1920*, 102.

26. McLester, et. al. *The Wisconsin Oneidas and the Episcopal Church*, xix.

27. Yearbook 1920–1931, SHNC, 25; Holy Apostles Church, *Ta Luh Ya Wa Gu*, 5–7, 27. Also, Church of the Holy Apostles—The "Grandmother Church" of the Diocese of Fond du Lac, holyapostlesoneida.com; McLester, et. al. *The Wisconsin Oneidas and the Episcopal Church*, xix.

28. Hall, "Last Chief of the Oneidas to be Ordained Episcopal Priest," n.d. [ca. 1903], SHNC.

29. Curtiss, *History of the Diocese of Fond du Lac and Its Several Congregations*, 4–5, 71; Holy Apostles Church, *Ta Luh Ya Wa Gu*, 8; "The History of the Oneida Indian Mission," *The People of the Red Stone*, 4; McLester et al., *The Wisconsin Oneidas and the Episcopal Church*, 89.

30. Reeves, "Hidden in Christ," 11; McLester et al., *The Wisconsin Oneidas and the Episcopal Church*, 168.

THE WISCONSIN ONEIDAS AND THE SISTERHOOD OF THE HOLY NATIVITY

The "Covenant Chain" metaphor symbolizes the relationship between the Oneida and the Episcopal Church. The Oneida did not consider missionaries the purveyors of civilization or the destroyers of Native culture, and they maintained a deep commitment to the Church. Several factors supported this centuries-old and ongoing relationship between the Oneidas and the Episcopal Church. The emphasis between the Episcopal Church and the Wisconsin Oneida focused on building relationships more than on theology. Cooperation with missionaries was centered on what benefitted the Oneida people in education, healthcare, economic development, and advocacy.[31] The Episcopal Church supported the agency of the Oneida by incorporating Iroquoian cultural and religious elements into the liturgy, music, and religious education. It accommodated their priorities and values, at least to some extent. Oneida Episcopalians became societal leaders, and church committees became a form of social organization. "One can see the conjoining of religious and social amelioration in the work of the Sisters of the Holy Nativity, . . . and in general in church women who served as upholders of Oneida community—just as women have always in Hodinöhsöni' life."[32]

The long relationship between the Oneida and the Episcopal Church must be considered within five centuries of Indigenous-Christian encounters in the Americas. This complex history suggests that the Covenant Chain between the Oneida and the Episcopal Church is constantly in flux and open to reconsideration. "These same missionaries [including the Sisterhood of the Holy Nativity] and bishops were the Oneidas' representatives to the national church, raised funds for Indian needs, brought medical care, taught at the mission school, developed self-help projects that benefitted the tribal economy and periodically served as cultural brokers between the Oneida and local, state, and federal officials to defend the Oneidas against outside threats. On the other hand . . . the Episcopal mission weakened the Oneida clan system and discouraged certain aspects of Iroquoian culture, including membership in medicine societies . . . the Oneida mission school

---

31. For an overview of the history of the Wisconsin Oneidas and the Episcopal Church, see "Owning Our Past: Christianity and Native Americans. Wisconsin Oneida and the Episcopal Church," Rodger Patience and Jennifer Webster, Grace Episcopal Church, Madison, Wisconsin, March 21, 2022. Accessed December 30, 2023. Interview, Rodger Patience, December 2, 2021.

32. McLester et al., *The Wisconsin Oneidas and the Episcopal Church*, 168–69. Hodinöhsöni' is a Seneca word for the peoples of the Iroquois Confederacy.

had an assimilationist focus and its teachers insisted on the use of English and not the Oneida language, a policy that was strictly enforced at times."[33]

The first contact between the Sisterhood of the Holy Nativity and the Wisconsin Oneidas was soon after the sisters arrived in the Diocese of Fond du Lac. The Sisterhood of the Holy Nativity was the first Episcopal sisterhood to undertake missionary work among Indigenous peoples. They eventually lived among the Oneidas for over fifty years. During the 1930s and 1940s, the Episcopal Church formally recognized their work among the Oneida; the sisters were officially appointed United Thank Offering (UTO) women missionary workers. At the time, the UTO was the primary funding source for women missionaries in the Episcopal Church. The funds were raised mainly by women across the Episcopal Church and promoted the values of prayer, study, and supporting missions among children and youth.[34]

The Sisterhood of the Holy Nativity viewed their missionary role as supporting the spiritual and physical welfare of the Oneida people. The first sisters arrived among the Oneida just as measles, smallpox, and diphtheria debilitated the people. The bitter cold and the harsh living conditions cut short Sister Christina's work at Oneida. She died of tuberculosis in 1894 at the age of thirty-six, four years after her profession.[35] During subsequent epidemics of polio in 1916 and influenza in 1918, the sisters were quarantined, and the church closed. Yet, they remained at Oneida to organize food distributions from the mission house, preventing starvation among the people.[36]

Sister Katherine and Sister Margaret were assigned to the Oneida mission house in 1895. Sister Katherine was a nurse before she entered religious life, and Sister Margaret was talented in languages. The two sisters later worked together at mission houses in Maine and Philadelphia. Conditions at Oneida remained challenging, especially during the cold winters when the sisters were subject to chilblains. Reports frequently mention the challenge of working in an unheated church and sacristy where water froze in the basin. True to the mission of the sisterhood, they offered a wide range of classes, including Bible studies for over fifty people and instruction on the

33. McLester et al., *The Wisconsin Oneidas and the Episcopal Church*, xvii–xx, 170–72.

34. Donovan, *A Different Call*, 76–78. When the Sisterhood of the Holy Nativity needed to close the mission house due to a lack of sisters, they were replaced there by the Order of Saint Anne in 1946–1959 and then by the Order of the Teachers of the Children of God from 1959–1967.

35. Reeves, "Hidden in Christ," 10; "The History of the Oneida Mission," *The People of the Red Stone*," 6.

36. Yearbook 1902, 171; Yearbook 1915–1918, 1919–1920, 71, 173, SHNC.

sacraments, often with the assistance of an interpreter. Home medical care, including hospice care, was offered at the mission house. They coordinated relief for Oneida families, including food, clothing, and other provisions. Both sisters contributed to worship at the church by teaching hymns and prayers to the children. The church had a choir for men and boys that sang Episcopal hymns in the Oneida language; the sisters started a choir for women and girls.[37]

The Oneida were Anglicans for almost two hundred years before any contact with the Sisterhood of the Holy Nativity. Thus, the sisters' role was less about evangelization than supporting the deep catholic faith already present. "The Church's liturgy seems to meet the religious aspirations of the Indian people more fully than the form of worship followed by any other body of Christians," commented Sister Katherine in 1904.[38] Early accounts by the sisters reveal a deep appreciation for the Oneida's commitment to the sacraments, particularly Baptism, mixed with white cultural chauvinism—for example, an account by Sister Lillian regarding three families. The two Oneida families showed "their childlike love and obedience" by getting babies immediately baptized and the elder children to church school by walking five miles in the rain on a Sunday. The white family put the sisters off until a more convenient time.[39] That the Oneida took tithing seriously, even in poverty, was also a source of appreciation. Noted one missionary priest when the mission offering of the Hobart Church exceeded the other churches in the diocese: "You can see that the Oneida Indians are desirous that the white people should be properly Christianized (!), hence their offering in excess of what is generally given in white congregations."[40]

In 1898, the Sisterhood of the Holy Nativity built the St. Michael's Mission House next to the church, with a chapel, a classroom, rooms for two sisters plus two or three novices, and additional rooms for guests and longer-term residents needing nursing care. The sisters oversaw the sacristy, altar guilds, and the church's interior; Sister Ann Fidelia painted the chapel when required.[41] Sister Phillipa organized an altar guild for young women. Sister Amy worked with the guild auxiliary, mostly of married women. The guild auxiliary made quilts and clothing to donate to the needy, sponsored

---

37. Reeves, "Hidden in Christ, 11; McLester et al., *The Wisconsin Oneidas and the Episcopal Church*, 168.

38. Sister Katherine, SHN, *The Spirit of Missions*, 119.

39. Sister Lillian, SHN, "Visiting in Oneida," *The Spirit of Missions*, 273–74.

40. Burleson, "$9.49 from Indians of the Hobart Church," *The Spirit of Missions*, 265.

41. "Our New Hill Memorial Chapel," *The People of the Red Stone*, 4.

a monthly dinner, and performed other church work.[42] "There has been much work at the Church," states the annual report for 1898. "Care of the sanctuary, sweeping, dusting; care of vestments and candles, and for any special decoration . . . .The organ was taken for Sunday services and the Thursday celebrations, for all choir rehearsals on Sunday nights and many other times, for all funerals, and for extra services and lectures; for daily Lenten services."[43] Children needing rest, food, and medical care or who lived far from their parents also stayed at the mission house. [44]

The Oneidas were exposed to Western education via missionary schools in New York as early as the 1760s. On the Oneida reservation, there were several schools for children; the parochial schools were the smallest. The Episcopal parochial school where the Sisterhood of the Holy Nativity had their primary association, also known as the Hobart Mission Day School, averaged about thirty students. The Methodist school, also known as the Advent Mission Day School, was slightly smaller, averaging about twenty-five students. There were two other Oneida day schools and an Oneida boarding school, all of which the sisters referred to as "the government schools," with a combined student body of 250 students. The Sisterhood of the Holy Nativity taught religion at the government schools and hosted the children and youth for study and recreation at the mission house. Statistics indicate that in 1910, the capacity for all these schools combined was 305 students, for an estimated 692 Oneida school-age children. While the parochial schools on the reservation provided religious education in addition to primary education in reading, writing, and arithmetic, they did not have the capacity or funding to meet the educational needs of all the Oneidas. One scholarly analysis states that the mission schools were "inadequate to meet either the white societal goals of absorbing the Indians or the reservation community's aspirations to educate their children." [45]

The limitations of educational access on all grade levels factored into how the Oneidas responded to the options available to educate their children. Although missionaries emphasized the need for school attendance in

---

42. McLester et al., *The Wisconsin Oneidas and the Episcopal Church*, 146–47, 149; Yearbook 1898, 34–35, SHNC.

43. Yearbook 1898, SHNC, 34–35.

44. "Holy Apostles—Oneida. One Hundred-Fifty Years, *The Diocese of Fond du Lac*, 1; "Our Parochial School Has a Birthday," *People of the Red Stone*, n.d. [ca 1941] 2; Campisi and Hauptman, eds., *The Oneida Indian Experience*. 71.

45. Hauptman and McLester, *The Oneida Indians in the Age of Allotment*, 1860–1920, 68, 41. Accounts of the starting date of the parochial school vary. The date of the 1760s is from Oneida sources.

the parochial day schools, poverty was a significant factor in keeping children out of school. For some families, the lack of emphasis on schooling was less about parents' resistance to Western education than the need to have children working in the fields. In the late nineteenth century, no local secondary schools or professional training options existed. By the early twentieth century, public schools opened on or near the reservation, lessening the need for schooling elsewhere in the country.[46]

The Hobart Mission Day School served the Oneida from 1816 (in New York) until 1967 in Wisconsin and became the longest-surviving Episcopal school in the state. Instruction at the Episcopal parochial school was in the Oneida language until the late 1840s, after which it was in English. Translation from Oneida or Mohawk into English was present in church services. The emphasis on English in church, along with the harsh treatment children received in government schools for speaking Oneida, contributed to a decline in Oneida language skills among the young.[47] Two sisters from the Sisterhood of the Holy Nativity taught religion and music at the parochial school for grades one through eight. They provided outreach to the children and their families. The sisters worked at the school with an Oneida teacher, Alice Cornelius. In 1898, Bishop Grafton raised the funds to renovate the building and added a band room. Eventually, the curriculum met state standards, and the staff grew to include three sisters, two lay teachers, and the missionary priest as headmaster. There were, at times, as many as fifty children. Efforts were made to include lessons directly related to the cultural heritage of Oneida children. For example, the curriculum on the formation of American democratic government included lessons on the ideals of the Iroquois Confederacy.[48]

In addition to the Hobart Mission Day School, the Sisterhood of the Holy Nativity provided religious instruction and music education for children at the government school at the mission house once per week. On Sunday morning, the catechism class for government school children hosted over one hundred children. The sisters' curriculum included the Bible, church history, and studies on the *Book of Common Prayer*. They also offered lace-making, basketry, and music. The response from over fifty girls was positive enough for the sisters to add beadwork to the curriculum.[49]

---

46. Hauptman and McLester, *The Oneida Indians in the Age of Allotment, 1860–1920*, 8, 60–62.

47. Hauptman and McLester, *The Oneida Indian Journey*, 80–82; McLester et al., *The Wisconsin Oneidas and the Episcopal Church*, xx–xxi.

48. Hanson, "School News," 12.

49. Yearbook 1901, 139, SHNC; Yearbook 1902, 172, SHNC; Reeves, "Hidden in Christ," 11; Holy Apostles Church, *Ta Luh Ya Wa Gu*, 18: "Our Parochial School Has

Instruction in rug weaving was added to the curriculum and was successful enough to introduce basketry as an additional cottage industry.[50] Sister Katherine purportedly found the best teacher available to teach her how to weave using the yellow willow available on the reservation so that she could encourage the art.[51]

The Hobart Mission Day School provided the primary source of recreation for young people, including youth groups, weekend activities, dinners, dances, and special occasions like May Day celebrations and diocesan Bishop's Day. Devotional activities such as quiet days, Holy Week liturgies, and Sunday Benediction were also incorporated into the schedule. Former students at the Oneida Mission School remember the care given by the sisters who served the school. One student reflected: "I believe that, besides my parents, those wonderful women affiliated with our church who were so nurturing had the greatest influence on me ... In my mind, Jesus' message about "love" has always been a verb, meaning action. The women of the church followed this message of the Gospel."[52]

THE WISCONSIN ONEIDA AND RESIDENTIAL SCHOOLS

As part of the forced assimilation policies for Indigenous peoples established by the United States government, beginning with the Indian Civilization Act of 1819 and continuing through the 1960s, a system of residential boarding schools was established with the racist agenda of "civilizing" Indigenous peoples under the guise of humanitarian impulse. This system of government-sponsored education intended to force native children and youth to assimilate into white culture, thus leaving their own traditions and cultural identities behind. Indigenous parents were forced to send their children to these schools, a great distance from their families and lands. Although the federal government acknowledged that the assimilation policies were an abject failure by the 1930s, the brutal physical, psychological, and spiritual treatment of the children and their families had already taken its toll. Survivors carried the trauma of the residential boarding schools to

---

a Birthday, 125th Anniversary," *The People of the Red Stone*, 15; McLester et al., *The Wisconsin Oneidas and the Episcopal Church*, 155–56; Yearbook 1898, 34–35, SHNC

50. Annual Report of Convent and Mission Houses, 1940–1943, SHNC, 63.

51. Yearbook 1901, 139–40, SHNC; Yearbook 1902, 171–72, SHNC; McLester et al., *The Wisconsin Oneidas and the Episcopal Church*, 70; McLester III and Hauptman, eds. *A Nation within A Nation*, 4–5, 81–82.

52. McLester et al., *The Wisconsin Oneidas and the Episcopal Church*, xix, 159–60.

subsequent generations. Families whose children died in the system were left without answers or even knowledge of their final resting place. As one scholar of the impact of Indian residential schools, writes: "It is in the dark reality of the residential schools that the civilizing mission is revealed as the hard edge of colonialism, and where the lofty ideal blurs into a more prosaic desire to eliminate the potential problems that cultural difference poses for an emergent nation state."[53]

Under the Dawes Act of 1887, the federal government promised the Oneidas that a boarding school would be established on reservation lands in Wisconsin. The lands were across Duck Creek from the Episcopal mission. Influential Episcopal missionary Edward Goodnough advocated for the project, and the school opened in 1893. The focus of the educational process was on assimilation. Education for boys centered on agriculture; girls focused on domestic work. One of the significant differences between the Oneida government school and other residential schools across the country was that it allowed students to go home over the weekends, thus alleviating some of the loss of family bonds, culture, and language experienced by students sent further distances. By 1900, the school employed over twenty staff, thirteen of whom were Oneidas in various roles, including teachers. However, the diminishing land base of the Oneidas increased financial pressures. By 1907, attempts were made to convert the government school into a day school to prevent it from closing altogether. Despite support from the tribal council and Reginal Weller, then bishop of the Episcopal Diocese of Fond du Lac, the school closed in 1918. During the 1980s, the Oneida Nation formed a task force to return the property to the tribe.[54]

Young Oneidas from Wisconsin also attended the Hampton Institute, a residential boarding school in Williamsburg, Virginia. The school was founded during Reconstruction as an industrial education school for African Americans. The educational model was rooted in the belief that it was possible to solve the "race problem" of the United States without disrupting the socioeconomic status quo. Integral elements in industrial education at Hampton focused on building "character," fostering self-reliance, and appreciating the dignity of labor. In addition to manual labor and an academic education geared toward practical skills, the school aimed to provide moral development and assist students in reaching material prosperity. At the boarding school, the students received instruction designed to "civilize" their behavior through Christian morality, cleanliness, and other

53. Woods, *A Cultural Sociology of Anglican Mission and the Indian Residential Schools in Canada*, 3; McNally, "Boss Women," 44–45.

54. Hauptman and McLester, *The Oneida Indians in the Age of Allotment, 1860–1920*, 63–70.

attributes designed to earn the respect of the white community. Graduates of the program went home and infused their schools with similar values. That Hampton received substantial support from whites made it increasingly likely that industrial schooling would be the only education available for African Americans. Not surprisingly, given that the model of industrial education employed at Hampton served to perpetuate the subordination of African Americans, the model was heavily criticized by W. E. B. Du Bois and other black intellectuals.[55]

In 1877, the Hampton Institute began to admit Indigenous people despite objections made by African American students. Although only 1388 Indigenous students ever attended Hampton, the school was influential in shaping federal policies. The Hampton ideal for Indigenous students was perpetuated through acculturated African American teachers who were upheld as role models. Scholars argue Hampton constructed the relationship between African American and Indigenous students to defuse the anger and betrayal of Black students at Reconstruction policies and Native students at treaty abrogation and the exploitation of tribal lands. The program at Hampton for Indigenous students was eventually closed in 1923.[56]

The other residential boarding school where the Wisconsin Oneidas attended was the Carlisle Indian Industrial School in Pennsylvania. Founded by Richard Henry Pratt in 1879, the school was the first residential school exclusively for American Indians. Pratt believed that giving students a marketable skill would make them more easily assimilated into American culture. The curriculum and philosophy of the school were based on the Hampton Institute. The school stressed religious education, and students attended non-Indian churches and Sunday schools. This policy of sending students into non-Indian contexts was known at Carlisle as the "outing system." Instead of returning home for vacations and the summers, students would live with non-Indian families and earn a minimum wage. Because the English language skills of the Oneida were higher than other students, they benefitted from higher graduation rates. However, not all students survived the residential school experience. During the years the school was in operation, 1879–1918, nearly two hundred students died there. The former school site is now affiliated with the Army War College. In 2019, Oneida tribal leaders and members of the Episcopal Church collaborated with the army to repatriate the remains of three Oneida girls who died at the school.[57]

55. For an overview of the Hampton Institute, see Anderson, *The Education of Blacks in the South, 1860–1935*; Peabody, *Education for Life*.

56. Lindsey, *Indians at Hampton Institute, 1877–1923*; Hauptman and McLester, *The Oneida Indians in the Age of Allotment, 1860–1920*, 60–62.

57. Hauptman and McLester, *The Oneida Indians in the Age of Allotment, 1860–1920*, 4855.

The Oneida Nation stresses that their responses to the residential school system were diverse. That the boarding school system was harsh and, for some children, fatal is undeniable. This said, the Oneida are resilient, and those who attended the schools were more than victims. The impact of the boarding school experience varied depending on where the children were sent and the quality and cultural sensitivity of the teachers, administrators, and staff at a given school. Some students, like Nancy Cornelius (1861–1908), one of the first Indigenous women to be educated as a nurse, and Josephine Hill Webster (1873–1978), a lace-making teacher and musician, became significant leaders within the Oneida Nation. Some sent outside Wisconsin did not return to Oneida, but some did and worked at the Oneida boarding school until it closed. Many benefited from contacts and friendships with other Native peoples. Some Oneidas pushed to save the government schools and gain better healthcare. For others, the experience deepened their connections with the Church. For Oneida women, the lace-making guild and leadership training at a residential school provided national recognition and supplemental income for families. For Oneida men, the cultural benefits of music education enabled them to become professional musicians and an integral part of community life. Both the lace-making and music industries became sources of community pride and identity. "Sometimes they used tried and true strategies; at other times they innovated. In either case, Indians responded to new contexts on their own terms."[58]

THE LACE-MAKING INDUSTRY

One of the most publicized examples of Episcopal mission work among Indigenous women was the celebrated lace-making project attributed to Deaconess Sybil Carter. In 1890, Carter worked among the White Earth Band of Ojibwe and expanded the project to other reservations in Minnesota, New York, Nebraska, South Dakota, California, and Oneida. In 1904, Carter founded the National Indian Mission and Lace Industry Association, which she supported until she died in 1926. The Sisterhood of the Holy Nativity was notified of the project and believed that lace-making could become an income source for Oneida women. The sisters already encouraged the beadwork industry. While the Oneida were proficient at beadwork long before they encountered the sisters, the sisters encouraged them to make practical items to be sold beyond collectors. Sybil Carter invited lace-making

---

58. Hauptman and McLester, *The Oneida Indians in the Age of Allotment, 1860–1920*, 8, 86.

teachers from the Hampton Institute to the Oneida reservation to conduct a first round of instruction with the sisters and a few students, who could then teach others on the reservation and at the government school. Associates of the Sisterhood of the Holy Nativity covered the cost of the materials and marketed the lace. In addition to income, both bead and lace work were considered part of the "civilizing" agenda of white missionaries. They believed that handwork wrought "a refining influence among the young girls, as shown in greater neatness of person and quietness of manner."[59]

In July 1898, the sisters taught six young girls to make lace; by the autumn, fourteen women were interested in learning, and the number soon expanded to over one hundred women. The sisters observed that many Oneida women were skilled at needlework and quickly learned to make exquisite lace. The sisters provided the women with materials to do the work at home. The finished lace was returned to the sisters to be pressed, registered, ticketed, and stored before beginning the process again. In 1899, an Ojibwe lace-maker and teacher, Annie Jackson, visited Oneida to assist with the instruction. By 1900, approximately 150 Oneida women earned $650 for their lace at a time when a weekly laborer earned four dollars. By 1904, the Oneida lace-makers won prizes for their lace in competitions in St. Louis, Buffalo, New York City, and Paris.[60] One of the finest examples of Oneida lace is an altar set, including superfrontal, credence covers, and chalice veil, preserved at the Cathedral of St. John the Divine in New York City. The twenty-five-piece lace set was given to the Cathedral for its opening in 1911.[61]

The lace-making tradition is an essential artifact in the material history of the Oneidas in the Episcopal Church. The patterns found in Oneida lace work evolved. Early lace work resembled traditional bobbin lace. The original patterns provided by the Sybil Carter Lace Association were stereotypical white translations of "Indian motifs"—bows and arrows, canoes, tepees—designed to appear "exotic" to non-Native consumers and unlikely to have originated with the lace-makers themselves. However, the Oneida Nation Museum found the images evolved as the lace-makers gained more industry control. Gradually, the lace featured traditional Oneida symbols of the sky dome and the tree of life.[62]

59. Bloomfield, *The Oneidas*, 345; McLester et al., *The Wisconsin Oneidas and the Episcopal Church*, 160–161.

60. Yearbook 1898, 35–38, SHNC; Yearbook 1899, 62–63, SHNC; Reeves, "Hidden in Christ," 12; Curtiss, *History of the Diocese of Fond du Lac and Its Several Congregations*, 37; McLester et al., *The Wisconsin Oneidas and the Episcopal Church*, 160–61.

61. McLester III and Hauptman, eds. *A Nation within A Nation*, 4–5, 81–82.

62. "Now online: Lace from the Oneida Nation Museum," www.oneida-nsn.gov. Accessed December 12, 2021.

Ongoing concerns about the importance of cleanliness during the lace-making process run through the sisters' reports to the Convent. For example, a report on the Oneida lace-makers stated that the women repeated the phrase, "Be always washing your hands."[63] This emphasis on the "gospel of soap" is evidence of underlying assumptions about Oneida culture dictated by white housekeeping standards. Stereotypes of Indigenous peoples as not only dirty but also lazy were underlying white attitudes in the industry. Both Sybil Carter and the sisters observed that Indigenous women were surprisingly idle and believed their lives would improve if they were more industrious. "They are so much happier with something to do," remarked one of the lace-making teachers.[64] Although the sisters recognized the skills of Indigenous women and were more inclined than their male counterparts to confront negative attitudes toward the Oneida, they also felt obliged to emphasize the importance of industry. They stressed the difficulties of protecting the lace from soiling when manufactured in the women's homes.[65] "The lace teachers show the Indian women how to make lace, and pay them when it is made, so that they not only learn to make the lace well and keep it white and clean, but they can also by it make their own living and be more comfortable in their homes," wrote Carter.[66]

The Sisterhood of the Holy Nativity was active in the lace-making industry until 1909 and then transferred leadership to Josephine Hill Webster, a daughter of Chief Cornelius Hill. The sisterhood discerned that it was time for the Oneida to take leadership of the project and offered their prayers and interest after that.[67] Webster returned to Oneida from boarding school at the Hampton Institute, where she excelled academically and learned to make bobbin lace. Sometimes referred to as the "last Oneida Princess," Josephine Hill Webster was an outstanding leader in the community. After the Sybil Carter Indian Lace Association was discontinued in 1926, Webster assumed leadership of the lace-making operation, including sixty workers at Oneida; after the first year, workers created and sold over 500 lace items. Webster won twenty-six first-place awards for her lace work at the Northeastern Wisconsin Fair.[68] An Episcopalian and an accomplished musician, Webster

63. Holy Apostles Church, *Ta Luh Ya Wa Gu*, 15. "Our Oneida Lace Work—Its History, *The People of the Red Stone*, 11.

64. Sybil Carter, "The Indian Women and Lace-Making," 657; McLester III and Hauptman, eds. *A Nation within A Nation*, 67–82.

65. McNally, "Boss Women," 46.

66. Quoted in McNally, "Boss Women," 46; Bloomfield, *The Oneidas*, 347–48.

67. "Our Oneida Lace Work—Its History, 11.

68. Holy Apostles Church, *Ta Luh Ya Wa Gu*, 16; "Our Oneida Lace Work—Its History, 11; Campisi and Hauptman, *The Oneida Indian Experience*, 116–17.

served as the church organist for a brief period. As the demand for lace waned in the 1930s, Webster became the first woman postmaster at Oneida until her retirement. She continued lace-making until 1953. After retiring, Webster supported the Episcopal Church through women's guilds.[69]

Little of what occurred in church-sponsored guilds for Oneida women was never written down as it was part of an oral tradition separate from the control of English-speaking missionaries.[70] Methodist missionaries in New York built their lay devotional societies on women's groups already in place in the 1720s. By the mid-nineteenth century, women elders met at the church every Thursday to make quilts, moccasins, and dolls. The several hundred dollars a year raised by the women's guild was an essential contribution to the building fund for the stone church.[71] According to missionary Ellen Saxton Goodnough, women associated with the Episcopal Church in Oneida had functioning women's guilds as early as 1853. Goodnough came to Oneida as a teenager with her husband, Edward A. Goodnough, who served as a missionary priest there. More so than her husband, the Oneida saw Ellen Goodnough as someone who advocated for them during famine and political threats.[72] Although the Goodnoughs were attributed with starting the Oneida women's guilds, they were probably building on social networks already in place. Groups of women working together in guilds replicated ancient Indigenous traditions, deepened relationships, and elevated their societal position. Friendship circles among women, particularly among older women active in church affairs, were closely aligned with the denominational affiliation of members. While Oneida voluntary societies superficially resembled their white counterparts, which may have contributed to missionaries' belief that they started them, closer study reveals the interplay of family status, gender, kinship, age, and religious boundaries.[73] "We have lists of priests, sisters, their orders, and their titles who have served at Holy Apostles. However, it is next to impossible to name all of the women, both Native and non-Native, who worked side by side with the male clergy . . . Indeed the women were and continue to be the backbone

---

69. Campisi and Hauptman, *The Oneida Indian Experience*, 116–18; Hauptman and McLester, *The Oneida Indians in the Age of Allotment, 1860–1920*, 109–11.

70. McNally, "Boss Women," 46–47.

71. Holy Apostles Church, *Ta Luh Ya Wa Gu*, 10–11.; McNally, "Boss Women," 46; Bloomfield, *The Oneidas*, 27084; "The History of the Oneida Mission," *The People of the Red Stone*, 4.

72. McLester et al., *The Wisconsin Oneidas and the Episcopal Church*, 53, 60

73. McLester III and Hauptman, eds. *A Nation within A Nation*, 16–18.

of every effort, challenge, and responsibility that has followed our church's history," writes Judy Cornelius-Hawk.[74]

Lace-making, beadwork, and basketry projects supported by the Sisterhood of the Holy Nativity contributed to social cohesion as they utilized group structures already prevalent among the Oneida in the Episcopal Church. The women who produced lace, beads, and baskets also worked for the Church.[75] Sybil Carter and the Sisterhood of the Holy Nativity praised lace-making as a cottage industry. It allowed women to work together in their homes rather than turning them out to work like "the brave girls in factories."[76] Analyzing the interplay between race, gender, and colonialism in the inauguration of the lace-making industry among the Oneida yields complex results. Modern critiques of the colonialist, paternalistic, and racist attitudes behind the lace-making industry are justified. At the same time, the industry contributed to the self-determination and self-esteem of Oneida women and counteracted the negative impact of the federal Dawes Act. Based on a cooperative model, the industry included the artisans who made the lace, packers, transporters, and marketers. The funds raised offset crop failures and saved lives.[77]

The Episcopal Church guilds among the Oneida became viable social institutions because they were led by people esteemed in the community who had recognized authority beyond the Church. The earliest guilds and auxiliaries for Oneida women supported by the Sisterhood of the Holy Nativity were initially conceived as a resource to train Indigenous women in the intricacies of white women's church work. Over time, through the resilience and agency of Oneida women, these groups performed services critical to their people's spiritual and material well-being. In this way, it is not at all surprising that the organization of the lace-making industry was eventually given over to the lace-makers themselves, for they were already engaged in translating the resources provided by the Church into goods sold for the benefit of their community. Through their work among the Oneidas, the Sisterhood of the Holy Nativity had the opportunity to serve as "upholders of Oneida community."[78]

The stories of Indigenous Christians are often told from the perspective of the missionaries, not from the Indigenous peoples themselves. This is

---

74. McLester et al., *The Wisconsin Oneidas and the Episcopal Church*, 159.

75. Carter, "The Indian Women and Lace-Making," 657; Hauptman and McLester, *The Oneida Indians in the Age of Allotment, 1860–1920*, 94.

76. Carter, "The Indian Women and Lace-Making," 657.

77. McLester III and Hauptman, eds. *A Nation within A Nation*, 76–78; 81–82.

78. McLester et al., *The Wisconsin Oneidas and the Episcopal Church*, 169.

also the case for narratives relating to the Oneida and the Episcal Church, including their relationship with the Sisterhood of the Holy Nativity. While the living memories of the Oneida regarding the sisterhood are positive, the historical analysis of the relationship is more nuanced.[79] There is limited data from the perspective of the Oneida themselves during the years the Sisterhood of the Holy Nativity ministered among them. The relationship was highly publicized from the perspective of the missionaries. Bishop Grafton was deeply committed to the work and adept at obtaining publicity and raising funds through the Board of Missions of the Episcopal Church. Although the Board of Missions considered Grafton's churchmanship "extreme," they also appreciated his "sympathetic touch" with people of all "races," wherein they included Indigenous peoples, African Americans, Eastern Christians, Old Catholics, and European white immigrants.[80]

Beginning in 1891 through the early 1920s, there were regular stories on the Oneida in the leading Episcopal Church mission magazine, *The Spirit of Missions*, including church school curricula based on "Our Oldest Indian Mission," written for the centenary celebration in 1921. At that time, the "Oldest Indian Mission" in the Episcopal Church had a membership of 1500 and was considered "among the poorest people in the Church."[81] The stories are told from the white missionary perspective, including those written by the Sisterhood of the Holy Nativity. The sisters' work was often subordinated to the work of the clergy missionaries. The stories suggest that the missionaries and the sisters who lived among the Oneida exercised their roles with compassion and a commitment to alleviate human suffering. They were progressive for their era in their recognition of the heritage, gifts, and dignity of the people. The sisters also understood when it was time to relinquish their control to facilitate leadership from the Oneida. At the same time, they did not question white cultural superiority, nor were they publicly critical of federal policies assumed to be in the Oneida's best interests.[82]

The earliest observations shared by the Sisterhood of the Holy Nativity living at Oneida often conveyed white values regarding religion, children, gender roles, productivity, and housekeeping standards. "First of all, the Church has a firm hold upon these children, from (almost) the moment

---

79. Interview, Rodger Patience, December 2, 2021.

80. "Charles Chapman Grafton, Obituary," 710.

81. Watson, "Our Oldest Indian Mission," 448–53; "Twelve Places Every Young Churchman Should Visit," 685.

82. For example, see "severe trials" of missionary Edward Goodnough when he protested the proposal to remove the Oneida to Montana, "The History of the Oneida Indian Mission," *The People of the Red Stone*, 5.

of their birth," wrote Sister Katherine.[83] Sunday afternoon classes at the mission house included at least 150 children, one hundred of whom were church members. It was noted that entire families came to church, and the children were always well-behaved.[84] In 1904, Sister Katherine reported that the government school teachers approved of the sisters' work with the children. "Not only did the children and their families share a strong sense of the importance of Baptism," wrote Sister Katherine, but they also received a religious education that reminded them of "home." Initially, Sister Katherine betrayed no sense of concern about "what they [the Oneida children] become after Uncle Sam takes them in hand" and viewed the "traces of refinement and the beginning of gentle manners" exhibited by the children as signs of progress.[85]

As the number of Oneida children and youth served by the sisters grew, the Diocese of Fond du Lac launched a major campaign to build a multi-functional community center. The facility was eventually named Bishop Grafton Parish Hall. Grafton envisioned a facility that included a hall for 300, a gym, library, reading room, kitchen, band room, work room for women, guild rooms, and additional classrooms. "It seems useless to send the Indian boys and girls away for such an education as Hampton and Carlisle provide and then do nothing when they return to the reservation," said missionary Frank Wesley Merrill. Merrill and the sisters observed that the students returning to the reservation from boarding school were a pastoral concern for the Church, "for they come back to their homes educated out of harmony with their old surroundings . . . ."[86] Much in the records goes unstated, and neither the missionaries nor the sisters were likely to criticize the federal government publicly. Instead, they focused on what they believed to be the Church's role among the Oneida. For them, that meant a compassionate response to help transition young people back home to their families and reservation life. They believed that giving young people access to "a social and religious center" would help them adjust and unleash "real power for good among them."[87]

Over their years at Oneida, the Sisterhood of the Holy Nativity gained more profound insights into the trauma children and families experienced through the residential school system. In 1911, Sister Lillian and Sister

83. Sister Katherine, SHN, "With the Indian Boys and Girls at Oneida," 116.
84. "The People of the Stone," 991.
85. Sister Katherine, SHN, "With the Indian Boys and Girls at Oneida," 114.
86. "A Parish House of the Oneida Indians," 862; Merrill, "A Parish House Among the Oneida Indians," 303–4.
87. Merrill, "A Parish House Among the Oneida Indians," 303–4.

Amelia reported that they were often asked whether it was worthwhile for them to teach at Oneida, given that at the age of fourteen, children were sent away to a distant state—Pennsylvania, Virginia, Kansas, or South Dakota—for three to seven years, with no way to contact their families. "I reply that it is even more worthwhile than it is to teach white children," responded Sister Lillian. "It matters greatly before going that they have been trained in Christian ideals and religious priorities according to the faith of the Church. If they have been so trained it will be a great protection to them, and they are far more likely to return to the reservation loyal and faithful to the Church which they have learned to love and prepared to carry on the work and perpetuate the atmosphere so dear to the hearts of their ancestors."[88]

HEALTHCARE AND HUMANITARIAN ASSISTANCE

The Oneidas brought their traditional healing practices to Wisconsin. The first hospital for the Oneidas was founded in 1898 by Bishop Grafton, ten years before the federal government responded to the need. Associates of the sisterhood raised funds for medical care and humanitarian aid.[89] The Sisterhood for the Holy Nativity was responsible for the new Oneida dispensary, providing home remedies, visits, and hospice care. The sisters' work served as a bridge between traditional remedies and medical professionals, and they performed the spiritual care indicative of chaplains today: "At the hospital weekly visits were made when advisable, and when there were any very sick patients the visits were more frequent," noted the annual report for 1898. Sr. Katherine watched one night with a dying man; another woman was prepared for the sacraments and death. "The Sisters had prayers with such patients as could understand English; friendly visits were made to Lavinia [Cornelius], the Indian nurse, and to old Mary Ann [Bread], an inmate but not ill, to whom some delicacy was carried whenever possible."[90] They often soothed the dying with music: "The Sisters took their harp and sang for the dying man. Restless as he was, music would quiet him." They revisited the hospital at Easter, with the choir, providing a long "sing" for the patients.[91] The sisters also offered "personal help" at the hospital, such

---

88. "The People of the Red Stone," 992.

89. Annual reports from the Oneida Mission detail the Associates' financial support. For example, see Yearbook 1931–1932, 13, SHNC.

90. Yearbook 1898, 34, SHNC.

91. Yearbook 1899, 63–64, SHNC.

as writing letters for patients.[92] In the case of confinements, the sisters assisted the midwives and provided clothing for women and infants, soup and fruit for the mother, and sheets and other bedding.[93] At least one missionary priest did not want the sisters working in the dispensary, but the Oneidas overruled him. After his death, the Oneidas refused to allow one of his sons to become the new priest out of fear that the sisters would not be allowed to work at the hospital.[94]

The hospital was administered by two of the first Indigenous nurses; both were Oneidas: Lavinia Cornelius, who worked at the government school, and Nancy Cornelius Skenandore, who worked there until 1904. Zilpha Rinehard Wilson, M.D., was a white woman, not Oneida, though they honored her for her medical service. Employed as a physician for the government school from 1901–1904, Wilson volunteered at Oneida Hospital and worked with the sisterhood. She made over 400 home visits during her first year and vaccinated over 700 people. Oneida physician Josiah A Powless, M.D., administered the hospital until 1916, when he was sent overseas during World War I.[95]

Sister Amy came to Oneida in 1923 and served there for over twenty-five years. The Oneida referred to Sister Amy as "Our Mother." She worked in the dispensary and assisted the physician, Rosa Minoka-Hill, M.D. Hill was born into the Mohawk Nation and forcibly adopted by Quakers in Philadelphia. There, she became the second Indigenous woman to obtain a medical degree. While working at a charity school for Indigenous girls, she met Anna Hill, a Wisconsin Oneida student who introduced Rosa to Charles Abram Hill. The two were married and returned to Oneida where Minoka-Hill was a physician for over forty years. She was formally adopted by the Oneida in 1947. Sister Amy assisted Minoka-Hill with patients. Aware that many people could not afford a doctor and pay for their medication, Sister Amy raised critical medical relief funding by giving talks to Woman's Auxiliaries across the Episcopal Church.[96]

---

92. Yearbook 1899, 65, SHNC.

93. Yearbook 1895, n.p. SHNC.

94. McLester et al., *The Wisconsin Oneidas and the Episcopal Church*, 53–54, 138–39, 149.

95. Cornelius, Jourdan, Metoxen, "Oneida Healers: Hospitals, Doctors and Nurses," *Oneida Cultural Heritage Department*. Accessed February 12, 2022; Hauptman and McLester, III, eds., *The Oneida Indian Journey*, 77.

96. Yearbook 1920–1931, 9, SHNC; Holy Apostles Church, *Ta Luh Ya Wa Gu*, 350; "The Oneida Mission," by W.F. Christian, Missionary and the Sisters of the Holy Nativity 1934; Feature story on Dr. L. Rosa Minoka-Hill, *The Milwaukee Journal* (October 19, 1947), n.p. SHNC.

The Sisterhood of the Holy Nativity understood from the beginning of their ministry among the Oneida that it was their responsibility to demonstrate that they were a compassionate presence; they did not assume that trust would be given to them. Like other Episcopal missionaries, the sisters saw themselves as reformers, hopeful that the Church's spiritual resources, humane assimilation, adequate education, and work opportunities could alleviate the poverty and social chaos the Oneida people experienced.[97] They did not consider that this agenda might in any way contribute to the poverty and social chaos experienced by the Oneida.

As the twentieth century progressed, the Oneida gradually assumed many roles initially held by the Sisterhood of the Holy Nativity. For example, Oneida laywoman Pearl Archiquette House became the organist and choir director at the Church of the Holy Apostles in 1930, serving in that capacity until 1963. House developed youth music programs for the Episcopal Church and the young people who visited the parish hall from the government school. She also taught dance and musical instruments. House worked with the sisters in several capacities; in addition to the music program, she was a member of the altar guild, a leader in the women's guild, and served as the cook at the Oneida parochial school.[98]

It is difficult to assess the relationship between the Sisterhood of the Holy Nativity and the Oneidas in binary terms. The Episcopal Church and the Oneidas secured religious, political, and economic gains through their relationship.[99] As two of the foremost scholars in the field argue, the Church provided the Oneidas with more than spiritual support; it also served as an extension of kinship ties and was a dominant social institution for centuries.[100] Missionaries (and the Sisterhood of the Holy Nativity, by extension) both advised the tribal council and took direction from them. While Episcopal missionaries exerted influence on secular matters, it is also true that tribal leaders exerted influence on religious affairs. As one recent study of the Oneidas argues: "The [white] ministers [and sisters] were outsiders who carried out their religious duties and offered their advice, but they did not form or direct public opinion. The church councils, made up of Oneidas, provided the mechanisms to bear approbation or condemnation on community members."[101] The sisterhood developed cottage industries among the Oneida, contributing to social cohesion and the tribal economy.

97. For an analysis of missionary motivations, see McNally, "Boss Women," 44–45.
98. Campisi and Hauptman, *The Oneida Indian Experience*, 123,
99. McLester et al., *The Wisconsin Oneidas and the Episcopal Church*, xx.
100. McLester III and Hauptman, A *Nation within A Nation*, 17.
101. McLester III and Hauptman, eds. *A Nation within A Nation*, 17.

They raised critical funding to meet humanitarian needs and ensured their participation in ecclesiastical structures. In local, state, and federal contexts, they leveraged their positions and whiteness to defend the Oneidas from external threats.[102]

The Sisterhood of the Holy Nativity served among the Oneidas for nearly sixty years. When they withdrew in 1946 due to insufficient sisters, they were replaced by the Order of St. Anne until 1959, followed by the Order of the Teachers of the Children of God from 1959-1967. Two Oneida women eventually became sisters of the Order of the Teachers of the Children of God, Mother Superior Alicia Torres, TCG, attended the Oneida Mission School as a girl and was directly influenced by the Sisterhood of the Holy Nativity. The Order of St. Anne encouraged Sister Theresa Rose, TCG, in her vocation.[103]

MISSION HOUSE IN MILWAUKEE

In 1909, the Sisterhood of the Holy Nativity expanded the order's ministry in Wisconsin by establishing a mission house at All Saints' Cathedral in the Episcopal Diocese of Milwaukee. William Walter Webb (1857-1933), the bishop of the Diocese of Milwaukee, was a former president of Nashotah House and an ardent promoter of the catholic faith. Under Webb's leadership, "Milwaukee continued to present a solid front favoring the highest conceptions of the Catholic heritage of the Episcopal Church."[104] A graduate of the Berkeley Divinity School, he was consecrated bishop co-adjutor in 1906 and soon envisioned the possibilities for the sisterhood in the diocese.[105]

For most of their history in the Diocese of Milwaukee, three sisters lived in the mission house and supported All Saints' Cathedral and local parishes. The sisters in Milwaukee had access to the Convent in Fond du Lac and were involved in community life there at least once a month. Sister Etheldreda was most associated with the Milwaukee mission house, arriving there as Sister-in-Charge in 1926 and serving in that capacity for many years. At the Cathedral, the sisterhood was included in weekly staff meetings, active in the altar guild and guilds for women and girls and taught in the primary department of the church school. They also provided religious

---

102. McLester et al., *The Wisconsin Oneidas and the Episcopal Church*, xx–xxi.
103. McLester et al., *The Wisconsin Oneidas and the Episcopal Church*, 156–57.
104. Wagner, *The Episcopal Church in Wisconsin, 1847–1947*, 146–48.
105. Wagner, *The Episcopal Church in Wisconsin, 1847–1947*, 146–48.

education for the mothers of primary school children.[106] Once resident in Milwaukee, the sisters actively supported the diocesan Woman's Auxiliary, hosting meetings and retreats for women in parishes across the diocese.[107] Sister Etheldreda taught monthly at the Wisconsin Industrial School, a reform school for girls; girls from the school were confirmed with the Cathedral class.[108] The mission house in Milwaukee also initiated a Christmas card project, sending cards from the sisterhood to charitable organizations such as the Soldier's Home and County Hospital.[109]

One of Bishop Webb's priorities was strengthening college work among University of Wisconsin, Madison, students. This work was undertaken by sisters from the Convent and the Milwaukee mission house, often hosting students on retreats away from campus.[110] Sister Patricia was deeply interested in college ministry and spent at least two days a month on campus.[111] One sister from the Sisterhood of the Holy Nativity, either from the Milwaukee mission house or the Convent in Fond du Lac, typically visited the students once a month, offered spiritual programs and talks on religious life.[112] In the 1920s, the sisters extended their campus outreach to include Downer College, a women's liberal arts college in Milwaukee, and Sister Patricia's alma mater. The college women were invited to the bishop's residence for tea and programs.[113]

All Saint's Cathedral in the Episcopal Diocese of Milwaukee played an essential role among the Oneidas. Ruth Baird, an Oneida Nation, and Cathedral congregation member formed an Indian Women's Guild. The guild raised funds for the Oneida mission and sponsored traditional activities, such as a dance program and an arts and crafts program.[114] Milwaukee Associates of the Sisterhood of the Holy Nativity actively supported the Oneida mission. "We are most grateful to the Community, Milwaukee Associates, and personal friends who supplied two-thirds of our relief funds during these months," the 1930 annual report states.[115]

106. Yearbook 1931–1932, 19–20, SHNC

107. For Sister Etheldreda's work with the Woman's Auxiliary and St. Luke's, Bay View, see Yearbook 1931–1932, 19, SHNC.

108. Yearbook 1935–1936, 146–47, SHNC.

109. Yearbook 1920–1931, 38, SHNC.

110. For example, Yearbook 1933–1934, 75, SHNC.

111. Yearbook 1935–1936, 134, SHNC.

112. Wagner, *The Episcopal Church in Wisconsin, 1847–1947*, 117–18, 174–77; Yearbook 1931–1932, 19–20, SHNC.

113. Yearbook 1920–1931, 269–70, SHNC.

114. McLester III and Hauptman, eds. *A Nation within A Nation*, 88–89.

115. Yearbook 1920–1931, 264, SHNC.

In Milwaukee, the Sisterhood of the Holy Nativity also worked in the African American community at the Cathedral's mission congregation, St. Michael and All Angels. There, the sisters offered instruction at least once per month.[116] The mission was related to the National Board of the Woman's Auxiliary. The sisterhood prepared candidates for the sacraments, supporting the young people's fellowship, the St Agnes Guild for girls, and the altar guild. Given their charge to advance the catholic faith, the sisters were pleased when the mission held their first solemn evensong: "There is a Master of ceremonies, acolytes, crucifer, vested choir, all black—also music and incense."[117] St. Michael's mission "continued to grow despite cramped quarters and lack of funds."[118] The ministry of the Sisterhood of the Holy Nativity at the mission extended the outreach of the Episcopal Church to the African American community in Milwaukee.

THE MISSION DISTRICT OF NEVADA

The Sisterhood of the Holy Nativity's experience with recent immigrants and Indigenous peoples in Wisconsin resulted in an invitation from the Missionary District of Nevada in the 1940s. The sisterhood was invited to the Missionary District of Nevada by Thomas Jenkins (1871–1955), missionary bishop from 1929–1942, and his successor, William F. Lewis, missionary bishop from 1942–1949. Jenkins noted, "Beginning in the middle 1850s, hundreds of emigrants, traveling principally from New York, Ohio, and Pennsylvania, on their way to the California gold districts settled in what became Nevada. Many were members of the Protestant Episcopal Church."[119] In 1930, Bishop Jenkins brought Deaconess Lillian Todd to the district. Ten years later, the Sisterhood of the Holy Nativity came to Moapa, Nevada, with Sister Hilary and Sister Esther Beulah being the first sisters to arrive.[120]

The first mission for the Sisterhood of the Holy Nativity in Nevada was St. Matthew's Church in Moapa. The Moapa Indian Reservation is home to the Moapa Band of Piutes, about fifty miles northeast of Las Vegas. Thomas Jenkins took an interest in the Moapa as soon as he was consecrated bishop and proceeded to repair the former mission. The mission had previously been served by an Episcopal laywoman worker, Eva Fenner, who also taught

---

116. Yearbook 1935–1936, 146, SHNC.
117. Yearbook 1935–1936, 147, SHNC.
118. Yearbook 1920–1931, 269, SHNC.
119. Bishops of the Episcopal Diocese of Nevada (nvdiocese.org).
120. Chase, *History of the Episcopal Church in Nevada*, 171–74.

at the government school there. After that, the mission was served by a succession of Episcopal deaconesses: Deaconess Lucy Carter came in 1926, Deaconess Florence I. Omerod in 1937, and Deaconess Clare E. Orwig in 1938. Eight years after her mission year in Moapa, Omerod joined the Sisterhood of the Holy Nativity and, in 1950, was professed as Sister Isabel.

Before entering religious life, Sister Hilary was a medical doctor and missionary, and Sister Esther Beulah was a retired World War I nurse and a former deaconess. They spent the first weeks rehabbing the parish and mission houses at Moapa for regular use. The sisters did home visits and distributed clothing and other goods from the Woman's Auxiliary. They offered home nursing classes, maintained the church, and offered church school for children, hoping the adults would grow interested.[121] Until the 1940s, Moapa was served by a priest from Las Vegas and the bishop, providing Holy Communion infrequently. When clergy were unavailable, services were conducted by the Sisterhood of the Holy Nativity, deaconesses, or laywomen missionaries.[122]

After the first year in Nevada, the sisters were moved to Christ Church, Las Vegas. They began working with the rector there, spending several days per week at Moapa and visiting five other missions: Boulder City, Nelson, Sloan, Lake Tahoe, and Searchlight. The sisters believed that their work in Nevada brought "results for the Kingdom of God, by teaching the Catholic Faith without apology, dilution, or compromise, of course varying the presentation of the Faith according to the needs, backgrounds, and capacities of our people."[123] Tremendous population growth in the Las Vegas area moved the bishop to expand the sisters' work to additional missions where they taught Christian education for all ages, organized guilds, started Episcopal organizations like the Girls Friendly Society (GFS), created camps and vacation Bible schools, and trained the altar guilds. "We aim, of course, to produce men and women whose social, political, economic, and moral action will be determined by the religion of the Incarnation," reported one of the sisters to the diocesan newspaper.[124] Through their missionary efforts, the sisters aimed to avoid high-pressure tactics, narrow parochialism, and excessive fundraising. "These are the direct fruits of Catholic Faith and

---

121. Annual Reports of the Convent and Mission Houses, 1940–1943, Las Vegas, 1940, 26, SHNC.

122. Chase, *History of the Episcopal Church in Nevada, 1860–1959*, 173.

123. Kerstetter, "The Las Vegas-Boulder City Field," SHNC.

124. Kerstetter, "The Las Vegas-Boulder City Field," SHNC; Annual Reports of the Convent and Mission Houses, 1940–1943, Las Vegas, 1940, 26; 1941, 52, 1942, 77–78. SHNC.

Practice."[125] The Sisterhood of the Holy Nativity continued its work in the Missionary District of Nevada for eight years until 1948.

Through the efforts of the Sisterhood of the Holy Nativity, the catholic faith became known throughout the Diocese of Fond du Lac, Wisconsin, and the wider Episcopal Church. Their ministries among Indigenous peoples and African Americans sought to support spiritual lives and address humanitarian needs. Though not without limitations as white missionaries, the Sisterhood of the Holy Nativity contributed to communities underserved by the Church and societal institutions and met humanitarian needs. As the official journal of the Diocese of Fond du Lac noted, "Everywhere they have been they have won the hearts and confidence of our people, and all have seen the immediate fruits of their labors in the large numbers prepared and presented for Baptism and Confirmation. Their teaching has been a great help to many in a better understanding of the Church, her doctrines and ceremonies, as well as the deepening of their spiritual life."[126]

---

125. Kerstetter, "The Las Vegas-Boulder City Field," SHNC.

126. *Journal of the Sixteenth Annual Council of the Protestant Episcopal Diocese of Fond du Lac*, 1890, 52–53.

4

Missionary Spirit

THE FIRST SEVENTY-FIVE YEARS after the founding of the Sisterhood of the Holy Nativity in 1882 were marked by the rapid growth and expansion of short-term and long-term missions. The sisterhood's commitment to the "Missionary Spirit of Christ himself" translated into various ministries within individual parishes and extending beyond, working directly among the poorest of society. Typically, the Anglo-Catholic parishes served by the Sisterhood of the Holy Nativity were "free" churches, with membership open to all people, regardless of background or social status. Rooted in the theology of the Incarnation, the sisterhood emphasized the catholicity of their faith through the liturgy and the sacraments. A vision of the Church as the Body of Christ compelled the sisterhood to understand social witness as a sacramental action.

For the Sisterhood of the Holy Nativity, missionary spirit was focused on parishes and dioceses in the United States. Although the sisters supported international mission activities such as the Red Cross, their direct work was concentrated in the informal network of Anglo-Catholic dioceses and parishes within the Episcopal Church. Just as *The Book of Common Prayer* was designed to address the entirety of the human lifecycle, from birth to death, within the liturgical life of the Church, in the same way, the parishes served by the Sisterhood of the Holy Nativity stressed intentional catechesis for all ages, including Christian education; instruction in the sacraments—Baptism, first Confession, first Holy Communion, Confirmation, anointing of the sick—education for the lapsed; altar guild training; guilds for women, youth, and children; retreat and quiet day facilitation, and Bible studies. Forming guilds for all ages within churches was a form of pastoral outreach that provided for members' spiritual, social, and material needs before public education and social welfare services were available. In addition to the guilds typical across Episcopal churches, local guilds were founded to address needs in specific locations.

The missionary spirit of the Sisterhood of the Holy Nativity served as an icon for the embodiment of the consecrated life and the compassionate care of the Church. "The living of a religious life within the parish is the most important part of our work," said Sister Veronica, who was Sister-in-Charge in Providence for almost a decade. "Most intelligent lay people can do what we do but that is not the point. The sacrifice of the religious life is what provides strength."[1] The sisters balanced their work within churches with extensive missionary outreach through parish visits, hospital visits, and ministries among African Americans, Indigenous peoples, community youth, and recent immigrants. These ministries placed the Sisterhood of the Holy Nativity in a relationship with social and cultural groups different from most of their own. For many of those served, it was their first encounter with a sisterhood in the Episcopal Church. In some cases, the sisters converted souls for Christ through their evangelism. But generally, in Episcopal churches, the emphasis was more on education than evangelism, particularly when visiting the sick and teaching children. "One nursed the sick, aided the poor, and visited captives in prison because Christ had mandated such practices for his disciples— not to add members to the Episcopal Church."[2] The Anglo-Catholic emphasis on the movement for Christian Unity moved the Sisterhood of the Holy Nativity to seek out local ecumenical relationships where their mission houses were located to deepen understanding and provide additional resources for those in need.

The Sisterhood of the Holy Nativity was most active during an era in Christian history when the Church's understanding of its mission evolved to include a commitment to the poor and the wider society. The Oxford Movement instilled in the hearts and minds of the founders and succeeding generations of the Sisterhood of the Holy Nativity the importance of service to those most in need. Due to economic uncertainty and rapid social change in the years after the American Civil War, the Church participated in the ecumenical Social Gospel movement (1870s-1920), the precursor to contemporary urban ministries. This movement stressed Jesus' healing and serving ministry as the model for the Church in the world. The origins of most modern social services are connected to religious charity and benevolence, including the modern profession of social work. "The working of the

---

1. Scotti, "Their Sacrifice Gives Strength," 14.
2. Donovan, *A Different Call*, 16.

church cannot but spill over into the needs and people around it," wrote one early social worker in the 1920s.[3] Theologically, the Social Gospel movement was fueled by the call to bring forth the Kingdom of God on earth through biblical charity and justice. The movement began among religious leaders in the urban northeast in the 1870s, gaining momentum and influencing the Church's role in society through World War I.[4]

The Episcopal Church was a leading voice in the Social Gospel movement and, in northeastern cities like New York City, was considered the most influential denomination after Roman Catholicism. Ministry among African Americans was also an urgent need after the Civil War, and the Sisterhood of the Holy Nativity served Black churches in major cities such as Baltimore, Philadelphia, Milwaukee, and Los Angeles.[5] Given the shortage of African American clergy and the financial insecurity of many Black churches, many became missions of white congregations. Anglo-Catholics like Bishop Grafton, rooted in the doctrine of the Incarnation, believed that parish membership should be open to all, resulting in congregations like St. Stephen's, Providence, that were, to some degree, racially integrated.[6]

Although upper-class white Episcopalians did not wholly abandon moralistic and paternalistic attitudes toward the poor, the Social Gospel exhorted members to consider the sociological causes of poverty and develop ministries for the wider community. Many large, urban Episcopal churches, like those served by the Sisterhood of the Holy Nativity, developed "sister" mission congregations for their poorer neighbors. While it was common for these large city churches and their mission congregations to meet on special occasions, they generally operated separately. The social vision did not extend to a diverse society worshipping together in a single church.[7]

The first waves of urban Irish, German, and Jewish immigrants in northeastern cities lived in overcrowded housing, subject to unsanitary conditions and outbreaks of disease. In an era without social services or public education, the Social Gospel movement inspired Episcopal churches to initiate children's charities, schools, orphanages, fresh air programs, services for the disabled, medical care, kindergartens, support for working mothers, clubs for working young people, and lodging houses—many of which were staffed by women religious like the Sisterhood of the Holy

---

3. Hall, "Social work in the churches, 1922, quoted in Placido, "A History of Charity and the Church," www.nacsw.org. Accessed January 10, 2022.

4. Kujawa-Holbrook, *By Grace Came the Incarnation*, 73.

5. Kujawa-Holbrook, *By Grace Came the Incarnation*, 73.

6. Pettingell, "Bethlehem in Providence," 147.

7. Kujawa-Holbrook, *By Grace Came the Incarnation*, 74.

Nativity, deaconesses, and lay church women. The poor were left behind in an era of unbounded prosperity and commercial growth for the upper classes. Those who organized these "modern" programs hoped they would provide resources and skill training to give the poor and recent immigrants access to a middle-class life.

By the 1880s, a second wave of immigrants from Eastern Europe and Italy exacerbated the crowding and poverty in major cities. Landlords felt little accountability for housing conditions without regulation and in an era of real estate speculation. Popular sentiments against immigrants blamed poverty on their moral fiber and personal habits. One of the impacts of the Social Gospel movement ecumenically was an expanded theology of sin to include not only personal vice but also the collective manifestation of evil, emphasizing the need for church and society to take responsibility for corporate sin. Thus, the Kingdom of God necessitated both individual and social salvation.[8] The changing demographics within American cities affected Episcopal Church worship through the 1892 revision of the *Book of Common Prayer*. The 1892 prayer book was translated into more languages than any other edition for immigrant congregations; portions were available in German, Italian, Swedish, Hungarian, Chinese, and other languages.[9]

The Sisterhood of the Holy Nativity's missionary spirit reflected the growth in Episcopal organizations that focused on the needs of women and girls after the Civil War. Between 1850 and 1920, various women's organizations, including sisterhoods, created structures and networks to advocate and authenticate women's vocations in the Episcopal Church. The Sisterhood of the Holy Nativity integrated these organizations into parishes and dioceses. In local churches, the sisters supported parish chapters of the Woman's Auxiliary to the Episcopal Church's Board of Missions, founded in 1872 by the Emery sisters of Massachusetts, to support women's missionary work. Through the agency of the Woman's Auxiliary, the elaborate domestic and foreign missionary expansion of the Episcopal Church was developed and supported. The work of women like those in the Sisterhood of the Holy Nativity moved the whole church to greater compassion for the poor and laboring classes. "It was precisely because these women were at the opposite end of the socioeconomic scale from the people with whom they worked that they were able to initiate such ministries. Rigid social conventions kept upper-class Episcopal women from gainful employment but encouraged benevolent and charitable work . . . That the Episcopal Church could tap such a large force of capable volunteer labor was key to its primacy in the

---

8. Kujawa-Holbrook, *By Grace Came the Incarnation*, 74.
9. Kujawa-Holbrook, *By Grace Came the Incarnation*, 69.

social-gospel movement."[10] By the 1920s, the charity and outreach of the Church were transformed, and the pattern of social service as a gospel imperative was set for the Church in future generations.[11]

The Sisterhood of the Holy Nativity also supported local chapters of the Girls' Friendly Society (GFS)—an international Anglican organization started in 1875 to mentor working-class girls and young women. Founded in the United States in 1878, parish chapters of the organization provided recreation and instruction in the arts, such as music, drama, and painting. As seen in the history of the Sisterhood of the Holy Nativity, GFS encouraged the creation of "houses of rest" where working women and girls could have quiet retreat time in a religious house. In the case of the Sisterhood of the Holy Nativity, these "houses of rest paved the way for the founding of formal retreat houses for women."[12]

While clergy were the theological and ideological promulgators of the Social Gospel movement, women provided most of the workforce for the Church's social agenda. By the 1850s, Episcopal women were involved in education, healthcare, and work with the poor and disabled. Women's participation in these ministries predates clergy participation in the Social Gospel movement by at least twenty years. As prominent historian Mary Sudman Donovan writes, "The women accomplished the social gospel with their actions, not their words . . . Clergy learned from women already at work, examples of which are many."[13] Women were restricted from many of the institutional roles of the Episcopal Church—clergy, vestries, diocesan deputies, and deputies to the General Convention. Yet many, such as the educated, skilled, and devout women who entered the Sisterhood of the Holy Nativity, found deeply satisfying vocations in parish work and mission. Though generally appreciated by the clergy and laity who worked with them most closely, women church workers—sisterhoods, deaconesses, laywomen, volunteers—were institutionally considered an expendable workforce. For those in paid positions, salaries were meager without benefits or pensions until well into the later twentieth century.[14] Similar trends are found in the Sisterhood of the Holy Nativity records. Though they were resident in some parishes and dioceses for decades, there is a paucity of records related to their contributions beyond the archives of the sisterhood. Financial records reveal the extent to which the sisterhood was often challenged to obtain

10. Donovan, *A Different Call*, 15–16.
11. Donovan, *A Different Call*, 17.
12. See chapter 5 on "Soul Work" in this book.
13. Donovan, *A Different Call*, 11.
14. Donovan, *A Different Call*, 75–76.

even minimal financial support from some parishes or dioceses they served. Without the Associates, who raised funding to support the Sisterhood of the Holy Nativity, much of their mission involvement would have been dramatically curtailed.

MISSION IN NEW YORK CITY

The Sisterhood of the Holy Nativity's first mission house in New York was situated in Kingston, about ninety miles from New York City on the Hudson River. In 1891, Paul Watson, the rector of St. John's Episcopal Church in Kingston, founded the Church of the Holy Cross— a catholic parish with a special mission to the poor of the city. Sister Harriet and Sister Constance opened the house in 1896; Sister Annette joined them in 1897. In addition to parish visits, the sisters were responsible for the sacristy, taught in the Sunday school, and completed many hospital visits. The sisters were in contact with another Episcopal sisterhood, the Community of St John the Baptist, that worked at the state girls' reformatory in Mamaroneck, New York. By 1899, the Sisterhood of the Holy Nativity regularly visited the almshouse and prepared people for the sacraments. "In January, a class of thirty was confirmed, most of them prepared by the sisters, and there were about the same numbers of Baptisms in the course of the year."[15] Although the records of the sisterhood are often silent regarding personal feelings, one entry for the Parish of the Holy Cross in Kingston is unusually revealing: "The Sisters wish to place on record their thankfulness to God for the favorable conditions under which they labour, for the good and faithful Priest, and for the affection and confidence among the people among whom they are privileged to work."[16]

Also in 1899, the Sisterhood of the Holy Nativity began its long association with the Church of St. Mary the Virgin in New York City. The sisterhood resided in the parish for sixty-five years, from 1899–1907, and after a two-year gap, from 1909–1966. Sister Katherine Edith, Sister Harriet, and Sister Annette arrived in New York City to find a warm welcome and a dilapidated mission house: "The walls throughout the house were very bad, dirty and with large cracks; and in December the Trustees had the whole house kalsomined."[17] (Kalsomine was a whitewash used to cover walls and fences to prevent mites.) Given the architecture of the mission house, the

---

15. Yearbook, 1897, Kingston, 11; 1899, Kingston, 69, SHNC.

16. Yearbook 1899, Kingston, 69, SHNC.

17. Yearbook 1899, Report from the Mission House of St. Mary the Virgin, New York, 70, SHNC.

sisters soon realized that they would either need a third sister or a woman from the parish to help with reception. "The house being five stories high, without [an] elevator, it is almost a necessity that someone should be in the office on the ground floor, to answer the door and to report through the speaking tube to the Sister-in-Charge, whose office is two flights up."[18] After the mission house was sorted, the sisters started making parish visits and training women to assist with the guilds.

The Church of St. Mary the Virgin was founded by Thomas McKee Brown (1841–1898), one of the leading Ritualists in the Episcopal Church at the end of the nineteenth century. A graduate of Trinity College in Hartford and the General Theological Seminary in New York City, Brown's theology blended the high churchmanship of John Henry Hobart, bishop of the Diocese of New York from 1816–1830, and the vision of the Church and sacraments as articulated by the Oxford Movement. The climate of the Diocese of New York at the time embraced the teaching of the Tractarians and thus provided a foundation for the emergence of ritualism. In the 1850s and 1860s, Ritualists introduced ceremonial, vestments, vessels, and church appointments more commonly associated with Roman Catholicism into the Episcopal Church. Social, cultural, and economic developments after the close of the Civil War paved the way for changes in the Episcopal Church away from more understated high churchmanship "by a vibrant and emphatic theology which sought to link the Catholic theology of Anglicanism with a sensuous, colorful, and dramatic liturgy that gave a voice and a tangible expression to be a perceived religious truth."[19]

Between the years 1865 and 1871, the height of the Ritualism controversy in the Episcopal Church, four ritualistic churches were founded in New York City: St Alban's Church, the Oratory of the Blessed Sacrament, the Church of St. Mary the Virgin, and the Church of St. Ignatius. Brown's vision for St. Mary the Virgin was a free Episcopal Church based on catholic liturgy, spirituality, and the sacraments, and committed to pastoral outreach, social witness, and community service. After conversations with Horatio Potter, bishop of the Diocese of New York, concerning possible locations, and John Jack Astor, Jr. regarding funding, the Church of St. Mary the Virgin opened in December 1870. Charles Grafton preached there in 1873 before he was elected bishop of the Diocese of Fond du Lac. The association of Episcopal religious orders with the Church of St. Mary the Virgin began early in its history. A mission house was donated to the church in

---

18. Yearbook 1899, Report from the Mission House of St. Mary the Virgin, New York, 71, SHNC.

19. Platt, "The Rise of Advanced Ritualism in New York City," 331–38, 340.

1888, and Brown founded the Sisters of the Order of the Visitation of the Blessed Virgin Mary to work in the parish among the city's poor. The Sisters of the Order of the Visitation were eventually received into the Community of Sister Mary and moved to other houses after Brown died in 1898.[20]

In 1909, Joseph G. H. Barry (1858–1931), a graduate of Nashotah House and a canon of St. Paul's Cathedral in Fond du Lac, was called to be rector of the Church of St. Mary the Virgin in New York City. A committed Anglo-Catholic, Barry gained a reputation as an elegant preacher. The move was well-timed; Barry was not content in Fond du Lac, as he considered Wisconsin a less-than-ideal location, and he had significant differences of opinion with Bishop Grafton on matters of ritual and architecture. He was keen to have the assistance of the Sisterhood of the Holy Nativity in New York and was hired there with the understanding that they would be invited to the parish. "Here in the heart of the city, the Divine Office is recited regularly, in union with all the other Sisters in various parts of the country," writes one sister.[21]

The location of the Church of St Mary the Virgin, near Times Square in what is referred to as New York's Hell's Kitchen, was named for the high rate of violence that occurred there. This location offered many opportunities for social work. Before she came to the Sisterhood of the Holy Nativity, Sister Harriet, an art student in New York City, became Sister-in-Charge and opened the mission house. Sister Mary Elizabeth, a native of Philadelphia, assisted Sister Harriet. The sisters soon created a "clothing bureau" for local families as they did in Kingston. Given the working conditions in factories in New York City, the sisters supported workers' petitions for the sixty-hour work week.[22]

In addition to advancing the catholic faith through teaching, guilds, and altar work, the sisterhood managed the parish's summer home in Keyport, New Jersey. The home served over one hundred individuals and families annually, providing parishioners who could not otherwise enjoy the seashore with worship and fellowship. One of the challenges for the sisterhood in running the summer home was the schedule. Typically, the sisters' mission houses were open for eight or nine months, allowing the sisterhood to gather annually as a community for retreat and recreation. Mission houses were usually closed from the end of June until the beginning of October, with some regional variations. But in New York, the break was limited to

20. Pratt, "The Rise of Advanced Ritualism in New York City," 340–367; Monastics at Saint Mary's — The Church of Saint Mary the Virgin (stmvirgin.org).

21. 'The Sisterhood of the Holy Nativity," brochure on mission houses, n.d. [ca. 1950s] SHNC.

22. Reeves, "Hidden in Christ," n.d., 8–9, SHNC.

three weeks. The sisters were supported by Associates who ran the kitchen and assisted in the sacristy. The sisters thanked the parish each year for their generosity in supporting the summer home. However, fatigue is noticeable in the reports: "The season just completed passed quietly, therefore successfully . . . There was no serious sickness. Fortunately for those who needed something to complain about to complete their happiness, there was an abundance of mosquitos, so nothing at all was missing."[23]

The summer home of the Church of St. Mary the Virgin in Keyport was located near the largest munitions factory in the world, an unsettling location during wartime. "It was an anxious season at Keyport," wrote one sister in 1916. "But the household was mercifully protected from infantile paralysis, typhoid fever, man-eating sharks, munitions explosions, etc."[24] The protection did not last long. Shortly before the war's end in October 1918, the Morgan Ammunition Depot Explosion killed scores of people and caused damage throughout Middlesex County, New Jersey. The explosion was so powerful that the impact was felt twenty miles away, and unexploded shells are still found there. "It was providential that the great explosion of munitions at Morgan occurred after the home was closed," wrote one sister, "for dangerous amounts of plaster were shaken down from the ceilings."[25] The explosion was attributed to worker error, though German sabotage was suspected. Thousands of homes were destroyed, leaving the evacuees homeless and vulnerable to the Spanish flu.

During World War I and the 1918 Spanish flu epidemic, the sisters in New York were engaged in extensive relief work. All the guilds were involved in war work, including knitting, and making bandages for the Red Cross. One sister continued the sewing school for girls started by the Order of the Visitation when the church was founded. The sisters founded new guilds for women and girls of diverse needs: St. Anne's Guild "for business women," a group for faculty and students at Teachers College, Columbia University, and Barnard College, a group for "fallen girls" from the state reformatory, and a group for girls from the Spence School interested in the spiritual life.[26] Given their location in Hell's Kitchen, it was not uncommon for the Sisterhood of the Holy Nativity to have over four thousand visitors yearly, more than any other mission house. For example, from 1921 to 1922, the New York house received 4,649 visitors, and the sisters made 2,238 visits. In addition, the sisters gave eighty-five classes and 598 private

23. "What is Saint Mary's Summer Home?"
24. Yearbook, 1915–1918, 1919–1920, New York, 66, SHNC
25. Yearbook, 1915–1918, 1919–1920, New York, 138–39. SHNC.
26. Yearbook, 1915–1918, 1919–1920, New York, 66, 177–78, SHNC

instructions, prepared twenty-nine for Baptism and seventy-four for first Confession, and conducted 295 guild meetings.[27]

In addition to social work, the mission house in New York City was an important spiritual center. The mission house provided regular hospitality for parish and diocesan retreats and holiday dinners for the poor. New Associates, both women and clergy, joined the New York chapter of the sisterhood to share in its work. Episcopal organizations, such as the Woman's Auxiliary, scheduled retreats at the mission house. The Society of the Companions of the Holy Cross (SCHC), a devotional society for Episcopal women committed to intercessory prayer, spiritual growth, and a Rule of life, met monthly at the mission house, as did the Girls Friendly Society.[28] James Otis Sargent Huntington, OHC, one of the founders of the Order of the Holy Cross for men, was chaplain to the Society of the Companions of the Holy Cross and would regularly hear confessions and lead retreats at the New York mission house. The sisters also taught at the Chapel of the Intercession, a chapel of Trinity Church on West 155th Street, and other parishes on invitation.[29]

While rector of the Church of St. Mary the Virgin, Joseph Barry became the Chaplain- General of the Sisterhood of the Holy Nativity. In addition to the traditional work of retreats and confessions, Barry initiated weekly classes on spiritual theology for the sisters. He actively supported the sisters in their efforts to offer retreats and was instrumental in securing resources for the sisterhood's retreat house in Bay Shore. Barry made no secret of his opinion that Fond du Lac was a backwater town, and he and Mother Katharine Edith developed plans to move the motherhouse to Bay Shore on Long Island. Mother Katharine Edith believed that more vocations would be found in East Coast parishes rather than in Fond du Lac. Statistics on the states where sisters were born support this assumption. More sisters were born in New York than in any other state, followed by Massachusetts and Pennsylvania. Out of eighty-seven sisters, fifty were born in New England of the Mid-Atlantic states.[30] Further, after Bishop Grafton died in 1912, he was succeeded by Reginald Weller (1857—1935). Mother Katharine Edith

---

27. Yearbook 1920-1931, New York, 38-39, SHNC

28. Yearbook, 1915-1918, 1919-1920, New York, 96-98, SHNC

29. Yearbook, 1915-1918, 1919-1920, New York, 177-78; House diary, November 14, 1928-February 29, 1932, SHNC

30. See Appendix, Life Professed Sisters. Of the 87 sisters who remained in SHN for life, 13 were born in New York, 11 in Massachusetts, and 9 in Pennsylvania. The regional distribution is as follows: New England (18), Mid-Atlantic (32), Midwest (22), the South (5), and the West (3). In addition, six sisters were born in Canada and in Europe; one birthplace is unknown.

never developed an effective working relationship with Weller, even though he demonstrated his pastoral concern for the sisterhood and appreciated all their efforts on behalf of the diocese. It is unclear if there was a conflict or if, as a person with his own family, Weller was not as available as Grafton. For Mother Katherine Edith, other bishops were just not on the same level as Grafton.[31] Barry and Mother Katharine Edith believed that a move to New York would bring the sisterhood closer to the Chaplain-General and other sympathetic clergy and associates.

In early 1919, Mother Katherine Edith brought the possibility of a move to the sisters' Council, and shortly afterward, the Roman Catholic Agnesian sisters took a real estate tour of the Fond du Lac Convent. But soon, the dynamics changed, and the possibility of a move was tabled. Barry resigned as Chaplain-General in October, complaining that he did not have enough authority over the sisters. A month later, Mother Katherine Edith died seventeen days after a diagnosis of liver cancer. It is unclear if the sisterhood would have moved out of Fond du Lac in 1919 had she lived. By 1922, the Sisterhood of the Holy Nativity was the largest sisterhood in the Episcopal Church, though concerns about access to vocations remained an ongoing issue.[32]

Despite stepping down as Chaplain-General, Barry maintained his enthusiasm for the Sisterhood of the Holy Nativity. He encouraged their participation in Annual Catholic Congresses where laity and clergy gathered to hear from the world's most notable Anglo-Catholics. The end of World War I through the 1920s was considered the "Golden Age" of Anglo-Catholicism, and an advantage of the New York City location was access to events and visitors from around the Anglican Communion. Barry and other leaders of the Catholic Movement were conscious that the first phase of the Oxford Movement was a century old, and thus, a theological vision needed to be articulated for a new century. "Rather let us remember that we have represented one stage in a Movement and not the end of a dispensation. We should passionately desire that there should be no end till the goal is reached—the reunion of the catholic Church of Jesus Christ," preached Barry at the Third Annual Catholic Congress in 1927.[33] Barry was concerned that the Catholic Movement was intellectualizing too much about dogma and neglecting to translate it into "visibly incarnate" sacramental practices and devotions. He did not want the Catholic Movement known for giving

31. House Diary, Convent, 1919; Yearbook, 1915–1918, 1919–1920, Convent, 172, SHNC; Reeves, "Hidden in Christ," 14.

32. House Diary, Convent, 1919; Yearbook, 1915–1918, 1919–1920, Convent, 172, SHNC; Reeves, "Hidden in Christ," 14.

33. Barry, "The Congress Sermon," Accessed February 1, 2022.

ceremonial primacy over holy living: Holiness of life was the Christian's first and most important vocation. "Catholicity is not and cannot be an individual thing," said Barry. "It is social and the true catholic is an energetic force for righteousness in the community to which he belongs."[34] Barry resigned as rector of the Church of St. Mary the Virgin in 1928 after a nineteen-year tenure. Notably, he was praised for his ability to eschew high society.[35]

During the late 1920s, the sisters expanded their work among faculty and students at Columbia University. The mission house offered the university community an annual retreat, and the sisters provided instruction on the sacraments and facilitated reading groups. A parish lending library was instituted to provide devotional reading. A new guild for nurses was started; each month, the nurses would meet for a partial retreat day. The sisters provided retreat opportunities through the mission house for growing numbers of professional women. "The formation of a devotional guild for nurses has been a big work this past year and promises to be far-reaching. It is not parochial, but it started at St. Mary's. An experiment of a semi-retreat last year has met with great success. So many business and professional women cannot take a full day off."[36]

Notably, the social ministries of the Sisterhood of the Holy Nativity greatly expanded during the years of the Great Depression. At the outbreak of World War II, the parish instituted prayers for the country's defense, for those in action, grounded in the belief that the Christian response to war should "be the fruit of prayer and should not be prompted by the selfish desire for physical safety or for a false peace."[37] Opportunities for prayer for the war effort included the Exposition of the Blessed Sacrament, intercessions followed by Benediction each Wednesday at noon, and special Votive Masses on Friday at noon. The St. Mary's Ward of the Confraternity of the Blessed Sacrament was considered a missionary organization of the Church.[38] During the war years, the sisters assumed responsibility for the sacristy work as all the acolytes were drafted.[39] In 1944, the "Guild of Help" worked with the Diocese of New York Youth Consultation Service on a "forward looking plan" to establish an interracial office on 110th Street with

---

34. Barry, "The Congress Sermon," Accessed February 1, 2022.

35. "Dr. Barry leaves St. Mary's Church," *New York Times,* December 15, 1928, 29.

36. Yearbook 1920-1931, New York, 178-79, 208-09, 266-67, SHNC

37. *Ave* 11.3 (January 1942) 2.

38. *Ave* 11.3 (January 1942) 3-4.

39. An Annual Reports of Convent and Mission Houses, 1940-1943, New York, 64, SHNC.

Annual Reports of Convent and Mission Houses, 1940-1943, New York, 64, SHNC.

African American leadership.[40] As concern for young people grew in the postwar era, the sisterhood added guilds to attract young adults in their twenties and thirties to the Church.

From the late 1920s through the 1960s, the Sisterhood of the Holy Nativity was considered integral to the parish's mission and, thus, was listed on the masthead of the monthly bulletin, *Ave,* along with clergy leadership and the trustees. However, by the 1960s, there were not enough sisters to maintain all the mission houses, and difficult choices were made. The diocesan bishop, the rector of St. Mary's, the New York Associates of the sisterhood, and many parishioners made strenuous efforts to keep them in residence, to no avail. The Sisterhood of the Holy Nativity withdrew from the Church of St. Mary the Virgin in July 1966. At the same time, they withdrew from the Baltimore mission house, and both churches were challenged to replace them and the services they provided. "I have been encouraged by the evident will of the parish to go forward and maintain so many of the things done by the Sisters. Their presence among us contributed much more than these things, however," wrote Donald L. Garfield, rector of St. Mary the Virgin, upon the sisters' departure.[41]

MISSION HOUSE IN MAINE

In 1907, the Sisterhood of the Holy Nativity was invited by Robert Codman, the bishop of the Episcopal Diocese of Maine, to establish a mission house there. Codman was the son of one of the sisterhood's first Associates, Catherine E. Hurd Codman. Bishop Codman was raised at the Church of the Advent in Boston; his father, Robert, was senior warden when Charles Grafton was the rector. After the death of his mother (1892) and brother (1893), Codman attended the General Theological Seminar in New York. He was ordained priest in 1894 by Bishop Grafton and served in two parishes in Massachusetts, including the Anglo-Catholic All Saints Parish in Ashmont, before being elected bishop in 1900.[42] One of his first actions as bishop was to build a chapel in memory of his mother in the Town of St. George, Maine. The Sisterhood of the Holy Nativity made the altar and dossal hangings in her memory.[43]

During his tenure as bishop, Codman built a dozen missions in the Diocese of Maine. An Anglo-Catholic, he invited the Society of St. John

40. *Ave* 13.8 (November 1944) 120.
41. *Ave* 25.7 (October 1966) 98.
42. On Bishop Robert Codman, Our History (episcopalmaine.org).
43. "Built By Bishop Codman," *Boston Daily Globe* (December 1, 1901), 23.

The Evangelist to staff churches north of Bangor. Mother Katherine Edith, who took her annual rest time in Maine, seized the opportunity to establish a mission house there despite the low churchmanship of the diocese. "The churchmanship is v. Protestant," wrote Mother Edith about the diocese. However, the Sisterhood of the Holy Nativity was received kindly, even by those less than comfortable with the liturgical direction Bishop Codman was taking the diocese.[44]

In the Diocese of Maine, the sisters guided the sacristy work at the Cathedral Church of St. Luke in Portland. They also focused on parochial mission work, home visiting, instruction for the sacraments, and Christian education classes. In a typical year, they made 842 visits and received 1593 guests. The sisters offered fifty-nine group classes and 276 private instructions, primarily women and girls, focusing on preparation for Baptism, first Confession, and Confirmation. Retreat leaders offered retreats at the mission house. Sometimes, the sisters went on retreat with the Society of St. Margaret at their house in Duxbury, Massachusetts. In addition to the Cathedral in Portland, the Sisterhood of the Holy Nativity served All Saints mission on Orr's Island. The sisters were happy to report that their accommodations were upgraded from a barn to a neighboring house.[45]

In Portland, at St. Luke's Cathedral, the sisters' contributed to the children's music program and led the Daily Office when the dean was out of town. Bishop Codman enlarged the Cathedral in Portland by adding the Emmanuel Chapel as a memorial to his brother, Archibald Codman, who was also an Episcopal priest. (The architect was another brother, Stephen Russell Hurd Codman.) It was there where the Sisterhood of the Holy Nativity attended the monthly vespers with the Confraternity of the Blessed Sacrament. The sisters' work in Maine did not revolve around guild activities as it did in other mission houses but focused on the rich liturgical life of the Cathedral and preparing women and girls for the sacraments.[46]

Tragically, Bishop Codman died in 1915 while on his honeymoon. The Sisterhood of the Holy Nativity continued at the mission house in Maine after the bishop's death, funded by his sister Catherine Amory Codman. In 1923, that funding stopped, though the sisters continued home visits and instruction until they were dispersed to other mission houses.[47]

44. Diary, Portland, 1907, SHNC, Our History (episcopalmaine.org).

45. Yearbook, 1915-1918, 1919-1920, Portland, 27, 104, 156-57; SHNC.

46. Yearbook 1920-1931, Portland, 36-37 SHNC. On Emmanuel Chapel (Codman Memorial), History & Architecture - St Luke's Cathedral of Portland (stlukesportland.org).

47. Yearbook 1920-1931, Portland, 58, 80-81, SHNC.

MISSION IN BALTIMORE

In 1917, the Sisterhood of the Holy Nativity was invited to Mount Calvary Episcopal Church on Eutaw Street in Baltimore.[48] Mount Calvary was known in Baltimore for its outreach to the African American community. Joseph Richey, an Anglo-Irish immigrant, attended Trinity College in Hartford and the General Seminary in New York. Upon ordination in 1870, Richey became an assisting priest at the Church of the Advent, Boston, when Charles Grafton was rector. He became rector of Mount Calvary in 1872 and brought new vitality and purpose to the congregation. The mission congregation that became St. Mary the Virgin was founded by "two earnest" African American laymen, James Thompson and C.M. Mason. Elizabeth Oliver purchased a church building for them. "We have given you an altar no whit inferior to that in the parish church: your services shall be the counterpart to those in Mount Calvary, and everything that is necessary for the edification of the people there, its likeness shall be given to you," promised Richey to the African American Congregation.[49] "You will no longer be treated as outcasts to whom it should be considered a sufficient favor if the smallest trifle is given, but as children of One Father, bought by the Blood of One Redeemer, and sanctified by One Holy Ghost."[50]

Richey invited the All Saints Sisters of the Poor from London to Baltimore, and together, they established All Saints School. Along with his assistant, Calbraith Bourn Perry, who became the priest at St. Mary's, Richey worked among the African American community in Baltimore until his death. Richey and the All Saints Sisters of the Poor established an African American sisterhood, the Sisterhood of St. Mary and All Saints. The three African American and four white English sisters established a school for girls and an orphanage for boys at St. Mary's mission. It also became a training center for African American clergy.[51]

---

48. Mount Calvary Church became Roman Catholic in 2012. The two African American chapels, St Mary the Virgin and St. Katherine's, are parishes of the Episcopal Diocese of Maryland.

49. "History of St. Mary's," 1953, from the leaflet for the Consecration of the Chapel of Saint Mary the Virgin, SHNC.

50. "History of St. Mary's." 1953; Mary Klein, "From the Archives: The Church of St. Mary the Virgin, Baltimore, n.p.

51. On Joseph Richey, Rev Joseph Richey (1843–1877)—Find a Grave Memorial; on Calbraith Bourne Perry, Rev Joseph Richey (1843–1877)—Find a Grave Memorial; on Mount Calvary Church, Mount-Calvary-Church-Baltimore—Photographicus Baltimorensis (19thcenturybaltimore.com); "The Sisterhood of the Holy Nativity," *Holy Cross Magazine*, 237. Also, Perry, *Twelve Years Among the Colored People*. Klein, "From the Archives."

In 1891, St. Katherine's Chapel was established as an African American mission of the Chapel of St. Mary the Virgin, and by extension, Mount Calvary Church. Established on the feast of St. Katherine of Alexandria, the congregation moved several times as its membership increased. A sewing school for girls, an industrial school for women, and eventually St. Katherine's Home for Colored Girls were established at the chapel.[52]

The Sisterhood of the Holy Nativity was invited to Mount Calvary by the ninth rector, William Adams McClenthen, who remained at the church from 1908 until he died in 1948. McClenthen was concerned that the intensity of the Anglo-Catholic ethos of Mount Calvary had lessened. Fewer people attended daily Mass, vespers on Sundays, and parish activities. He believed the presence of a sisterhood was integral to reestablishing the priorities of spiritual life. Joseph G.H. Barry of the Church of St. Mary the Virgin in New York knew the great need that Mount Calvary was facing. He connected them with the Sisterhood of the Holy Nativity, even though only three sisters were available when four were needed. The sisters were to work at Mount Calvary and the two chapels, the Chapel of Saint Mary the Virgin and Saint Katherine's Chapel. The sisterhood started with the usual commitment to teach Sunday school, coordinate guilds, and undertake home visits. They moved into Mount Calvary mission house to enhance the whole parish's spiritual life and create a place of welcome for women. "A Catholic parish needs sisters not merely because they are unusually useful workers, but because it needs the power and inspiration which only the religious life can contribute," wrote McClenthen. "We should think of our Sisters as being here first of all to live this dedicated life in our midst, and then secondly, as being here to express the fruits of this life in good works among our people."[53] All Parishioners were encouraged to cultivate a missionary spirit and to reach the unchurched in the community.[54]

McClenthen emphasized the importance of demonstrating "intense loyalty to the Sisters." He hoped the parish would someday have "spiritual children" in the Sisterhood of the Holy Nativity. He reminded everyone in the parish, including the priests, that all Christians are called, like the sisterhood, to give "first place to God and prayer."[55] In addition to the Sisterhood of the Holy Nativity, Mount Calvary also had a relationship with the brothers of the Order of the Holy Cross, who conducted preaching missions

---

52. Klein, "From the Archives: The Church of St. Katharine of Alexandra, Baltimore," n.p.

53. *Mount Calvary Magazine* 9.1 (November 1917) 4

54. *Mount Calvary Magazine* 9.1 (November 1917) 5.

55. *Mount Calvary Magazine* 13.2 (December 1921) 8.

in the parish. The parish further supported the brothers as they provided pastoral care to wounded American soldiers in France during World War I, and in opening their new mission in Liberia.[56]

The first generation of the Sisterhood of the Holy Nativity in Baltimore were Sister Fredrica, Sister-in-Charge; Sister Caroline, who was at St. Mary's; and Sister Agatha, who worked at both Mount Calvary and St. Mary's. Mother Katherine Edith chose sisters for the mission house who were between the ages of thirty-nine and forty-five and who had experience in other mission houses. Though newly life professed, Sister Fredrica was the daughter of an Associate of the sisterhood and granddaughter of a founding Associate. Sister Agatha was also newly life professed and contributed her library experience. Sister Caroline was the youngest and the longest professed. Her background in the hardware business helped with the constant repairs needed in the mission house.[57]

The sisters strove to serve the parish church and the African American chapels equally and, thus, believed in a consistent presence among the people to build relationships and trust. The living conditions of the African American community were atrocious, with sweltering summer temperatures, a lack of sanitation, and poor housing conditions. Scarcely was a parish newsletter published that did not praise the work of the sisterhood, encourage participation, and request the practical support needed to make the mission more effective. At Mount Calvary, the sisters' prepared women for the sacraments and gave retreats. They started new evening groups for working girls with dinner and devotions and a sewing group. The sisters who focused on the Chapel of Saint Mary the Virgin's work taught in the church school and the Dorcas Society, a guild for church women. These opportunities included evening classes and short retreats for women with work and family obligations that limited their participation. The "quiet afternoons" were scheduled from 3:30–6:00 p.m. and offered three meditations and supper. The sisterhood recruited Associates from Baltimore, Washington D.C., and other cities in Maryland. Monthly retreats for Associates were held at the sisters' chapel in the mission house. During Lent, the Associates gathered daily for intercessory prayers; during wartime, they offered novenas for peace. Eventually, the sisters were enlisted to coordinate Advent and Lenten retreats for the entire parish.[58]

56. *Mount Calvary Magazine* 9.1 (November 1917) 8; *Mount Calvary Magazine*, 9.2 (December 1917) 7.

57. *Mount Calvary Magazine* 9.2 (December 1917) 7.

58. *Mount Calvary Magazine* (March 1922) 5; *Mount Calvary Magazine* (April 1922) 5; *Mount Calvary Magazine* (November 1924) 3–4, *Mount Calvary Magazine* (November 1931) 7; *Mount Calvary Magazine* (April 1945) 3; *Mount Calvary Magazine* (December 1947) n.p.; Yearbook, 1931–1932, Baltimore, 25, SHNC.

The sisters organized the sacristy at St. Katherine's Chapel for African Americans and started guilds for women and girls. The work intensified at St. Katherine's with frequent clergy changes; they had three different vicars in one year.[59] During World War II, the guilds and sacristy work of the two African American chapels were seriously hampered, as few lay people were left in the Church. Women instead went to work in the defense industry, including domestic workers. "We have been much affected by war conditions; the acute transportation problem has curtailed church attendance and visiting," says the sisters' annual report for 1942–1943. "To all the Sisters' work was added the housekeeping, cooking, and part of the laundry, as the maids have become defense workers."[60]

Although the sisters' annual reports tended not to mention the accomplishments of individual sisters, it appears that Sister Esther Beulah's work in Baltimore was exceptional: "The splendid work of Sister Esther has blazed a trail for more interests than it has been possible for us to carry out."[61] Sr. Esther Beulah, a former deaconess and a nurse, secured public funding to open a nursery school at St. Mary's. Along with several other nurses and the head of obstetrics at the Johns Hopkins Hospital, she provided certification training to thirteen members of the "Guild of the Guardian Angels," formed by young women of the Chapel of Saint Mary the Virgin. Sister Esther Beulah taught nursing at Provident Hospital in addition to coordinating church guilds and "handling problem cases."[62] She was instrumental in organizing student nurses to help in the community.[63]

The work of the Sisterhood of the Holy Nativity at Mount Calvary in Baltimore advanced the catholic faith and provided healthcare for almost fifty years. At times, the sisters felt over-extended: "At St. Mary's, everything has been on a large scale, as usual, the Guilds bigger than ever and consuming and innumerable number of hours."[64] The sisters also reported the kindness and generosity of the people at Mount Calvary. The parish women held periodic "pound parties" where parishioners donated food staples

---

59. Annual Reports of the Convent and Mission Houses, 1940–1943, Baltimore 1940–1941, 15, 1942–1943, 70, SHNC.

60. Annual Reports of the Convent and Mission Houses, 1940–1943, Baltimore 1942–1943, 70, SHNC

61. Annual Reports of the Convent and Mission Houses, 1940–1943; Baltimore 1940–1941, 15; 1941–1942, 41. SHNC.

62. Annual Reports of the Convent and Mission Houses, 1940–1943; Baltimore 1940–1941, 15; 1941–1942, 41;
1942–1943, 69, SHNC.

63. Yearbook, 1931–1932, Baltimore, 25, SHNC.

64. Yearbook, 1931–1932, Baltimore, 25, SHNC.

to the sisters' pantry and gave cash donations.[65] "Much personal work is done," reads one annual report. "Two of the Associates have been very generous with their cars this year, which has been a great help in visiting far-off parishioners."[66] The sisterhood closed the mission house in Baltimore in July 1966, when the mission house in New York City was also closed, with deep regret. Mother Alicia Theresa and most of the Council (there was one negative vote) believed that there were insufficient sisters to staff the houses adequately.[67]

MISSION IN PHILADELPHIA

The first parish work of the Sisterhood of the Holy Nativity in Pennsylvania began soon after its founding when the motherhouse was in Providence. The sisters conducted parish missions with James Otis Sargent Huntington, OHC, in churches outside Philadelphia, New York, and New Jersey. Many of these missions aimed to reach workers in mill towns, where Huntington concentrated his missionary efforts. When possible, the sisters stayed a week in a parish before the preaching mission to provide instruction, staying several weeks during the mission itself. One of these churches was St. Timothy's in Roxborough, a neighborhood of Philadelphia. There, the sisters conducted church school classes, preparation for the sacraments, Bible study, and guild work, and made over 600 visits. They also visited the parish's Memorial Hospital and House of Mercy patients.[68]

The Sisterhood of the Holy Nativity first worked at St. Clement's in Philadelphia in the 1880s, but there were not enough sisters to establish a mission house there. Sisters from All Saints Sisters of the Poor worked in the parish until 1917 when they decided to devote themselves to institutional work full-time. The Society of St. Margaret worked in St. Clement's from 1917 until 1923, until they decided to devote their energies to their city convent. Considered by Bishop Grafton to be "the Mother of Catholicism in America," St. Clement's invited the Sisterhood of the Holy Nativity a second time, and they moved into the mission house in January 1924.[69]

65. *Mount Calvary Magazine* (February 1922) 4.
66. Yearbook, 1931–1932, Baltimore, 25, SHNC.
67. Acts of the Council, 1957–2004, 91–92, SHNC.
68. Yearbook 1894, St Timothy's, Roxborough, PA, n.p.; 1895, Report of Temporary Mission at St. Luke's, Utica, October 17, 1895–November 27, 1895, n.p, SHNC.
69. Lilly, *The Story of St. Clement's Church, Philadelphia*, 41; Much of Lilly is taken from the following: Joiner, Franklin, "The Early Days of St. Clements, Philadelphia," 100–08, 220–31, 298–306. "The Sisterhood of the Holy Nativity," *The Holy Cross Magazine*, 238.

St. Clement's was founded as a neighborhood Episcopal Church. Its connection to the catholic revival in the Episcopal Church came with the election of Herman Griswold Batterson (1927–1903) as rector in 1869. Batterson was a native of Connecticut and a financial contributor to the Church of St. Mary the Virgin in New York City. "Dr. Batterson began immediately upon his accession to teach the Catholic faith and laid the foundation stones for all that St. Clement's has been able to accomplish in the past, and for which she bears witness today."[70] Batterson's tenure precipitated seventeen years of ritual controversy at St. Clement's. He remained there until he was assured that the congregation would continue in the catholic faith. The Society of St. John the Evangelist had sent Oliver Sherman Prescott to the parish to assist Batterson. Consequently, the vestry immediately requested the Society of St. John the Evangelist to assume leadership of the parish under the direction of Prescott as rector. A conflict ensued when William Bacon Stevens (1815–1887), the bishop of the Diocese of Pennsylvania, accused Prescott of "ritualistic rascality," charged him with heresy, and inhibited another of the Cowley Fathers,[71] Basil William Maturin (1847–1914), for his sermon on the Real Presence. Despite the controversy in the diocese, St. Clement's flourished under the Society of St. John the Evangelist. Prescott resigned in 1881. Maturin became the rector and, within a year, restored all the old ceremonial and added the use of incense and fiery hour-long sermons. "It was during Father Maturin's rectorship that St. Clement's achieved its greatest glory and reputation ... What the newspapers of the day called 'a mass of seething humanity' crowded the corridors and aisles of the church. People tell how week after week they have seen the windowsills, the choir, and the pulpit steps jammed with the overflowing congregations."[72]

Conflicts with the diocese ended with Bishop Steven's death in 1887. A small hospital for the poor was added to the parish. Two other members of the Society of St John the Evangelist, Duncan Convers (1851–1929) and Charles Neale Field (1849–1929) became the rector, further strengthening St. Clement's outreach and reputation as "the church of those in trouble."[73] The Cowley Fathers served the parish for a total of fifteen years. Their withdrawal from the parish was predicated by concerns common in the lifecycle

---

70. Lilly, *The Story of St. Clement's Church, Philadelphia*, 2–6, 7.

71. "Cowley Fathers" is the colloquial name of the Society of St. John the Evangelist (SSJE).

72. Quoted in Smith, SSJE, "The Cowley Fathers in America: The Early Years," n.p. Lilly, *The Story of St. Clement's Church, Philadelphia*, 12–14.

73. Lilly, *The Story of St. Clement's Church, Philadelphia*, 18.

of religious orders. They were concerned that the community's mission work was draining the society's corporate life.[74]

When the Sisterhood of the Holy Nativity arrived at St. Clement's in 1924, it was considered one of the most prominent Anglo-Catholic churches in the United States. The rector, Franklin Joiner (1887–1960), who arrived four years earlier, was ordained in the Diocese of Milwaukee and had served churches in Michigan before his move to St. Clement's. The parish secured funding for a new mission house and an endowment to support the sisterhood's work there. The mission house was opened by Sister Katharine and Sister Margaret, who had worked together at Oneida and the mission house in Portland, Maine. They were later joined by Sister Agatha and Sister Helen, who had experience in urban mission houses. Within the first six months in residence in Philadelphia, the sisters made 550 visits, received 705 guests, conducted forty-five guild meetings, twenty-four sacristy training sessions, seventy-three classes, 152 individual instructions, and prepared fifty-nine people for the sacraments.[75] The number of visitors (1205) and guests (1207) significantly increased the following year, indicating interest in what the sisters offered the parish.[76] In keeping with the sisterhood's mission to women and children, the sisters offered weekly chapel, supper groups, and rummage sales for mothers. They provided separate retreats for women, men, and individual guilds. Eventually, the sisters formed a group for business and professional women, "filling a long-felt need, the work has grown beyond all expectations."[77]

The Sisterhood of the Holy Nativity was closely associated with the liturgical life of St Clement's. There, as well as in other Anglo-Catholic churches, membership in the altar guild required high accountability. Altar guild service was an extension of the eucharistic spirituality of altar guild members. Those who were commissioned into the altar guild and received the medal designating their office prayed that they may "be fortified with heavenly might," "unblemished faith," "steadfast hope," and "fervent charity."[78] The sisterhood oversaw altar guild training, which included preparation for services, instruction in ecclesiastical art and embroidery, and baking "pure and seemly" altar bread "to beautify the sanctuaries of

---

74. Lilly, *The Story of St. Clement's Church, Philadelphia*, 18.

75. Yearbook 1920–1931, 1924, Philadelphia, 94–95, SHNC.

76. Yearbook 1920–1931, 1925, Philadelphia, 139, SHNC

77. Annual Reports of the Convent and Mission Houses, 1940–1943, Philadelphia 1942–1943,73, SHNC

78. *Altar Guild of S. Clements Philadelphia*. Philadelphia: St Clement's Church, n.d., SHNC.

God's worship for the glory of God and the Good of Souls."[79] In addition, the sisters were in charge of the sacristy laundry, mending and changing linens, repairing lace, cleaning vestments, polishing gold and silver vessels, hosting altar guild parties, and providing acolyte breakfasts and dinners. The sisters also shared their expertise with other churches by giving talks for the diocesan altar guild.[80]

One activity beyond the parish was Sister Helen's outreach to college women. Just as she worked with college women at Columbia University in New York City, Sister Helen counseled at Bryn Mawr College. Eventually, the sisters added a weekly Bible study for mothers during the summer months and field trips for their young children.[81] As the sisters became more known in Philadelphia, the number of retreats at the mission house increased, as did their work with diocesan women's groups, such as the Woman's Auxiliary, the Women's Department at the Philadelphia Divinity School, and the Church Periodical Club.[82]

In 1934, Sister Ruth Vera, an artist, and a vestment designer, returned to Philadelphia, where she served at the mission house until 1943 and again from 1950–1953. She was a college student in Philadelphia studying art when she discerned her vocation at St. Clement's. Her artistic talents were used at the church, where she completed expert pen and ink sketches of the interior décor and the outside of the church. Sister Ruth Vera also produced a highly acclaimed annual May Pageant in honor of the Virgin Mary.[83]

Despite all the ministries undertaken first by four sisters, and by the 1930s, by three sisters, St. Clement's rector was concerned that not enough was accomplished. Surviving correspondence between Mother Matilda and Franklin Joiner reveals the conversations between parish clergy and the Mother Superior of the Sisterhood of the Holy Nativity regarding the personnel in a mission house. In 1932, one of the older sisters in the house died, providing the rector, or so he anticipated, with the opportunity to make some changes. He wrote: "Do you realize how few of your Sisters we have

---

79. *Altar Guild of S. Clements Philadelphia.* Philadelphia: St Clement's Church, n.d., SHNC.

80. Yearbook 1920–1931, 1924, Philadelphia, 94–95, SHNC; Yearbook 1920–1931, 1927–1928, Philadelphia, 190, SHNC.

81. Yearbook 1920–1931, 1926–1927, Philadelphia, 164; Yearbook 1920–1931, 1929–1930, Philadelphia, 253, SHNC.

82. Annual Reports of the Convent and Mission Houses, 1940–1943, Philadelphia 1942–1943,73–74, SHNC

83. Saint Clement's Church Ordo Kalendar," 2021. Pencil drawings of the church's interior and exterior by Sister Ruth Vera, SHN. The author thanks Max Manuel and Andrew Nardone for the tour of S. Clement's, including the sacristy and vestment collection, on January 7, 2023.

had here in the 9 years you have been in charge of the work?...I do not see how the work can go on here with 3 sisters, unless all 3 are young and active....You once said that you might have to remove your Sisters from the work here. That is the last thing I want ... These are very strategic years for S. Clement's ... It is most necessary that the work here be aggressive and zealous, and it must be definitely pro-Western in its expression, if we are to survive. It demands the adventurous spirit that alone is the prerogative of youth."[84]

Mother Matilda's reply confirmed the availability of no more than three sisters and the complex matrix with which she managed multiple mission houses. She advised Joiner that the older sister he was concerned about "has more devoted friends than you have any idea of. She has her faults and limitations, but is a splendid woman, known only to the few who have gotten close to her, through some need which has called forth her love and sympathy."[85] Mother Matilda also confirmed that she knew about the inequitable workload at the mission house. Joiner's choice of Sister-in-Charge was unavailable to go to Philadelphia, as each sister's work was discerned within the context of the needs of the whole sisterhood: "If I cannot put her in St. Clement's, I will try to give you the one next best, but it will require many moves in the Houses, and I must give it months of consideration; in fact, it will be impossible to plan until I have seen the Sisters this summer. If I can find no one suitable, you shall have ample time to make a change of Community, which I trust may not be needful."[86]

While the personnel issues with the sisters were resolved at St. Clement's in 1932, Mother Matilda wrote the rectors in parishes served by the sisterhood again in September 1939 to notify them that she might have to make changes and to request their feedback. "It may not be necessary to make any change there, but I must be prepared to act in any emergency," she confirms.[87] The correspondence of Mother Matilda reveals the complexity of managing the mission house system, significantly as the number of sisters declined in the second half of the twentieth century. It also illustrates the role of the Mother Superior in negotiating the work in mission houses and her authority over the placement of sisters.

84. Franklin Joiner to Mother Matilda, 18 February 1932, Archives, S. Clement's Church, Philadelphia.

85. Mother Matilda to Franklin Joiner, 14 May 1932, Archives, S. Clement's Church, Philadelphia.

86. Mother Matilda to Franklin Joiner, 14 May 1932, Archives, S. Clement's Church, Philadelphia.

87. Mother Matilda to Franklin Joiner, 8 September 1939, Archives, S. Clement's Church, Philadelphia.

MISSION IN LOS ANGELES AND SAN DIEGO

The Sisterhood of the Holy Nativity opened its first mission house in California on All Souls Day in 1927 at St. Matthias Church in Los Angeles. Associates on the West Coast widely anticipated the event as an opportunity to advance catholic faith and practice in the region. It was also seen as a broader opportunity to serve the poor in Los Angeles, as the sisters would not "limit their efforts to St. Matthias or to the Episcopal Church, but in a broad and charitable way will try to reach and help all who are in need and the doors of their home will be open to all. It will be a great boon to our city."[88] St. Matthias became a parish in 1910, having previously served as a mission of St. John's Cathedral in Los Angeles. The church was built in 1905 by the first bishop of Los Angeles, Joseph Horsfall Johnson (1847–1948), with the proviso that private donors, not the Board of Missions, would cover the costs if Alfred Morton Smith would serve as missioner. Smith was a native of Philadelphia and a recent graduate of the Philadelphia Divinity School. As the sisters' diary notes, "Daily Mass and Reservation [of the Blessed Sacrament] began immediately."[89]

St. Matthias invited the Sisterhood of the Holy Nativity because of their capacity to undertake parish and social work. Irving Spencer, the rector of St. Matthias, came to Los Angeles after serving in Chicago, Appleton, Wisconsin, and the Philippines. A graduate of the Episcopal Theological School of Cambridge, Massachusetts, Spencer, and a committee of three lay people secured a portion of the funding for the sisters to cover three years and a donated house. They envisioned the sisters organizing Christian education programs, home visiting, and working among the poor, particularly women and girls. They also hoped that the sisters' presence would "bring many outsiders under the influence of the religious life."[90] The mission house in Los Angeles inspired vocations. By 1935, three aspirants came to test their vocations with the sisterhood.[91]

The House of the Holy Nativity, St. Mattias Parish, was opened through the efforts of Sister Emily Caroline, Sister Agatha, and Sister Grace, with the help of Clara Evans, an area Associate. They spent three weeks in Pasadena touring Los Angeles, visiting Anglo-Catholic parishes, and experiencing their first earthquake. The Associates furnished the house, including an altar

---

88. St Matthias Parish, Newsletter, February 20, 1927, SHNC.

89. "The 'Protestant Episcopal' Church and the City of Los Angeles," in Diary of the House of the Holy Nativity, n.p.1927, SHNC.

90. "The 'Protestant Episcopal' Church and the City of Los Angeles," in Diary of the House of the Holy Nativity, n.p.1927, SHNC.

91. "The Sisterhood of the Holy Nativity," *Holy Cross Magazine*, 238.

for the chapel considered "a sacred relic of the Catholic movement in this diocese, having been used in a mission chapel in downtown Los Angeles." [92]

The first years of the mission house in Los Angeles were filled with optimism and promise. The sisters were delighted when Spence Burton, SSJE (1881–1966), gave the first Associates' retreat. The house proved popular among individual retreatants and as a hospitality center for guild meetings and events sponsored by diocesan women's groups. The sisters supervised the altar guild and taught classes for all ages. They were gratified to offer regular talks around the diocese on religious life and a devotional guild for young women. Sister Agatha led Bible studies and Lenten studies in parishes. The sisters were also invited to attend the Provincial Synod in San Francisco. Despite the onset of the Great Depression in 1929, the sisters made 1137 visits in 1929–1930 and received 979 guests. They also offered 175 classes and 220 private instructions and supported 297 guild meetings. The parish hosted a pantry shower for the mission house that yielded 150 food articles. "The many instructions to the children and the faithful work of the Girls' Choir and with college groups have done much for the faith," notes the annual report. [93]

Despite the warmth and enthusiasm of the people of St. Matthias Parish, they could not financially support the mission house after July 1932. The financial responsibility for the house then shifted to the Los Angeles Branch of the Associates. Work in the Sunday school at St. Matthias continued. However, most of the ministry of the sisterhood thereafter focused on the diocese. Although initially disappointing, this reorientation of their work brought the sisters into contact with new mission possibilities. They began work with the chaplaincy office at the University of California at Los Angeles (UCLA) and at Los Angeles City College. Other parishes in the Diocese of Los Angeles quickly invited the sisters to give addresses and retreats. During 1932–1933, visits, guests, classes, instruction, and guild meetings increased by one-third over previous years.[94]

During the 1940s, the Sisterhood of the Holy Nativity's work increased in Los Angeles to include women's evening Bible studies and summer programming for children in a new mission near Beverly Hills. In addition to steady war-related work, such as supporting the Red Cross, the sisters issued publications that were very popular and related to the meaning and role of prayer during wartime. They sponsored weekly intercessory prayer

92. Note by Mrs. L Montgomery, Diary of the House of the Holy Nativity, Los Angeles, June 10, 1956, SHNC.

93. Yearbook 1920–1931; 1927–1928, Los Angeles, 192–93; 1928–1929; 224–25; 1929–1930; 250–51; 1930–1931, 279–80, SHNC.

94. Yearbook 1932–1933, Los Angeles, 65–66, SHNC

gatherings for the war effort. They also focused on social work throughout Los Angeles. For example, Sister Katrina began ministry among African American communities in Watts and Pasadena. Sister Ruth Vera continued this work. The sisters also worked at the Church Home for the Aged in Alhambra. During the postwar years, the sisterhood in Los Angeles was instrumental in starting St. Mary's Retreat House in Santa Barbara, one of the primary Episcopal retreat centers on the West Coast. The importance of Sister Agatha's work on college campuses was recognized through her participation in training conferences for college workers offered through St. Margaret's House, the deaconess training school in Berkeley. College work allowed the sisters to meet girls with little or no church background. "During the year, contacts have been made with between forty and fifty girls: ten to twelve of them have been more or less regular in the classes; one is ready to be confirmed on June 4. A few of the college girls' mothers have come with their own problems."[95]

During their years in Los Angeles, the Sisterhood of the Holy Nativity worked with the Episcopal City Mission Society as chaplains in institutions for indigent and low-income individuals requiring lengthy hospitalizations. In 1938, Sister Grace began visiting and providing follow-up care for three tuberculosis treatment centers: the Olive View Sanitarium, the Santa Anita Sanitarium, and the City of Hope. Before the availability of treatment, tuberculosis killed as many as 100,000 Americans per year.[96] To prevent the spread of the disease, patients were quarantined from others. Many tuberculosis facilities were in the southwest because the dry climate was considered helpful to patients. With medication to successfully treat tuberculosis available after World War II, these institutions were converted to convalescent centers or merged with larger hospitals. The sisters worked primarily in the wards for women and children. The sisters were primarily concerned with the spiritual care of the patients; transportation was provided to the church when requested, as was sacramental instruction.[97]

Sister Paula began visiting Los Angeles hospitals in 1946 and continued into the 1960s. She worked for nine years in Providence with Richard Lief, then the director of Christian Social Relations. When he came to Los Angeles as director of the City Mission Society, she continued to work in hospitals with children and elders. At Olive View, Sister Paula would visit critically ill children. At the Santa Anita Sanitarium, she often worked with

95. "Annual Report of the Los Angeles House, 1940–1941,4–6; Annual Reports of the Convent and Mission Houses, 1940–1943, Los Angeles, 1941, 47–48; 1942–1943, 75–76; "The Los Angeles House Annual report: June 1, 1938–June 1, 1939, SHNC.

96. Mercado, "The Los Angeles Sanitarium Then and Now," n.p.

97. "The Los Angeles House Annual Report," June 1, 1938–June 1, 1939, SHNC.

one hundred Episcopalians at one time, primarily the elderly; most of them were baptized and confirmed due to her efforts. One famous story involved a woman who was dying at the age of 107. She requested Baptism, and Sister Paula administered the rite because no priest was available. The woman recovered, and Sister Paula made sure that she was confirmed! When priests were unavailable, Sister Paula would coordinate services for forty to sixty wheelchair-bound patients. The Sisterhood of the Holy Nativity supported 35,000 hospital patients annually through their connection with the Episcopal City Mission.[98] In 1961, Sister Paul was honored by the Episcopal Diocese of Los Angeles for her work in the community.[99]

In 1959, the Sisterhood of the Holy Nativity was invited to begin a mission house at All Saints' Church in San Diego. With the declining number of sisters, a move to San Diego meant that a house in another location would need to close. After deliberation, it was decided that the Los Angeles mission house would close in 1960 to allow the sisters to move to San Diego. After thirty-three years in Los Angeles, it was not an easy decision, but the sisters believed it was essential to invest in a parish that was not as firmly rooted in the catholic faith as St. Matthias. Moreover, the location in San Diego would allow an ongoing relationship with Olive View, City of Hope, and other institutions where the sisters formed relationships. The Los Angeles Associates could commute to San Diego and St. Mary's Retreat House in Santa Barbara.[100] The work of the Sisterhood of the Holy Nativity at All Saints, San Diego, involved teaching religion in the parish day school, visiting families, working in the nursery, and visiting hospitals in Los Angeles.[101]

In addition to the Sisterhood of the Holy Nativity, All Saints' Church was supported by two long-term deaconesses, Emily T. Mould and Charlotte Gregory Massey.[102] Paul Satrang, rector of All Saints' from 1951–1985, was the most committed of the church's Anglo-Catholic priests and worked assiduously to bring the sisters there. The sisters remained at All Saints' until 1974, when it became necessary to reevaluate the number of mission houses once again.[103]

98. Bussing, "Visit from a welcome stranger," 1924.

99. "Five Win Honors of Episcopal Church Work," I, 24, SHNC.

100. Acts of the Council, 1959, 86–87, SHNC.

101. Macy, "Sisterhood Aids in Parish School," n.p.: Interview, Michael Kaehr, November 30, 2022.

102. Cox, *Changing and Remaining*, 86.

103. Cox, *Changing and Remaining*, 107–113, 189, 297; Acts of the Council, 1974, 110, SHNC.

MISSION IN OREGON

The Sisterhood of the Holy Nativity continued its missionary spirit in the mid-twentieth century to advance the catholic faith where it was less established. There was hope of finding new vocations and associates in the churches once they were exposed to religious life. The sisters worked among missionary clergy who shared their commitment to the catholic faith and welcomed the gifts the sisterhood brought to parishes and dioceses.

The Sisterhood of the Holy Nativity's first venture into the Pacific Northwest was in 1938 at St. Mark's Episcopal Church in Portland, Oregon.[104] The Missionary District of Oregon and Washington was founded in 1854, covering the territories of Oregon, Washington, Idaho, and Western Montana. The Episcopal Church also worked collaboratively with the Anglican Church of Canada in nearby British Columbia. The first Episcopal parishes in Oregon were founded in the 1850s. An Episcopal School, St. Helen's Hall, was founded in 1869. When the Sisterhood of the Holy Nativity started the mission house in Oregon, the diocesan bishop was Benjamin Dunlap Dagwell (1890–1963). Dagwell planted twenty-three congregations during his term, more than half of the Episcopal churches in Oregon at the time. St. Mark's Church in Portland was founded in 1887 and was known for its commitment to traditional liturgy. The rector, Reginald A'Court Simmons, was born in Hertfordshire, England, and educated at Trinity College, Toronto. Simmons served at St. Mark's from 1924 to 1951.[105] The Community of Saint John the Baptist was also in Oregon at the time, staffing St. Helen's Hall. The two sisterhoods celebrated Thanksgiving dinner together at the rectory; the rector showed his motion picture of Fond du Lac as the evening's entertainment.[106]

Both enthusiastic teachers, Sister Patricia and Sister Marie opened the Portland House of the Holy Nativity. Situated on the second floor of the parish house, the mission house provided a base for canvassing the neighborhood for church school members "and growing acclimated to the incessant rain and fog which long thwarted the promised glimpses of snow-capped Mt. Hood."[107] Soon, the first house guests visited, an Associate, Gertrude

---

104. St. Mark's left the Episcopal Church when the 1979 *Book of Common Prayer* was introduced and now lists itself as a Continuing Anglican congregation: The Anglican Parish of Saint Mark, Portland, Oregon (stmarkportland.org)

105. On Simmons, see, Collection: Reginald A'Court Simmonds papers | Special Collections and University Archives Collections Database (uoregon.edu).

106. Annual Report, Portland, 1937–1938, 1, SHNC.

107. Annual Report, Portland, 1937–1938, 1, SHNC.

Morrison of Seattle, and the Mother Superior of the Community of Saint John the Baptist.

The sisters' initial ministry focused primarily on St. Mark's. Both sisters oversaw the church school, with Sister Marie chiefly responsible for the younger children, and a "discouraging and difficult" youth group, which she eventually disbanded, instead offering education and programming for St. Elizabeth's Guild for girls. Sister Patricia mainly worked with the older girls and mothers, sometimes taking them to the church school's services. A squad of twenty cadets from Hill Junior Military School attended church school in military regalia. Another of Sister Patricia's roles was to infuse devotion into the altar guild, "which had gone out of existence except for the faithful if somewhat incompetent work of two or three members." What time remained was devoted to a group of student and graduate nurses from Good Samaritan Hospital.[108]

The newness of what the Sisterhood of the Holy Nativity brought to Oregon fueled the enthusiasm for the mission house. The sisters and the rector used the opportunity to introduce a range of catholic devotional practices to the people of St. Mark's. With the availability of six rooms for retreatants, the sisters hosted forty women during their first year in Oregon. For many, this was their first retreat and exposure to a religious house. The schedule included "quiet evenings" for girls and nurses. During Holy Week, they introduced the Stations of the Cross for children and the first twenty-four-hour watch on Maundy Thursday—an "intense atmosphere of unbroken prayer." The sisters instructed first Confessions and encouraged more frequent participation in Holy Communion. "After this first winter of experience and getting acquainted, the scope of the work seems particularly that of our dedication—making known the Faith. St. Mark's stands for full catholic practice, but many of the people are new to it . . . ," wrote Sister Patricia. "There is great opportunity, a sympathetic Bishop, a devotional atmosphere in the Church, a deeply spiritual and missionary-minded Priest who is taking infinite care to provide truly a *Religious* House and to support and safeguard the living of our life."[109]

Over the next two years, the sisters' ministry in Oregon expanded to include other churches and Episcopal organizations. They worked each summer at diocesan summer youth conferences on the Oregon shore. Sister Patricia's skills in adult education were well-utilized by the Woman's Auxiliary through a range of mission classes, Bible studies, and participation in the Ecumenical World Day of Prayer. Sister Patricia took on an active role

---

108. Annual Report, Portland, 1937–1938, 3–4, SHNC.
109. Annual Report, Portland, 1937–1938, 4–5, SHNC.

at the Provincial Synod. The sisters returned to Fond du Lac from 1939 to 1940 but returned a year later to resume work. One innovation was a series of "cottage meetings" led by the sisters and the rector at homes in different neighborhoods of Portland to facilitate Lenten instruction. "With a clearer knowledge of conditions, needs, and also difficulties, the Sisters are more than ever aware of the opportunity, realized at the first, of teaching and training in catholic faith and practice in a large field where it is little known or understood."[110]

Despite the enthusiasm of the sisters and the local people, the mission house in Portland, Oregon, proved to be financially unsustainable by 1941. During the outbreak of war in the Pacific, the sisters were engaged in first aid training and all-night blackouts. Shortly after Christmas, the rector decided that the parish could no longer sustain the mission house. Though the sisters returned to the Convent in May, the Associates remained firm in their commitment to the catholic faith and hoped there would be a mission house in Portland again after the war.

The missionary spirit of the Sisterhood of the Holy Nativity advanced the catholic faith, inspired the Church to adopt innovative ministries, and instilled greater compassion for the needs of children, women, the elderly, and poor families. Their efforts, along with the support of their Associates and other organizations inspired by the Social Gospel movement, eventually expanded the range of church-related institutions in local communities and beyond.

---

110. Annual Report, Portland, 1938–1939, 1–2; Annual Report, Portland, 1940–41, 1–2; Annual Reports of the Convent and Mission Houses, 1940–1943, Portland, 1941, 50–51, SHNC.

5

Soul Work

THE PRACTICE OF SPIRITUAL RETREAT — a time away in silence for rest and reflection —was part of the Christian tradition from Jesus when he withdrew into the desert to pray. In the third and fourth centuries, the practice was furthered by the Desert Fathers and Mothers who lived as solitaries and in communities of hermits. The Benedictine tradition of the sixth century established a daily rhythm of prayer, silence, and work. The opportunity for laity to reflect on their relationship with God became prominent in 1548, with the *Spiritual Exercises* by Spanish Jesuit Ignatius Loyola (1481–1556). Ignatius introduced a spirituality of service to those outside of monastic communities, along with the practice of discernment—the reflection on the presence of God within daily life.[1]

While Anglicans practiced forms of spiritual retreat during the seventeenth and eighteenth centuries, the development of the tradition dates most directly to the Oxford Movement. The founders of the Oxford Movement, who profoundly influenced the Sisterhood of the Holy Nativity and other religious orders, were concerned with reclaiming Anglicans' place within the catholic tradition and stressed the importance of the holiness of life within the Church's fellowship. As a renewal movement within Anglicanism, the Oxford Movement inspired Anglicans to live more spiritually aware, holier lives. Practices once considered medieval, such as processions, the Stations of the Cross, Marian devotions, adoration of the Blessed Sacrament, and silent meditation, appealed to clergy and laity. Periodic spiritual retreats were regarded as a means for discerning one's sacred purpose. Advancements in

---

1. Tyers, *Borrowed Silence*, 2–8.

rail and steamship travel allowed the founders of the first Anglican religious orders to travel to European religious houses to seek spiritual direction and study retreat practices.[2]

The first retreats in the Church of England were conducted under the auspices of a society of Ritualist priests who worked among the poor, the Society of the Holy Cross. Richard Meux Benson, who belonged to the society and later founded the Society of St. John the Evangelist in 1866, conducted the first retreat for clergy in 1858. Benson studied Continental retreat practices and adapted them to Anglicanism. His approach to leading retreats through silent meditation, worship based on the *Book of Common Prayer*, and leadership by a parish priest was shared with other catholic clergy, including Charles Grafton.[3] Anglican sisterhoods participated in annual retreats beginning in the mid-nineteenth century, including the Society of St. Margaret in East Grimsted, the mother community to the Sisterhood of the Holy Nativity. Though retreats were not yet widespread in Anglican circles by the end of the nineteenth century—due in part to fear of association with "papist" practices—religious orders began to establish the first retreat houses.[4]

When the Sisterhood of the Holy Nativity first began hosting retreats in 1883, the practice was relatively unknown in the United States. The number of retreat houses in England, mainly dedicated to clergy, steadily increased. Retreatants yearned for rest, solitude, and a liturgical experience beyond what they experienced in their local church. Although few options were available for laymen, laywomen were better served due to more sisterhoods than religious communities for men. Associates of sisterhoods, clergy spouses, teachers, nurses, and school alumni were laywomen who participated in early retreats. Parish retreats and parish preaching missions for entire congregations also grew in popularity, with religious communities like the Sisterhood of the Holy Nativity preparing the laity for the experience.[5]

Growth in the retreat movement within Anglicanism further accelerated during the "Golden Age" of Anglo-Catholicism in the 1920s. Participation in the Anglo-Catholic Congresses dramatically increased; an international gathering of 13,000 heard a plenary address on the efficacy of retreats in 1920. The study of mysticism was on the ascendency, both within the Church and for seekers outside of it, accompanied by the desire for silence after the stress and suffering of World War I. Retreat conductors

2. Tyers, *Borrowed Silence*, 27–30.
3. Tyers, *Borrowed Silence*, 30–33.
4. Tyers, *Borrowed Silence*, 30–33.
5. Tyers, *Borrowed Silence*, 52–60.

during the era were invariably male religious and secular clergy. The one exception to this rule was Evelyn Underhill (1875–1941), a popular retreat leader, primarily for women, whose works on mysticism and the spiritual life remain in print today. By the 1940s, retreats were considered a regular part of Anglican devotional life, with higher participation among women.[6] By the mid-twentieth century, the repertoire of retreat experiences within the Anglican tradition included private retreats, retreats with spiritual direction, residential retreats, preached retreats with a conductor in a group setting, closed retreats for specific groups, and parish retreats in a retreat house or parish church, allowing retreatants to live at home.[7]

The number of Anglican retreatants increased overall in the 1950s, corresponding to a period of post-war church growth on both sides of the Atlantic. This period coincided with growth in the number of diocesan retreat centers and retreat centers founded by religious orders, often through the re-purposing of buildings formerly used by larger communities as housing. Generally, women were not considered primary retreat leaders in Anglicanism until the 1960s. However, by then, sisterhoods, like the Sisterhood of the Holy Nativity, had hosted retreats and quiet days for eighty years and offered spiritual direction in their retreat houses, primarily for women. The decline in church membership during the 1960s lessened the number of retreatants and encouraged adjustments in the format. An increased number of ecumenical experiences, mixed retreats with men and women together, more women and lay retreat leaders, and a growing interest in spiritual direction and contemplative practice within parishes are some of the changes in retreat practices at the end of the twentieth century. This period also saw a decline in the number of retreat houses for reasons that affected the Sisterhood of the Holy Nativity. The financial burden of extensive repairs to aging buildings and increasing standards and regulations made the operating costs of many retreat houses untenable. In addition, the gradual decline in the numbers of religious from the mid-twentieth century onward meant that many religious orders were consolidating property and moving to smaller accommodations, thus closing their large houses. Trustees and owners of retreat houses, like the Sisterhood of the Holy Nativity, became increasingly challenged to provide a welcoming and affordable environment while managing housekeeping, staffing, and finances.[8]

---

6. Tyers, *Borrowed Silence*, 71–90.
7. Tyers, *Borrowed Silence*, f 4, 3–4.
8. Tyers, *Borrowed Silence*, 100–101; 168–70.

THE SISTERHOOD OF THE HOLY NATIVITY AND THE RETREAT TRADITION

From its inception, the Sisterhood of the Holy Nativity considered "soul work"—supporting the laity's spiritual growth in parishes—integral to their mission of advancing the catholic faith. "We are working directly with souls. The best work is done individually," said Sister Veronica, a former deaconess who was a member of the Sisterhood of the Holy Nativity for over fifty years.[9] The Sisterhood of the Holy Nativity considered soul work as "a hidden way, without much to be seen upon the surface, but we trust all the work acceptable to God because of the quiet way in which it is performed."[10]

One of the priorities for the sisterhood at its founding in 1882 was to ensure the availability of a house, first in Rindge, New Hampshire, and later in Nantucket, Massachusetts, where the sisters could rest and retreat.[11] The first generation of the Sisterhood of the Holy Nativity included those from families with summer homes where they spent time away each year for rest and recreation. Community rest and retreat during the summer months became part of the annual cycle of the sisterhood. In addition to yearly rest periods, the sisters' formation included individual and community retreats to support their formation and corporate life.[12]

When the Sisterhood of the Holy Nativity founded retreat houses, they did not consider themselves formal spiritual directors, then within the purview of the clergy. Still, they understood the importance of the many conversations on prayer that they shared with retreatants. "Regard any soul sent to you as directly from God," wrote the Mother Foundress, Mother Ruth Margaret.[13] Their confessors were ordained male clergy, as were their Chaplain-Generals and Bishop Visitors, and male clergy conducted their annual retreats until the end of the twentieth century. It wasn't until the late 1980s and the 1990s that the sisterhood invited an Episcopal woman religious to give their annual retreat and explored the efficacy of an "adjunct visitor"—a woman religious from another sisterhood who would, in addition to their diocesan bishop, be available to the sisters for spiritual direction.[14]

---

9. Scotti, "Their Sacrifice Gives Strength," 14.

10. "Beginnings of the House of Rest, Tiverton, R.I.," SHNC.

11. Reeves, "Hidden in Christ," 20, SHNC.

12. Thornton, *English Spirituality*, 76.

13. The Mother Foundress, *Mission Houses of the Sisterhood of the Holy Nativity,* 18, SHNC.

14. Letter from SHN to Bishop Stevens, February 1, 1988, Visitation Reports, Bishop Stevens, Episcopal Visitor, SHNC.

The "soul work" undertaken in mission houses and retreat centers of the Sisterhood of the Holy Nativity took the form of formal and informal spiritual guidance, directly with women and young people and indirectly with clergy. The role of Chaplain-General or Bishop Visitor did not diminish the spiritual authority of the Mother Superior or the counsel she gave the women in her charge. From the first letter written by a woman interested in exploring the sisterhood through to her life profession, the voluminous correspondence of the superiors of the Sisterhood of the Holy Nativity is an indication of the intentional spiritual guidance they gave to those seeking vocational advice. One of the primary roles of the Mother Superior was to care for the spiritual progress of the sisters and to ensure that the unique charism of the sisterhood was nurtured and passed along to each generation. Novice Mistresses also had a distinctive role in the vocational formation of sisterhood members in providing spiritual guidance, formal instruction, and, at times, consolation. It took a great deal of spiritual stamina, wisdom, discernment, and, at times, restraint to form an intergenerational group of women from different backgrounds into a cohesive religious community. In addition to the officers of the sisterhood, all the sisters participated in instruction on the sacraments; though priests heard Confessions, the sisters prepared people for those Confessions. Members of the sisterhood in each mission house and retreat house oversaw the spiritual formation of the Associates, who committed to participate in regular retreats. The Sisterhood of the Holy Nativity had great respect for traditional religious authority. The sisters always respected the counsel of Chaplain-Generals and Bishop Visitors. They ultimately made their own decisions about the readiness of individual sisters for vows or the appropriateness of specific ministries.[15]

The sisters' spiritual guidance benefitted the Church through the work the Sisterhood of the Holy Nativity performed in mission houses and retreat houses and, by extension, wrote devotional materials, made altar bread, designed vestments, and distributed devotional cards. Through their instruction on the sacraments, the Sisterhood of the Holy Nativity prepared thousands for Baptism, first Confession, and Communion. They counseled thousands of lapsed Christians back into the Church. The sisters provided spiritual guidance for the laity through formal classes and hundreds of guilds. Providing access to rest and retreat for working women and mothers was consistently emphasized as an essential part of the "soul work" of the Sisterhood of the Holy Nativity. Motivated by the missionary imperative to advance the catholic faith, members of the Sisterhood of the Holy Nativity

---

15. Ranft, *A Woman's Way,* 116–19.

influenced laity who did not otherwise have access to spiritual guidance and lived out their vocations through secular work and family life.

THE HOUSE OF REST, TIVERTON AND ST. HELENA'S REST, BARRINGTON, RHODE ISLAND

The Sisterhood of the Holy Nativity's establishment of houses for rest and refreshment intentionally served the working poor on coastal Rhode Island. While it was common for wealthy Episcopalians to occupy summer homes during July and August and attend church there, the idea that workers would benefit from rest and refreshment was considered an innovation. Shortly after they established the motherhouse in Providence, Rhode Island, in 1888, the Sisterhood of the Holy Nativity founded two "houses of rest" near the sea for working women needing a place of "spiritual as well as physical refreshment."[16] The House of Rest in Tiverton, Rhode Island, started with a Boston-area Associate of the sisterhood who was a summer resident there. In 1890, two years after the Sisterhood of the Holy Nativity was established in Rhode Island, Elizabeth Cobb of the Church of the Advent in Boston offered her house to Mother Ruth Margaret for mission work, agreeing to open it "as a House of Rest" for tired people at a small rate of board."[17] At the time, Tiverton had a community of seemingly unchurched recent immigrants, and Cobb was concerned that "some effort must be made to convert if possible, and teach them the truths of the Christian Religion."[18]

In addition to local townspeople, Elizabeth Cobb wanted teachers and other self-supporting women of limited income to use the Tiverton house during the summer months. Cobb furnished the house, and the sisters outfitted one of the rooms to serve as a chapel. As in all the Sisterhood of the Holy Nativity houses, the chapel was considered the spiritual center. Thomas Clark (1812–1903), bishop of the Episcopal Diocese of Rhode Island, consecrated the chapel and blessed all the rooms to show his support, and local clergy agreed to offer services. On the East Coast in the latter part of the nineteenth century, clergy in "fashionable" congregations developed the ritual of ministerial vacations during July and August, leaving them free to go to the coast and take services in establishments such as the House of Rest in Tiverton. Some fashionable clergy followed members of their congregations to holiday venues. Large city churches were left in the care of curates or partially closed with scheduled repairs during the summer months.

16. *The Churchman* [Episcopal Diocese of Rhode Island] April 19, 1893, 9.
17. "The Beginnings of the House of Rest, Tiverton, R.I.," SHNC.
18. "The Beginnings of the House of Rest, Tiverton, R.I.," SHNC.

Although the transition never entirely occurred, in 1880, it was predicted that city churches in New York and Boston would close completely for July and August.[19]

Soon, the chapel in Tiverton had a regular schedule of services and was frequented by a larger congregation than the sisters initially anticipated, including summer Episcopalian residents, "many [who] came out of curiosity, and some seemed really interested."[20] The sisters' chapel eventually became the Church of the Holy Trinity, Tiverton. Elizabeth Cobb's daughter organized a Sunday school in her home "in the Sisters' name" for about twenty children, recruiting other Associates as teachers to prepare children and adults for Baptism. She also recruited her husband, "not a churchman," to establish a children's choir.[21] Concerned that some catechumens consorted with the local "Baptist element," the sisters and Associates worked tirelessly to support the mission. Although the Sisterhood of the Holy Nativity had limited success in converting Italian immigrants to the Episcopal Church, they were motivated to ensure that the children received religious instruction. As Sister Rebecca notes in the house diary, "While it seems impossible, at least now, to do much for the men and women in the place, there are still the children who *can* be reached, and who, if they are God's children *now*, must by and by do God's work."[22]

As a mission house of the Sisterhood of the Holy Nativity during an era of economic depression, the House of Rest in Tiverton provided direct care to those in need throughout the community. During the Depression of 1892, the sisters and Associates provided food and clothing to impoverished families. In this way, the House of Rest was a practical model of religious devotion and community service.

Eventually, the House of Rest in Tiverton offered spiritual talks and book groups led by the sisters and Associates, augmented by "much individual instruction." Typically, the house was open during July and August; the census for the summer of 1897 reported 34 visitors who stayed a week or more and another dozen who stayed for a day or two.[23] "Many teachers and tired nurses coming from far away glad to avail themselves of so restful and quiet a home for their summer vacation . . . Their return from year to year shows how fully they appreciate the blessed privileges of this

---

19. Kujawa-Holbrook, *By Grace Came the Incarnation*, 70–71.
20. "The House of Rest," 1890, Motherhouse, Providence, Rhode Island, SHNC.
21. "The House of Rest," 1890, Motherhouse, Providence, Rhode Island, SHNC.
22. House Diary, Tiverton, R. I., SHNC.
23. "Report from the House of Rest," 1897,12. Yearbooks, 1894–1939, SHNC.

house."[24] As one Associate observed, "One can never know the amount of spiritual good that has been done in this house by our dear Sisters."[25] The women who came to the House of Rest for summer retreats were enthusiastic about what the sisters offered. Guests and sisters alike appreciated chapel services, instruction, silence, and recreation. "The evenings were gay with music, impromptu charades etc. until the Compline bell sounded, and silence reigned."[26]

The first "little retreat" at the House of Rest in Tiverton was given by Charles Neale Field, SSJE, and included the sisters, household staff, Associates, and guests. It was designed to initiate those with little formal retreat experience. Field was known for his deep catholic spirituality and ministry among the poor. He founded two African American parishes in Boston and a home for African American women with tuberculosis and other diseases. His retreat schedule included vespers during the first evening, the daily offices, Mass, meditations, instruction, and confession on the first day. The retreat concluded with a choral Mass and breakfast on the third day. Retreat lore recounts an episode where Field spoiled his pie by pouring salad dressing over it (thinking it was custard) and then breaking the Rule by refusing to consume it! Field's teaching urged against rigid religious practice, instead considering retreats as opportunities for spiritual refreshment. "To speak of the closer, more individual, more interior experiences of the Retreats is a different matter. Each soul has its own thankfulness for what God has done for it—which is better *lived* than talked about."[27] The sisters believed that the house fostered a profound spiritual experience, but it was impossible to determine the outcome for each person. "It is much like explaining a good joke—the ludicrous would be lost in the telling. It takes the circumstances and the surrounds of the Retreat with the temper of the Retreatant—the time and the place to best appreciate the occurrence."[28]

At the same time, the Sisterhood of the Holy Nativity founded a similar retreat house in Barrington, Rhode Island, known as St. Helena's Rest. Associate E. G. Hartshorne funded the project. Popular wisdom endorsed the benefits of fresh air and the countryside for children who lived in urban tenements. The focus was on providing rest and support for working women, girls, and families of limited income. The sisters hosted primarily women and children at St. Helena's Rest for a week or two. St Andrew's

---

24. "The Beginnings of the House of Rest, Tiverton, R.I.," SHNC.
25. "The Beginnings of the House of Rest, Tiverton, R.I.," SHNC.
26. House Diary, Tiverton, R. I., SHNC.
27. "The Retreats," instructional talk on the purpose of retreats, SHNC.
28. "The Retreats," instructional talk on the purpose of retreats, SHNC.

Episcopal School used the building in the winter, and the land provided vegetables for St. Helena's in the summer. The diocesan newspaper noted that the Rhode Island homes in Tiverton and Barrington were "wisely managed and mothered by the Sisters."[29]

"THE FIRST RETREAT HOUSE IN THE AMERICAN CHURCH"

The retreat houses that the Sisterhood of the Holy Nativity founded in Rhode Island were the model for their work in the Diocese of Newark. In 1915, the sisters were invited to expand the growing social work undertaken In West Orange, New Jersey. "During the thirty years of its existence, the Parish has found it necessary to enlarge the parish house three times. Situated as it is, the Church ministers to many souls who greatly need a gathering place for recreation, such as the parish house gives them."[30] Associate Margaret Van Wagenen deeded a house to the parish with the expressed purpose that the proceeds be used toward the sisters' support.[31]

In addition to advancing the catholic faith and participating in social service for the community, the Sisterhood of the Holy Nativity started a retreat house near the parish. Margaret Van Wagenen donated the rent of another house in West Orange for a trial period of three years. The intention was to open the house to women for short rests, "especially for such as desired to make retreats, of a day or longer."[32] An unpublished history of "The Beginnings of the First Retreat House in the American Church," by Sister Julia Elizabeth, SHN, notes that the retreat house was formally opened on May 31, 1915. While it is difficult to verify that the retreat house in West Orange was the first retreat house in the Episcopal Church, it was undoubtedly one of the earliest. "The Reverent Mother [Katharine Edith] with Sister Emily came here this afternoon to open this house . . . .It will be used for a house of Retreat and will be a place where ladies may come for rest and spiritual help."[33] Statements acknowledging the House of Retreat at All Saints Church in West Orange as the first retreat house in the American

---

29. *The Churchman* [Episcopal Diocese of Rhode Island], April 19, 1893, 9.

30. Episcopal Diocese of Newark, *Forty-First Annual Convention of the Diocese of Newark*. Trinity Church, Newark, N.J. May 18, 1915, 115.

31. Episcopal Diocese of Newark, *Forty-First Annual Convention of the Diocese of Newark*. Trinity Church, Newark, N.J. May 18, 1915, 115.

32. Yearbook, 1915–1918, 1919–1920, West Orange, May 30, 1915, 37, SHNC.

33. [Sister Julia Elizabeth, SHN] "The Beginnings of the First Retreat House in the American Church," 1–2; House Diary, West Orange, SHNC, 1.

church appeared in publications many years after its founding, supporting the claim.[34]

Planning for the House of Retreat in West Orange began shortly after the Sisterhood of the Holy Nativity established the mission house in New York City in 1909. Through participation in their own Rule of life, the Associates in the region yearned for opportunities to develop their spirituality. "The need for a House of Retreat where women could come and be spiritually refreshed was already evident as more people came under the influence of the great leaders of the Catholic movement within the American church."[35]

Sister Emily was the tenacious spirit and forward vision behind the House of Retreat in West Orange. A music teacher before she entered the sisterhood, Sister Emily possessed administrative skills combined with a deep commitment to the spiritual life. It is unknown when she became convinced that the sisterhood should open a retreat house, but she spent years praying and researching.[36] The desire for a retreat house among the Sisterhood of the Holy Nativity Associates was great. As one Associate wrote: "For many women, of diverse types, opened their hearts, from time to time, to the Religious of the New York Mission House, whose burden was, 'If I could only get away for a few days of quiet and of peace, and maybe have some time to think about my soul!'"[37] The same Associate noted that there were Roman Catholic retreat houses, as well as retreat houses in England, but neither were viable for "women of refinement and education" who had fewer options than the working women who frequented summer homes and city programs. The answer was to have retreat houses for women in New York City and other high-population centers.[38] Sister Emily worked intensely, putting together furniture, organizing construction, coordinating workers, and praying. As she noted in the house diary with exasperation and fatigue, "The day, after Mass, was spent in work about the house. Will it ever be settled?"[39]

---

34. [Sister Julia Elizabeth, SHN] "The Beginnings of the First Retreat House in the American Church," 1–2; SHNC.

35. [Sister Julia Elizabeth, SHN] "The Beginnings of the First Retreat House in the American Church," 1.

36. "A Tribute to Sister Emily, SHN," by a Sister of the Community, n.d. (1927), SHNC.

37. Miss Edmunds, "Bay Shore Retreat House," 4, SHNC.

38. Miss Edmunds, "Bay Shore Retreat House," 4, SHNC.

39. "The Beginnings of the First Retreat House in the American Church," 1–2; Yearbook 1915–1918, 1919–1920, 37, 39; House Diary, West Orange, SHNC,

The retreat house was located a few blocks from All Saints Church in West Orange, making it convenient for the sisters to live near their place of worship. The grounds included lush landscaping, fruit trees, and room for a vegetable garden to generate food. Associate Florence Jones gave the chapel an altar of Italian walnut, in memory of her mother, along with velvet hangings for the chancel. Gifts came in for other chapel appointments and fifty copies of the *Book of Common Prayer* and *The Hymnal*. The Sisterhood of the Holy Nativity created beautiful vestments for the chapel that impressed many visiting clergy. A notation from the sisters' yearbook records an observation made by Frederic Cecil Powell, SSJE, "He had no idea we had anything so beautiful."[40]

The sisters' parish work in West Orange engaged them in the local community. They settled into a rhythm of attending the early service at the larger church, St. Mark's, followed by the children's service at All Saints every Sunday. With two sisters assigned to the church for the year and two additional sisters as summer coverage, the Sisterhood of the Holy Nativity provided all the church support for women and girls, the parish guilds, as well as the Woman's Auxiliary, the Junior Auxiliary, the Girls' Friendly Society, visiting the sick, and instruction in the sacraments for the retreat house. During their first three months in West Orange, the sisters made 80 visits, received 245 guests, taught 121 private classes, thirty-three group classes, and facilitated over forty guild meetings.[41] Their work in the community increased interest in the retreat house. In the same year, the retreat house received twenty-seven visitors within this same period and hosted a Baptism.[42]

The first summer in West Orange, the sisters hosted a retreat for thirteen "Sisters in the Eastern houses who could be in attendance," led by Shirley Carter Hughson, OHC (1867–1949), superior of the Order of the Holy Cross. Soon, other prestigious leaders of the Catholic Movement in the Episcopal Church gave retreats, including Joseph G.H. Barry, rector of St. Mary the Virgin in New York, and James Otis Sargent Huntington, OHC. Huntington was particularly interested in the retreat house; he gave a quiet day attended by over two hundred people. Additional retreatants soon arrived in West Orange: three women from St. James Church in Brooklyn for a day's retreat, one of whom was eventually professed as Sister Mary Constance, SHN.[43]

---

40. Yearbook 1915–1918, 1919–1920, West Orange, 117, SHNC.
41. Yearbook 1915–1918, 1919–1920, West Orange, 37–39, 75, SHNC.
42. Yearbook 1915–1918, 1919–1920, West Orange, 37–39, 75, SHNC.
43. [Sister Julia Elizabeth, SHN] "The Beginnings of the First Retreat House in the American Church," 2–4, SHNC.

Within the year, the interest in private retreats among the Sisterhood of the Holy Nativity Associates gained momentum. In 1916, the sisters hosted a picnic for seventy-five New York Associates at the House of Retreat. The house once again hosted a retreat for sisters living on the East Coast from other Episcopal sisterhoods. By 1917, the requests had expanded beyond the rooms available in the retreat house. The age and condition of the house in West Orange meant that Sister Emily spent a great deal of time responding to emergencies, such as frozen water pipes. Associates Elizabeth Cobb and Florence Jones donated funds toward an endowment for a better-equipped retreat house. At the same time, Sister Emily and Sister Harriet began searching for a permanent location outside New York City.[44] Site visits to Cold Spring Harbor, Norwalk, Connecticut, Chappaqua, New York, and the Graymoor property on the Hudson were unsuccessful. The harsh winter of 1918 brought more frozen pipes and hardships for the sisterhood. "The work of the winter of 1918, at All Saints Church, Orange, was much interrupted by the scarcity of fuel, which necessitated closing the Sunday School, GFS, and Guilds." The lack of heat also meant closing the retreat house for the winter. The sisters continued their work in the parish despite the harsh weather through private instruction, visiting, and attending Red Cross classes.[45]

With the lease on the West Orange property expiring in May 1918, Sister Emily and Sister Harriet received word that Sarah Lawrance offered them her home at Bay Shore on Long Island.[46] Bay Shore was an ideal location for a retreat house, given its proximity to New York and accessibility by train. The estate had lush landscaping and sat on ten acres, including a farm, a gardener's cottage, a grapery, and a hot house. A visit from Mother Katharine Edith confirmed the property was ideal for what the sisterhood envisioned as a permanent retreat house. As Sister Emily recorded in the house diary that day, "How wonderful it is that God has moved Miss Lawrence to give this: May much work be done there for His glory."[47]

---

44. [Sister Julia Elizabeth, SHN] "The Beginnings of the First Retreat House in the American Church," 4; House Diary, West Orange, 1917, SHNC.

45. [Sister Julia Elizabeth, SHN] "The Beginnings of the First Retreat House in the American Church," 5; Yearbook 1915–1918, 1919–1920, West Orange, January 1918–June 1918, 148, 150, SHN.

46. Some sources report this surname with the more popular spelling "Lawrence." However, sources from the period and location designate the spelling of family name as "Lawrance."

47. [Sister Julia Elizabeth, SHN] "The Beginnings of the First Retreat House in the American Church," 6; House Diary, West Orange, 1918, SHNC.

In addition to moving the retreat house to Bay Shore, the Sisterhood of the Holy Nativity continued to carry a heavy workload in West Orange until 1925. By 1916, the sisters noted that the "local clergy want more work."[48] A year later, two sisters were assigned to the house and two added sisters in the summer months. Together, they undertook 912 visits, received 404 visitors, offered 160 classes, 169 private instructions, and facilitated 141 guild meetings and forty-nine private retreats. The house also welcomed five new Associates.[49] One of the tensions for the sisters was the growing needs of the parish while the retreat work was expanding in another direction. When the retreat house moved to Bay Shore in 1918, two sisters moved into the parish house in West Orange, funded primarily by a regular offering of groceries. Their work shifted from focusing on retreats to the needs of Italian immigrant families and the parish's children. During the 1918 Spanish flu epidemic, the sisters made 1214 visits and received 295 visitors.[50] By 1921, the number of parish visits burgeoned to 2135, with another 430 visitors received, 122 classes given, 130 private instructions provided, and 334 guild meetings.[51] For the next four years, the work of the house in West Orange expanded, including outreach to the Associates and new ministries, including a mother's guild and a weekly Bible class during Lent. Yet, by 1925, despite all the efforts of the Sisterhood of the Holy Nativity for over ten years, leadership changes at All Saints triggered the decision to leave: "The Curate's attitude toward the sisters made our residence there very undesirable, so by mutual agreement of the Rector, the Mother, and the Council, we withdrew on December 17."[52]

THE HOUSE OF RETREAT AND REST, BAY SHORE, LONG ISLAND

The House of Retreat and Rest, founded by the Sisters of the Holy Nativity in Bay Shore, Long Island, served the Church from 1918 until its closure in 1980.[53] "In retrospect," wrote Sister Julia Elizabeth, "these first three years of the beginnings of the Retreat House read like a modern version of the

---

48. Yearbook 1915–1918, 1919–1920, West Orange, 75, SHNC
49. Yearbook 1915–1918, 1919–1920, West Orange, 117, SHNC.
50. Yearbook 1915–1918, 1919–1920, West Orange, 180, SHNC.
51. Yearbook 1920–1931, West Orange, 67, SHNC.
52. Yearbook 1920–1931, West Orange, 16, 67, 91, 118. SHNC.
53. "House of the Holy Nativity Forced to Close in September," *Tidings*, June 1980, n.p.

Book of Foundations in Spain by St. Teresa of Avila."[54] The estate sat on land known as "Compwams" by the region's indigenous peoples.[55] Owner Sarah Lawrance hired one of the most famous architects in New York, Stanford White (1953–1906), to renovate the site from a private home to a retreat house. A leading architect of the Beaux-Arts movement, White designed homes for wealthy clients and civic monuments, such as the Washington Square Arch in New York City. Though the house required adaptations, the sisters and Associates were undaunted. Three years later, Lawrance deeded a separate lot to the sisterhood to provide an endowment to ensure the future of the retreat house.[56]

The first step in ordering the new retreat house was to prepare a chapel. A game room was converted for this purpose, and the library became the sacristy. Within two weeks of occupancy, the sisters began to say vespers in the chapel. The sisters also started to attend services at the local parish, St. Peter's.[57] The response from women who wanted to participate in retreats was immediate. Joseph G.H. Barry, then Chaplain-General, gave the first retreat in September 1918 on "Joy." Twenty-six women attended; another fifteen came on another retreat two weeks later. Many early retreatants expressed "what it meant for them to be in the atmosphere of a religious house."[58]

During its first six months in 1919, the House of Retreat and Rest in Bay Shore hosted 113 women for forty-two retreats. The sisters began a series of twelve talks on spiritual topics and gave private instruction to seventy-five guests. During the 1918 Spanish flu epidemic, one guest, a superintendent of nurses from Philadelphia, reported: "That she could have never gotten through the terrible siege of influenza if it had not been for what she got at Bay Shore."[59]

In 1920, central heating allowed the sisters to celebrate their patronal feast, the Feast of the Nativity, in the retreat house for the first time. Preparations involved much housework for Sister Emily while Sister Harriet

54. [Sister Julia Elizabeth, SHN] "The Beginnings of the First Retreat House in the American Church," 4, SHNC.

55. "Convent passes as time does," *Islip Bulletin*, July 24, 1980, 16; "Lawrence Estate Sold; Dates Back to Indian Days, newspaper clipping without source, [1918], saved by Suffolk Real Estate, SHNC.

56. [Sister Julia Elizabeth, SHN] "The Beginnings of the First Retreat House in the American Church,"9, SHNC.

57. Yearbook 1915–1918, 1919–1920, Bay Shore, 1919, 185, SHNC.

58. [Sister Julia Elizabeth, SHN] "The Beginnings of the First Retreat House in the American Church,"5; Yearbook 1915–1918, 1919–1920, Bay Shore, 1919, 185, SHNC.

59. Yearbook 1915–1918, 1919–1920, Bay Shore, 185, SHNC.

painted the floors. "But finally, all was ready, and the midnight Mass was celebrated with Christmas hymns. It was a holy time, a time of gladness and thanksgiving."[60] The rhythms of the liturgical year meant that both sisters were soon involved in preparations for a Lenten retreat. The sisters also hosted women for private retreats every week of the year. "The Sisters were daily giving instructions in the Sacraments, first confessions were being heard by the Chaplain, and more women were being admitted as Associates."[61]

The Sisterhood of the Holy Nativity's commitment to offering retreats was rooted in their understanding of the importance of prayer and silence in advancing the catholic faith. Through prayerful discernment, they were motivated to make the catholic faith and sacraments accessible. With many demands on their time, the sisters understood the challenges of other women seeking a more profound spiritual experience. By 1922, at least two other Episcopal sisterhoods in the region also offered women rest and retreat: the Community of St. Mary in Peekskill, New York, and the Community of St. John the Baptist in Mendham, New Jersey. Roman Catholic convents and retreat houses also offered opportunities, although attending retreats there was less common for Episcopal laity.[62]

The retreat house in Bay Shore was blessed on May 3, 1921, Rogation Tuesday, in a series of celebratory events, including a Requiem Mass for Sarah Lawrance's parents, in whose memory the property was given. "The entire house was blessed, and the procession went through every room, including the grounds, the stations, the fields, & the garden."[63] Soon afterward, Sister Emily and Sister Harriet began planning the expansion of the sisterhood's retreat ministry. The two women shared a sense of humor and brought energy and creativity to the retreat house. Sister Harriet possessed great administrative expertise, held several offices in the sisterhood, and was almost elected superior. On more than one occasion, she was sent to mission houses to assist in troublesome situations. The two sisters developed plans to build a cottage for a resident priest. The retreat schedule expanded to include pre-Advent and pre-Lenten retreats, altar guild retreats, and additional individual retreats. The foremost retreat conductors in the Episcopal Church, including brothers from the Order of the Holy Cross

60. [Sister Julia Elizabeth, SHN] "The Beginnings of the First Retreat House in the American Church," 8, SHNC.

61. [Sister Julia Elizabeth, SHN] "The Beginnings of the First Retreat House in the American Church," 9, SHNC.

62. M'Comas, "Havens of Rest: Houses Conducted by Sisters of the Anglican Communion," 8.

63. House Diary, Bayshore, May 3, 1921, SHNC.

and the Society of St. John the Evangelist, as well as Reginald Heber Weller, Jr., bishop of the Diocese of Fond du Lac, gave their full support. Joseph Crookson, the founder of the Society of St. Francis in the Episcopal Church in 1919, also conducted retreats there. As Sister Emily wrote in her annual report: "This House has done much for souls during the year which does not show in the above statistics, and its influence steadily increasing and extending to different states . . . The future is most encouraging."[64]

By 1923, the retreat house had expanded, adding an extra wing of guest rooms, offices, separate refectories for the sisters and visiting clergy, and renovations to the chapel. Resident in the office was Grey-friar, Sister Emily's devoted cat, who helped her navigate when her eyesight failed from acute glaucoma.[65] The sisters named each guest room after a saint and cut larger rooms in half to meet the demand: "Today we cut St. Perpetua half in two!" wrote Sister Emily to the Convent in Fond du Lac.[66] The retreat house was fully appointed to support Anglo-Catholic devotion. In addition to the Stations of the Cross, friends donated a crucifix, monstrance, veils, processional cross, and Angelus bell.[67]

Between 1925 and 1927, the House of Retreat and Rest in Bay Shore grew from hosting sixty retreats per year to hosting 115 individuals and groups. The gift of a car gave the sisters a means to increase their visits to local churches and hospitals. The sisters offered regular retreats for college women as well as for Associates. Representatives from local altar guilds were so impressed by Sister Harriet's talks that they requested further instruction. Chapel worship attracted the wider community: solemn vespers on Saturdays, Sundays, and saints' days, and the Adoration of the Blessed Sacrament on Sunday afternoons.[68]

For the Sisterhood of the Holy Nativity, 1927 was a turning point in their history of retreat work. It was the year when Sister Emily's health began to fail, and she became bedridden. The entire sisterhood was griefstricken. "The Sisters were able to listen over a friend's radio to the welcome of President Coolidge to Lindbergh, but their hearts were yearning over Sister Emily. She was failing rapidly, and there was nothing they could do."[69]

64. Yearbook 1920–1931, Bay Shore, 69–70, SHNC.

65. [Sister Bernadine, SHN] "A Tribute to Sister Emily, SHN," SHNC.

66. [Sister Julia Elizabeth, SHN] "The Beginnings of the First Retreat House in the American Church," 6, SHNC.

67. [Sister Julia Elizabeth, SHN] "The Beginnings of the First Retreat House in the American Church," 10, SHNC.

68. Yearbook 1920–1931, Bay Shore, 102, 113–114, 136–137, 162. SHNC

69. [Sister Julia Elizabeth, SHN] "The Beginnings of the First Retreat House in the American Church," 7.

Sister Emily died on July 12, 1927, leaving a rich legacy in retreat ministry in the name of the Sisterhood of the Holy Nativity. "In our report for this House, our first thought is of the passing of Sister Emily, who accepted such a great service of Our Lord, not only in the establishment of this work but in the souls of the many who came to her for instruction and advice," records the house dairy for 1927–1928. "This house might well be called her memorial." Sister Bernadine, a sister mentored by Sister Emily wrote: "Sister Emily taught the Juniors how to present the Faith and how to prepare persons for the Sacraments. Any success [I had] in that Junior's life as a Religious; in giving instructions, is due, under God, to Sister Emily."[70]

HOUSE OF RETREAT AND REST, BAY SHORE, 1930s–1980s

During the mid-twentieth century, the House of Retreat and Rest in Bay Shore expanded its mission. Mother Matilda considered the house to be second in importance after the Convent in Fond du Lac.[71] Now, four sisters were resident in the house full-time, compared to two in the past, with an extra two sisters during the summer months. "Many women who have here been taught the Catholic Faith have become Associates of the Community and now are living under the voluntary obligation of a Rule for those whose way of life is in the world. Several have found vocations as Religious."[72] By the 1930s, the house was attracting younger people who were less active in churches but had their own "strivings" and who were searching for "the still dews of quietness."[73] "Many others have been drawn nearer to God by the daily offering of the Mass, by the most Holy Presence in the Reserved sacrament, and by the sweet sacrifice of praise and thanksgiving of the Choir Offices. Numbers of troubled souls have found here peace and absolution. Many sad or lovely hearts have been brought consolation by the atmosphere of love, so reassuring of the greater love of God."[74]

By 1935, the sisters organized the Friends of the House at Bay Shore, responsible for fundraising and promoting retreats in parishes. Though "effective on the spiritual side," the sisters were concerned about costs. Members of the advisory board included women Associates, the diocesan

70. [Sister Bernadine, SHN] "A Tribute to Sister Emily, SHN," SHNC.
71. Letter from Mother Matilda to Fr. Joiner, Philadelphia, Feast of St. Matthias [1932], SHNC.
72. Miss Edmunds, "Bay Shore Retreat House," 5, SHNC.
73. Miss Edmunds, "Bay Shore Retreat House," 5, SHNC.
74. Miss Edmunds, "Bay Shore Retreat House," 5, SHNC.

bishop, clergy friends, a professor of ecclesiastical history at the General Theological Seminary in New York, Frank Gavin (1890–1938), pioneer social worker Mary Kingsbury Simkhovitch (1867–1951), and ecclesiastical architect Ralph Adams Cram 1863–1942).[75]

World War II nearly decimated the retreat movement in England due to damage caused by frequent bombings, a downturn in charitable giving, and overall changes in priorities. While the Sisterhood of the Holy Nativity in Bay Shore did not experience enemy action during the 1940s, the realities of the war were never far from their awareness: "We are constantly reminded of the war by the great number of army and navy planes that fly over the house daily, making it quite necessary to take out a war damage insurance policy. We have had plenty of dim-outs and black-outs."[76] During the war years, the sisters hosted an average of 300 guests annually. Quiet days, such as those given in 1941 by Sister Mary Josephine, SHN, were conducted by the sisters.[77] Recognition came in 1942, when the newly consecrated bishop of the Diocese of Long Island, James P. DeWolfe (1896–1966), visited the retreat house—the first diocesan bishop to do so in its twenty-four-year history. "He is a strong Anglo-Catholic and promises to be a good advance in this low church diocese, the next to the smallest in area (R.I.), but one of the highest in communicants—over 60,000."[78] The sisters welcomed DeWolfe's support, believing that "the full catholic faith would be made known through him."[79] DeWolfe recognized the value of a retreat house in his diocese. He encouraged parish retreats hosted by the sisters, and the diocesan altar guild held retreats there.[80]

The 1940s brought expanded outreach on Long Island through visits to Pilgrim State Hospital, a state psychiatric facility that opened in 1929. The retreat house continued to host over 300 guests annually for retreats. "In these troubled times, women who are working under great pressure and strain find refreshment and peace here and return to their work with

---

75. Letter from Frank Gavin to the Rt Rev. dear Father Sturtevant, May 16, 1935, SHNC,

76. Annual Reports of Convent and Mission Houses, 1940–1943, Bay Shore, 1942–1943, 71, SHNC.

77. Annual Reports of Convent and Mission Houses, 1940–1943, Bay Shore, 1940–1941, 17, SHNC.

78. Annual Reports of Convent and Mission Houses, 1940–1943, Bay Shore, 1942–1943, 71, SHNC.

79. [Sister Julia Elizabeth, SHN] "The Beginnings of the First Retreat House in the American Church," 7, SHNC.

80. [Sister Julia Elizabeth, SHN] "The Beginnings of the First Retreat House in the American Church," 7, SHNC.

renewed strength."[81] Instead of the sisters teaching in the church school, classes from St. Peter's came to the retreat house for instruction and devotions in the chapel. Soon, the entire church school of St. Peter's was visiting the retreat house for the Rogation Day procession. Interest in inviting the sisters to parishes spread throughout the surrounding villages: they hosted retreats for local parishes, displayed religious books and cards at parish bazaars, organized new altar guilds, and taught in church schools in Farmingdale and Babylon. Interest in the spiritual talks the sisters gave also grew, and the retreat house hosted local writers and artists. By 1949, the name of the retreat house was updated to "House of the Holy Nativity." Sister Harriet, who started the retreat house with Sister Emily, was Sister-in-Charge until three months before her death on October 20, 1949, notably while the house was full of retreatants![82]

By the early 1950s, the House of the Holy Nativity was known as a spiritual center and pilgrimage destination for church women in the Episcopal Diocese of Long Island. The number of conducted retreats per year grew to seven, and the sisters offered quiet days for women and young people regularly, as well as retreats for other sisterhoods, with a focus on "*renewal* of the souls, and minds, and bodies of those who come here."[83] In 1954, Gregory Mabry (1890–1970), the retired rector of St. Paul's Church in Brooklyn, became the chaplain at the House of the Holy Nativity. Mabry was an authority on the Oxford Movement and considered one of the foremost retreat conductors in the Episcopal Church. He believed that the Oxford Movement stood for social reform, in addition to the catholic faith and ritualism.[84] Mabry soon organized retreats for clergy and "days of recollection"—quiet days focused on themes related to the Christian life. Mabry also offered conferences for parish clergy on organizing quiet days and retreats. He authored monthly "spiritual notes from the House of the Holy Nativity, including meditations on the liturgical year."[85] Mabry's teaching extended the reach of the House of the Holy Nativity to people in parishes who could not visit in person. The House of the Nativity became a center for diocesan groups, such as the Woman's Auxiliary, Diocesan Altar

---

81. Letter from SHN to Friends of the House of Retreat and Rest, June 1947; Annual Reports of Convent and Mission Houses, 1940–1943, Bay Shore, 1941–1942, 43, SHNC.

82. Letter from SHN to Friends of House of the Holy Nativity, April 1949, SHNC

83. Letter from SHN to Friends of the House of the Holy Nativity, May 1951, May 1952, SHNC.

84. "Theology Degrees Awarded to 53 . . . 24L.

85. [Sister Julia Elizabeth, SHN] "The Beginnings of the First Retreat House in the American Church," 7, SHN.

Guild, Young People's Fellowship, and the St. Ursula's Guild for teachers. Church school children who wanted to see "a real live Nun" also visited the retreat house.[86] Financial support by Associates and friends was augmented by collecting Betty Crocker coupons to keep the house stocked with dishes and utensils.[87]

In April 1951, a radio show sponsored by the United Council of Christian Women devoted twelve minutes to the Sisterhood of the Holy Nativity and the retreat house. Other outreach projects included bi-weekly spiritual talks given by the sisters, a question box on the front porch during the summer months, a weekly intercession period in the chapel, and retreats geared explicitly for girls and young women. The sisters became active in the youth program at Camp DeWolfe. "In such ways as these, we extend the knowledge of the spiritual life to our people, and, we hope, the impetus to practice its principles."[88]

During the 1960s, the Sisterhood of the Holy Nativity, in addition to over twenty conducted retreats per year, monthly days of recollection, quiet days, and group pilgrimages, increased their support of the national Episcopal Church. Sister Ruth Angela, Sister-in-Charge of the retreat center in Bay Shore, became chair of Prayer and Worship for the Episcopal Church Women (ECW). The sisterhood also embraced the ecumenical movement. The Second Vatican Council of the Roman Catholic Church, under the leadership of Pope John XXIII and Pope Paul VI, ushered in a new era of ecumenical cooperation concerned with restoring unity among Christians. Although the sisters at Bay Shore House were familiar with local Roman Catholic sisterhoods such as the Daughters of Wisdom at Good Samaritan Hospital and the Nursing Sisters of the Sick Poor at West Islip since the 1920s, forty years later, the sisters sought to cultivate ecumenical relationships intentionally. Sister Ruth Angela, SHN, a gifted networker and ambassador, represented the Sisterhood of the Holy Nativity at ecumenical gatherings and encouraged participation among her sisters. The Sisters of Mercy from St. Patrick's in Bay Shore called on the Sisterhood of the Holy Nativity at their retreat house after Sister Ruth Angela drove them home from the train station in the rain. "It has been my privilege to have had warm relationships with Roman Catholic sisters and lay people even prior to my entry into holy religion," she said.[89] The Sisters of the Holy Nativ-

86. Letter from SHN to Friends of the House of the Holy Nativity, May 1951, SHNC.

87. Letter from SHN to Friends of the House of the Holy Nativity, May 1952, February 1958, June 1959, SHNC.

88. Letter from SHN to Friends of the House of the Holy Nativity, February 1958, SHNC.

89. Bosco, "Anglican Nuns," n.d., n.p., SHNC.

ity in Bay Shore participated in a study day with other religious at Pius XI Preparatory Seminary in Uniondale, New York, as well as a week-long ecumenical gathering for women religious from fourteen Roman Catholic, ten Anglican, and one Greek Orthodox community. "For one week we were living the religious life together," said Sister Ruth Angela. "It was one of the greatest experiences of our lives."[90]

By the time the sisters celebrated the fiftieth anniversary of the House of the Nativity in 1968, the number of monthly retreats had tripled since the work began. Given increased access to public transportation, the retreat house hosted retreatants from all over the United States, Canada, and beyond. "Drawn to God, the very Core and Center of our life and being concentrating upon His Word; responding with all our heart and soul to His love...." wrote Sister Ruth Angela.[91]

ST. MARY'S RETREAT HOUSE, SANTA BARBARA, CALIFORNIA

The Sisterhood of the Holy Nativity established retreat ministry on the West Coast when they opened St. Mary's Retreat House in Santa Barbara, California. Having been residents in the Diocese of Los Angeles since 1927 at St. Matthias Church, the sisters had active Associates and friends in the region. The dream of an Episcopal retreat house for women on the West Coast was spearheaded by Latitia Merrill, an Associate of the Community of St. Mary, a member of the English Association for the Promotion of Retreats (APR), and the devotional chair for the diocesan Woman's Auxiliary. James L. McLane, rector of St. Matthias Church, the first parish served by the sisterhood in Southern California, took an enthusiastic lead by driving sisters to see properties and by encouraging participation among the people of his parish. He considered retreat work an opportunity to enrich the interior spiritual lives of people in his parish and the diocese. "We first went into the Chapel with the Holy Cross fathers for devotions before the Blessed Sacrament and to give thanks for the fulfillment of this dream," he wrote his parish.[92]

---

90. Bosco, "Anglican Nuns," n.d., n.p., SHNC

91. [Sister Ruth Angela, SHN], "House of the Holy Nativity Celebrates Golden Jubilee," 5.

92. McLane, Service Leaflet, St. Matthias Church, Los Angeles, California, July 11, 1954, SHNC.

St. Mary's Retreat House in Santa Barbara was, at its founding in 1954, the first Episcopal retreat house for women in the Southwest.[93] The first prior of Mt. Calvary Retreat House for men in Santa Barbara, Karl Tiedemann (1890–1968) of the Order of the Holy Cross, a friend of the Sisterhood of the Holy Nativity, and Francis Eric Bloy (1904–1993), bishop of the Episcopal Diocese of Los Angeles, supported the project and agreed that the retreat house should be in Santa Barbara so that priests from the Order of the Holy Cross would be available. Mt. Calvary Retreat Center had been in operation for five years, and thus, Tiedemann was well-connected in the area. He found donors interested in the project and served as the first chaplain for St. Mary's Retreat House. Tiedemann recognized the value of the sisters and encouraged collaboration between them and the Order of the Holy Cross rather than presuming he was to give oversight. "In these days of the emancipation of women and the growth of women's work, it is only right and fitting that Sisters should give retreats and say prayers as well as priests."[94] Initially, the Community of St. Mary was invited to run the retreat house but turned down the opportunity as they were already over-extended. The Sisterhood of the Holy Nativity was then offered the project. "It was a venture of faith, for there did not seem to be Sisters enough available to open another House," wrote Sister Patricia, Sister-in-Charge, but the sisterhood decided to move forward. She opened the retreat house in Santa Barbara with Sister Helen. "There was no endowment, no certainty as to financial support. In the years since, the Sisters have often repeated, 'God must have meant the House to be because He has blessed it so.'"[95]

The property chosen for St. Mary's Retreat House previously belonged to the Hazard family. Rowland Hazard II and Margaret Hazard, originally from Rhode Island, were vacationing in Santa Barbara and purchased land adjacent to the historic Old Mission with views of the Pacific Ocean and the Channel Islands. The property was known for its incredible beauty, with the Pacific Ocean to the south and views of the mountains across Mission Creek Canyon to the north.[96] Known as "Mission Hill," the Hazards built a house on the five-acre site and leased the adjacent property from the Franciscans in 1885. In 1916, they built the Dial House, named after the sundial, mounted on a section of the lower wall in the gardens. Mission Hill became St. Joseph's, the sister's house, with an office, kitchen, and refectories for both sisters and guests. The Dial House became St. Mary's Retreat House.

93. "Episcopal Women Plan Silver Tea to Aid Sisters," D-7, SHNC.
94. Tiedemann, OHC, "Double Barreled," 153.
95. Sister Patricia, SHN, "St. Mary's Retreat House in Santa Barbara," 32.
96. "Lux Dei Vitae Viam Monstrat Sed Umbra Horam Atque Fidem Docet," SHNC.

The Hazards' adult children, Caroline Hazard, and Rowland Gibson Hazard II, continued the family's philanthropic commitments. Caroline Hazard was the president of Wellesley College from 1899 to 1910 and spent her summers on the property. A nephew, Rowland Hazard III, was a leader in the nascent Alcoholics Anonymous Movement (AA) and held meetings in the Dial House living room. The sisterhood added devotional beauty to the grounds with sculpture, an outdoor altar, and the Stations of the Cross.[97]

With the opening of St. Mary's Retreat House scheduled for July 1954, the work of making it ready for guests began in earnest. The original plan was to host fifteen women. "As a retreat house, it will provide a place where women may come for retreat, or for rest and spiritual refreshment in the quiet atmosphere of a religious house.... It is the sisters' intent to always be ready to help with the planning of a private retreat or to give instruction in such subjects as prayer, the Church or the sacraments," read the first news release.[98] The Associates ensured the house was renovated and supplied. Associates Esther P. Fullenwider and Harry Thompson addressed the interior decorating. Karl Tiedemann procured donations of furniture and arranged for dedicated amateur painters. The Hazard family donated the china and silver. Sister Patricia provided oversight and ensured the guestrooms were "simple, friendly, not secular."[99] A graduate of Downer College in Wisconsin, Sister Patricia was the daughter of a Supreme Court judge and worked as a parish secretary before entering religious life in her twenties. She served the sisterhood as the Novice Mistress, was an accomplished writer and speaker, and was an adept administrator. Sister Helen, who worked alongside Sister Patricia to open St. Mary's Retreat House, was an artist and art teacher before she entered the sisterhood. During the 1920s, when she lived at the mission house in New York City, Sister Helen met weekly with students at Columbia University and other schools in the city. The chapel at St. Mary's Retreat House was designed by Sister Helen's brother, architect Thornton M. Carson of Alhambra, California.[100]

By August 1954, one month after the opening of the retreat house, the sisters had hosted two retreats for Associates, known then as "the Pioneers,"

---

97. Sister Patricia, SHN, "St. Mary's Retreat House in Santa Barbara," 32–33; Keith, "Some Facts about the Property behind Santa Barbara Mission now Occupied by the Sisterhood of the Holy Nativity," n.d., SHNC.

98. "Dial House, Mission Hill to Be Episcopal Retreat," *Santa Barbara News Press* (February 5, 1953) n.p., SHNC.

99. Sister Patricia, SHN, "St. Mary's Retreat House in Santa Barbara," 32–33; [Sister Julia Elizabeth,] "A Brief Historical Sketch for Our Centennial," 3. SHNC.

100. Jean Storke Menzies, "Anglican Sisters' Chapel Dedication to be September 8," SHNC.

amid ongoing renovations. St. Mary's Retreat Center had the added advantage of cook Carolyn Davis, known for her many friends, imaginative food preparation, and dedication to the house. (In contrast, the House of the Nativity in Bay Shore once employed sixteen cooks in one year!) Davis considered cooking as her service to God, and it was considered an integral part of the hospitality of the retreat house.[101]

Bishop Bloy formally dedicated St. Mary's Retreat Center in Santa Barbara on the Feast of the Nativity of the Blessed Virgin Mary, September 8, 1954. Mother Ruth Mary arrived from Fond du Lac for the widely publicized event. Included in the procession were nine sisters of the Sisterhood of the Holy Nativity, three sisters from the Community of St. Mary, two sisters of the Society of the Transfiguration, Karl Tiedemann, OHC, Kenneth Abbott Viall, SSJE, the suffragan bishop of Tokyo, and over 200 guests.[102] "St. Mary's Retreat House belongs not alone to California but to the entire Community, and the prayers of each Associate are needed in support of this venture of Faith," wrote Esther P. Fullenwider, the secretary general of the Associates.[103] Local clergy welcomed the sisters. "St. Mary's Retreat House and Mount Calvary Monastery make Santa Barbara *the* center on the Pacific Coast for the Church's Retreat Movement, announced the rector of Trinity Church, Santa Barbara."[104]

As was the custom of the Sisterhood of the Holy Nativity, the retreat house charged no fixed fees. Instead, the sisters accepted voluntary donations from retreatants based on their ability to pay. By 1963, more than 4500 individual retreats were made by women at St. Mary's Retreat House, but finances were still tight. The Los Angeles branch of the Associates of the Sisterhood of the Holy Nativity became the largest branch in the country. They became concerned that too much of the sisters' time was spent making ends meet. Therefore, the Associates began raising an endowment to cover costs, building maintenance, and to provide an emergency fund.[105]

Following the pattern of the sisterhood's houses, an appropriate liturgical space to anchor the spiritual life of the retreat house was a priority.

---

101. Sister Patricia, SHN, "St. Mary's Retreat House in Santa Barbara," 33.

102. "New Retreat House Opens for Women," 8, SHNC; Leaflet, "Dedication of St. Mary's Retreat House in Santa Barbara, California on the Feast of the Nativity of the Blessed Virgin Mary, September 8, 1954, SHNC.

103. Letter from Esther P. Fullerwider to the Associates of the Sisterhood of the Holy Nativity," September 15, 1954, SHNC.

104. Annual Report of Trinity Church, Santa Barbara. The Rector's Report. January 1955, SHNC.

105. "Associates Launch Fund Raising Project to Maintain St. Mary's Retreat House," 10.

The original chapel space, a small portion of the patio portioned for the purpose, quickly proved inadequate. Sister Patricia and the chaplain started a chapel fund. A large donation from Louise Woodruff, who never met the sisters, enabled Bethlehem Chapel to be completed in 1956 and consecrated two years later. An appropriate environment for worship—daily Mass, the divine office, individual prayer—was considered integral to retreat ministry and critical to the spiritual life of the sisters, making Bethlehem Chapel an essential asset.

The retreat pattern at St. Mary's Retreat House was parallel to the schedule of the sisters' other houses. Retreats typically started with vespers on Friday evenings and concluded after Sunday lunch. Guests were invited to all the daily offices but were required to attend vespers and compline. In addition to daily Mass (at 7:15 a.m.), priests from Mount Calvary Monastery were available to hear confessions, conduct retreats, and officiate the Exposition and Benediction of the Blessed Sacrament on Thursday evening. "Appreciation of the Divine Office, of its regularity and rhythm, of the opportunity to pray in the Lord's sacramental Presence has developed beautifully," wrote Sister Patricia.[106]

Although the sisters were initially concerned about how they would publicize St. Mary's Retreat Center, they found that women were eager to come there. By 1965, the retreat house served nearly one thousand retreatants per year, with reservations made a year in advance. "The influence of the House is amazingly far-reaching," wrote Sister Patricia.[107] Women came to the house from California, Oregon, Washington, Alaska, Vancouver, and other locations. One of the primary groups the sisters served were stressed young wives and mothers: "People get so involved in life and do so many things," Sister Patricia said. "We try to help them not be so busy, and we try to show them how to pray and how to be silent."[108]

The constituency attracted to St. Mary's Retreat House included retreatants from parishes with varied churchmanship and socio-economic backgrounds, from junior high school-aged young people to great-grandmothers. The sisters found the number of young women interested in retreats encouraging. Although the retreat house did not reach the unchurched per se, it did "deepen, stabilize, and make practical the spiritual life of women of potential influence and leadership to become leaven in their various

---

106. Sister Patricia, SHN, "St. Mary's Retreat House in Santa Barbara," 35, SHNC; Sylvia Brickley, *St. Mary's Retreat House (Anglican)*, Santa Barbara Weekly Bulletin, n.d., 14.

107. Sister Patricia, SHN, "St. Mary's Retreat House in Santa Barbara," 35.

108. Sylvia Brickley, "St. Mary's Retreat House (Anglican)," 14.

parishes."[109] The popularity of the retreat center meant there was little room available for women experiencing a moment of crisis or bereavement. A "vocations" retreat co-sponsored with the Order of the Holy Cross became part of the annual schedule. The sisters also hosted an extended retreat for sisterhoods in the West to cultivate relationships between the Sisterhood of the Holy Nativity, the Community of St. Mary, and the Sisters of the Transfiguration.[110] The proximity between Mount Calvary Monastery and St. Mary's Retreat House also allowed couples to be on retreat simultaneously, if not in the same facility.[111]

The sisters and Associates intentionally provided an orientation for first-time retreatants at St. Mary's Retreat House. As E. L. Hicks presented to her parish:

> Arriving at St. Mary's retreat home in Santa Barbara, I was met by a sister of the house, who showed me to my room, and gave me to read a paper with the order and instructions of the retreat. She waited as I read it. And then pointed to the white Cap on the dresser, which all retreatants wear as guests of this house. A symbol of obedience to the Rule and order of that house . . . . I wondered if I would get lonesome . . . if I would miss at all, those persons and places that made up my life at home . . . . The only reality was His presence . . . Our Lord's presence seemed to fill that room and settle upon me, and envelop me in His peace.[112]

For the Sisterhood of the Holy Nativity, St. Mary's Retreat House was an opportunity to gain Associates in the West and grow their mission "to teach the Catholic Faith, to help spread its practical, livable influence."[113] Anglican Benedictine Dom Francis Hilary Bacon, OSB (1903–1967), a Chaplain-General of the Sisterhood of the Holy Nativity, and one of the founders of St. Gregory's Priory at Three Rivers, Michigan, visited the retreat house to care for the spiritual needs of the sisters. Active in the Movement for Christian Unity, Bacon preached widely on the topic. The sisters in Santa Barbara participated in ecumenical events, such as the "Mass for Christian Unity" sponsored by the Order of the Holy Cross at Trinity Episcopal Church in Santa Barbara. A guitar Mass, followed by supper, was geared toward college and university students.[114]

109. Menzies, "Marriage Counsel Services Vital," A06, SHNC.
110. Sister Patricia, SHN, "St. Mary's Retreat House in Santa Barbara," 35.
111. Tiedemann, "Double-Barreled," 153–54.
112. Hicks, "What is a Retreat," (Given in Our Prayer Group) n.d. [ca. 1965], SHNC.
113. Sister Patricia, SHN, "St. Mary's Retreat House in Santa Barbara," 35.
114. O'Brien, "Anglican Benedictine Monk Makes First Visitation to Retreat," n.p; "A 'Mass For Christian Unity,'" *Santa Barbara News-Press*, n.d., SHNC.

As the Sisterhood of the Holy Nativity became better known throughout the West, the sisters' work expanded, though they emphasized the retreat house. Four or five resident sisters visited parishes, nursing homes, hospitals, and Episcopal dioceses in California and the region while maintaining a rigorous retreat schedule. Both sisters and clergy conducted retreats. A Twelve-Step Retreat and a retreat for charismatic Christians were added to the schedule. Even the sisters' feline friends became known throughout Santa Barbara, particularly Elizabeth, who arrived at the retreat house and promptly delivered a litter of kittens. The Associated Press wire service picked up the story, and all the kittens found homes except for one who moved East with one of the sisters. Brother Bernard, the sisters' dog, was the sole male resident of the retreat house. The tradition of feline excellence was continued when Pansy won fourth place among seventy household cats at the Fiesta City Cat Club Show in Santa Barbara. The house menagerie grew to include cats Punkin, Misty, Charlie, Thomas, and Joseph, the amazing blind dog.[115] Sister Patricia moved back to the Convent in Fond du Lac shortly before her death at ninety-one. She lived to see the twenty-fifth anniversary of St. Mary's Retreat House in 1979; the other founder of the retreat house, Sister Helen, died at the age of ninety-two in 1976.

St. Mary's Retreat Center was the last house outside of Wisconsin owned by the Sisterhood of the Holy Nativity. Like many other retreat houses owned by religious orders, challenges due to the declining number of sisters available impacted the work. Conflict developed over balancing the retreat house's workload and the needs of local churches and the community. But the closure of St. Mary's Retreat House did not stop the retreat tradition of the Sisterhood of the Holy Nativity. The sisterhood's "soul work" tradition continued in Wisconsin at the Convent in Fond du Lac and later at Bethlehem-by-the-Lake through 2013. The history of the Sisterhood of the Holy Nativity is intertwined with the history of the retreat movement in Anglicanism and the Episcopal Church. The "soul work" of the Sisterhood advanced the catholic faith and enriched the spiritual lives of thousands of people, including the faithful Associates. This legacy is alive today, nourished through the rich spiritual tradition of the Sisterhood of Holy Nativity over its long history.

---

115. "Brother Bernard Will Reign Again," n.p., SHNC.

6

Navigating Change
Hoping for Renewal

As the twentieth century progressed, many Episcopal religious orders, including the Sisterhood of the Holy Nativity, faced decisions to close long-standing ministries due to the unavailability of sisters and the realities of aging communities. From 1910 to 1960, the average number of sisters in the Sisterhood of the Holy Nativity was 51. But from 1960–1980, the average number of sisters dropped to 40. Over the same twenty-year period, the sisterhood experienced the most significant number of deaths; twelve sisters died between 1960 and 1969, and thirteen between 1970–1979. During the 1970s, the Sisterhood of the Holy Nativity admitted a record number of aspirants and novices, but very few of those women remained through life profession. Between 1970 and 1980, there were 28 sisters in the community; a decade later, in 1980 and 1990, there were 16 sisters. By 1990–2000, the number of sisters decreased to 13, and from 2000–2010, to 10. Between 2010 and today, the sisterhood decreased from 8 to 2 sisters.[1]

As early as the 1940s, when the Sisterhood of the Holy Nativity had its highest number of sisters (55–56), they recognized that the community was aging and that growth was necessary if the sisterhood was to staff existing

---

1. Statistics derived from life professed sisters and do not include novices, those in their junior vows, or life professed sisters who left the sisterhood. Though sisters who were not life professed undoubtedly contributed to the work of the sisterhood, as did those who left, the stability of the mission houses was calculated on the life professed. In contrast, Anglican sisterhoods in the UK began to decline during World War I (1914–1918), see Dunstan, "The Revival of the Religious Life," 9.

mission houses and potential new ministries successfully.[2] Mother Foundress Ruth Margaret originally conceived the system of mission houses as agile and responsive to shifts in the sisterhood and local needs. Discernment about the number of ministries the sisterhood undertook was an ongoing reality. The "mixed life" of the sisterhood always combined the active and contemplative life and sometimes made course corrections when situations warranted. For example, soon after the Sisterhood of the Holy Nativity moved to Providence, two sisters agreed to a trial ministry working in an orphanage. But after two years, it was discerned that the work involved was out of balance with the Rule of the sisterhood. The mission houses in Kingston (1905) and Portland, Maine (1923) were closed after local financial support dissipated. The closure in West Orange (1925) was made, despite the significant needs there, because the curate devalued the sisters, and they had organized another retreat house in the region. These strategic closures were made when the number of sisters was substantial. Requests for sisters to open new mission houses or reopen closed ones continued to arrive at the Convent and were discerned by the sisterhood at each Council meeting.[3]

In the early 1940s, two short-term mission houses were closed. The first, in Portland, Oregon, shut in 1941; after two years, the parish could no longer support the mission house financially. The mission in the Missionary District of Nevada continued for eight years (1940–1948) but was largely dependent on external missionary funding and was unlikely to contribute to future vocations. The mission house in Newport closed in 1953 to consolidate the sisters in Rhode Island into one location. In the 1960s, the Sisterhood made wrenching decisions to close four long-standing mission houses: Milwaukee and Philadelphia closed in 1962, and Baltimore and New York City in 1966. Mother Alicia Theresa and the Council argued that there were insufficient sisters to staff the houses adequately because fewer women joined the sisterhood, and the remaining sisters were aging.[4]

The closures fueled anxieties about the survival of the Sisterhood of the Holy Nativity, aggravated by tensions regarding the mandate of the Rule for "missionary spirit" and the belief that without vibrant ministries, new vocations would not be attracted to the sisterhood. A direct result of the closure of mission houses was that the sisters were less visible in parishes, an essential source for new vocations. In some parishes, the Sisterhood of the

2. The most professed sisters in the sisterhood were 56 (1930–1949). See U.S. Census 1940 and 1950. These numbers include the life professed sisters only, not novices or those in junior vows.

3. Acts of the Council, 1957–2004, 1961, 1962, 1963, 1964, 1965, 1967, 1968, 1969, and following, SHNC.

4. Acts of the Council, 1957–2004, 91–92, SHNC.

Holy Nativity was visible in the sacristy, church school, guilds, and outreach ministries for decades. Once they began to withdraw from parish mission houses, the vocation of the sisterhood was no longer visible. "If we are not going to accept some new challenges on faith," said one sister who eventually left the sisterhood, "we will contribute to losing vocations and creating discontent within the community."[5] In this instance, the Council rejected Grace Church's (Newark) request to continue a ministry formerly staffed by the Society of St. Margaret and another offer to start a mission house in Guatemala.[6]

During the closures, sisters who favored renewing the sisterhood's missionary spirit urged moving to new locations rather than returning to previous sites. "It is better for SHN to go to new places now," argued Sister Margaretta. "The days of St. Mary the Virgin and the High Church parish are over."[7] Seattle, San Francisco, Hollywood, and Phoenix were "lively possibilities" for short-term missions staffed by two sisters. Still, these and many other options were not confirmed as none came with viable financial plans. The financial infrastructures that had made the sisterhood's late nineteenth and early twentieth-century missionary expansion possible were no longer available. While the requests from dioceses and parishes for sisters were ongoing, few offered financial assistance. The already consolidated ministries in Los Angeles and San Diego were closed in 1974. Though these closures were traumatic for the sisterhood and the parishes involved, the legacies of the sisterhood remain. Volunteers staffed Sister Isabel's gift shop in San Diego until the 1980s. The sisters returned periodically to San Diego to offer quiet days and retreats for over a decade after the closure. "It was reported, and believed in the parish, that their prayers had healing power."[8] One of the most visible legacies that remains of the Sisterhood of the Holy Nativity's mission houses is Sister Ruth Vera's artwork of St. Clement's Church, Philadelphia. Her drawings are still published in the parish's Ordo Kalendar.[9]

---

5. Acts of the Council, 1957–2004, 1968, 105, SHNC.
6. Acts of the Council, 1957–2004, 1968, 105, SHNC.
7. Acts of the Council, 1957–2004, 1976, 1977, 115–17, SHNC.
8. Cox, *Changing and Remaining*, 107–113, 189, 297; Acts of the Council, 1974, 110, SHNC.
9. Saint Clement's Church Ordo Kalendar," 2021.

CHANGES IN THE TWENTIETH-CENTURY EPISCOPAL CHURCH

In the early twentieth century, institutional support for women's ministries in the Episcopal Church grew. National suffrage passed in 1920 in the United States, and women were increasingly visible in the professions. The Sisterhood of the Holy Nativity, along with other sisterhoods, deaconesses, women missionaries, and the leaders of national women's organizations, were part of a movement that, from 1850–1920, demonstrated their commitment and administrative acumen through mission, education, and service. Though many expected the General Convention in 1919 to give women full membership rights in the Church, the reverse happened; women were given neither voice nor vote. Women's right to participate in church governance was again before the General Convention in 1943. Although women were elected from their dioceses in 1946 and 1949, they were not formally seated as deputies in the General Convention until 1970. In that same year, the ordination of women to the diaconate was officially approved; ordination to the priesthood was approved in 1976, two years after the first eleven women (the Philadelphia 11) were ordained. The latter half of the twentieth century also included women's formal entry into the Church's seminaries, giving them access to theological education training schools for deaconesses and women workers. [10]

While some Episcopalians rejoiced in women's ordination, others did not. Increasing numbers of women seeking ordained vocations further eclipsed the ministries of lay women, many of whom already faced marginalization in the Church. "There were few of my church worker colleagues who wished to be ordained, once it became possible, not because they didn't approve of women priests, but because we felt secure in our own vocation as theologically educated lay professionals," wrote one lay women church worker. "What we found offensive was the complete lack of respect for our own work and vocation on the part of women who sought ordination and were committed to their vocations as ordained ministers. Moreover, once ordination was available for women, most of us were no longer able to work in the church. The church's clericalism saw to that."[11]

For Episcopal sisterhoods, where the number of women seeking religious life was already declining, the ordination of women brought challenges, including questions about whether a particular sisterhood would admit deacons or priests or allow sisters to be ordained. Sister Ellen Stephen of the

---

10. Fredrica Harris Thompsett, 'Introduction,' 7.
11. Morgan, "Women's ordination: not all consequences were positive," n.p.

Order of St. Helena, who worked with the Sisterhood of the Holy Nativity in the 1980s-1990s, described religious life as "the road less traveled." Lay people typically divide their lives into three areas: faith, home, and work, emphasizing one of these. But in the religious life, faith, relational status, and work are all united in one commitment. "This makes for a very intense lifestyle," Sister Ellen wrote.[12]

In 1977, the Order of St. Helena was the first Episcopal sisterhood to ordain a sister to the priesthood. The transition was challenging. Some sisters in the community were opposed to women's ordination and, thus, felt they could not participate if a sister priest presided at the community Eucharist. The sisters who approved of women's ordination did not want to exclude the other sisters but were challenged by the suggestion that only an outside (male) priest should preside during community worship. The solution the Order of St. Helena enacted was a compromise whereby no sister was wholly satisfied or wholly ignored.[13]

Similar challenges with women's ordination surfaced in the Sisterhood of the Holy Nativity, exacerbated by having houses in dioceses with different perspectives. The Diocese of Fond du Lac, where the Convent was located, did not ordain women to the priesthood until 2002. However, St. Mary's Retreat House in Santa Barbara was directly related to the dioceses of Los Angeles and San Diego, which had growing numbers of women clergy. Some in the Sisterhood of the Holy Nativity were vociferously opposed to the ordination of women, some preferred silence on the issue, some sisters approved, and a few quietly nursed a call to ordination in the hope the community would eventually be open to the possibility in the future.[14]

Another significant theme in Episcopal Church history during the mid-twentieth century included revising the *Book of Common Prayer*. For Episcopalians, an outcome of the mid-twentieth-century Liturgical Movement included the approval of a new edition of the *Book of Common Prayer* in 1979. The 1979 prayer book was a substantial revision and modernization of the 1928 version. In a tradition like the Episcopal Church, where identity is so closely tied to worship, changes in the liturgy elicited volatile reactions despite the lengthy decades-long planning process. Many traditionalists, both Anglo-Catholics and evangelicals, felt alienated by changes in language and ritual to the extent that in 2000, the General Convention formally apologized to those offended during the transition to the 1979

---

12. Ellen Stephen, "Apart and Together," 16.
13. Ellen Stephen, "Apart and Together," 19.
14. The opinions of individual sisters on women's ordination are based on data found in correspondence or interviews from the time in question.

Book of Common Prayer.[15] Though opposition to the new prayer book was less pronounced in the Sisterhood of the Holy Nativity than the ordination of women to the priesthood, the resulting liturgical changes caused conflicts among the Associates and friends that contributed to the ferment of the era.[16]

There were differences in opinion among the sisters in the Sisterhood of the Holy Nativity about how to respond to the changes in the Episcopal Church in the mid-twentieth century. For some, the response was isolation from the larger church or feelings of anger because they believed the changes made the catholic faith unrecognizable. Others believed the sisterhood needed to be more visible and effectively articulate its mission within the larger Church. "I am very concerned about our involvement (or lack of it) in the total life of the Church," wrote one sister to the bishop of Fond du Lac in 1966. "We seem to blame the Church for not understanding us, But I think we share a large portion of the guilt. So often we say that the Church has nothing to say about certain aspects of our life—as if we have any life without the Church!"[17]

By the 1970s, the challenges that beset many sisterhoods made continuing the retreat house at Bay Shore untenable for the Sisterhood of the Holy Nativity. The cost of maintaining an aging twenty-four-room building with more than seven acres of land and a cottage grew steadily. Fewer sisters were available to staff the retreat house, which added to the financial issue of providing adequate salaries for an increasing number of lay employees. The sisterhood eventually discerned that their primary mission was advancing the catholic faith, not maintaining properties, so reluctantly, the retreat house was closed in 1980. The "soul work" of House of the Holy Nativity was carried forward by the many Associates, laity, and clergy who continued the rich spiritual tradition by offering retreats and quiet days in thanksgiving for the generations of sisters who served there.[18] "The number of souls reached and helped over the years is countless. Those who have made a spiritual pilgrimage or quiet retreat know what deep meaning it has had for them."[19]

15. 2000 General Convention of the Episcopal Church. "Resolution 2000-B034: Apologize to Those Offended During Transition to the 1979 Prayer Book". *Acts of Convention*.

16. For an overview, see Sumner, "Episcopal History From 1940–1980: A Brief Chronology," 83–87.

17. Correspondence, Sister Mariana, SHN, to the Rt. Rev. William Brady, March 13, 1966, SHNC.

18. "House of the Holy Nativity Forced to Close in September," n.p. SHNC.

19. [Sister Julia Elizabeth, SHN] "The First Retreat House in The American Church," 31, SHNC.

The Sisterhood of the Holy Nativity remained in Providence until 1983 when conflicts with St. Stephen's rector precipitated the mission house's closing. The declining number of sisters and financial pressures also factored into the decision. "The religious life today is not exempt from undergoing many changes and is being challenged to meet the needs of those seeking Community living," wrote one sister for the diocesan newspaper, *The Churchman*. "New structures for the Conventual life are taking place in both the Roman Catholic and Anglican Churches and we pray that we can meet these challenges."[20]

The Oneida mission was the only location where the Sisterhood of the Holy Nativity returned long-term after they discontinued their ministry there. The sisterhood's work was closed in 1946 and continued by the Order of St. Anne and, thereafter, the Order of the Teachers of the Children of God. The Sisterhood of the Holy Nativity returned to the Church of the Holy Apostles at Oneida to teach in the church school from 1967 through the 1970s. The legacy of the sisterhood is part of the fabric of the Church of the Holy Apostles, considered the "Grandmother Church" of the Diocese of Fond du Lac today. With the resurgence of activism among Indigenous peoples in the 1960s, the Episcopal Church began to confront its complicity with colonialism and cultural genocide. Taking accountability for the long-term impact colonialism and cultural genocide have had on Indigenous peoples remains a central issue within global Anglicanism.[21] Recent headlines illustrating the appalling history of the residential school system suggest any history between Indigenous peoples and the Episcopal Church must reassess the narratives of those encounters. In 2019, Oneida tribal leaders and members of the Episcopal Church collaborated with the Army to repatriate the remains of three Oneida girls who died at residential schools.[22] Two years later, the Episcopal Church released a statement pledging to investigate "how this history has harmed the families of many Indigenous Episcopalians," and to commit to the work of truth and reconciliation.[23]

Although records are scattered and incomplete, most major Christian denominations obtained government funding to operate Indigenous

20. Sisterhood of the Holy Nativity, a draft for the *Rhode Island Churchman*, [ca. 1957], SHNC.

21. Woods, *A Cultural Sociology of Anglican Mission and the Indian Residential Schools in Canada*, 1–3.

22. Hauptman and McLester, *The Oneida Indians in the Age of Allotment, 1860–1920*, 48–55.

23. "Statement on Indigenous boarding Schools by Presiding Bishop Michael Curry and President of the House of Deputies Gay Clark Jennings," July 12, 2021, Office of Public Affairs, The Episcopal Church.

boarding schools, at least nine of which were operated by the Episcopal Church.[24] In the case of the Oneida, the Diocese of Fond du Lac did not own the residential school. The clergy missionaries and the Sisterhood of the Holy Nativity welcomed the residential school students to the church and mission house for religious instruction, medical care, recreation, and hospitality. Recent studies of the relationship between the Oneida and the Episcopal Church, which includes the contributions of the Sisterhood of the Holy Nativity, stress that the Indigenous peoples and the white missionaries both adapted through centuries of contact, resulting in a cooperative, syncretized, and unique religious tradition.[25] During their years at Oneida, the Sisterhood of the Holy Nativity supported the lace-making, beadwork, and basketry industries. The lace-making tradition at Oneida is considered an essential artifact in their material history. One of the finest examples of Oneida lace is a twenty-five-piece altar set, including superfrontal, credence covers, and chalice veil, preserved at the Cathedral of St. John the Divine in New York City.[26] Efforts to revive the lace-making industry among the Oneida date as recently as 2010.[27] These efforts include a weekly women's crafts group that does lacework, beadwork, and basketry.[28]

In addition to the Sisterhood of the Holy Nativity's work through mission houses and retreat centers, there were innovative contributions to the ecclesiastical arts. The sisterhood continued the tradition of ecclesiastical embroidery as late as 1988; vestments created by the sisters are preserved in collections today. The ecclesiastical embroidery made by the Sisterhood of the Holy Nativity and other sisterhoods paved the way for the renewal of the art form by the current generation of Anglican embroiderers.[29]

Before quality theological books were widely available, the Sisterhood of the Holy Nativity discerned the need for quality theological resources to advance the catholic faith among those who did not otherwise have access to printed resources. The Margaret Peabody Lending Library was closed in 1988—104 years after its inception. Books and pamphlets were distributed freely or at cost through the lending library and later through the Parish Press of the Cathedral Church of St. Paul in Fond du Lac. After the 1970s, researchers looking for archival materials in church history, the history of

24. Petersen, "Council Focuses on Indigenous Boarding Schools," 5.
25. Interview, Roger Patience, December 2, 2021; McLester et al., *The Wisconsin Oneidas and the Episcopal Church*.
26. McLester III and Hauptman, eds. *A Nation within A Nation*, 4–5, 81–82.
27. McLester III and Hauptman, eds. *A Nation within A Nation*, 76–78; 81–82.
28. McLester et al., *The Wisconsin Oneidas and the Episcopal Church*, 54, 161,
29. Huntley, "Stitching the Sacred," 7–11, 28–29.

liturgy, and the Oxford Movement referred to the collection. The remaining materials were donated to Nashotah House. The Margaret Peabody Lending Library met a unique need until inexpensive theological materials became widely available. The Parish Press was founded at St. Paul's Cathedral in Fond du Lac in the 1920s by the clergy and the Sisterhood of the Holy Nativity to advance the catholic faith and "to plant and expand the principles of the Offord Movement." They produced tracts, framed cards for the altar, the sacristy, the narthex of churches, and other devotional materials. Though the Cathedral sold the press in the 1990s, the Parish Press continues to recognize the Sisterhood of the Holy Nativity as part of its legacy.[30]

ST. MARY'S RETREAT HOUSE, SANTA BARBARA

St. Mary's Retreat Center was the last house outside of Wisconsin owned by the Sisterhood of the Holy Nativity. The 1990s through the early 2000s at St. Mary's Retreat House in Santa Barbara were marked by creativity and challenges. Like many other retreat houses owned by religious orders, the declining number of sisters available impacted the work. Conflicts developed between the sisters over balancing the retreat house's domestic workload and opportunities for ministry in local churches and the wider community.

Though the Santa Barbara location was attractive to many secular individuals and groups, the sisters consistently emphasized the spiritual purpose of the retreat house. "We are not a hotel. [One's visit] must be a retreat for the spirit," said Sister Kathleen Marie, one of the two African American sisters in the Sisterhood of the Holy Nativity, appointed Sister-in-Charge in Santa Barbara in 1993.[31] Although the Episcopal Church first ordained women to the priesthood in 1974, twenty years later, the Sisterhood of the Holy Nativity did not allow ordained women to celebrate the Holy Eucharist in Bethlehem Chapel. The policy caused friction between the sisterhood and the Diocese of Los Angeles and the Diocese of San Diego, limiting the groups who would hold retreats there. While the decision banning women celebrants in the chapel was overturned in 2000, the earlier policy had repercussions for the reputation of the retreat center among the groups it served on both sides of the issue.

The Sisterhood of the Holy Nativity made significant efforts to connect with the greater Santa Barbara community to interest more local women in the retreat house, including groups not traditionally served by the ministry.

30. Interview, Keith Ackerman, December 1, 2021;https://theparishpress.com.

31. Kuryla, Of Peace and Prayer. Gracious Santa Barbara Retreat Houses Are Oases for Contemplation, Growth," 5, SHNC.

One of the sisters taught a program on mysticism, "A Journey Toward the Deeper Love of God," focusing on a different mystical tradition each session.[32] Another sister facilitated outreach in the Latinx community by working with the Hispanic Ministries Team of All Saints Episcopal Church in Oxnard, California, attending Sunday services, making home visits, and collaborating with the Episcopal Diocese of Los Angeles. Members of the Latinx community were invited to the retreat house, and initial plans for Spanish-language retreats were in process before the work was halted. The Sisterhood of the Holy Nativity was also active in the renewal movement, Cursillo. A friend of the sisterhood, Liberian priest John Kpoto, a former member of the Order of the Holy Cross, served the retreat house as a landscape gardener and said Mass in the chapel at least once weekly. His social witness connected the sisterhood to the homeless community. Distrusting social institutions, Kpoto eventually lived among the homeless community while continuing in active ministry until he died in 2020.[33]

St. Mary's Retreat House became a primary focus of the Sisterhood of the Holy Nativity as a source of potential vocations and an active ministry site. In 1999–2000, the sisters there met intensively with a Roman Catholic sister and psychologist for "family therapy" and spiritual direction to ease tensions and grow community spirit. Like the situation in the Fond du Lac Convent, there were generational differences among the sisters regarding communication styles and the vision for the sisterhood's ministry in the present and the future. Other sisterhoods faced similar challenges. The generation gap placed considerable responsibility on the shoulders of younger women, some of whom were still in formation, leaving comparatively little time for the generative ministries that motivated them to enter religious life. There were also tensions in leadership styles, with some sisters favoring a more collaborative, less hierarchical approach to decision-making. In contrast, other sisters were comfortable with the hierarchical leadership style prevalent when they entered religious life. During the years that St. Mary's Retreat Center housed the sisterhood's novitiate, it was at the center of the struggles women new to the sisterhood experienced as they arrived to discern their vocations. The unfortunate result was that most left the sisterhood, including some professed members considered future leaders. Despite struggling with internal strife during tremendous change and uncertainty, the Sisterhood of the Holy Nativity hosted over 1000 retreatants

---

32. Kuryla,, Of Peace and Prayer. Gracious Santa Barbara Retreat Houses Are Oases for Contemplation, Growth," 5, SHNC.

33. The Reverend John Kpoto - Episcopal Diocese of Los Angeles (diocesela.org).

annually at St. Mary's Retreat Center, including thirty-nine group and ninety-six individual retreats.[34]

The last major events in the history of St. Mary's Retreat Center reveal the profound generosity of the Sisterhood of the Holy Nativity to Associates, retreatants, and other religious orders, even as concerns for the future of their community escalated. In 2003, when three Roman Catholic Sisters of Bethany were evicted from their home by the Archdiocese of Los Angeles so the funds could be used for abuse payouts, the Sisterhood of the Holy Nativity offered them a place of privacy and peace for as long as they needed. This hospitality gave the Roman Catholic sisters, based in Guatemala, time to organize a more permanent home. Sister Abigail, then Sister-in-Charge at St. Mary's Retreat House, responded, "They are my sisters," and hoped that the media would not intrude on the retreat house.[35] A similar act of generosity occurred after the 2008 Montecito Tea Fire when Mount Calvary Monastery of the Order of the Holy Cross burned to the ground. The Sisterhood of the Holy Nativity did not hesitate to invite their brothers, who so actively supported them, to live at St. Mary's Retreat House and continue retreats there.

In 2013, as the sisterhood grew unable to continue running St. Mary's Retreat House, they decided to deed the property to the Order of the Holy Cross. The brothers there continued to use the property as a monastery and retreat house until they, too, were called to consolidate their brothers at the monastery in West Park, New York, thus ending seventy years of service to the Diocese of Los Angeles.[36] The closure of St. Mary's Retreat House did not end the Sisterhood of the Holy Nativity's commitment to the retreat tradition. The sisterhood's "soul work" continued at Green Lake in Wisconsin for as long as the sisters remained in residence. It persists today, alive in all the individuals and parishes nourished through the work, generosity, and spiritual enrichment the Sisterhood of Holy Nativity provided over its history.

In 2014, the Sisterhood of the Holy Nativity generosity contributed funds toward purchasing an eighteenth-century house near Emery House, the rural monastery of the Society of St. John the Evangelist in West Newbury, Massachusetts. The house was named Grafton House after Charles Grafton, and its chapel, the Chapel of the Holy Nativity, in honor of the Sisterhood of the Holy Nativity and the shared history between the two

34. Session Reports, Suzanne Dunn and SHN, Sessions 1–14, 1997–1999. St, Mary's Retreat House, Annual Report, 1999–2000, SHNC.

35. "Sisters Helping Sisters," 6; Trounson, "Nuns facing eviction get help," n.p.

36. Kawamoto, "Order of the Holy Cross will close monastery and retreat center in Santa Barbara, Calif," www.episcopalnewsservice,org; Interview, Scott Borden, OHC, October 8, 2021.

communities. Grafton House has been used as the site for the Society of St. John the Evangelist's monastic internship program. In this way, the legacy of the Sisterhood of the Holy Nativity lives on in the formation of those who participate in the monastic internship program.[37]

MISSION IN WEST VIRGINIA

The last mission house of the Sisterhood of the Holy Nativity opened in 2000. The lure of the Diocese of West Virginia caught the imagination of the new superior, Mother Maria. It was considered an opportunity for renewal after other missions were closed. Still, the size and average age of the sisterhood made it more practical to commit to shorter-term missions rather than administer a network of mission houses. In 1996, Lada Hardwick, a priest and missioner in the Greenbriar Cluster in West Virginia, shared her dream of having the sisters work with her. A possible church site at White Sulfur Springs was identified but proved too costly to renovate. The following year, John Smith, the bishop of the Diocese of West Virginia, investigated the possibility of locating the sisters on the grounds of Sandscrest, an Episcopal conference and retreat center in Wheeling, West Virginia. There was also an option of having a presence at Peterkin Camp and Conference Center in Romney, West Virginia, and teaching in the diocesan School for Spirituality. The sisters immediately began to discern if God was calling them to the Diocese of West Virginia. Though some sisters stressed the challenge of taking on mission commitments given their diminished numbers, others were hopeful about an opportunity to return to active ministry. After deep discussion, the Sisterhood of the Holy Nativity pursued the opportunity and moved into Emmaus House, a cottage on the Sandscrest property. The house was blessed, and the Blessed Sacrament was reserved in the sisters' oratory in January 2000.[38]

The energy behind the mission house in the Diocese of West Virginia was attractive to the sisters because it reflected the missionary spirit that had characterized the Sisterhood of the Holy Nativity for over one hundred years. It was an opportunity to bring the catholic faith and a contemplative presence to a traditionally Protestant diocese in a region with significant human needs and without affluent resources. Participation in an active and vibrant mission could also attract vocations, as the Diocese of West Virginia had no other sisterhoods at the time. There were also challenges. The

37. Monastic Internship Program, www.ssje.org. Accessed November 10, 2023.

38. [Sister Barbara Jean, SHN,] "Sisterhood of the Holy Nativity. The West Virginia Mission," n.d., SHNC.

Diocese of West Virginia could not fully fund the endeavor; thus, the sisters needed to contribute financially to the mission. Given the few available clergy in the diocese, a daily celebration of the Eucharist at Emmaus House was unlikely. Some sisters had reservations about working with women priests, which was typical in the diocese.[39]

The Sisterhood of the Holy Nativity closed Emmaus House in 2002. Despite energy and intention, the Council determined there were not enough sisters available to give the work the stability the mission required.[40] Younger sisters were leaving the community, and the remaining sisters found it impractical to operate distant mission houses—though ongoing offers for potential ministries continued. The sisterhood continued its "missionary spirit" through shorter-term work—such as Sister Grace's three-year mission at St. Christopher's Church in Anchorage, Alaska. Missionary spirit lives on today through Sister Abigal's and Sister Charis' ministries and the Associates and friends who continue the legacies of the Sisterhood of the Holy Nativity.

HOPE FOR RENEWAL

"Whatever knowledge concerning the future is still withheld from us, we can at least be certain of one thing," wrote Mother Boniface during the centenary of the Sisterhood of the Holy Nativity in 1982, "and that is that our life—both in the context of our baptismal commitment and as individuals, and in our commitment as a Community—can produce its richest fruit only insofar as we are faithful to the Gospel of Christ, and insofar as we correspond with God's grace so that we become channels of His life, love, and hope, to the world."[41] Within this future vision, Mother Boniface anticipated a role for the sisterhood and other religious communities in the twenty-first century. "The twenty-first century will have no use for mediocre Christians and will tolerate no mediocre Religious. Thus, we are thrown back to the very roots of our Community: the primary importance of a deep, all-encompassing love of God, a profound commitment to His cause, and a strong, personal faith in Christ our Lord."[42] Despite the challenges experi-

---

39. [Sister Barbara Jean, SHN,] "Sisterhood of the Holy Nativity. The West Virginia Mission," n.d., SHNC.

40. Acts of the Council, 1957–2004, 2001–2002, 149–51, SHHC.

41. Mother Boniface, "The Sisterhood of the Holy Nativity offers thanks for one hundred years of blessings, 1882–1982." SHNC.

42. Mother Boniface, "The Sisterhood of the Holy Nativity offers thanks for one hundred years of blessings, 1882–1982." SHNC.

enced by the Sisterhood of the Holy Nativity in the twentieth century, they hoped to discern opportunities for renewal without large houses to manage but open to the possibility of short-term missions where they could meet more significant numbers of people.

One of the challenges of renewal for religious orders such as the Sisterhood of the Holy Nativity was the tension between revisioning the charism and customs inherited from the nineteenth century for the twenty-first century while remaining true to their tradition. The Sisterhood of the Holy Nativity was not alone in this endeavor. Almost all Episcopal sisterhoods founded in the nineteenth century inherited the ethos of nineteenth-century English foundations, derived from Roman Catholic congregations on the Continent in the same period. The inheritance from English foundations was "high Victorian, steeped in neo-gothic sensibility and the romantic movement. Yet this was exactly what many in the mid-twentieth century were trying to banish."[43] Reviewing and modifying their formularies and customs for the twenty-first century caused anguish for many of the sisters, and neither those who resisted change nor those who made radical changes were spared the decline.[44] "The habited nuns when seen were viewed as something from a previous generation, while those who had donned ordinary clothes no longer seemed to be distinct from any other social worker."[45] Sister Ellen Stephen, OSH, describes the renewal process for women's religious orders as "finding a voice" or "letting go of inessentials while faithfully keeping the essentials of the life."[46] To continue as a living organism, a sisterhood needs to be committed to ongoing renewal while remaining traditional. "A healthy community perseveres in the discernment of reconfiguring itself to nurture the real needs of its members without losing its essential configuration."[47]

A significant challenge for the Sisterhood of the Holy Nativity was that for a critical mass of the sisters (mostly older sisters but not exclusively so), their experience of a stable, prosperous community was rooted far more in the realities of the nineteenth century than contemporary life. Despite the richness of Anglo-Catholicism, the tradition also developed weaknesses, including a tendency to reinforce clericalism, a rigidly hierarchical view of the Church and society, and a tendency to self-isolate by creating a world within a world.[48] "The Tractarians unconsciously made religion a life sub-

43. Dunstan, "The Revival of the Religious Life," 9.
44. I Dunstan, "The Revival of the Religious Life," 9.
45. Dunstan, "The Revival of the Religious Life," 10.
46. Ellen Stephen, "Apart and Together," 17.
47. Ellen Stephen, "Apart and Together," 23.
48. Leech, "The Radical Anglo-Catholic Social Vision," 7–8.

stitute rather than a life revealer, not a way into the splendors of the visible world but a way out. That habit of mind is fixed in us still, and ultimately it is destructive of religion itself."[49]

Many older sisters entered the community when approximately fifty life professed sisters, along with juniors and novices, were distributed through the Convent and as many as eight mission houses. They valued their well-defined roles amid a clearly defined hierarchy. Much of the work was within established catholic parishes and became routine: sacristy work, religious education, parish visiting, and instruction in the sacraments. The authority of the Mother Superior was absolute. The system provided stability and security if a sister did not cause significant problems, turned up in chapel on time, respected her superiors, and generally did what she was told. However, it did not equip individual sisters with skills in navigating interpersonal relationships, conflict resolution, institutional change, collaborative leadership, or problem-solving. The sisters who entered a vibrant community had difficulty adapting to uncertainty. They felt that renewal had a negative connotation and meant throwing off the old ways without introducing effective solutions, thus causing a vacuum. Within this framework, it was easy for some sisters to develop a fatalistic outlook, expressed through tearing down each other, the sisterhood, and the Church. The emotional toll of living in a religious community with protracted internal tensions was highly costly, personally and spiritually, for all involved.[50]

The community environment needed to be more supportive of sisters who advocated a positive definition of renewal or were still discerning their religious vocations. Some sisters in the Sisterhood of the Holy Nativity were committed to reconfiguring the order for its next iteration. A few sisters of the bridge generation, along with some of the older sisters, some novices and junior professed, were interested in forming the nucleus of a new community. The spirit demonstrated among these sisters was the honest questioning of the sisterhood's roots and purpose, the search for vital future ministries, and creating an environment characterized by love and mutual support. Although there were various degrees of understanding about why sisters who underwent formation in an earlier era resisted renewal, there was no wish to exclude them. For decades, the Sisterhood of the Holy Nativity tried to unite the whole community. Over time, some sisters began to believe that not enough change was occurring to ensure the community's survival. Some sisters felt frustrated, inhibited, uninspired, or thwarted in

---

49. Pitt, "The Oxford Movement: A case of cultural distortion?" 233.

50. This illustration of a faction of the sisterhood is distilled from correspondence between Mother Boniface and Bishop William Louis Stevens, Bishop and Episcopal Visitor, 1985, SHNC; Argulo, "The Unnamed Presence," 16.

their vocations. The need for a more cooperative and participatory form of governance was also characteristic of the renewal agenda. The sisters who advocated for renewal had challenges and shortcomings, but the qualitative difference was their desire to remain in communication. "Renewal is not change, but a chance to take a look at ourselves and our life together," wrote the Renewal Committee to the sisterhood. "This is not pleasant. It requires courage. However, we move forward in a spirit of thanksgiving for the rich spiritual heritage that is ours with a sure and certain hope for the future."[51]

The Sisterhood of the Holy Nativity facilitated several renewal processes starting in the 1960s when reports from the wider church indicated that women interested in religious life were discouraged from considering them. "It was generally accepted that SHN was definitely dying."[52] The inability to resolve the resentments between sisters surfaced as an issue twenty years later in the renewal discussions centered on the centenary anniversary of the sisterhood. The relatively frequent occurrence of sharp speech among community members was the focus of many reports on the morale within the sisterhood amid deep concerns regarding the quality of community life. One chaplain general resigned because he saw the sisterhood as "an aggregation of units, rather than a community."[53] A report from the mid-1970s suggested that although "a tornado had been unleashed in our midst" regarding institutional change, "The ministry of death has been transformed into a ministry of life. There is hope."[54]

One concern among some sisters was the perceived drift of the Sisterhood of the Holy Nativity toward contemplative life, a pattern familiar to religious orders founded with a mixed lifestyle as the membership ages. Some sisters welcomed the possible shift, while others felt the sisterhood was abandoning their missionary heritage. Those in favor of an increased focus on the contemplative life argued that this shift was not about limiting exterior ministries as much as it was about building up the interior life of the community. Like other aspects of renewal, a more contemplative lifestyle for the Sisterhood of the Holy Nativity could only be discerned through the prayers and participation of the whole community. A critical mass of the remaining sisters was unable or unwilling to participate constructively in

---

51. Memo, Renewal Committee, to the SHN, May 15, 1984, SHNC; Argulo, "The Unnamed Presence," 18.
52. Correspondence, Mother Boniface to Bishop Stevens, 1985, SHNC.
53. Correspondence, Mother Boniface to Bishop Stevens, 1985, SHNC.
54. Sister Mariana, SHN, "Sisterhood of the Holy Nativity," n.p.

efforts at group discernment, breaking down renewal efforts, and disillusioning those who supported them.[55]

By the mid-1980s, there was a consensus in the sisterhood that continuing renewal was necessary, or they faced inevitable decline. However, there was deep uncertainty about how the process should resume. "I would hope that the community could relax in the common understanding that 'renewal' no longer has to do with great changes in the religious habit, community worship or the customs and Rule of the community," wrote Bishop Stevens, the Episcopal Visitor for the Sisterhood of the Holy Nativity at the time. "Renewal has more to do with rediscovering and implementing the vision of the founders, or growing in charity toward one another, and of 'dreaming dreams and seeing visions' of what SHN can become in the hands of the Lord who said, 'Behold I make all things new.'"[56]

Additional house meetings whereby sisters could develop healthier communication patterns and tools such as the Myers Briggs Personal Indicator (MBPI) to develop a more profound understanding of personality styles were some of the resources explored by the sisterhood, in addition to psychotherapy, group dynamics, and spiritual direction, to address resistance and unresolved conflicts.[57] The ongoing commitment to renewal led the sisterhood to issue a "Covenant for Rebirth" in May 1997, shortly after the election of Mother Maria as superior. Twelve of the sixteen sisters who signed the covenant remained in the Sisterhood of the Holy Nativity. Mother Maria and the sisterhood shared excitement about the possibility of a new ministry in West Virginia and Bethlehem-by-the-Lake as the new motherhouse. Attempts were made to update the Rule for a new century. Though a new Rule was never fully approved, guidelines were developed to reframe the core values of the Sisterhood of the Holy Nativity for the twenty-first century.

Despite these signs of progress, resistance, fear, and anxiety about dialogue and renewal continued. Mother Maria, struggling with personal health issues and disillusioned with the progress toward renewal, believed the situation was intractable and that the interpersonal relationships among the sisters continued to deteriorate as they decreased in numbers. In 2004, she proposed that the sisterhood develop a plan to ensure the skilled

---

55. William Lewis Stevens, Bishop and Episcopal Visitor, to SHN, April 2, 1986, SHNC.

56. Correspondence, William Louis Stevens, Bishop and Episcopal Visitor to SHN, February 1, 1985, SHNC.

57. Correspondence, William Louis Stevens, Bishop and Episcopal Visitor to SHN, February 1, 1985; Sister Marilyn to Mother Boniface, 1987; Mother Boniface to St. Mary's Retreat House, January 17, 1989, SHNC.

management of its affairs as the remaining members lived out their vocations. Against her wishes, Mother Maria was re-elected to a third term. In the same year, she was authorized by the Chapter to investigate the possibility of a merger or affiliation with other sisterhoods, which proved inconclusive.[58]

The Associates of the Sisterhood of the Holy Nativity provided crucial support during the transitional years and, in difficult times, were a source of friendship and renewal. The Associates continued to pray for the sisters, follow their Rule, and always hoped for the renewal of the community. Many Associates continue to strive to live their Rule today.[59]

An innovation occurred in 1984 when the Companions of the Sisterhood of the Holy Nativity was formed. The Companions were young people between the ages of fifteen and twenty-one who desired a Rule of life to grow in their commitment to Jesus Christ. Like other Associates, candidates were admitted as Companions only after a period of discernment. The program was significant for the young people who participated as it acknowledged their spiritual hunger and allowed them to learn more about religious life.[60] In 1997, the Sisterhood of the Holy Nativity also launched a successful Oblate program, which grew from some Associates' desire to deepen their connection to religious life. Fifteen oblates were enrolled from 2000 to 2009.[61] The program was another visible affirmation of the Sisterhood of the Holy Nativity's positive impact on the spiritual lives of their Associates and others who benefitted from their ministries and the fervent desire that the spiritual inheritance survive in some form. In addition to following a Rule of life, Oblates supported the sisterhood's retreat ministry. [62]

---

58. Correspondence, Mother Maria to SHN, 2004. After Mother Maria died, Mother Boniface was approached by Mother Miriam, CSM, with a proposal that SHN and CSW (Western Province) move to Greenwich, where CSM (Eastern Province) was located. But the move did not come to fruition. As Mother Miriam, CSM, noted: "The familiar was too strong an influence for either community to contemplate an amalgam of similar souls." Email between Sheryl Kujawa-Holbrook and Mother Miriam, CSM, October 26, 2021.

59. Interview, Phoebe Pettingell, February 24, 2022; Interview, Don Langlois, January 14, 2022; Interview, Dorsey Henderson, January 21, 2022; Interview, Nancy Kuhn and Lynn Shaw, February 18, 2022.

60. "Companions Program," The Bishop's Column, 2; Interview, Paul Aparico, December 1, 2021.

61. "Oblates of the Sisterhood of the Holy Nativity," enrollment book, 2000–2009, SHNC.

62. "A Trial Program: Oblates," 1997, SHNC.

BETHLEHEM-BY-THE-LAKE

During discernment about the potential ministry in West Virginia, back in Fond du Lac, the Sisterhood of the Holy Nativity decided to sell the Convent—which was far too large and inaccessible for the current sisters, and build Bethlehem-by-the-Lake, a new religious house on the order's property in Green Lake, Wisconsin. Though a retreat ministry was beginning to grow at the Convent in downtown Fond du Lac, the maintenance of the large facility proved challenging. The West Virginia and Green Lake projects were designed to signal a season of new life for the Sisterhood of the Holy Nativity. "We are all excited about moving to our new home," said Mother Maria, the superior. "We are thankful to be able to respond to (the Diocese of) West Virginia and look forward to the possibility of new ministries in other places."[63] Though the ministry in West Virginia was not viable, Bethlehem-by-the-Lake provided a supportive home environment for several sisters in their last years, and the beautiful setting nourished Associates and friends for retreats and social gatherings. Although the sisters fully expected to grieve over their departure from the Convent in Fond du Lac, those regrets never materialized. The building committee, along with the efforts of Mother Maria and Sister Boniface, managed to design Bethlehem-by-the-Lake to evoke the feeling of the old Convent, accentuated by the property's natural beauty.[64] At the same time, the move out of Fond du Lac distanced the sisterhood from the activity of the diocese and the Cathedral.[65]

The unresolved tensions in the sisterhood and the need to close the West Virginia mission weighed heavily on Mother Maria, and she grew increasingly discouraged. At the time of her death in 2007, eight sisters remained, two of whom lived in nursing facilities to ensure proper care. There were no longer enough active sisters available to pursue the renewal of the sisterhood. Eventually, three more sisters moved to nursing facilities. Despite her health challenges and many years as superior, Mother Boniface provided leadership for another four years until she died in 2011, after which Mother Abigail was elected. The remaining sisters moved to a smaller home in Ripon, Wisconsin in 2014.

---

63. "New Mission in West Virginia for Sisters of the Holy Nativity," 6.
64. Newsletter to Associates, Mother Maria, January 2001, SHNC.
65. Interview, Russ and Jerrie Jacobus, November 4, 2021.

LEGACIES—VOCATION AND WITNESS TO THE RELIGIOUS LIFE

Throughout its history, the Sisterhood of the Holy Nativity made incalculable contributions to the Episcopal Church, local catholic parishes, and the spiritual lives of individual Christians. The history of the Sisterhood of the Holy Nativity shows how they advanced the catholic faith of the Oxford Movement through an extensive network of parishes, mission houses, retreat centers, and missionary enterprises. The vocation of a consecrated life rooted in prayer and compassionate action was central to those called to the Sisterhood of the Holy Nativity. The depth of their spiritual vision and the scope of their ministries illustrate the powerful impact of vocational living. Fueled through prayer and the sacraments, they focused on those needing spiritual companionship and humanitarian aid. Their vocations enhanced the ministries of the laity and clergy they served. Their labors also supported Episcopal women's organizations such as altar guilds, parish aid societies, and national organizations such as the Church Periodical Society, Girls Friendly Society, and Woman's Auxiliary.[66]

Research on Roman Catholic sisterhoods suggests the importance of racial and cultural diversity as a sign of renewal in religious orders today. Historically, Episcopal sisterhoods have not been racially integrated overall or reflective of the ethnic and cultural diversity of the Church, even though globally, most Anglo-Catholics are Black, with traditional strongholds in the Caribbean and in Central and South Africa.[67] Where racial diversity occurred, it was often in religious orders with overseas houses. The sisterhoods for African American women that did exist, such as the Sisterhood of St. Mary and All Saints, founded in Baltimore in 1876, were much smaller and less well-supported than their white counterparts.[68] While there may be women (and men) in the Latinx community interested in religious life, there needs to be more recruitment by traditional religious orders in these contexts.[69] The experience of both Anglican and Roman Catholic sisterhoods confirms the importance of developing intergenerational and intercultural communities and addressing the challenges and isolation experienced by sisters who are the only members of their racial or cultural group in a religious community.[70]

66. Thompsett, "Introduction," in *Deeper Joy*, 7.

67. Leech, "The Radical Anglo-Catholic Social Vision," 7.

68. For example, Perry, *Twelve Years Among the Colored People*; Klein, "From the Archives: The Church of St. Mary the Virgin, Baltimore, n.p.

69. Interview, Anthony Guillén, February 11, 2022.

70. Gaunt and Do, *New Faces, New Possibilities*, 167–68.

Data on women's religious orders suggests that the ethnic composition and class stratification of a given society influence whether women have an opportunity to respond to their vocational calling. Another factor that mediates vocational choice for women, closely related to race and class, is their level of education.[71] Most women in the Sisterhood of the Holy Nativity were from white affluent and middle-class backgrounds, with the educational credentials needed to support a teaching ministry as a criterion for admission. Many had a college education or professional training before entering religious life; some were active in professions.[72] With the possibility of one biracial (white and Indigenous) sister professed in 1917, the Sisterhood of the Holy Nativity was all white until the first African American sister, Sister Charis, was professed in 1983. Sister Kathleen Marie, also African American, was received from the Order of St. Anne four years later.[73] Sources suggest that until the late twentieth century, white clergy affiliated with sisterhoods discouraged racial integration and that African American clergy discouraged women from considering religious life as a vocational choice.[74] Two Oneida women with religious vocations, Mother Superior Alicia Torres and Sister Theresa Rose, were inspired by the Sisterhood of the Holy Nativity and the Order of St. Anne. Yet they joined a sisterhood with ties to the Latinx community in Arizona, the Order of the Teachers of the Children of God.[75]

Presently, the Sisterhood of the Holy Nativity is a member of the Conference on Anglican Communities in the Americas (CAROA). Across the nineteen member communities, there are 130 religious and eight novices.[76] Data from the wider Anglican Communion reveals the Global South's

71. Wittberg, et al., *God's Call is Everywhere*, 2002–2010.

72. Family and occupational data for the Sisterhood of the Holy Nativity are included in the sisters' obituaries, entrance data, and correspondence. Biographical data confirmed on Ancestry.com for each sister listed in the Appendix of Life Professed Sisters.

73. One SHN document suggests that Sister Mary Kathleen, SHN, was biracial and of Indigenous and white ancestry, but it is not confirmed. Sister Charis, SHN, was the first African American woman professed in the SHN. Sister Kathleen, also African American, transferred from the Order of St Anne in 1987.

74. Interview, Patty Allen, June 8, 2023. Ms. Allen is completing a monograph on Mother Ruth Younger, a biracial sister who founded the Community of the Holy Spirit in New York; Interview, Valerie Bailey, October 13, 2021; Interview, Regina Christianson, October 14, 2021.

75. McLester et al., *The Wisconsin Oneida and the Episcopal Church*, 156–157.

76. Statistics confirmed by David Brinton, OGS, General Secretary of CAROA, January 31, 2024. Of the 19 religious communities constituting CAROA, thirteen are women's communities, five are men's, and one is for women and men. Some communities have admitted non-binary persons; the data here correlates with the categories on the site.

growth in sisterhoods (and religious orders). The ninety-eight celibate and vowed religious communities on the current Anglican Religious Life Yearbook website include 1,075 religious, 467 novices, and 26 postulants. The largest sisterhood is the Chama cha Mariamu Mtakatifu (Community of St. Mary of Nazareth and Calvary, CMM). CMM has a convent and eleven houses in Tanzania and Zambia with eighty-two sisters, eleven novices, and three postulants. The Community of the Holy Name (CHN) has thirty-six sisters in Zululand, ten in Lesotho, fourteen in Australia, and thirteen in Yorkshire, United Kingdom. Anglican sisterhoods are also flourishing in Oceania. The Community of the Sisters of Melanesia (CSM) includes forty-nine sisters and forty-eight novices in the Soloman Islands, Papua New Guinea, and Vanuatu. Also in the Pacific region is the Solomon Islands Community of the Sisters of the Church (CSM), with twenty-seven sisters, ten novices, seven postulants, and other smaller women's communities.[77]

Although numbers are not the only indicator of vitality, there are regions where traditional Anglican, celibate, vowed sisterhoods are growing. The communal cultures of the Global South support growth in religious orders for women and men. Communal prayer and work are interwoven in people's lives from birth. "It is through mission and spending time with people that young women are attracted to our community," writes Sister Veronica Vasaethe, CSM, from the Soloman Islands. "Women do not read about us in the newspaper or see us on the Internet but find out about us through human contact. This is Incarnational mission, the Word becoming flesh (JN 1.14)."[78]

The legacies of the Sisterhood of the Holy Nativity have contributed to generating new forms of religious life. Although sisterhoods do not typically consider the ministries of sisters who left the community as part of its legacy, that perspective might be shortsighted. Just as the Sisterhood of the Holy Nativity claimed its early formation in the Society of St. Margaret, one-third of the women who left continued in some form of religious life after their departure, building on and expanding their early formation. Some went on to other sisterhoods or church ministries, and at least three established new traditional or dispersed religious communities.[79]

---

77. Statistics from the Anglican Religious Life Yearbook website, www.aylyb.org.uk. Of the ninety-eight celibate and vowed religious communities listed, thirteen did not provide updated data. Thus, the total of 1,075 religious, 467 novices and 26 postulants may be lower than the actual numbers. Accessed February 1, 2024.

78. Vasaethe, "Sisters of the Church in the Solomon Islands," 146.

79. Acts of the Council, 1957–2004, SHNC, confirmed with interview data; Interview, Sister Barbara Jean, AF, July 28, 2021, Sister Julian Wilson, AF, January 11, 2022.

The proliferation of dispersed religious communities in the Anglican Communion and the Episcopal Church signals a deep spiritual yearning among many people for an ordered life of prayer and service during this challenging time in human history. Dispersed religious communities bring together the values of historic monasticism without geographical boundaries. The Anglican Religious Life Yearbook website reports two celibate dispersed religious communities with a combined membership of seventy-three plus sixteen novices. In addition, there are twenty-six acknowledged religious communities with various vows and promises, many dispersed. The Third Order Society of Saint Francis (TSSF) is the largest dispersed community, with 2677 women and men and 399 novices worldwide living their Franciscan vocations.[80] These numbers suggest to those concerned with formation that there are people today who carry the gift of a vocation to a traditional or dispersed religious community but also need support and encouragement to explore the path for themselves. Making more aware that God continues to call people to the consecrated life would represent a significant shift in awareness throughout the Church.

Archbishop of Canterbury Justin Welby speaks to the urgent need within Anglicanism to support the religious life today. He recently launched the Community of St. Anselm, a new religious community designed to unite young people in prayer and service at Lambeth Palace. Convinced that the Church of the twenty-first century will not grow by watering down the demands of Christian discipleship, Welby believes in the importance of religious communities that bring together people "seeking a spirituality with rigour, vitality, and truthfulness, through stages of life, and death, and in a serious community."[81] Although modern life provides avenues for human flourishing unavailable in the past, spiritual hunger and the search for lives of meaning and purpose persist. The core missionary spirit of the Sisterhood of the Holy Nativity must continue to evolve and express itself in the current age. "Religion, as well as religious life, must find its place in the secular world, not the other way around. In this secular world the whole Christian community seeks to express what it knows to be true about life and meaning. This is the only world in which religious life can express its faith."[82]

Discussing the future with members of Anglican and Episcopal religious orders today reveals several common themes: acknowledgment of uncertainty, recognition that the size and organization of religious orders

---

80. Anglican Religious Life Yearbook, www.arlyb.org.uk.
81. Justin Welby, "Afterword: The Vowed Life," 175.
82. Merkle, *Sensing the Spirit*, 147–147.

will differ from the past, and the frank admission that, at least in Western cultures, there is a resistance to the ideals of voluntary poverty and lifelong commitment. At the same time, there is palpable enthusiasm for religious life, deep faith in the love of God, and confidence that their experience, grace, and imagination will create a sustainable future.[83]

Because of the witness of the Sisterhood of the Holy Nativity and other religious communities who courageously offer lives of prayer and service to the Church, in 2022, the 80th General Convention invited the Episcopal Church to observe "Religious Life Sunday" each year on the Third Sunday of Epiphany.[84] It is an opportunity to learn more about the history and witness of the sisters, brothers, nuns, monks, oblates, and others who are part of our religious communities, to pray for them and their vocations, and to support those who might consider giving their lives to the world and the Church like the women of the Sisterhood of the Holy Nativity did.[85] Religious Life Sunday is a reminder to uphold religious life as a viable vocational option, along with other lay and ordained vocations.

"Religious life expresses a vision of the human person who is not only a creature of God but a partner with God."[86] The need for flexibility and adaptability anticipated by Mother Foundress Ruth Margaret in 1882 remains an essential trend among religious communities. The Sisterhood of the Holy Nativity's missionary spirit was always broader than any single ministry. Not only did they teach, counsel, and provide relief for thousands of people over the past 140 years, but their efforts also contributed to the Episcopal Church's spiritual vitality. While clergy promoted the theological and liturgical tradition of the Oxford Movement, advancing the catholic faith among the laity was central to the work of sisterhoods. Their dedication transformed local parishes and dioceses in the Episcopal Church. They deepened the catholic revival's impact by cultivating the laity's spirituality and responding to critical human needs.

---

83. Interview, Sister Barbara Jean, AF, July 28, 2021; Interview, Brother Scott Borden, October 8, 2021; Interview, Sister Ellen Stephen, OSH, December 12, 2014; Interview, Sister Julian Wilson, AF, January 11, 2022; Interview, Brother Samuel Timothy, AF, January 18, 2022; Interview, Sister Elizabeth Rolfe-Thomas, SSJD, Sister Constance Joanna Geffert, SSJD, Sister Elizabeth Ann Eckert, SSJD, February 1, 2022; Interview, Sister Greta Ronningen, CDL, February 18, 2022; Interview, Sister Madeleine Mary, CSM, February 22, 2022; Interview, Sister Monica Clare, CSJB, March 4, 2022.

84. See Resolution 2022-B004 on the General Convention website, generalconvention.org.

85. "Episcopalians invited to observe Religious Life Sunday on January 22," www.episcopalchurch.org/publicaffairs.

86. Merkle, *Sensing the Spirit,* 155.

The Sisterhood of the Holy Nativity started with six sisters, a priest, and a rented house. Throughout Christian history, small groups inspired by the Gospel and a shared vision accomplished great things for the Church and the world. Today, the Church's mission has shifted from bringing the Gospel to the poor to standing in solidarity with them. Reflecting this shift, members of Anglican and Episcopal religious orders are moving toward smaller grassroots ministries, serving in churches, agencies, prisons, and other institutions, but still with the flexibility to change course to respond to pressing human needs. Religious orders in the twenty-first century are more likely to respond as individuals with loving hearts and a desire to be present to those in need than as members of an institution. As the earthly witness of the Sisterhood of the Holy Nativity passes into history, their lives demonstrate a steadfast love of the catholic faith for all willing to open their hearts. May their hidden way of holiness inspire new generations to devote their lives to loving service in God's name.

Appendix A
The Sisterhood of the Holy Nativity (SHN) Life Professed Sisters

1. *Sister Mary Margaret, SHN* (1837–1916). Born Mary Robertson in Charleston, New Hampshire. Professed February 2, 1878, the Feast of the Purification. Formerly of the Society of St. Margaret and a founding sister of SHN. Served as Novice Mistress. Active in Boston, Kansas City, Providence, and Fond du Lac.

2. *Sister Hannah Margaret, SHN* (1840–1904). Born Hannah Hagadorn Grosvenor in Pomfret, Connecticut. Professed September 29, 1878, the Feast of St. Michael & All Angels. Formerly of the Society of St. Margaret and a founding sister of SHN. She served as the first superior on the condition that it was a one-year term, from late 1882 to January 1884. Sister Hannah edited the first Rule and Constitution for publication. Also served in Boston, Providence, and Fond du Lac. She died of pneumonia after the doctor declared her on the road to recovery. Buried in Swan Point Cemetery, Providence, Rhode Island.

3. *Sister Ruth Margaret, SHN* (1826–1910). Born Ruth Tufts Vose in Boston, Massachusetts. Professed on Corpus Christi 1881. Her religious vocation was delayed until her mid-fifties as she cared for aging parents. Formerly of the Society of St Margaret (Novice Mistress). Daughter of Elisha Vose and Rebecca Gorman Bartlet. Sister of Judge Henry Vose of Boston. Raised Unitarian. Mother Foundress, co-founder with Charles Chapman Grafton, Mother Superior (1884–1908). She suffered from rheumatism and a heart ailment in her later years. Served in Boston, Providence, and Fond du Lac. She is known for her moral authority, practical wisdom, and example as a religious.

4. *Sister Katharine, SHN* (1858–1934). Born Effie Adelaide Dunbar in Lynn, Massachusetts. Professed January 1, 1884, the Feast of the Circumcision. Formerly of the Society of St. Margaret and a founding sister of SHN. Served at Oneida, Portland (Maine), Philadelphia, and New York City. A trained nurse and an astute administrator.

5. *Sister Rebecca, SHN* (1846–1937). Born Rebecca Gorham Vose from a prominent Boston family. Professed on February 2, 1884, the Feast of the Purification. Formerly of the Society of St. Margaret and a founding sister of SHN. The niece of Mother Ruth Margaret. Served in Boston, Providence, Tiverton, and Fond du Lac. She served as Assistant Superior for eighteen years, Sister-in-Charge of the mission house in Fond du Lac, Guest Mistress, and administrative assistant for Bishop Charles Chapman Grafton. As Guest Mistress, she counseled many friends and Associates of SHN, both laity and clergy. Gifted with children and godmother to many, she took a particular interest in Grafton Hall School and held Sunday classes for faculty and students there. Sister Rebecca coped with chronic migraines and nearly died of pneumonia twice. At the Convent in Fond du Lac, she acted as superintendent of the building and was instrumental in converting the former private home into a religious house.

6. *Sister Agnes, SHN* (1847–1932). Born Annie A. Morrill in Salisbury, Massachusetts. Professed on the Feast of All Saints, November 1, 1884. Formerly of the Society of St. Margaret and a founding sister of SHN. Served in Boston, Providence, and Fond du Lac. Sister Agnes was challenged by increasing dementia after a major fall in 1926.

7. *Sister Augustine, SHN* (1840–1930). Born Emmaline K. Bradford in Maryland. Professed October 2, 1889. One of twelve children of Maryland governor Augustus Bradford. Sister Augustine experienced progressive deafness. Served in Providence and Fond du Lac. She was often seen with her cat, Gypsy.

8. *Sister Margaret, SHN* (1854–1932). Born Martha M. Smith in Mystic, Connecticut. Professed on February 2, 1890, the Feast of the Purification. Fluent in French and German. Served at Oneida, Philadelphia, and Portland (Maine). Adept at languages and skilled in music.

9. *Sister Christina, SHN* (1858–1894). Born Sara Hallett Bovey in Nantucket, Massachusetts. Professed on the Feast of the Visitation 1891. She is considered the first martyr of SHN, as she died of tuberculosis in service at Oneida. She also served in Barrington (Rhode Island). Buried in Swan Point Cemetery, Providence, Rhode Island, she left SHN a legacy.

10. *Sister Adelaide, SHN* (1841–1934). Born Lydia Adelaide Barrows in Ohio. Professed on the last Thursday in Eastertide 1892. Daughter of a clergyman in New York. Sister Adelaide coped with migraines and survived surgery for "a rupture" on the dining table at the Convent when there was no room at the hospital. Sister Adelaide served in Providence, Fond du Lac, and Philadelphia. She was a skilled seamstress.

11. *Sister Katharine Edith, SHN* (1848–1919). Born Katharine Edith Peirce in Boston. Professed September 21, 1872, the Feast of St. Matthew. Former Mother Superior of the Community of the Holy Name, Boston. Assistant Superior SHN (1894–1908), Mother Superior (1908–1919). Sister Katharine Edith died of liver cancer shortly after her diagnosis, having started the process for the election of a new superior upon returning to the Convent after her diagnosis. Served in Providence and Fond du Lac. A gifted academic and writer, she wrote several books, edited Charles Grafton's writing, and served faithfully as superior despite wanting to step down. Her plans (with the SHN chaplain) to move the motherhouse to Bay Shore and out of Fond du Lac were thwarted by her final illness. Served in Boston, Providence, New York City, and Fond du Lac.

12. *Sister Alice, SHN* (1851–1929). Born Martha Alice Sperry in Delafield, Wisconsin. Professed September 21, 1872, the Feast of St. Matthew. Formerly of the Community of the Holy Name, Boston, with Sister Katharine Edith. She taught music and Sunday school before entering the religious life. Her father was a physician influenced by the preaching of James DeKoven, and she worked as a teacher before entering religious life. Her maternal grandparents ran the Hawks Inn, now the home of the Delafield Historical Society. Sister Alice struggled with mental illness and lived for five years in a state hospital; SHN later brought her home and cared for her. She served at Oneida, Boston, Providence, and Fond du Lac.

13. *Sister Emily Constance, SHN* (1857–1943). Born Emily Stafford in Mississippi. Professed on the Feast of All Saints, November 1, 1892. Daughter of a Mississippi judge. A notable retreat leader. Sister Emily Constance suffered from eye problems. She was the author of the widely circulated paper "The Religious Life," originally presented to the Society of the Companions of the Holy Cross (SCHC) in Massachusetts. Served in Providence, Fond du Lac, and Kingston.

14. *Sister Carlotta Mary, SHN* (1862–1898). Born Charlotte Mary Henkel in Indiana. Professed on the Feast of All Saints, November 1, 1894. Daughter of a merchant, Phillip Melancthon Henkel, from a family of seven generations

of Lutheran clergy. Served in Providence and Tiverton. Died from an infection after surgery for fibroid tumors. Buried in Swan Point Cemetery, Providence, Rhode Island.

15. *Sister Annette, SHN* (1870–1953). Born Sarah Anne "Brightie" Rogers in Ontonagon, Michigan. Professed on Whitsun Tuesday 1896. The first SHN profession in Fond du Lac. The daughter of a merchant from Appleton, Wisconsin, her brother was Benjamin Talbot Rogers, a clergyman who served as Archdeacon of the Diocese of Fond du Lac and Bishop's Chaplain at the Cathedral of St. John the Divine in New York City. Sister Annette attended Kemper Hall in Kenosha, Wisconsin. Her family moved to Appleton in 1873 to a house on the Fox River. Her sister was the vice president of the *New York Tribune*. Sister Annette served in Fond du Lac, Oneida, Providence, Kingston, New York City, Portland (Maine), Milwaukee, and Bay Shore.

16. *Sister Alice Ernestine, SHN* (1864–1906). Born Alice Halsey in New York. Professed on August 7, 1896, the Feast of the Holy Name. Served in Fond du Lac. Sister Alice Ernestine suffered from rheumatoid arthritis and served while in chronic pain.

17. *Sister Harriet, SHN* (1860–1948). Born Harriet Hayes Smith in Minnesota. Professed on the Feast of Purification 1897. The daughter of a paper manufacturer, she was an art student for two years in New York City before coming to SHN. Served as Sister-in-Charge in Fond du Lac. Known for her energy, vision, and administrative ability, she was an effective "troubleshooter" and was sent to serve in several mission houses. She was almost elected superior in a tied election. Sister Harriet served in Fond du Lac, Providence, Tiverton (Rhode Island), Kingston (New York), New York City, Milwaukee, and Bay Shore. Sister Harriet received treatment for pulmonary illness and was known as a lively member of the infirmary community – she even grew apricots there. She is buried in the Swan Point Cemetery in Providence, Rhode Island.

18. *Sister Sophia Margaretta, SHN* (1848–1940). Born Sophia Margaretta Swainson in Stoke Fleming, Devon, England. Professed on All Saints, November 1, 1900. Sister Margaretta served for many years at Oneida as Sacristan and Sister-in-Charge. She also served in Providence and Bay Shore. She was very proud of her English ancestry.

19. *Sister Elizabeth, SHN* (1855–1925). Born Eliza Delaplaine Opdycke in New York City. Professed on September 8, 1897, the Feast of the Nativity of the Blessed Virgin Mary. Skilled in mathematics and plumbing. Sister Elizabeth ran the Altar Bread Department for twenty-seven years until she

stepped down due to tuberculosis. She was blind for the last two years of her life. Served in Fond du Lac.

20. *Sister Mary Elizabeth, SHN* (1864-1919). Born Mary Elizabeth Warnock in Germantown, Philadelphia. Professed on September 8, 1898, the Feast of the Nativity of the Blessed Virgin Mary. She was the daughter of a master builder who opposed her religious vocation. She served in Fond du Lac, Tiverton, Kingston, Philadelphia, New York City, and Milwaukee. A clerestory window at All Saints Cathedral in Milwaukee is in her memory. Sister Mary Elizabeth was unstoppable, even with a brace on one foot. She was known for her skills as a Confirmation instructor.

21. *Sister Matilda, SHN* (1863-1942). Born Matilda Richardson Lorrieiére in Philadelphia of French ancestry. Professed on August 24, 1903, the Feast of St. Bartholomew. Served as Novice Mistress before she was elected Mother Superior (1919-1942). She served in Fond du Lac, Providence, East Providence, Kingston, and Green Lake. She is known for her energy, sense of humor, administrative gifts, and diplomatic skills. Mother Matilda was an astute administrator of the many logistics involving the mission houses. She was gifted with a challenging German Shepherd, Rex, by the SHN physician at Christmas 1928. Rex was affectionate and lovable but held a grudge against Agnesian sisters. He is buried at Green Lake (Ripon); Mother Matilda outlived him briefly.

22. *Sister Lillian, SHN* (1887-1942). Born Lillian McNaughton in Wisconsin. Professed in the Octave of the Holy Name, August 10, 1904. Served many years at Oneida, Fond du Lac, and Thornton. Survived surgery for a stomach ailment, probably ulcers.

23. *Sister Amy, SHN* (1870-1953). Born Amy Fenner Murray in Toronto. Professed in the October of the Holy Name, August 10, 1904. Sister Amy became a naturalized US citizen in 1948. She served for over twenty years at Oneida and was considered "our mother" by the people there, where she assisted in the infirmary, among other roles. Sister Amy also served in Kingston and Milwaukee.

24. *Sister Barbara, SHN* (1867-1955). Born Babette (Babetta) Diem in Paris of German ancestry. Professed April 25, 1906, the Feast of St. Mark. She was the daughter of the bookkeeper for a German mining company in the United States. Served in Fond du Lac and West Orange.

25. *Sister Amelia Christine, SHN* (1860-1934). Born Emma Amelia Christine Battles in Georgia. Professed January 18, 1909, the feast of St. Prisca.

Her family was originally from New England; her father worked as an agent for a cotton factory. She was trained as a music teacher. First refused election to profession despite Bishop Charles Grafton's support. Her novitiate was extended before permission was granted. She served at Fond du Lac, Oneida, Providence, Thornton, and Milwaukee.

26. *Sister Frances, SHN (1868–1936)*. Born Arabella Frances Rich in New York. Professed on September 8, 1909, the Feast of the Nativity of the Blessed Virgin Mary. Her grandfather was the American ambassador to Spain, and her family lived in several European cities. Her father was William Alexander Rich, a Canton, New York, missionary priest. She served at Oneida as Sacristan and in Milwaukee and Philadelphia.

27. *Sister Emily, SHN (1849–1910)*. Born Emilie Susan Phillips in Watertown, Maine. Professed on September 29, 1910, the Feast of St. Michael & All Angels. Sister Emily was a music teacher in Maine before entering religious life. She was deeply committed to providing places where the laity could go for retreats and was instrumental in founding SHN retreat houses in West Orange and Bay Shore. She also served in New York City and Milwaukee. Greatly loved for her "soul work," Sister Emily supported the work of the Bay Shore retreat center until two months before her death from abdominal cancer. She was also a beloved Novice Mistress.

28. *Sister Clare Margaret, SHN (1863–1911)*. Born Margaret Robinson Bragg in North Carolina, the daughter of a sea captain. Professed on September 8, 1911, the Feast of the Nativity of the Blessed Virgin Mary. Sister Clare died of stomach cancer. She served in West Orange and Milwaukee.

29. *Sister Emily Caroline, SHN (1870–1934)*. Known as *Sister Caroline*. Born Emily Josephine Parker in Connecticut. Professed on October 28, 1911, the Feast of Saints Simon & Jude. The last sister (with Sister Dorothea) that Bishop Charles Grafton professed. The daughter of William, the vice president of a hardware company in New Britain, Connecticut, she worked as an English teacher before entering the religious life. Served in Tiverton, West Orange, Portland (Maine), Los Angeles, and Baltimore.

30. *Sister Dorothea, SHN (1884–1980)*. Born Amelia Dorothea "Nonnie" Nydegger in Chicago. Professed on October 28, 1911, the Feast of Saint Simon & June. The last sister professed by Bishop Charles Chapman Grafton, along with Sister Caroline. From a German-Swiss family, her parents were deceased when she entered the SHN. She started visiting the Convent as a child. Served in mission houses for fifty-five years at Oneida and Fond du Lac, Providence, Bay Shore, Baltimore, Newport, and Milwaukee. Sister

Dorothea served as Sister-in-Charge in Newport and Baltimore. She is known for the added skip in her genuflection as she processed out of the chapel. Sister Dorothea was the last sister to have personally known Bishop Grafton and died on the anniversary of his consecration to the episcopate. In her later years, she was known for making beautifully woven scarves.

31. *Sister Etheldreda, SHN* (1877–1966). Born Ethel Mariette Green in Summit Lake, Wisconsin. Professed on November 11, 1912, the Feast of St. Catherine of Alexandria. Served many years in Milwaukee at All Saints Cathedral, as well as in Providence and Bay Shore. She was a skilled seamstress and made wimples.

32. *Sister Juliana, SHN* (1863–1949). Born Mabel Wilder Baldwin in East Orange, New Jersey. Professed on the Octave of All Saints, November 8, 2013. Her parents were deceased by the time she entered sisterhood. Sister Juliana was a gifted calligrapher and made devotional cards. She served in Fond du Lac.

33. *Sister Caritas, SHN* (1876–1946). Born Carrie May Sentenne in Milwaukee. Professed on the Feast of the Annunciation, March 25, 1938. Deeply influenced by Sister Julia Elizabeth in her vocation, Sister Caritas trained as a nurse. She overcame a severe stammer. Served in Newport and Baltimore. Sister Caritas was killed by a car with brake failure near the Baltimore mission house.

34. *Sister Frederica, SHN* (1871–1943). Born Frederica Christie Bowman in Canada. Professed on the Feast of the Purification, February 2, 1916. Sister Frederica was the daughter of an SHN Associate and the granddaughter of a founding Associate. Served in Fond du Lac, Kansas City, Providence, West Orange, Newport, and Baltimore.

35. *Sister Katrina, SHN* (1887–1978). Born Emma Katharena Coop in Rhode Island. Professed on the Feast of the Holy Name, August 7, 1916. Introduced to the SHN as a physical education teacher at Grafton Hall. Her mother opposed her religious vocation, claiming that her daughter was in poor health. Sister Katrina lived until the age of ninety-one. She hurt her back while teaching and wore a brace. She was also challenged by deafness in her later years. Sister Kartina loved to stage liturgical dramas with children, especially Nativity plays. Served in Fond du Lac, Bay Shore, Providence, Los Angeles, Baltimore (twice for thirty years), Portland (Oregon), and Milwaukee.

APPENDIX A

36. *Sister Mary Gertrude, SHN* (1877–1962). Born Charlotte Mary Louisa Jarrett in New York City. Daughter of Thomas Jarrett and Lucy Jane Alma Elow. Professed on the Feast of the Nativity of the Blessed Virgin Mary, September 8, 1916. Served at Oneida and Fond du Lac, Tiverton, Providence, Bay Shore, New York City, and Baltimore.

37. *Sister Mary Kathleen, SHN* (1879–1954). Born Kathleen McMurray in Chicago. Professed on the Feast of St. Bartholomew, August 24, 1917. Sister Mary Kathleen was possibly biracial of white and Indigenous ancestry. She served as Sister-in-Charge of the Philadelphia mission house and in New York City, Kingston, Bay Shore, and Fond du Lac.

38. *Sister Ruth Mary, SHN* (1879–1968). Born Ruth Lee Gifford in New York. Her father was Elihu Gifford, a bookkeeper, and her mother was Matilda Andrews Gifford. Professed on Ascension Day, May 15, 1918. Sister Ruth Mary was first admitted to SHN in 1906, left to discern her vocation more, and returned in 1913. She was a holy woman with a kind and gentle demeanor. She served as Mother Superior from 1942 to 1961 in Fond du Lac. Also in West Orange, Bay Shore, and New York City.

39. *Sister Agatha Bernice*, SHN (1878–1962). Born Bernice A. Jones in Kansas. Professed on March 19, 2017, the Feast of St. Joseph. Sister Agatha Bernice served many years in the Margaret Peabody Lending Library. Also in Bay Shore, Los Angeles, Newport, Baltimore, Philadelphia, and Milwaukee.

40. *Sister Harriet Patricia, SHN* (1889–1980). Born Harriet Hersey Haney in Plankinton, South Dakota. Known as *Sister Patricia*. Her father was a Supreme Court Judge. Professed on the Feast of Saints Phillip & James, May 3, 1920. A graduate of Downer College in Wisconsin, she was a parish secretary before entering the SHN. Academically gifted and a skilled writer, speaker, and teacher. Sister Patricia was a popular Novice Mistress for fifteen years and Assistant Superior for a year. She was the first Sister-in-Charge of the house in Portland, Oregon (twice), founded the retreat house in Santa Barbara, and served there for fifteen years. Sister Patricia also served in Providence (twice – once as Sister-in-Charge), Newport, Los Angeles, and Baltimore. Though she returned to the Convent in Fond du Lac to "retire" in 1974, she contributed to novitiate training and the revision of the SHN rule. Sister Patricia played a central role in building the summer cottage at Green Lake (Ripon) in 1923, where she was the first member of SHN (and perhaps the first woman religious) to drive a Model T automobile.

41. *Sister Helen, SHN* (1884–1976). Born Helen Dearing Carson in St. Paul, Minnesota. Professed on the Feast of St. Luke, October 18, 1920. Sister

Helen was an artist and art student when she joined the SHN. Her brother Thornton Carson designed the chapel at the retreat house in Santa Barbara. Sister Helen was active in college ministry with students from Columbia University when she served in New York City. Sister Helen served in Philadelphia for thirty years. She also served in Santa Barbara, Bay Shore, Long Island, and Baltimore.

42. *Sister Mary Jeanette, SHN* (1869-1929). Born Mary Jane McCloughey. Professed on August 1, 1921, the Feast of St. Peter's Chains. Despite a "successful" surgery for cancer in 1926, Sister Mary Jeanette died three years later. She served in Portland (Maine) and Milwaukee.

43. *Sister Mary Constance*, SHN (1876-1968). Born Constance Mary Jowitt in New York. Her parents were from England. Her father, Joseph F. Jowitt, was a Staten Island, New York priest. Professed on August 1, 1921, the Feast of St. Peter's Chains. Sister Mary Constance was known for her quick humor and her talent as a seamstress – she made habits for the sisters. In addition, she served in Kingston, Providence, Bay Shore, New York City, Newport, and Milwaukee.

44. Sister Carlena, SHN (1875-1950). Born Carlena Arnd in Wisconsin. Her parents were from Germany. Professed on the Feast of the Epiphany, January 6, 1923. Sister Carlena worked as a music teacher before she entered the SHN. She served in Providence, Newport, Philadelphia, Baltimore, Milwaukee, and Portland (Maine).

45. *Sister Mary Gabriel, SHN* (1873-1960). Born Mary Emma Clarkson in Spring Lake, New Jersey. Professed on the Feast of the Epiphany, January 6, 1923. Sister Mary Gabriel was dismissed from the community in 1919 but returned to the SHN thirteen months later. She served in Portland (Oregon), Bay Shore, Santa Barbara, Los Angeles, Milwaukee, and Philadelphia.

46. *Sister Anita, SHN* (1890-1974). Born Nita Weichers in Brighton, Michigan. Professed on the Feast of Saints Phillip & James, May 3, 1923. She was raised in a family that emigrated from Germany to Grand Rapids, Michigan. A graduate of Wellesley College, Sister Anita worked as a teacher at Grafton Hall before she entered the SHN. Sister Anita was a trained musician and served as the Convent organist in Fond du Lac. She was also the Sister-in-Charge of the Margaret Peabody Lending Library and served in New York City, Newport, Milwaukee, and Bay Shore.

47. *Sister Grace SHN* (1886-1980). Born Gracie Frances Blood in Medfield, Massachusetts. Professed on the Feast of the Transfiguration, August 6,

1923. Her family was from Vermont, and her father worked as a teamster. Sister Grace worked as a teacher and occupational therapist before entering the SHN. She later served as an occupational therapist at the hospital and home for the aged in Fond du Lac. She loved producing Mystery Plays with children. In addition, she served in West Orange, Newport, Los Angeles, Milwaukee, and Nevada.

48. *Sister Laura, SHN* (1888–1975). Born Laura Crosby Sturtevant in Chippewa, Minnesota. Professed on October 28, 1923, the Feast of Saints Simon & Jude. Sister Laura was a skilled nurse and the first cousin of Bishop Harwood Sturtevant of the Episcopal Diocese of Fond du Lac. She served in Bay Shore, Newport, Milwaukee, and Nevada.

49. *Sister Mary Josephine, SHN* (1877–1962). Born May Caroline Spalding in Michigan. Professed on May 3, 1924, the Feast of Saints Philip and James. The daughter of a clergyman, she received her undergraduate degree from Vassar College and a PhD in Middle English from Byrn Mawr College. Before she entered the SHN, Sister Mary Josephine was a professor of English at Wilson College in Pennsylvania. She served in Providence, Bay Shore, New York City, Philadelphia, Los Angeles, and Milwaukee.

50. *Sister Mary Virginia, SHN* (1878–1952). Born Mary Vernon Young in Quebec City, Canada. Professed on the Feast of the Holy Name, January 3, 1924. Before entering the SHN, Sister Mary Virginia was a graduate nurse at Montreal General Hospital. In Fond du Lac, she oversaw the Picture Department. Her nursing skills were highly regarded at Oneida. In addition, Sister Mary Virginia served in New York and Providence.

51. *Sister Elisabetha, SHN* (1899–1970). Born Elisa Betha Coster in Irvington-on-the-Hudson, New York. Professed on August 27, 1927, the Feast of St. Monica. Sister Elisabetha struggled with epilepsy. She served in Providence.

52. *Sister Bernadine, SHN* (1892–1969). Born Edith Gertrude Burton in Fulham, London, England. Professed in the Octave of Michaelmas, 1927. Sister Bernadine lived in Fond du Lac and oversaw the orphanage there. She was a puppeteer. Her brother, Arthur Alfred Burton, was a priest at St. Paul's Cathedral in Fond du Lac and St. Michael's, North Fond du Lac. He is buried in the Nashotah House Cemetery. Her sister, Mary Brinton, was the Fond du Lac Children's Home matron. In addition to Fond du Lac, Sister Bernadine served in New York City, Bay Shore, Newport, Baltimore, and Philadelphia. She was the last sister buried in Swan Point Cemetery, Providence.

53. *Sister Hildegarde, SHN* (1881–1965). Born Helen De Forest in New York City. Professed on the Feast of the Epiphany, January 7, 1929. She worked as a secretary before entering the religious life. Sister Hildegarde oversaw the Embroidery Department in Fond du Lac and served in Providence, Newport, Philadelphia, New York City, and Bay Shore. She also avidly wrote children's plays.

54. *Sister Edwina, SHN* (1903–1947). Born Edwina Dorothy Irwin in Baltimore. Sister Edwina was the first SHN sister born in the twentieth century. Professed on Whitsun Tuesday, 1929. Sister Edwina suffered from epilepsy. She oversaw the Altar Bread Department in Fond du Lac and served in Milwaukee.

55. *Sister Esther Beulah, SHN* (1886–1962). Born Beulah Esther Frederick in Kentucky. Known as *Sister Esther*. Professed on March 1, 1930, the Feast of St. David. She worked as a clerk and then as a Red Cross nurse during World War I. She also attended Episcopal deaconess training school before she entered the SHN. She later served in Baltimore, Newport, Los Angeles, and Nevada. She is buried in Swan Point Cemetery, Providence.

56. *Sister Faith, SHN* (1884–1968). Born Christine Percival Skelton in Lowell, Massachusetts. She was professed on November 4, 1930. Before entering the SHN, Sister Faith obtained a diploma in domestic science from the Pratt Institute. Sister Faith was released from her vows in 1937 and returned to the SHN in 1945, remaining in the sisterhood for the rest of her life. She served at Oneida, in Providence, and for a short time in Michigan.

57. *Sister Harriet Vincent, SHN* (1884–1931). Born Harriet Storer Fisk in Boston. Professed on the Feast of St. Mark, April 25, 1931. Her father was Dr. Everett Fisk, a prominent Methodist and President of the Boston Methodist Social Union and Boston Missionary and Church Extension Society. Before entering the SHN, Sister Harriet Vincent was valedictorian of her class at Wyoming Seminary Prep School and worked as a teacher. She received her undergraduate and master's degrees from Boston University, where she was president of the sophomore class, active in the College Women and Mozart clubs, and a member of the Intercollegiate Socialist Society. Sister Harriet Vincent served in Bay Shore and died there four months after her profession.

58. Sister Regina, SHN (1867–1938). Born Regina Garrigues in Pennsylvania. Professed on October 10, 1931, the Feast of Teresa of Avila. Sister Regina delayed entering the SHN to care for her mother. As an adult, Sister Regina lived in Baltimore and got to know the sisters there. She served in Baltimore and oversaw the Embroidery Department in Fond du Lac.

APPENDIX A

59. *Sister Mary Louise, SHN* (1884–1971). Born Louise Nowlin Peck in Fincastle, Botetourt, Virginia. She was professed on the Feast of the Annunciation (transferred) on April 4, 1932. Before entering the SHN, Sister Mary Louise was the supervisor of nurses at Children's Hospital in New York. She served in New York and Bay Shore.

60. *Sister Veronica, SHN* (1892–1978). Born Marjorie Hume Peck in Toronto, Ontario, Canada. She was professed on the Feast of the Annunciation (transferred) on April 4, 1932. Sister Veronica, a relative of Sister Mary Louise, served as a deaconess before she entered the SHN. She served in Bay Shore, Providence (twice), Philadelphia, and Newport (twice). Sister Veronica served as Sister-in-Charge in both Philadelphia and Newport. Poor vision prompted her return to the Fond du Lac Convent from her beloved Newport.

61. *Sister Marie, SHN* (1899–1942). Born Mildred Marie Lund in Minnesota to a Swedish family. Her father was an attorney. She was professed on the Feast of the Annunciation (transferred) on April 4, 1932. Sister Marie was a musician. She served in Philadelphia, Portland (Oregon), and Providence.

62. *Sister Alicia Theresa, SHN* (1894–1972). Born Alice Theresa Starr in Waupun, Wisconsin. Known as *Sister Alicia*, she worked as an elementary school teacher and was in contact with the sisters at Oneida through family in Green Bay before she entered the SHN. Professed on June 12, 1933, the Feast of St. Barnabas. Served as Novice Mistress, Assistant Superior, and Mother Superior, 1961–1972. Intelligent, practical, fun, and highly generous, Sister Alicia is credited with holding the community together through the turbulent 1960s. In addition to the Convent in Fond du Lac, she served in Baltimore.

63. *Sister Jeanne Elizabeth, SHN* (1896–1961). Born Gertrude Elizabeth Huff in Guilford, Piscataquis, Maine. Known as *Sister Jeanne*. Professed on All Saints Day, November 1, 1935. She trained as a dancer before she entered the SHN and was a member of the Church of the Advent in Boston. Served at Oneida, Baltimore, Providence, Philadelphia, Bay Shore, and Portland (Oregon). Buried at Swan Point Cemetery, Providence.

64. *Sister Philippa, SHN* (1887–1970). Born Käthe Louise Philippine Peters in Magdeburg, Germany. Became an American citizen in 1919 and was a member of Calvary Church in New York City. Professed on Trinity Sunday, June 7, 1936. Served at Oneida for many years and in New York City. She became a naturalized US citizen in 1914 while living in New York with her family.

65. *Sister Hilary, SHN* (1897–1983). Born Leigh Stoek in State College, Pennsylvania. Professed on All Saints Day, 1937. Sister Hilary's father was a mining expert for the University of Illinois in Champaign, Urbana. There, she was active in the local chapter of the Episcopal Church Women at St. Stephen's Episcopal Church. Sister Hilary graduated from Vassar College and received her M.D. from the Women's Medical College of Pennsylvania. Before entering the SHN, she served as a medical missionary in Puerto Rico. Sister Hilary taught First Aid during World War II. She served in Providence, Philadelphia, Bay Shore, Milwaukee, and Nevada. After surgery for her hip and a fractured leg, Sister Hilary returned to the Convent in Fond du Lac. She was an avid knitter and contributor to the Mouse Factory at St. Paul's Cathedral, where she served at least one tour of duty as the parish visitor.

66. *Sister Ruth Angela, SHN* (1905–2006). Born Hazel K. Fitz in Upper Darby, Pennsylvania. Her family were members of the Church of the Advocate in Philadelphia. Professed on June 6, 1938, Whitsun, Monday. Sister Ruth Angela was from a family of teachers and a Bryn Mawr College and Drexel School of Library Science graduate. She worked as a librarian before entering the SHN. Sister Ruth Angela held the positions of Novice Mistress and Assistant Superior. She served in Fond du Lac as Sister-in-Charge of the House of Rest and Retreat in Bay Shore for twenty-two years and in Milwaukee, Los Angeles, and Santa Barbara. In 1990, as Associates' Secretary, Sister Ruth Angela began a ministry visiting Associates around the country via the Greyhound bus, car, taxi, train, and airline at the age of eighty-five. In 2002, she covered 85 cities in 26 states. Known as the "Apostle of Sunshine," Sister Ruth Angela attended the General Convention of the Episcopal Church as a representative of the religious life.

67. *Sister Ruth Vera, SHN* (1904–1990). Born Ruth Alice Findon in Washington, D.C. She was influenced in her religious vocation by the SHN sisters at St. Clement's in Philadelphia where she attended art school at Moravian College. Professed on September 8, 1936, the Nativity of the Blessed Virgin Mary. Sister Ruth Vera was noted for exquisite work as an artist and designer of liturgical vestments and altar hangings. Her pen-and-ink drawings are still used at St. Clement's in Philadelphia. The Embroidery Department was reopened due to her artistic skills, and she taught the novices how to cut, sew, and embroider vestments. Sister Ruth Vera also served as a Sacristan. She served in Philadelphia (four times), Baltimore, Los Angeles (twice), Providence, and New York City. Known for her work among African

Americans, while in Wisconsin, Sister Ruth Vera commuted to Milwaukee on weekends to teach children at St. George's Episcopal Church.

68. *Sister Mary Angela, SHN* (1904–1976). Born Edith Angela Tyler in California and was raised in Los Angeles. Professed May 23, 1940, the Feast of Corpus Christi. Received deaconess training at St. Margaret's House, Berkeley. She served in Providence and New York City.

69. *Sister Ann Fidelia, SHN* (1911–1978). Born Rosella Ann (Amy) Woolsey in Vancouver, Washington, and raised in nearby Minnehaha, Sister Ann Fidelia came from a family of ranchers. Professed on May 23, 1940, the Feast of Corpus Christi. Studied at the Art Institute of Chicago and designed liturgical vestments. Sister Ann Fidelia served at Oneida and in New York City, Milwaukee, Baltimore, Newport, Philadelphia, San Diego, Bay Shore, Providence (twice), Los Angeles, and Santa Barbara (twice.) Sister Ann Fidelia was Sister-in-Charge in Philadelphia for eight years and in Providence for three years. She oversaw the Embroidery Department at the Convent in Fond du Lac for five years.

70. *Sister Paula, SHN* (1881–1971). Born Juliet Roseberry Stackhouse in Germantown, Philadelphia, Pennsylvania. Her family were members of St. Luke's Episcopal Church in Germantown. Professed on the Feast of Corpus Christi on June 12, 1941. She was a businesswoman before entering the SHN. An effective missionary, Sister Paula was honored by the Diocese of Los Angeles for serving as a chaplain for over twenty years in children's hospitals, tuberculosis centers, jails, and prisons associated with the Episcopal City Mission Society. In addition to her chaplaincy, she taught at All Saints Episcopal School in San Diego. Sister Paula served in Providence, Nevada, Los Angeles, and San Diego.

71. *Sister Edith Sylvia*, SHN (1913–2000). Born Sylvia Edith Hiss in Newark, New Jersey. Her family belonged to St. Mark's Episcopal Church in Newark. Professed on the Feast of St. James, July 25, 1942. Known as *Sister Sylvia*, she entered the SHN despite her mother's objections. She graduated from Hiram College, majoring in literature and languages and minoring in history. After graduation, she attended the Drexel School of Library Science. She served the SHN for many years as the Margaret Peabody Lending Library librarian, oversaw the sisters' libraries, and was Assistant Sacristan. Sister Sylvia taught church school and Confirmation classes in many urban parishes. She served in Fond du Lac, New York City, Newport, Baltimore, Philadelphia, Providence (three times), Bay Shore (twice), and Santa Barbara.

72. *Sister Jane Frances, SHN* (1901–1989). Born Margaret Louise Lehrle in St John, New Brunswick, Canada. Professed on July 3, 1943, the Feast of the Visitation, trans. She was known for her humor, love of animals, and grace in suffering. She became a naturalized US citizen in 1944. Sister Jane Frances served many years in the Altar Bread and Embroidery Departments. She served in Providence, Fond du Lac, Bay Shore, Philadelphia, Santa Barbara, Milwaukee, and Oneida. Sister Jane Frances oversaw the Altar Bread Department for eight years and served as Novice Mistress and Assistant Superior. She attended the General Convention of the Episcopal Church as a representative of religious life.

73. *Sister Katherine Anne, SHN* (1887–1971). Born Katherine Anne Jones in New York. Professed on August 24, 1946, the Feast of St. Bartholomew. Before entering the SHN, Sister Katherine Anne was the home economics teacher at Grafton Hall. She was a member of All Saints Cathedral in Milwaukee. Sister Katherine Anne served at Oneida and in Fond du Lac.

74. *Sister Mary Grace, SHN* (1916–2016). Born Mary Grace Brinton in Richardson Park, Delaware. Her family belonged to St. Andrew's Episcopal Church in Wilmington. Professed on the Feast of St. Mark, April 25, 1950. Sister Mary Grace served parishes in Providence, Philadelphia, San Diego, Livonia, Michigan, Elm Grove (Wisconsin), Fond du Lac, and the SHN retreat houses in Bay Shore and Santa Barbara. She served in Anchorage, Alaska, for several years. She established the first chapter of the Girls Friendly Society there and was active in the Alaska Chapter of the Evangelical and Catholic Mission. Sister Mary Grace taught Vacation Bible School in Iowa, Michigan, Texas, Indiana, and Louisiana, youth camps in Long Island and Indiana dioceses, and parishes in Boston and Kansas. She also served on committees and commissions in the Diocese of Fond du Lac, including the Ecumenical Commission, and the city, including the County Board of Alcoholism and Other Drug Abuse, the Mental Health Board, and the Board for the Association of Retarded Citizens. At the Convent in Fond du Lac, she oversaw the building, often acting as an electrician, plumber, and carpenter.

75. *Sister Elsbeth, SHN* (1914–2011). Born Elizabeth Ellen Morris in Philadelphia. Professed on April 25, 1950. A trained dancer before she entered the SHN, Sister Elsbeth also had a keen interest in horticulture. Visiting St. Margaret's Convent in Boston influenced her vocation to religious life. She served in Fond du Lac, Philadelphia (twice), Bay Shore (four times), New York City (twice), Baltimore, Newport, Providence, Los Angeles, San Diego, and Santa Barbara (three times). Sister Elsbeth loved working with children

and assisted at Vacation Bible Schools and church camps. Known as a gracious listener and the most peripatetic sister who could make a valuable contribution anywhere, she also served as the Novice Mistress for five years.

76. *Sister Florence Isabel, SHN* (1906–2003). Born Florence Isabel Ormerod in St. Louis. Known as *Sister Isabel.* Set apart as a deaconess in 1933, she served as a UTO worker in Michigan, Ohio, and California parishes. She worked as a teacher among Indigenous people in the Dakotas and Nevada. Professed on the Feast of Saint Mary Magdalene, July 22, 1950. In the SHN, she served in New York City and as Sister-in-Charge in Los Angeles, San Diego, and Bay Shore. Sister Isabel also served for many years as the Secretary to the Associates.

77. *Sister Georgina Louise, SHN.* (1906–1952). Born Georgina Louise Gilchrist [Willing] in Brooklyn. Professed on the Feast of Saint Mary Magdalene, July 22, 1950. She worked as a switchboard operator in the garment industry before her marriage. Sister Georgina was married in 1938 to Carl F. Willing. Willing was a former choir boy from Grace Church in Manhattan who worked as a traveling salesman. The couple later divorced, and the marriage was annulled because he was also married to someone else. Visits to the SHN retreat house in Bay Shore inspired her vocation. Sister Georgina Louise served in Providence and died of cancer two years after her profession. She is buried in Swan Point Cemetery, Providence.

78. *Sister Mary Rebekah, SHN.* (1904–1957). Born Mary Rebekah Spofford in Haverhill, Massachusetts. Professed on the Feast of Corpus Christi, May 24, 1951. Sister Mary Rebekah's father was a carpenter, and she was a teacher at public schools in Massachusetts and New York before entering religious life. She was also an accomplished violin teacher. Sister Mary Rebekah served in Milwaukee. She was a musician who could play many instruments; the organ at All Saints Cathedral, Milwaukee was dedicated to Sister Mary Rebekah.

79. *Sister Julia Elizabeth, SHN* (1907–1999). Born Julia Elizabeth Wilson in Washington, D.C., Professed on the Feast of the Conception of the Blessed Virgin Mary, 1951. Medical librarian at the Johns Hopkins Medical School. Influenced in her vocation by Sister Caritas, SHN, Sister Julia Elizabeth was an academic and wrote a history of the retreat center at Bay Shore. She served in Fond du Lac, Philadelphia, Providence, Bay Shore, Los Angeles, and Santa Barbara.

80. *Sister Margaretta, SHN* (1927–2015). Born Margaret Bishop Kraft in Brooklyn, New York. Professed on the Feast of St. Peter in Chains, August 1,

1956. Sister Margaretta was a trained stenographer and worked in business before entering religious life. A talented artist and accomplished vestment designer, she oversaw the Embroidery Department for several years. She designed a magnificent banner for the Cathedral in Fond du Lac. A gifted musician, Sister Margaretta played the recorder for many years. She served in Fond du Lac, New York City, Santa Barbara and as Sister-in-Charge in Providence and Green Lake (Ripon). Her classes in theology and scripture were considered inspiring by children and adults. Her brother was the Rev. Harry Kraft, an Episcopal priest who served in Rhode Island, Arizona, and New York. After her move to Green Lake (Ripon), Sister Margaretta participated in Bible study at the local parish and organized the sisters' library.

81. *Sister Mary Frances, SHN* (1925–2008). Born Mary Frances Tudor in Baltimore, she was a Church of the Advent member there. One account suggests that she was an abandoned child and lived in an orphanage during her youth. Professed on the Feast of the Epiphany, January 6, 1958. She left the community in 1949 before taking her vows and returned in 1953. Sister Mary Francis served in Fond du Lac, New York City, Providence, San Diego, Santa Barbara, Bay Shore, and short-term missions in Kansas City and South Dakota. She had unique gifts for working with older adults and, during her years in Fond du Lac, visited nursing homes, especially the Lutheran Home.

82. *Sister Boniface, SHN* (1928–2011). Born Elenore Barbara Göetz in Würzburg, Bavaria, Germany. Her father was a tailor and taught her to sew. Sister Boniface survived the bombings of her hometown in Germany during World War II. After the war, she worked as a secretary for the US. Air Force. She immigrated to the United States in 1954 and became a naturalized citizen in 1961. Raised in the Roman Catholic church, Sister Boniface moved to Los Angeles, became an Episcopalian, and was a member of St. John's Church. A visit to the SHN retreat house in Santa Barbara and encouragement from Sister Patricia and others there inspired her call to religious life. Professed on the Feast of St. Teresa of Avila, October 15, 1962. Served as Novice Mistress, Sister-in-Charge, and Mother Superior, 1973–1996, 2007–2011. Known for her organizational gifts, she served in Fond du Lac, Providence, New York City, Bay Shore, and Green Lake (Ripon). As Mother Superior, she spoke widely and cultivated many friends for the SHN. She served as a trustee for Nashotah House. Mother Boniface received training in ministry with alcoholics and their families. Known for opening the Convent to all, she worked tirelessly to create Bethlehem-by-the-Lake and continued her service until her death.

83. *Sister Columba, SHN* (1934–2016). Born Joan Louise Moore in Sewickley, Pennsylvania to an armed forces family. She attended college and worked as a kindergarten teacher at a school run by the Order of Saint Anne before entering religious life. Professed in the Octave of the Nativity of the Blessed Virgin, September 15, 1964. She served in Fond du Lac, Providence, Bay Shore, Santa Barbara, San Diego, and on a short-term mission in South Dakota. She was active in the Cursillo Movement and ministry with the deaf. Sister Columba volunteered in the local hospital's emergency department in her later years. She later received Clinical Pastoral Education (CPE) training and served as a hospital chaplain at St. Agnes Hospital, Fond du Lac. At the Cathedral in Fond du Lac, Sister Columba sang in the choir, served as a lay reader and Chapter member, assisted in the Mouse Factory, and volunteered in the food pantry. Sister Columba was an avid bird watcher and animal advocate. She attended the General Convention of the Episcopal Church as a representative of religious life. Sister Columba was interred with her mother in St Paul's Cathedral Columbarium in Fond du Lac.

84. *Sister Kathleen Marie, SHN* (1924–2016). Born Kathleen Robertson [Wilson] in Morristown, New Jersey, into a Baptist family and raised in Chicago by her grandmother. She married Russell P. Wilson in 1951 and was a wife, mother of two sons, stepmother to two daughters, grandmother, and great-grandmother. Professed in the Order of St. Anne, Chicago, on September 29, 1981, the Feast of St. Michael & All Angels. She transferred to the SHN in 1987 and served as Assistant Sacristan and Assistant Housekeeper. Her efforts in the sewing room produced a new habit design for the sisters. Before entering the SHN, Sister Kathleen Marie was well known in the Diocese of Chicago and worked as a postal clerk, parish secretary at the Church of the Ascension in Chicago, and a teacher, and later principal, at St. Edmund's Episcopal School. She also studied theology at Loyola University in Chicago. Sister Kathleen was the second African American sister and the first widow in the SHN. Her daughter-in-law is an Episcopal priest. Sister Kathleen Marie served in Fond du Lac, as Sister-in-Charge in Santa Barbara, and in short-term missions in Louisiana and Kansas. Sister Kathleen Marie was Secretary to the Companions —teenage Associates of the sisterhood—from 1988 to 1999. She attended the General Convention of the Episcopal Church as a representative of religious life.

85. *Sister Charis, SHN* (1948–). Born Sharon D. Jones in Fort Riley, Kansas. Professed on December 27, 1983, the Feast of St. the Evangelist. Sister Charis was the first African American sister in the SHN. Her father was a professional soldier. Before entering the SHN, Sister Charis worked as

a math teacher in Columbus, Georgia. During her years in the SHN, she has worked extensively with young people in church schools, camps, and conferences. She served in Fond du Lac, Providence, Green Lake (Ripon), and short-term mission work in South Dakota and Wisconsin. While in Providence, Sister Charis ministered to mental health patients. She is active in St. Peter's Episcopal Church in Ripon, Wisconsin. (The SHN has been active at St. Peter's since the 1950s during summers at Green Lake and after their move there.) Sister Charis has also served the SHN by caring for her older sisters.

86. *Sister Maria, SHN* (1946–2007). Born Jane Karen Griffiths in Batavia, New York. Professed on March 15, 1991, the Feast of St. Mary the Virgin. She learned about SHN at the retreat center in Bay Shore and was encouraged in her vocation by Sister Margaretta. Sister Maria had a master's degree in education from the State University of New York and worked as an elementary school teacher before she entered the SHN. Sister Maria particularly enjoyed teaching first and second graders. She suffered from rheumatoid arthritis from the age of forty-two and briefly left the sisterhood to seek treatment for her illness. She served as Novice Mistress, Assistant Sacristan, and Mother Superior from 1996 to 2007. Sister Maria served in Fond du Lac, Bay Shore, Santa Barbara, and Green Lake (Ripon) and was a spiritual director for seminarians and their spouses at Nashotah House Seminary. Sister Maria had an ongoing relationship with a day school in the Diocese of Fort Worth. She was instrumental in building Bethlehem-by-the-Lake and selling the Convent building in Fond du Lac. She took charge of the retreat house in Santa Barbara in 2002 and refurbished it. Known for her love for all creation, Sister Maria became a vegetarian and advocated for conserving the planet.

87. *Sister Abigail, SHN* (b. 1951–). Born Margaret Joan Zacari in the Pittsburgh area. Professed on the Feast of Saints Phillip & James, May 1, 2005. Sister Abigail worked as a trained nurse (RN) for twenty-five before entering the SHN, first at Shadyside Hospital and then at East Liberty Family Health Care Center, a Christian outreach ministry. Sister Abigail served as Mother Superior from 2012 to 2023. Her medical skills were utilized at camps and conferences at the Convent in Fond du Lac, and Bethlehem-by-the-Lake. Sister Abigail served as Associates' Secretary, Assistant Superior, and Sister-in-Charge in Santa Barbara. She also served in West Virginia. In addition to conducting retreats, she provided generous hospitality and outreach through the retreat house in Santa Barbara, eventually deeding it to the Order of the Holy Cross. At St. Peter's Church, Ripon, she has helped

with the Godly Play program, Vacation Bible School, and diocesan summer camp.

Sisters included in this listing were life professed and are either currently living in vows or died in the SHN. Unless otherwise noted, deceased sisters are buried in the Rienzi Cemetery, Fond du Lac, Wisconsin—biographical data obtained through SHN records, obituaries, and correspondence and confirmed through Ancestry.com.

FOUNDING SISTERS (PREVIOUSLY OF THE SOCIETY OF ST. MARGARET)

Sister Mary Margaret, SHN

Sister Hannah Margaret, SHN

Sister Ruth Margaret, SHN

Sister Katherine, SHN

Sister Rebecca, SHN

Sister Agnes, SHN

MOTHER SUPERIORS

Sister Hannah Margaret, SHN, 1882–1884 (one-year term)

Mother Ruth Margaret, SHN (Mother Foundress), 1884–1908

Mother Katherine Edith, SHN, 1908–1919

Mother Matilda, SHN, 1919–1942

Mother Ruth Mary, SHN, 1942–1961

Mother Alicia Theresa, SHN, 1961–1972

Mother Boniface, SHN, 1973–1996, 2007–2011

Mother Maria, SHN, 1996–2007

Mother Abigail, SHN, 2012–2023

Appendix B
Convents, Mission Houses, and Retreat Houses— Sisterhood of the Holy Nativity

Brimmer Street, Boston (1882–1888)

House of the Holy Nativity, Providence (St. Stephen's Parish); St. Helena's Rest,

Barrington, Rhode Island; House of Rest, Tiverton, Mission of the Holy Nativity,

Thornton, and parishes in Olneyville, East Providence, Cranson, and other-Rhode Island churches (1888–1983)

Mission House of the Visitation; Mission House of the Holy Nativity; Convent of the Holy

Nativity, Fond du Lac, Wisconsin (1889–1999)

St. Michael's Mission House, the Oneida Nation, Wisconsin (1890–1946)

Mission House of the Holy Cross, Kingston, New York (1891–1905)

Mission House of the Holy Nativity, Church of St. Mary the Virgin, New York (Manhattan), and Summer Home in Keyport, New Jersey (1899–1907; 1909–1966)

Mission House of the Holy Nativity, the Diocese of Maine; St. Luke's Cathedral, Portland, and St. Timothy's, Orr's Island, Maine (1908–1923)

Mission House of the Holy Nativity, All Saints Cathedral, Milwaukee (1909–1962)

Mission House of the Holy Nativity, The Zabriskie Memorial Church of St. John the Evangelist, St. Michael's School, Newport, Rhode, Island (1914–1953)

Mission House of the Holy Nativity and Retreat House, All Saints Church, West Orange, New Jersey (1915–1925)

Mission House of the Holy Nativity, Mount Calvary Parish, Baltimore (1917–1966)

House of Rest and Retreat, Holy Nativity Retreat House, Bay Shore, Long Island (1918–1980)

Bethlehem-by-the-Lake, Green Lake, (Ripon) Wisconsin (1923–2014)

Mission House of the Holy Nativity, St. Clement's, Philadelphia (1924–1962)

Mission House of the Holy Nativity, St. Matthias Parish & the Episcopal Diocese of Los Angeles (1927–1959)

Mission House of the Holy Nativity, St. Mark's Church, Portland, Oregon (1938–1941)

Mission House, Missionary District of Nevada, included the Moapa Nation, Las Vegas, Boulder

City (1940–1948)

Saint Mary's Retreat House, Santa Barbara (1954–2013)

Mission House, All Saints Episcopal Parish & School San Diego (1960–1974)

Emmaus House, the Diocese of West Virginia (2000–2002)

Appendix C
Significant Dates in the History of the Sisterhood of the Holy Nativity (SHN)

1702 – The Oneida people accept Christianity

1820s – The Oneida founded a parochial day school (Hobart Mission day School)

1821 – Formation of the Domestic and Foreign Missionary Society (DFMS)

1822 – [1821–1823] – The Oneida bring Christianity to Wisconsin

1830s-1840s – THE OXFORD MOVEMENT

1825 – The Hobart Church built at Oneida

1826 – Ruth Tufts Vose, Mother Ruth Margaret, Mother Foundress, born in Boston

1830 – Charles Chapman Grafton was born in Boston

1834 – Jackson Kemper visits the Oneida at Duck Creek

1835 – Jackson Kemper consecrated the first missionary bishop of the Northwest

1842 – Nashotah House founded

1844 – Church of the Advent, Boston, founded

1845 – First Anglican Sisterhood, the Sisterhood of the Holy Cross, founded in England

1845 – Anne Ayres professed, Church of the Holy Communion, New York City

1848 – *Wisconsin Statehood*

1852 – First Episcopal sisterhood founded, Sisterhood of the Holy Communion

1855 – Society of St. Margaret (SSM) founded in Sussex, England; Charles Grafton ordained to the diaconate in the Diocese of Maryland

1858 – Charles Grafton was ordained to the priesthood

1858 – Publication of *Directorum Anglicanum* and revival of the ecclesiastical arts

1865 – Charles Grafton meets Pusey, Sellon, Benson, and others in England associated with the revival of religious orders in Anglicanism

1866 – Society of St John the Evangelist (SSJE) founded in Oxford, England

1867 – Confraternity of the Blessed Sacrament brought to the United States by Charles Grafton

1870s-1920s – THE SOCIAL GOSPEL MOVEMENT

1871 – SSM invited to Boston to staff the Children's Hospital

1872 – Charles Grafton becomes rector of the Church of the Advent, Boston

1872 – All Saints Sisters of the Poor (ASSP) arrive in Baltimore

1882 – Sisterhood of the Holy Nativity (SHN) founded on Brimmer Street, Boston, Sister Hannah was elected superior for a fixed term (November 1882- January 1884); the professed sisters renewed their vows on December 25, 1882

1882 – First SHN Associates

1883 – SHN begins retreats for working women in Rindge, New Hampshire—"First retreat for lay women in the Episcopal Church"

1883 – SHN mission at St. Timothy's, Roxborough, and other Philadelphia area churches

1884 – The first four SHN novices professed

1884 – Order of the Holy Cross (OHC) founded in New York City

1884 – Margaret Peabody Lending Library founded by an SHN Associate

1884 – First invitation to SHN to work at Oneida

1884 – Mother Foundress Ruth Margaret elected superior

1884 – SHN mission at St Mary's in Kansas City begins

1885 – SHN mission at St. Mary's in East Providence begins

1886 – Altar bread production begins

1886 – The Rule and Constitution completed by Sister Hannah, SHN.

1887 – SHN Community retreat, Nantucket, MA

1888 – Grafton elected bishop of the Diocese of Fond du Lac; SHN moves to St. Stephen's, Providence, Rhode Island. Charles Grafton resigns as rector of the Church of Advent, Boston; SHN reconciles with SSM

1889 – SHN begins work in the Diocese of Fond du Lac and Reservation of the Blessed Sacrament in Providence convent; Charles Grafton consecrated bishop of the Episcopal Diocese of Fond du Lac

1889 – First SHN mission house in the state of Wisconsin in Plymouth

1889 – The General Convention passes the Deaconess Canon

1890 – Ecclesiastical embroidery begins; House of the Visitation, Fond du Lac, opens

1890 – SHN houses for rest and retreat founded in Tiverton and Barrington, Rhode Island

1890 – SHN mission house at Oneida opens.

1891 – SHN opened a temporary mission at Oakfield, Wisconsin

1891 --SHN mission in Kansas City closed

1891 – SHN mission for English Mill Hands, Thornton, Rhode Island; work with girls and young women in Olneyville, Rhode Island, opened

1891 –SHN mission in Kingston, New York, opens

1892 – SHN begins social work with recent immigrants in Providence

1893 – SHN reaches twenty-five sisters

1895 – SHN temporary mission to St Luke's, Utica

1895 – (Renamed) House of the Holy Nativity, Fond du Lac, opens

1895 – Grafton Hall School founded; Grafton ordained Oneida Chief Cornelius Hill to the diaconate

1895 – SHN mission to Cleveland with James Otis Sargent Huntington, OHC; The picture department is opened at Huntington's urging.

1896 – SHN takes over the Margaret Peabody Lending Library

1897 – Lambeth Conference approves the revival of sisterhoods

1898 – SHN helps begin lace-making at Oneida

1899 – SHN mission to St Mary the Virgin, New York City.

1899 – Publication of Percy Dearmer's, *The Parson's Handbook,* revives catholic liturgy, English Use

1903 – Electricity and telephone installed in Fond Du Lac

1904 – Cornerstone laid for the Fond du Lac Convent

1904 – Oneida lace-makers win prizes in competitions

1905 -- SHN moved from Providence to Fond du Lac; Dedication of the Convent of the Holy Nativity

1905 – Grafton ordains Oneida Chief Cornelius Hill to the priesthood; Oneida Hospital converted to a dispensary

1905 – Mission House in Kingston, New York, closes

1906 – First SHN clergy Associates

1906 – Grafton Parish House built at Oneida

1907 – Mission house in Portland, Maine, opens

1907 – Charles Winifred Douglas tutors SHN on plainchant; SHN leaves New York City mission for one year

1908 – Mother Foundress resigns as superior for health reasons; Mother Katherine Edith elected superior

APPENDIX C

1909 – Mission house at St Mary the Virgin, New York reopens

1909 – Mission house in Milwaukee at All Saints Cathedral opens

1910 – Mother Foundress dies

1912 – Charles Grafton dies

1914–1918 – WORLD WAR I (THE GREAT WAR)

1914 – Mission house in Newport, Rhode Island, opens

1915 – Special Novena for the Allied war effort

1915 – Mission house and retreat house open in West Orange, New Jersey
– "The first retreat house for women in the Episcopal Church

1917 – Mission house at Mt Calvary Parish in Baltimore opens

1918 – House for Retreat and Rest, Bay Shore, opens

1919 – Mother Katharine Edith dies; Mother Matilda elected superior

1920s – "THE GOLDEN AGE OF ANGLO-CATHOLICISM"

1920s – The Parish Press was founded at St. Paul's Cathedral, Fond du Lac

1921 – Josephine Hill Webster named supervisor of Oneida Lace Industry

1922 – SHN named the largest sisterhood in the Episcopal Church

1923 – Mission house in Maine closes

1923 – SHN builds a summer cottage at Green Lake, Wisconsin—"The House that Mother Built"—and obtains a Model T automobile

1923 – The priest's cottage is built at Bay Shore

1924 – Mission house at St. Clement's, Philadelphia opens

1925 – Mission house and retreat house in West Orange, New Jersey, closes.

1927 – Mission house at St. Matthias and the Diocese of Los Angeles opens

1930 – First mission trip to Burlington, Vermont; Grafton Hall School closes

1938 – Mission house in Portland, Oregon, opens

1939–1945 – WORLD WAR II

1940 – Mission house in the Missionary District of Las Vegas opens

1941 – Mission house in Portland, Oregon, closes

1942 – Mother Matilda dies; Mother Ruth Mary elected superior

1946 – Mission house closed at Oneida; the Order of St Anne continued the work

1948 – Mission house in Nevada closes

1953 – Mission house in Newport closes

1954 – St Mary's Retreat House, Santa Barbara opens

1956 – Bethlehem Chapel, St. Mary's Retreat House built

1959 – Mission house in Los Angeles closes

1960 – Mission house at All Saints' Episcopal Church and School in San Diego opens

1961 – Mother Alicia Theresa elected superior

1962 – Mission houses in Milwaukee and Philadelphia close

1966 – Mission houses in New York and Baltimore close

1967 – Lightning strikes Mary's Retreat House

1967 – SHN returns to teach at Holy Apostles Church, Oneida, through the 1970s; the Oneida parochial school closed.

1970 – The General Convention approves women deputies and women's ordination to the diaconate

1972 – Mother Alicia Theresa dies

1973 – Mother Boniface elected superior, picture department and altar bread departments close

APPENDIX C 219

1974 – First ordinations of women to the priesthood in the Episcopal Church; mission house in San Diego closes

1976 – The General Convention approves the ordination of women to the priesthood

1979 – The *1979 Book of Common Prayer* approved by the General Convention

1980 – Holy Nativity Retreat House, Bay Shore, closes.

1982 – Centenary Celebration, Fond du Lac

1983 – Mission house in Providence closes

1984 – The Companions of the SHN program founded

1986 – Short-term mission to Alaska, St Christopher's, Anchorage

1988 – The ecclesiastical embroidery department closes

1996 – Sister Maria elected superior

1988 – Margaret Peabody Library closes

1997 – SHN founds the Oblate program

1999 – Dedication of Bethlehem-by-the Lake and the Chapel of the Incarnation, Green Lake, Wisconsin; SHN sells the Fond du Lac Convent

2000 – Emmaus House opens in West Virginia (Emmaus House); sale of Fond du Lac Convent

2001 – Work with Hispanic Ministries Team, All Saints, Oxnard, California

2002 – Mission house in West Virginia closes

2007 – Mother Maria dies; Sr. Boniface assumes leadership

2008 – Montecito Tea Fire – Order of the Holy Cross (OHC) moves to St. Mary's Retreat House

2011 – Mother Boniface dies

2012 – Mother Abigail elected superior

2013 – SHN closes work at St Mary's Retreat House and deeds the property to OHC

2014 – SHN donates funds to SSJE to build Grafton House and the Chapel of the Holy Nativity, West Newbury, Massachusetts

2014 – SHN sells Bethlehem-by-the-Lake; sisters move to a smaller home in Ripon, Wisconsin

2022 – The 80th General Convention approves the annual Religious Life Sunday on the Third Sunday after the Epiphany

Appendix D
Interviews for this Book

Interviews conducted by Sheryl A. Kujawa-Holbrook

January 11, 2021, September 16, 2021, Matthew A. Gunter

February 15, 2021, April 15, 2021, July 28, 2021, Barbara Jean, AF

September 12, 2021, Charis, SHN

September 13, 2021, Edwin B. Smith

September 13, 2021, Marie and Roger Funk

October 7, 2021, Kathleen Reeves

October 8, 2021, Scott Borden, OHC

October 14, 2021, Regina Christianson

October 22, 2021, Keith and Suzanne Whitmore

November 4, 2021, Russell and Jerrie Jacobus

November 4, 2021, Rebecca Dinovo

November 10, 2021, Kathy Whitt

November 10, 2021, David Klutterman

November 29, 2021, Neff and Dorothy Powell

December 1, 2021, Keith Ackerman

December 1, 2021, Paul Aparicio

December 2, 2021, Rodger Patience

December 14, 2021, Ellen Stephen, OHC

December 15, 2021, Richard Valantasis

January 11, 2022, Julian Wilson, AF

January 12, 2022, Carole Maddux

January 12, 2022, Sue von Rautenkranz

January 13, 2022, Ezgi Saribay Perkins

January 14, 2022, Donald Langlois

January 18, 2022, Samuel Timothy, AF

January 21, 2022, Dorsey Henderson

January 25, 2022, William Bippus, Jr and R. Edgar Wallace

January 25, 2022, Jaime Coats

January 26, 2022, Ana Clara, OSA

February 1, 2022, Wilson Roone

February 1, 2022, Elizabeth Rolfe-Thomas, SSJD, Constance Joanna Gefert, SSJD, Elizabeth Ann Eckert, SSJD

February 1, 2022, Michele Whitford

February 11, 2022, Anthony Guillen

February 18, 2022, Greta Ronnigen, CDL

February 18, 2022, Nancy Kuhn and Lynn Shaw

February 22, 2022, Madeline Mary, CSM

February 25, 2022, Karl Schaffenburg

February 24, 2022, Frank Tracy Griswold, III

February 24, 2022, Phoebe Pettingell

March 4, 2022, Monica Clare, CSJB

March 11, 2022, David M. Baumann

March 11, 2022, Ted McConnell

April 4, 2022, Carol Knox

April 20, 2022, Norman and Zulette Catir

May 26, 2022, Michael Corrigan

July 8, 2022, Anna Wager

July 22, 2022, Patricia Allen

November 30, 2022, Michael Kaehr

January 7, 2023, Maximillian Manuel and Andrew Nardone

June 8, 2023, Patricia Allen

Interviews recorded by Steven Peay

November 18, 2018, Mariana Keene

May 31, 2019, June 10, 2019, Charis, SHN, Abigail, DHN

June 10, 2019, Barbara Jean, AF

Appendix E
Illustrations

Charles Chapman Grafton (1830–1912). "Father Founder" of the Sisterhood of the Holy Nativity. Elected Bishop of the Episcopal Diocese of Fond du Lac in 1889. Photo from the Sisterhood of the Holy Nativity Collection (SHNC), used with permission.

APPENDIX E

Mother Ruth Margaret, SHN (1826-1910), "Mother Foundress," Superior 1884-1908. Photo from the Sisterhood of the Holy Nativity Collection (SHNC), used with permission.

Cornerstone, Convent of the Holy Nativity, Fond du Lac. Photo from the Sisterhood of the Holy Nativity Collection (SHNC), used with permission.

"The Heart of Christmas." The Christmas Altar with Holly-Covered Rood Screen, Convent of the Holy Nativity, Fond du Lac. Photo from the Sisterhood of the Holy Nativity Collection (SHNC), used with permission.

Music Class. Hobart Mission Day School, Oneida. Photo from the Sisterhood of the Holy Nativity Collection (SHNC), used with permission.

Oneida Lace-Makers. Seen here with a lace altar frontal. Photo from the Sisterhood of the Holy Nativity Collection (SHNC), used with permission.

Mother Katherine Edith, SHN, Superior 1908–1919. Photo from the Sisterhood of the Holy Nativity Collection (SHNC), used with permission.

APPENDIX E

Mother Matilda, SHN, Superior 1919–1942. Pictured with Rex, Her Notorious Dog. Photo from the Sisterhood of the Holy Nativity Collection (SHNC), used with permission.

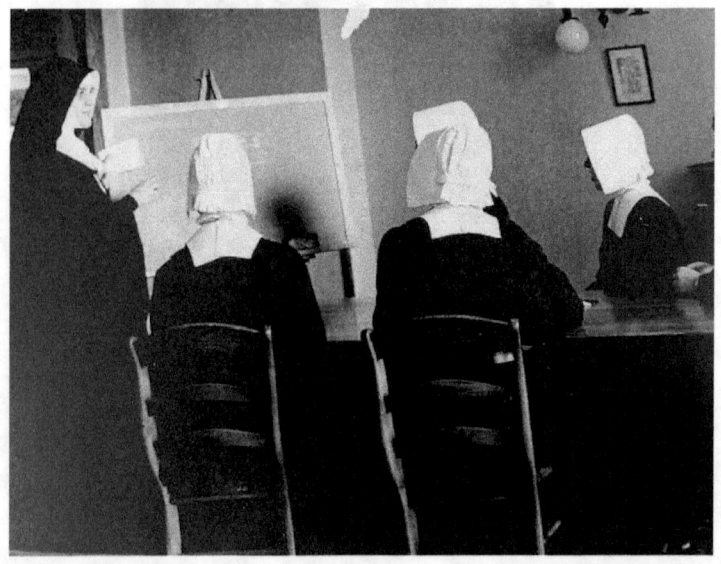

Novitiate Class. Photo from the Sisterhood of the Holy Nativity Collection (SHNC), used with permission.

APPENDIX E

Sister Sylvia, SHN, in the Margaret Peabody Lending Library. Preparing Books for Mailing. Photo from the Sisterhood of the Holy Nativity Collection (SHNC), used with permission.

Recorder Class. Photo from the Sisterhood of the Holy Nativity Collection (SHNC), used with permission.

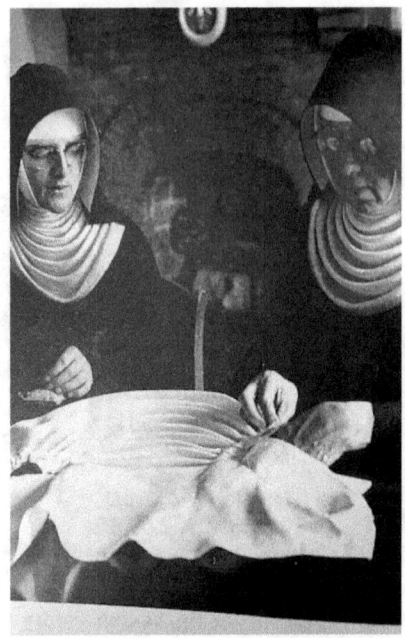

Sewing Wimples. Photo from the Sisterhood of the Holy Nativity Collection (SHNC), used with permission.

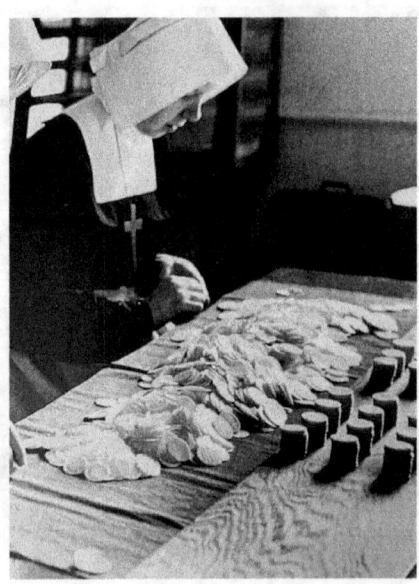

The Altar Bread Department. A Novice Counts and Sorts Communion Wafers. Photo from the Sisterhood of the Holy Nativity Collection (SHNC), used with permission.

APPENDIX E 231

The Embroidery Department. Sister Ruth Vera, SHN, Works on a Stole. Photo from the Sisterhood of the Holy Nativity Collection (SHNC), used with permission.

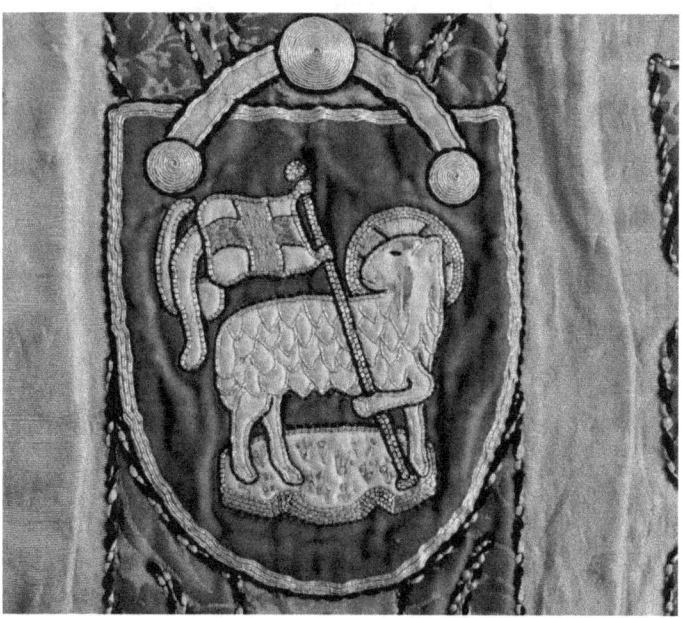

Sample Embroidery—Lamb of God (Angus Dei) by Sister Ruth Vera, SHN. Photo from the Sisterhood of the Holy Nativity Collection (SHNC), used with permission.

APPENDIX E

The Picture Department. The Picture Department of the Sisterhood of the Holy Nativity circulated countless devotional cards in parishes and through the mail to encourage prayer and reflection. Some included images of biblical scenes, the saints, or feasts. Some were purchased for distribution, while the sisters created others, like this calligraphy card. Photo from the Sisterhood of the Holy Nativity Collection (SHNC), used with permission.

The Sacristy. Sister Veronica, SHN, in the sacristy at St. Stephen's Church, Providence. In most of the parishes and retreat houses they served, and in their mission houses and the Convent, the Sisterhood of the Holy Nativity contributed to the liturgy as Sacristans. In many locations, they also provided training for Altar Guild members. Photo from the Sisterhood of the Holy Nativity Collection (SHNC), used with permission.

The Divine Office. The chapel was the heart of the Convent and every mission house and retreat house of the Sisterhood of the Holy Nativity. Photo from the Sisterhood of the Holy Nativity Collection (SHNC), used with permission.
"Seven times a day do we praise Thee, O God."

Intercessory Prayer. A central ministry of the Sisterhood of the Holy Nativity was to pray for the world's needs at the altar. "We hold up the world to God." Photo from the Sisterhood of the Holy Nativity Collection (SHNC), used with permission.

Sister of the Holy Nativity Participates in a Baptism, the Church of St. Mary the Virgin, New York City. Throughout their history, Sisterhood of the Holy Nativity members prepared the laity for the sacraments, including Baptism. Photo by Gladys Louise Rice, 1951. Published with the permission of the Church of St. Mary the Virgin.

Mother Ruth Mary, SHN, Superior, 1942–1961. Photo from the Sisterhood of the Holy Nativity Collection (SHNC), used with permission.

APPENDIX E   235

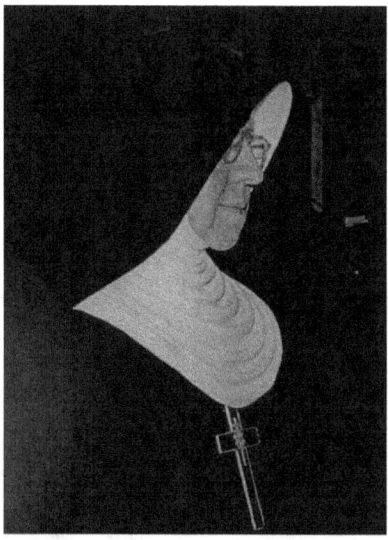

Mother Alicia Theresa, SHN, Superior 1961–1972. Photo from the Sisterhood of the Holy Nativity Collection (SHNC), used with permission.

Garden in Baltimore. The sisters planted gardens for food, flowers, and reflection whenever possible. Sister Dorothea, SHN, and Sister Bernadine, SHN, enjoy the garden at the mission house in Baltimore. Photo from the Sisterhood of the Holy Nativity Collection (SHNC), used with permission.

APPENDIX E

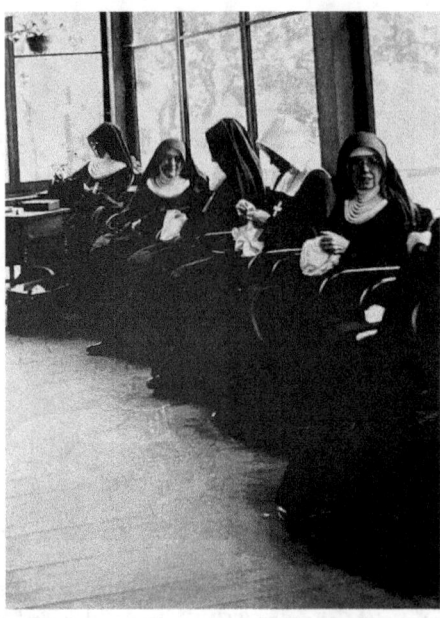

Recreation. Community time at the Convent. Photo from the Sisterhood of the Holy Nativity Collection (SHNC), used with permission.

Sisters in the Garden, Holy Nativity Retreat Center, Bayshore, Long Island. The beautiful grounds of the retreat center provided beauty and encouraged reflection. Photo from the Sisterhood of the Holy Nativity Collection (SHNC), used with permission.

On Retreat. A Retreatant is Shown to Her Room. Providing individuals, especially women, with accommodations and support for retreats was one of the earliest ministries undertaken by the Sisterhood of the Holy Nativity. SHN's retreat houses were among the first in the Episcopal Church. Photo from the Sisterhood of the Holy Nativity Collection (SHNC), used with permission.

Mother Boniface, SHN, 1973–1996; 2007–2011. Photo from the Sisterhood of the Holy Nativity Collection (SHNC), used with permission.

St. Matthias Church School, Los Angeles. Advancing the catholic faith through religious education for all ages was central to the mission of the Sisterhood of the Holy Nativity. Many of the sisters had a particular fondness for working with children. Photo from the Sisterhood of the Holy Nativity Collection (SHNC), used with permission.

Sister Paula, SHN, Recognized by the Diocese of Los Angeles. Shown here with Bishop Francis Eric Bloy and an SHN Associate, Sister Paula received a certificate of recognition for her many years as a chaplain in city hospitals and tuberculosis sanitariums. Photo from the Sisterhood of the Holy Nativity Collection (SHNC), used with permission.

Nursey School Worship, All Saints Episcopal School, San Diego. Sister Isabel, SHN, guides the children through the service. Photo from the Sisterhood of the Holy Nativity Collection (SHNC), used with permission.

Christmas at Bethlehem Chapel, St. Mary's Retreat House, Santa Barbara. Photo from the Sisterhood of the Holy Nativity Collection (SHNC), used with permission.

Sister Julia Elizabeth, SHN, and the Morris Award Winner —Best Household Pet. The award went to Mickie, one of several cats at St. Mary's Retreat Center. Photo from the Sisterhood of the Holy Nativity Collection (SHNC), used with permission.

Centenary Celebration 1982. Photo from the Sisterhood of the Holy Nativity Collection (SHNC), used with permission.

APPENDIX E   241

Mother Maria, SHN, Superior 1996–2007. Photo from the Sisterhood of the Holy Nativity Collection (SHNC), used with permission.

Sister Ruth Angela's 100th Birthday. Sister Ruth Angela, SHN, had many roles during her long history in the sisterhood. Still, perhaps the most popular was her role as the Associates' Secretary when she traveled around the country via the Greyhound bus, car, taxi, train, and airline to visit them. She was appropriately known as the "Apostle of Sunshine." Photo from the Archives, Episcopal Diocese of Fond du Lac, used with permission.

APPENDIX E

August 2007 Grafton Commemoration, Bethlehem-by-the-Lake. Photo from the Archives, Episcopal Diocese of Fond du Lac, used with permission.

Sister Abigail, SHN, Life Profession, Mother Superior 2012–2023. Photo from the Sisterhood of the Holy Nativity Collection (SHNC), used with permission.

APPENDIX E

Sister Charis, SHN, and Saint, The Parish of St. Peter, Ripon, Wisconsin. Sister Charis and her dog, Saint, are much-loved parish members. Photo from the Parish of St. Peter, used with permission.

Bibliography

PRIMARY SOURCES
Archival

Sisterhood of the Holy Nativity Collection (SHNC). The DeKoven Center Archives, Racine, Wisconsin. During the research for this book, this collection was held by the Episcopal Diocese of Fond du Lac, Appleton, Wisconsin. Includes original correspondence, newsletters, journals, published and unpublished articles, pamphlets, books, and photographs.

Sisterhood of the Holy Nativity Records, 1882-1976. Wisconsin Historical Society. Micro 753; Oshkosh Micro 14; Green Bay Micro 23. Housed at the Wisconsin Historical Society, Division of Library Archives and Museum Collections, the Archives & Area Research Center, Polk Library, University of Wisconsin Oshkosh, and the University of Wisconsin-Green Bay Archives and Area Research Center, owned by the Wisconsin Historical Society, Division of Library, Archives, and Museum Collections. The original documents are in the Sisterhood of the Holy Nativity Collection (SHNC). Digital collection.

Archives, Episcopal Diocese of Fond du Lac. Housed at the Diocesan Office, Appleton, Wisconsin. Includes Charles Chapman Grafton's episcopate, records about the Episcopal Church and the Oneida, Episcopal Visitors' reports (diocesan bishops and the SHN), correspondence related to the SHN, diocesan newsletters, newspaper, etc.

Other Archival Collections:

Archives, Church of the Advent, Boston. Materials related to Charles Chapman Grafton's rectorship, the founding of SHN, and the laywomen of the first SHN Associates in the parish.

Archives, Church of St. Mary the Virgin, New York City. Parish Newsletter, *Ave,* photographs related to the SHN.

Archives, the Episcopal Diocese of Maryland. Materials related to the SHN presence at Mount Calvary Parish.

Archives, the Episcopal Diocese of Nevada. Materials related to the work of the SHN in the Nevada Missionary District.

Archives, Order of the Holy Cross (OHC) West Park, New York. Issues of the *Holy Cross Magazine* related to or written by SHN. Materials related to St. Mary's Retreat House, Santa Barbara.
Archives, S.Clement's Church, Philadelphia. Artwork, vestments, and correspondence associated with the Sisterhood of the Holy Nativity.
Archives, Society of Saint John the Evangelist (SSJE), Cambridge, Massachusetts. Charles Chapman Grafton Correspondence.
Archives, the Society of St. Margaret (SSM) Duxbury, Massachusetts. The Archives of the Episcopal Church, Austin, Texas. Holdings related to the founding of SHN and the early years in Boston.

Unpublished Primary Sources (All in the SHNC)

"An Act to incorporate the Sisterhood of the Holy Nativity in the City of Providence, State of Rhode Island, In General Assembly, January Session, A.D. 1890." SHNC.
Bridge, Kenneth, and Dirk Reinken. "Saint Mary's Episcopal Church," 125th Anniversary booklet, 1995, 8, SHNC.
By a Sister, "The Drama of a Eucharist," n.d., SHNC.
Centennial Celebration of The Diocese of Fond du Lac, 1875–1975. Commemorative Booklet, SHNC.
The Constitutions, The Rule, The Customary, and the By-Laws of the Sisterhood of the Holy Nativity. Sisterhood of the Holy Nativity: Whitsuntide 1889, copyright 1890, revised Whitsuntide 1908, 1967, 1976, 1979, SHNC.
"Correspondence between the Sisterhood of the Holy Nativity and the Society of St. Margaret, transcribed by Sister Rebecca, SHN, 1888. Notebook, SHNC.
"Customary" personal notebook, 1977–1989, SHNC.
"The Dedication of Bethlehem-by-the-Lake and Consecration of the Chapel of the Incarnation, Green Lake, Wisconsin, December 26, 1999," Service Leaflet, SHNC.
"Dedication of the Convent of the Holy Nativity at Fond du Lac Wisconsin on the Feast of the Nativity of the Blessed Virgin Mary, September 8, 1905," Service Leaflet, SHNC.
"Dedication of St. Mary's Retreat House in Santa Barbara, California on the Feast of the Nativity of the Blessed Virgin Mary, September 8, 1954, Service Leaflet, SHNC.
Dr. L. Rosa Minoka-Hill, *The Milwaukee Journal* (October 19, 1947), n.p SHNC..
"Glory to God," vocations leaflet, Sisterhood of the Holy Nativity, n.d., SHNC.
Grafton, Charles Chapman. "A Letter Addressed to the Members of the Society of S. John the Evangelist." Boston: Sisterhood of the Holy Nativity. Printed not Published, n.d. [ca. 1883] SHNC.
———. "Meditations for Profession Retreat." Used for the first profession retreat of the Sisterhood of the Holy Nativity, December 26, 2883–January 1, 1884. Transcribed by Sister Rebecca, SHN, SHNC.
———. "The Religious Life: Meditations by Bishop C. C. Grafton" manuscript notebook, transcribed by Sister Rebecca, SHN, n.d. [ca. 1884]."
Hall, Edna Elizabeth, "Last Episcopal Chief of the Oneidas to be Ordained Episcopal Priest," n.d. [ca. 1903] SHNC.
Hierseman, Judy. "Oneidas plan more work on symbolic altar frontal," *Green Bay Press-Gazette*, n.d. [ca. 2001) SHNC.

Hicks, E. L. "What is a Retreat," (Given in Our Prayer Group) n.d. [ca. 1965], SHNC.
"The History of the Oneida Mission, 1702, 1822, 1940," *The People of the Red Stone,* The Oneida Indian Mission (Church of the Holt Apostles) January 1940, 3, 5, 7, SHNC.
"The History of the Oneida Mission, 1702, 1822, 1940," *The People of the Red Stone,* The Oneida Indian Mission (Church of the Holt Apostles) February 1940, 4, 9, 16, SHNC.
"The History of the Oneida Mission, 1702, 1822, 1940," *The People of the Red Stone,* The Oneida Indian Mission (Church of the Holt Apostles) March 1940, 4, 5, 11, SHNC.
"The History of the Oneida Mission, 1702, 1822, 1940," *The People of the Red Stone,* The Oneida Indian Mission (Church of the Holt Apostles) April 1940, 3,6, SHNC.
"The History of the Oneida Mission, 1702, 1822, 1940," *The People of the Red Stone,* The Oneida Indian Mission (Church of the Holt Apostles) June 1940, n.p. SHNC.
"The History of the Oneida Mission, 1702, 1822, 1940," *The People of the Red Stone,* The Oneida Indian Mission (Church of the Holt Apostles) July 1940, 3, SHNC.
"History of St. Mary's, [Baltimore]" 1953, from the leaflet for the Consecration of the Chapel of Saint Mary the Virgin, SHNC.
Holy Apostles Church, *Ta Luh Ya Wa Gu. Mission to the Oneidas,* 1822–1972. 150th Anniversary Booklet, SHNC.
"Holy Nativity Convent. Fond du Lac, Wisconsin," informational leaflet, n.d. [ca. 1940], SHNC.
"Holy Apostles—Oneida. One Hundred-Fifty Years," *The Diocese of Fond du Lac* 37.6 (June 1972) 1, SHNC.
"Junior Profession Retreat Notebook," n.d., SHNC.
Keith, Susan Bascom, "Some Facts about the Property behind Santa Barbara Mission Now Occupied by the Sisterhood of the Holy Nativity," n.d. SHNC.
Lee, Susan H. "Remembering Our Sisters: The Rhode Island Herstory Project," n.d. SHNC.
"Meditations for Profession Retreat," n.d. SHNC.
"Necrology," Fr. Wellares," devotional book, n.d. [ca. 1919–1942] SHNC.
"Notes from the Religious Life Conferences, Advisory Conference, 1963–1974," SHNC.
"Novice Classes," Part I & Part II," Notebooks, Sisterhood of the Holy Nativity, Providence, n.d. [ca. 1960] SHNC.
The Oneida Mission," by W. F. Christian, Missionary and the Sisters of the Holy Nativity 1934, SHNC.
"Other Beloved I Have…or Meet the Sisters of the Holy Nativity," by a Sister of St Agnes, n.d. [ca 1983] 4, SHNC.
"Our Anniversary Book, The Oneida Mission, 1922–1942," Oneida, Wisconsin, SHNC.
"Our Oneida Lace Work—Its History," *The People of the Red Stone,* The Oneida Indian Mission (Church of the Holy Apostles) October 1939, 4,10-11, SHNC.
"Our Parochial School Has A. Birthday," *The People of the Red Stone,* The Oneida Indian Mission (Church of the Holy Apostles) January 1941,2-3,15, SHNC.
Pettingell, Phoebe, "Bethlehem in Providence: The Sisters of the Holy Nativity at Saint Stephens," n.d.[ca.2019] SHNC.
"The 'Protestant Episcopal' Church and the City of Los Angeles," in "Diary of the House of the Holy Nativity," n.p. 1927, SHNC.

Reeves, Kathleen, "[Hidden in Christ:] A History of the Sisterhood of the Holy Nativity," n.d. [ca. 1982] SHNC.
"The Retreats," instructional talk on the purpose of retreats, n.d. (ca. 1916-1918) SHNC.
"Retreats and Confessions. Records of Postulants and Novices." Notebook, 1924-1973 SHNC.
Sister Boniface, SHN. "Theology Curriculum Notebook," n.d. [ca. 1973] SHNC.
[Sister Julia Elizabeth, SHN] "The Beginnings of the First Retreat House in the American Church by a Sister of the Holy Nativity," unpublished history, n.d. (ca. 1965) two versions, a one-part, and a two-part, SHNC.
———. "A Brief Historical Sketch for Our Centennial," *Alleluia* 10.2 (June 1982) 2–4 SHNC.
Sister Mary Kathleen, SHN, "The Interior Life," Four Addresses delivered at St. Ignatius Church, New York City, n.d. [ca. 1950].
Sister Katherine SHN, Sister Rebecca, SHN, Sister Agnes, SHN "A Letter Concerning the
Founding of Our Sisterhood," (Fond du Lac: Convent of the Holy Nativity, May 19, 1927), SHNC, 1. Privately bound extended narrative to the SHN novitiate by the three living founding sisters, SHNC.
"The Sisterhood of the Holy Nativity," Fond du Lac: Sisterhood of the Holy Nativity, 1928, SHNC.
"The Sisterhood of the Holy Nativity," brochure on mission houses, n.d. [ca 1950s] SHNC.
"Sisterhood of the Holy Nativity," *Conference on the Religious Life*, April 24–29, 2001, 13 SHNC.
"Sisterhood of the Holy Nativity, 1882," pamphlet, n.d. [ca. 1960s] SHNC.
"The Sisterhood of the Holy Nativity. By an Associate," pamphlet, n.d. [ca. 1883] SHNC.
"Sisterhood of the Holy Nativity, Formation: a Life Process," n.d. n.p. [ca. 1970s] SHNC.
Sisters of Saint Agnes. "Other Beloved I Have... Meet the Sisters of The Holy Nativity" n.d. SHNC.
[Sister Barbara Jean, SHN] "Sisterhood of the Holy Nativity. The West Virginia Mission," n.d., SHNC.
[Sister Bernadine, SHN] "A Tribute to Sister Emily, SHN," by a Sister of the Community, n.d. (1927) SHNC.
Sisterhood of the Holy Nativity. Curriculum folders for teaching the sacraments: Holy Baptism, Penance, Holy Eucharist, Confirmation, Holy Matrimony, Holy Orders, Holy Unction, Sacraments in General. n.d. [ca. 1909-1910], SHNC.
"Sisterhood of the Holy Nativity, 1882-1892," vocations leaflet, 1982 SHNC.
"St. Mary's Retreat House. Santa Barbara, California. Its Story: 1882, 1954, Today." Historical pamphlet, n.d., SHNC.

Published Primary Sources

Altar Guild of S. Clements Philadelphia. Philadelphia: St. Clement's Church, n.d.
An Associate of SHN, comp. *Before the Tabernacle*. Fond du Lac: Berndt Publishing Co, n.d.
"Associates Launch Fund Raising Project to Maintain St. Mary's Retreat House," *The Episcopal Review* (July–August 1963) 10 SHNC.

Barry, J. G. H. "The Congress Sermon." The Third Annual Catholic Congress: Addresses and Papers, Albany, New York, October 25-27, 1927," transcribed by Wayne Kempton for Project Canterbury, anglicanhistory.org.
Barry, J. G. H. *From A Convent Tower.* New York: Gorham, 1919.
Barry, J. G. H. "Mission Work and Prayer. A Description of the Sisterhood of the Holy Nativity, *The Holy Cross Magazine*, August 1919, 337.
"Bishop Grafton." Memorial Booklet, Diocese of Fond du Lac, ca. 1912, SHNC.
Bishop of Peterborough. "Anglican Sisterhoods: Their Inestimable Value in Rescue Work Among Fallen Women." April 15, 1886. Printed at the Directory Office, Torquay, 1886.
"Bishops of the Diocese," *The Fond du Lac Clarion*, 3. 10 (1984) n.p. SHNC.
Bloomfield, Julia K. *The Oneida.* New York: James Stewart, 1909.
Bodington, Charles. *Devotional Life in the Nineteenth Century.* London: SPCK, 1905.
Bosco, Antoinette, "Anglican Nuns," *The Long Island Catholic*," n.d. [ca. 1965], SHNC.
Brickley, Sylvia. "St. Mary's Retreat House (*Anglican*)," *Santa Barbara Weekly Bulletin* n.d., 14, SHNC.
"Brother Bernard Will Reign Again," *Santa Barbara New-Press* (June 1, 1966) n.p.
"Built By Bishop Codman," *Boston Daily Globe* (December 1, 1901) 23.
Burleson, S S. "$9.49 from the Indians of Hobart Church," *The Spirit of Missions* 56 (1891) 265.
Bussing, Elizabeth. "Visit from a Welcome Stranger," *The Episcopalians* (May 1964) 19-24.
By a Sister. "The Sisterhood of the Holy Nativity," *Holy Cross Magazine.* 71.1 (January 1960) 10-14.
By a Sister of the Holy Nativity. *The Early Days of the Christian Church.* Fond du Lac: Parish Press n.d. [ca. 1959-1960].
———. *A Journey Through History from Abraham to Christ. A Miniature Handbook.* Fond du Lac: The Parish Press, n.d. [ca. 1959-1960].
By an Associate. *The Sisterhood of the Holy Nativity.* Fond du Lac: Convent of the Holy Nativity, 1915.
Carter, Sybil. "The Indian Women and Lace-Making," *The Spirit of Missions* 70 (1905) 657-61.
Carter, T. T. *Spiritual Instructions: The Religious Life.* London: J Masters, 1879.
A Centenary Collect for Sisters and Associates," n.d. [ca. 1982], SHNC.
"Charles Chapman Grafton, Obituary," *The Spirit of Missions* 77 (1917) 710.
Constitutions and Rule of the Sisters of the Holy Nativity, Whitsunday 1889. Fond du Lac: P. B. Haber, 1905.
Craik, Dinah Mulock. "On Sisterhoods." In *A Women's Thoughts about Women*, edited by Elaine Showalter, 45-58. New York: New York University, 1995.
Dearmer, Percy. *The Parson's Handbook.* London: Grant Richards, 1899.
"Dial House, Mission Hill to Be Episcopal Retreat," *Santa Barbara News-Press*, February 5, 1953, n.p. SHNC.
"The Divine Office," unidentified publication, August 1983, SHNC.
Douglas, A. E. *The Worship of the Body: A Ceremonial for the Laity, compiled from the Best Anglican Authorities and Adapted to Use in the American Church.* 2nd ed. New York: Clayton & Co., 1869.
Dix, Morgan. *Instructions on the Religious Life Given to the Sisters of Saint Mary.* New York: Community of Saint Mary, 1909.

"Dr. Barry leaves St. Mary's Church," *New York Times,* December 15, 1928, 29.
"Episcopal Women Plan Silver Tea to Aid Sisters," *Santa Barbara News-Press,* April 19, 1964, D-7.
"Examen. Based upon the Rule of an Associate of the Sisterhood of the Holy Nativity," n.d., SHNC.
Fiske, George M. "A Sermon Preached at St. Stephen's Church, Providence, by the Rector, The Rev. George McClellan Fiske, D. D., from Bishop Grafton." Privately Printed, 1913.
"Five Win Honors of Episcopal Church Work," *Los Angeles Times,* January 31, 1961, I.24.
For the Associates of the Holy Nativity. Pamphlet by the Sisterhood of the Holy Nativity, n.d. [ca. 1900] SHNC.
"From Seder to Last Supper," *The Providence Journal,* March 16, 1962, n.p.
Gores, Stan, "Motherhouse Moved to City by Bishop Grafton in 1905," *Fond du Lac Commonwealth Reporter,* June 8, 1967, 13.
Grafton, Charles Chapman. *Catholicity and the Vincentian Rule.* Fond du Lac Tracts, No. 3. Milwaukee: Young Churchman Co., n.d. [ca. 1903].
———. *The Church of the New Testament.* Fond du Lac Tracts, No. 1. Milwaukee: The Young Churchman Co., n.d. [ca. 1900].
———. *A Journey Godward of Doulos Iêsou Christou [A Servant of Jesus Christ].* Milwaukee: Young Churchman Co., 1910. Vol. IV, *The Works of the Rt. Rev. Charles C. Grafton,* edited by B. Talbot Rogers. Revised. Edition. New York: Longmans, Green and Co., 1914.
———. [The Bishop of Fond du Lac]. *A Loving Word to Our Fellow Christians.* Pamphlet, Diocese of Fond du Lac, n.d. [ca. 1900].
———. "A Letter Addressed to the Members of the Society of S. John the Evangelist [Printed not Published]." Boston, November 1883. Anglican History Online, anglicanhistory.org/grafton/ssje_letter1883.html.
———. *Meditation.* Fond Du Lac: Sisterhood of the Holy Nativity, 1887.
———. *Meditations and Instructions.* Fond du Lac: Sisterhood of the Holy Nativity, 1923.
———. *Pusey and the Church Revival.* Milwaukee: The Young Churchman, 1908.
———. *Vocation: Or the Call of the Divine Master to a Sister's Life.* New York: E & J.B. Young, 1886.
Grou, Abbé. *Self-Consecration,* trans. An Associate of the Sisterhood of the Holy Nativity. New York: J. B. Young, 1887.
Father Founder. *The Statutes and Rule of Life of the Order of S. Anne.* Order of S. Anne, 1946.
Hanson, Virginia. "School News," *The People of the Red Stone* (March 1999) 12, SHNC.
Holcombe, Theodore I. *An Apostle of the Wilderness: James Lloyd Breck, D.D., His Missions and His Schools.* New York: Thomas Whittaker, 1903.
"Holy Nativity Convent Dedicated," *The Living Church,* September 16, 1905, 672–74.
"House of the Holy Nativity Forced to Close in September," *Tidings* (June 1980) n.p.
Joiner, Franklin, "The Early Days of St. Clements, Philadelphia," *American Church Monthly* 35 (1934), 100-108, 220-31, 298-306. Also, Project Canterbury, anglicanhistory.org.
Journal of the Sixteenth Annual Council of the Protestant Episcopal Church in the Diocese of Fond du Lac, 1890.

Journal of the Thirty-Third Annual Council of the Diocese of Fond du Lac, 1907.
Journal of the Thirty-Sixth Annual Council of the Diocese of Fond du Lac, 1910.
Journal of the Forty-Second Annual Council of the Diocese of Fond du Lac 1916.
Karst, Pat, "Traditional Religious in a Secular World," *Fond du Lac Reporter,* August 10, 1972, 14, SHNC.
Kerstetter, T. H. "The Las Vegas-Boulder City Field," *The Desert Churchman,* n.d. [ca. 1943].
Klein, Mary. "From the Archives: The Church of St. Katherine of Alexandria, *Maryland Episcopalian,* May 14, 2019, n.p.
Klein, Mary. "From the Archives: The Church of St. Mary the Virgin, Baltimore, *Maryland Episcopalian,* February 19, 2019, n.p.
Kremer, Ted. "Convent of the Sisterhood of the Holy Nativity, *Fond du Lac Reporter,* July 8, 1967, n.p. SHNC.
Kuryla, Mary. Of Peace and Prayer. Gracious Santa Barbara Retreat Houses Are Oases for Contemplation, Growth," *The Episcopal News,* March 1994, 5.
"Lace from Oneida Nation Museum," www.Oneida-nsn.gov. Accessed November 12, 2021.
[Lawson, Mary Sackville]. *Letters of John Mason Neale, DD / Selected and Edited by His Daughter.* London: Longmans, Green and Co., 1910.
Little, Caroline Frances. *The Three Vocations.* Milwaukee: Young Churchman Co., 1888.
"Lux Dei Vitae Viam Monstrat Sed Umbra Horam Atque Fidem Docet,'" *The Clarion* (January 1982) n.p. SHNC.
Macy, Sally, "Sisterhood Aids in Parish School," *San Diego,* ca. 1963, n.p SHNC.
Manual of the Associates of the Sisterhood of the Holy Nativity, 1883, revised 1996.
"The Margaret Peabody Lending Library," *Fond du Lac Clarion,* April 1983, n.p., SHNC.
The Margaret Peabody Lending Library for the Distribution of Church Literature by Mail. Fond du Lac: Convent of the Holy Nativity, Advent 1928, SHNC.
"A Mass for Christian Unity," *Santa Barbara News-Press,* n.d. [1965] SHNC.
McLane, James L. Service Leaflet, St. Matthias Church, Los Angeles, California, July 11, 1954, SHNC.
M'Comas, Joseph, "Havens of Rest: Houses Conducted by Sisters of the Anglican Communion, *New York Tribune,* 21 January 1922, 8.
Menzies, Jean Storke, "Anglican Sisters' Chapel Dedication to be September 8," *Santa Barbara News-Press,* n.d. [1956] n.p. SHNC.
Menzies, Jean Storke, "Marriage Counsel Services Vital," *Santa Barbara News-Press,* April 19, 1958, A06.
Merrill, Frank Wesley, ed. *The Church's Mission to the Oneidas.* Oneida: Oneida Indian Reservation, 1902.
Merrill, F [Frank] W [Wesley]. "Onon-gwat-go, A Priest of the Oneidas," *The Spirit of Missions* 68 (1903) 588–89.
"Minnesota Lace Schools," www.inhonorofthepeople.org.
Miss Edmunds, "Bay Shore Retreat House," *Adestes Fideles,* n.d. [1935] 4-5, SHNC.
Morgan, Alda Marsh, "Women's ordination: not all consequences were positive," *Episcopal News Service,* August 24, 2009.
Mother Eva Mary, CT. *Community Talks.* Glendale: Convent of the Transfiguration, n.d.
Mother Foundress [Mother Ruth Margaret, SHN] and Mother Ruth Mary, SHN. *Mission Houses of the Sisterhood of the Holy Nativity: An Instruction.* Sisterhood of the Holy Nativity, n.d. [ca. 1908] 4–5.

Mount Calvary Magazine, November 1917.
Mount Calvary Magazine, December 1917.
Mount Calvary Magazine, December 1921.
Mount Calvary Magazine, February 1922.
Mount Calvary Magazine, March 1922.
Mount Calvary Magazine, April 1922.
Mount Calvary Magazine, November 1924.
Mount Calvary Magazine, November 1931.
Mount Calvary Magazine, April 1945.
Mount Calvary Magazine, December 1947.
Neslund, Bob. "Native American Lace: An Experiment in Mission and Self Help." *The Historiographer* 41, 2 (Pentecost 2003) 18–21.
"New Mission in West Virginia for Sisters of the Holy Nativity," *The Living Church*, January 10, 1999, 6.
"New Retreat House Opens for Women," *Los Angeles Times*, September 12, 1954, 8.
O'Brien, Tom "Anglican Benedictine Monk Makes First Visitation to Retreat," *Santa Barbara News-Press* (April 9, 1959) n.p.
"Old Property Will Be Sisterhood Retreat," *Santa Barbara News-Press*, 1953, n.d.
"On the Patio. St. Mary's Retreat House," *The Clarion* (December 1983) 4.
"100% of the Easter Offering Returned," *The Spirit of Missions* 71 (1906) 468.
One of the Sisters, "The Sisterhood of the Holy Nativity," *Holy Cross Magazine*, September 1935, 235–38, SHNC.
"A Parish House Among the Oneida Indians," *The Spirit of Missions* 72 (1907) 303–304.
"A Parish House for the Indians," *The Spirit of Missions* 71 (1906) 862.
Pax Series. *A Visit to The Crib*. England, n.d. [ca. 1900] SHNC.
'The People of the Stone," *The Spirit of Missions* 76 (1911) 986–992.
Perry, Calbraith Bourn. *Twelve Years Among the Colored People: A Record of the Work of Mount Calvary Chapel of S. Mary the Virgin, Baltimore*. New York: James Potts, 1884.
Piggin, Julia Remine, "An Anglican Nun's Story," reprinted from *Forth*, n.d. [ca. 1950s] SHNC.
Potter, Henry C. *Sisterhoods and Deaconesses at Home and Abroad*. New York: E.P. Dutton, 1873.
The Pre-Christmas Antiphons. London: SPCK, 1910, SHNC.
The Proper Offices for the Sisterhood of the Holy Nativity. Providence: Snow and Farnham, n.d. [ca. 1900] SHNC.
Purchas, John, and Frederick George Lee, *The Directorium Anglicanum; Being a manual of directions for the right celebration of the Holy Communion, for the saying of matins and evensong, and for the performance of other rites and ceremonies of the church, according to the ancient use of the Church of England*. London: T Bosworth, 1858.
Religious Communities in the American Episcopal Church and in the Anglican Church in Canada. New York: Holy Cross Press, 1945, SHNC.
The Rule and the Constitution of the Community of the Transfiguration. Glendale, OH: The Convent, 1945.
Rules and Constitutions of the Sisters of the Holy Nativity. Fond du Lac: P. B. Haber Company, Whitsuntide 1889, revised Whitsuntide 1908, 1965, 25–31. (Original in unpublished manuscripts.)
Samter, James. "The Ordination of Women," *Clarion* 37.9 (November 1972) n.p. SHNC.

[Sister Emily Constance, SHN], *The Religious Life. A Paper Prepared and Read by A Sister of the Holy Nativity, At the Request of the Society of the Companions of the Holy Cross, During Their Eleventh Annual Conference Held at Their House, Adelynrood, South Byfield, Massachusetts, August 1906*. Fond du Lac: Sisterhood of the Holy Nativity, 1910, SHNC.

Sister Hilary CSM, "The Revival of Monasticism," *Holy Cross Magazine* (July 1945) 199–203. (August 1945) 234–38.

Sister Katherine, SHN. "With the Indian Boys and Girls at Oneida," *The Spirit of Missions* 69 (1904) 113–15.

[Sister Katherine Edith, SHN]. *Holy Warfare*. Milwaukee: Young Churchman Co., 1894.

———. *The King's Message: A Story of the Catacombs*. Milwaukee: Young Churchman Co., 1898.

———. *The New Creation*. Milwaukee: Young Churchman, 1891.

———. *Our Family Ways*. Milwaukee: Young Churchman, 1890.

Sister Lillian, SHN, "Visiting in Oneida," *The Spirit of Missions* 78 (1939) 273–74.

[Sister Patricia, SHN], *About Praying: A Series of Meditations*. Fond du Lac: Sisterhood of the Holy Nativity, n.d. [ca. 1960] SHNC.

Sister Patricia, SHN, "St. Mary's Retreat House in Santa Barbara," *Holy Cross Magazine* 77.1 (January 1966) 32–35.

[Sister Ruth Angela, SHN], "House of the Holy Nativity Celebrates Golden Jubilee," *Tidings* (September 1956) 5.

The Sisterhood of the Holy Nativity. Fond du Lac: Sisterhood of the Holy Nativity, 1928, SHNC.

The Sisterhood of the Holy Nativity. Fond du Lac: Sisterhood of the Holy Nativity, 1936, SHNC.

The Sisterhood of the Holy Nativity. Fond du Lac: Sisterhood of the Holy Nativity, 1958, SHNC.

Society of St. Margaret. *Some Principles of the Religious Life from the Writings of John Mason Neale*. London: SPCK, 1956.

"Statement on Indigenous Boarding Schools by Presiding Bishop Michael Curry and President of the House of Deputies Gay Clark Jennings," July 12, 2021, Office of Public Affairs, The Episcopal Church, www.episcopalnewsservice.org.

"Sybil Carter Indian Lace Association," https://www.minnpost.com/mnopedia/2021/07/the-sybil-carter-indian-lace-association-created-employment-for-women-on-minnesota-reservations/.

"Theology Degrees Awarded to 53…. Members Hear Dr. Mabry and Dr Stewart on Advances of the Oxford Movement," *The New York Times*, May 24, 1933, 24L.

Thorn, William B., "Twelve Places Every Young Churchman Should Visit, A Series of Sunday School Lessons, 1911–1912." *The Spirit of Missions* 76 (1911) 685.

Tiedemann, Karl, OHC, "Double Barreled," *Holy Cross Magazine* (May 1955) 153.

"To our dear Associates, Christmas Day, 1950," SHNC.

"Two Sisters," *The Minneapolis Sunday Tribune*, January 15, 1893, 20.

The Virgins That Be Her Fellows. Intercessions for Sisters, for the Associates, and Others Working in Religious Houses. Oxford: Mowbray, 1897, SHNC.

Walsh, Walter. *The Secret History of the Oxford Movement*. London: Swan Sonnenschein, 1899.

Watson, William, "Our Oldest Indian Mission" Vol. 86, 1921, 448–53.

Webb, Allan Beecher. *Sisterhood Life and Woman's Work in the Mission-Field of the Church.* Grahamstown, 1883.

Weller, Reginald Heber. "Religious Orders in the Anglican Communion," *The Hale Memorial Sermon.* Privately Printed: Western Theological Seminary, Diocese of Springfield, 1909.

Weller, Reginald Heber. "The Year's Work in Northern Wisconsin," *The Spirit of Missions* 71 (1906) 919.

"What is Saint Mary's Summer Home?" *Ave* 11.7 (October 1942) 105.

White, Greenough. *An Apostle of the Western Church: Memoir of the Right Reverend Jackson Kemper.* New York: Thomas Whittaker, 1900.

Williams, Thomas J. "The Influence of S. Augustine," *Holy Cross Magazine* 56. 8 (August 1945) 245–47.

Willmann, Henry. From a sermon by Fayette Durlin, "How Our Church Came to Wisconsin," *The Spirit of Missions* 81 (1919) 883–90.

"Wisconsin's "King of France," *The Milwaukee Journal*, April 29, 1947, n.p. SHNC.

SECONDARY SOURCES

Advisory Council for Religious Communities. *Anglican Religious Communities. A Directory of Principles and Practice.* Oxford: SLG,1976.

Advisory Council for Religious Communities. *A Directory of Religious Life.* Oxford: SLG, 1975.

Advisory Council on Religious Communities. *A Directory of Religious Life.* London: SPCK, 1943.

Advisory Council on the Relations of Bishops and Religious Communities. *A Handbook of the Religious Life.* Norwich: Canterbury, 2004.

Alexander, John D., "Grafton and the Religious Life: Address Given at the Grafton Festival,

August 27, 2011. In the Cathedral of Saint Paul, Fond du Lac, Wisconsin." Diocese of Fond du Lac, episcopalfondulac.org/grafton/documents/paper2011.pdf.

Allchin, A. M. "R.M. Benson: The Man in his Time." In *Benson of Cowley*, ed. Martin Smith, 1–26. Oxford, New York: Oxford, 1980.

———. *The Silent Rebellion. Anglican Religious Communities, 1845-1900.* London: SCM, 1958.

———. *Trinity and Incarnation in Anglican Tradition.* Oxford; SLG, 1977.

Anderson, James D. *The Education of Blacks in the South, 1860-1935.* Chapel Hill: University of North Carolina. 1988.

Anderson-Faithful, Sue and Catherine Holloway. *Women and the Anglican Congress 1861-1938, Space, Place and Agency.* London: Bloomsbury. 2023.

Anglican Religious Communities Yearbook, 2006-2007. London: Canterbury, 2005.

Anglican Religious Life, 2008-2009. London: Canterbury, 2007.

Anglican Religious Life, 2010-2011. London: Canterbury, 2009.

Anglican Religious Life, 2018-2019. London: Canterbury, 2017.

Anglican Religious Orders and Communities. A Directory. Cincinnati: Forward Movement, 1991.

Anson, Peter F. *Building Up the Waste Places. The Revival of the Monastic Life in Medieval Lines in the Post-Reformation Church.* Leighton Buzzard, UK: Faith, 1973.

———. *The Call of the Cloister: Religious Communities and Kindred Bodies in the Anglican Communion*. Revised and edited by A. W. Campbell. London: SPCK, 1964.

Argulo, Ianire. "The Unnamed Presence: Abuse of Power in the Consecrated Life," *Magistra* 28. 1 (Summer 2022) 3-28.

As Possessing All Things. All Saints Sisters of the Poor Centenary – America, 1872-1972. Catonsville, MD: All Saints Sisters of the Poor, 1972.

Ayres, Anne. *The Life and Work of William Augustus Muhlenberg*, Fifth Edition. New York: Thomas Whittaker, 1889.

[Ayres, Anne]. *Practical Thoughts on Sisterhoods*. New York: Thomas Whitaker, 1964.

Bailey, Sarah. *Clerical Vestments*. Oxford: Shire, 2011.

Barnabas, Christine. *Consecrated Celibacy: A Fresh Look at an Ancient Calling*. Durham, UK: Sacristy, 2022.

Berge, Clark, SSF. *The Vows Book. Anglican Teaching on the Vows of Obedience, Poverty and Chastity*. Mt Sinai, New York: Vest Pocket, 2014.

Bonham, Valerie. *Joyous Service. The Clewer Sisters and Their Work*. 2 Ed. Mendham, NJ: CSJB, 2012.

———. *Living Stones: The Community of St. John Baptist in America*. Mendham, NJ: CSBJ, 2016.

———. *A Place in Life. The Clewer House of Mercy, 1849-1883*. Self-published, 1992.

———. *The Second Spring. The Community of St. John Baptist in America from 1940 to 2020*. Mendham, NJ: CSJB, 2022.

Brown, Stewart J., Peter B. Nockles, James Pereiro, eds. *The Oxford Handbook of the Oxford Movement*. Oxford: Oxford, 2017.

Brunk, Quincealea. "Caring without Politics: Lessons from the First Nurses of the North and South." *Nursing History Review* 2 (1994) 119–36.

Calamari, Barbara, Sandra DiPasqua. *Holy Cards*. New York: Harry N. Abrams, 2004.

Campsi, Jack and Laurence M. Hauptman, eds. *The Oneida Indian Experience. Two Perspectives*. Syracuse: Syracuse,1988.

Catherine Louise, Sister, SSM, *The House of My Pilgrimage: History of the American House of the Society of Saints Margaret*. Glenside, PA: Littlepage, 1973.

———. *The Planting of the Lord. The History of the Society of Saint Margaret in England, Scotland, and the U.S.A., 1855-1995*. Boston: Society of St. Margaret, ca. 1995.

Case-Winters. *God Will Be All in All. Theology through the Lens of Incarnation*. Louisville: Westminster John Knox, 2021.

Catir, Norman J., Jr. *Saint Stephen's Church in Providence: The History of a New England Tractarian Parish*. Providence, RI: Saint Stephen's Church, 1964.

Chadwick, Owen. *The Victorian Church. Part One. 1829-1859*. London: SCM, 1987.

———. *The Victorian Church. Part Two. 1850-1901*. London: SCM, 1987.

Chase, Rolfe B. *The Episcopal Church in Nevada, 1860-1959*. Carson City, Nevada: [No Publisher], 2000.

Church of the Advent, Boston, MA. *The Parish of the Advent in the City of Boston: A History of One Hundred Years 1844-1944*. Boston: Church of the Advent, 1944.

Coakley, Sarah, and Matthew Bullimore, eds., *The Vowed Life. The Promise and Demand of Baptism*. London: Canterbury, 2023.

"Companions Program," "The Bishop's Column," *The Fond du Lac Clarion* (December 1984) 2.

Community of the Sisters of the Church. *A Valiant Victorian. The Life and Times of Mother Emily Ayckbowm, 1836-1900.* London: Mowbray, 1964.

Conference on the Religious Life in the Anglican Communion in the Americas. *Handbook of Guidelines for Anglican Religious Communities, Solitary Religious, and Those Taking Private Religious Vows.* Cambridge: Cowley, 1992.

Convers, Duncan. "Early Attempts to Organize Religious Communities." *American Church Monthly* 17(1925) 2108-18.

Cornelius, Carol, Judith L. Jourdan, Loretta V. Metoxen, "Oneida Healers: Hospitals, Doctors and Nurses," *Oneida Cultural Heritage Department*. Oneida.nsn.gov.

Cornelius-Grosskopf, Edna. *Traveling Home Blessed by Spirit-filled Songs: A Journey to Indian Boarding School and Home.* Phia Studios, 2019.

Cox, Stephen. *Changing and Remaining. A History of All Saints' Church San Diego.* Xlibrius, 2011.

Cramer, Jared. *Percy Dearmer Revisited. Discerning Authentically Anglican Liturgy in Multicultural, Ecumenical, Twenty-First-Century Context.* Eugene, OR: Wipf & Stock, 2020.

Crumb, Lawrence N. "Biography of James DeKoven." In *To Hear Celestial Harmonies: The Witness of James DeKoven and The DeKoven Center.* Ed. Robert Boak Slocum and Travis Talmadge DuPriest, 1–13. Cincinnati: Forward Movement, 2002.

Curtiss, Parker. *A History of the Diocese of Fond du Lac and Its Several Congregations.* Fond du Lac, Wisconsin: P.B. Haber,1925.

David, John W. *Dominion in the Sea. History of the Diocese of Long Island.* Hempstead, New York: The Georgin Foundation, 1977.

Dean, Beryl. *Ecclesiastical Embroidery.* London: B.T. Batsford, 1958.

DeMille, George E. *The Catholic Movement in the American Episcopal Church.* 2nd Edition. Philadelphia" Church Historical Society, 2016.

Dibbert, R.B. *The Story of the First Anglicans in Wisconsin, 1821.* Akron, OH: DeKoven Foundation, 2004) n.p.

Dix, Morgan. *Harriet Starr Cannon. First Mother Superior of the Sisterhood of St. Mary.* New York: Longmans Green,1896.

Donovan, Mary Sudman. *A Different Call: Women's Ministries in the Episcopal Church, 1850-1920.* Wilton, CT: Morehouse Barlow, 1986.

Doyle, Ann, RN. "Nursing by Religious Orders in the United States: Part V—Deaconesses, 1855-1928." *The American Journal of Nursing* 29.11 (November 1929), 1331–343.

Doyle, C. Andrew, ed. *Episcopate. The Role of Bishops in A Shared Future.* New York: Church Publishing, 2022.

Dunstan, Petà. "The Revival of the Religious Life in the Church of England: How Vows Became Newly Contentious in a Victorian Culture of Convention." In *The Vowed Life. The Promise and Demand of Baptism,* Sarah Coakley and Matthew Bullimore, eds., 3-14. London: Canterbury, 2023.

Ellen Stephen, "Apart and Together: Vocation in the Order of Saint Helena." In *Deeper Joy: Lay Women and Vocation in the 20th Century Episcopal Church,* edited by Fredrica Harris Thompsett and Sheryl Kujawa-Holbrook, 13–25. New York: Church Publishing, 2002.

Ellen Stephen, OSH. *Together and Apart. A Memoir of Religious Life.* New York: Morehouse, 2008.

"Episcopalians invited to observe Religious Life Sunday on January 22," www.episcopalchurch.org/publicaffairs.
Faught, C. Brad. *The Oxford Movement. A Thematic History of the Tractarians and Their Times.* University Park, PA: University of Pennsylvania, 2003.
Ferry, Kathryn. *The Old Convent. East Grinstead. John Mason Neale, George Edmund Street and the Society of Saint Margaret.* East Grinstead: Old Convent Residents Ltd, 2021.
Fox, Neva Rae. "Telling the Story of Our First Deaconesses," *The Living Church,* January 24, 2024.
Gaunt, Thomas P., SJ, and Thu T. Do, LHC. *New Faces, New Possibilities. Cultural Diversity and Structural Change in Institutes of Women Religious.* Collegeville, MN: Liturgical Press, 2022.
Gladwin, Michael. "Mission and Colonialism." In *The Oxford Handbook of Nineteenth Century Christian Thought* Joel Rasmussen, Judith Wolfe and Johannes Zachhuber, eds., 282–304. Oxford: Oxford, 2017.
Goodrich, Wallace. *The Parish of the Advent in the City of Boston. A History of One Hundred Years, 1844-1944.* Boston: Parish of the Advent, 1944.
Greene, Howard. *The Reverend Richard Fish Cadle. A Missionary of the Protestant Episcopal Church in the Territories of Michigan and Wisconsin in the Early Nineteenth Century.* Waukesha, Wisconsin: David-Greene, 1936.
Griffith, Bruce D. *Grace and the Incarnation. The Oxford Movement's Shaping of the Character of Modern Anglicanism.* Eugene, OR: Pickwick, 2020.
Griffiths, Alan. *Identity and Ritual.* Oxford: SLG, 2021.
Grilley, Sheridan. "Keble, Froude, Newman, and Pusey." In *The Oxford Handbook of the Oxford Movement,* edited by Stewart J. Brown, Peter B. Nockles, James Pereiro, 97-110. Oxford: Oxford University Press, 2017.
A Guide to Anglican Religious Communities in the United States and Canada. West Park: New York, 1965.
Hauptman, Laurence M., and Gordon McLester, III. *Chief Daniel Bread and the Oneida Nation of Indians of Wisconsin.* Norman: University of Oklahoma, 2002.
Hauptman, Laurence, and M. L. Gordon McLester, III, eds. *The Oneida Indian Journey. From New York to Wisconsin, 1784-1860.* Madison: University of Wisconsin, 1999.
Hauptman, Laurence, and L. Gordon McLester, III, eds., *The Oneida Indians in the Age of Allotment, 1860-1920.* Oklahoma City: University of Oklahoma, 2006.
Haws, Steven, CR. *The Cowley Fathers in Philadelphia.* Bloomington: Author House, 2019.
Heath, Jennifer, ed., *The Veil. Women Writers on Its History, Lore, and Politics.* Berkeley: University of California, 2008.
Hefling, Charles, ed., with Sister Ana Clara, OSA, Erica Gelser, Mary Meader, Sister Olga, OSA, Julia Slayton. *Catch The Vision. Celebrating a Century of the Order of Saint Anne.* Arlington, MA: The Order of Saint Anne – Bethany, 2010.
Heeny, Brian. *The Women's Movement in the Church of England, 1850-1930.* Oxford: Clarendon, 1988.
Herringer, Carol Engelhardt. "The Revival of the Religious Life. The Sisterhoods." In *The Oxford Handbook of the Oxford Movement,* edited by Stewart J. Brown, Peter B. Nockles, James Pereiro, 387–97. Oxford: Oxford University, 2017.
———. *Victorians and the Virgin Mary. Religion and Gender in England, 1830-1885.* Manchester; Manchester University, 2008.

Heyes, Sister Monica Mary, CT. *Women of Devotion. History of an Anglican Religious Community Begun in 1898.* Wilmington, OH: Orange Frazier, 2014.

Hill, Bridget, "'A Refuge from Men': The Idea of a Protestant Nunnery," *Past & Present* 17 (1987) 107–30.

Hill, Michael. *The Religious Order: A Study of Virtuoso Religion and its Legitimation in the Nineteenth Century Church of England.* London: Heineman, 1973,

Hogan, Anne, and Andrew Bradstock. *Women of Faith in Victorian Culture. Reassessing the Angel in the House.* London: Macmillan, 1998.

Hosmer, Rachel, and Joyce Glover, ed. *My Life Remembered. Nun, Priest, Feminist.* Cambridge: Cowley, 1991.

Huntington, James, O.S. "Beginnings of the Religious Life for Men in the Episcopal Church," *Historical Magazine of the Protestant Episcopal Church*, 2 (1933) 35–42.

———. *The Work of Prayer, A Manual for Those Who Would Pray Well.* Manchester, NH: Sophia Institute, 2005.

Huntington, William Reed. *A Short History of the Book of Common Prayer together with Certain Papers Illustrative of Liturgical Revision, 1878–1892.* New York: Thomas Whitaker, 1893.

James, Serenhedd. *The Cowley Fathers. A History of the English Congregation of the Society of St. John the Evangelist.* London: Canterbury, 2019.

John-Julian, Fr., OJN. "Blessed Charles Grafton 1830–1912." Paper presented during the Feast of Blessed Charles Chapman Grafton [tr.], August 29, 2009, at the Cathedral of St. Paul the Apostle, Fond du Lac, Wisconsin. Diocese of Fond du Lac, episcopalfonddulac.org/grafton/documents/paper2009.pdf.

Kaczynski, Bernice M. *The Oxford Handbook of Christian Monasticism.* Oxford: Oxford, 2020.

Kawamoto, Janet. "Order of the Holy Cross will Close Monastery and Retreat Center in Santa Barbara, Calif," *Episcopal New Service,* July 18, 2019, www.episcopalnewsservice.org.

Kelmsley, R., SLG. "The Religious Life: Aspects of Father Benson's Teaching." In *Benson of Cowley,* ed. Martin Smith, 98-118. Oxford: Oxford, 1980.

Kinny, John Mark. *Grafton of Fond du Lac.* Juneau: Mitre, 2019.

Kuhns, Elizabeth. *The Habit. A History of the Clothing of Catholic Nuns.* New York: Doubleday, 2003.

Kujawa-Holbrook, Sheryl A. *By Grace Came the Incarnation: A Social History of the Church of the Incarnation, Murry Hill, New York, 1852-2002.* New York: Church of the Incarnation, 2002.

Kujawa-Holbrook, Sheryl A. "Conclusions." In *Deeper Joy: Lay Women and Vocation in the 20th Century Episcopal Church,* edited by Fredrica Harris Thompsett and Sheryl Kujawa-Holbrook, 277–83. New York: Church Publishing, 2002.

Kujawa-Holbrook, Sheryl A. "Women and the Episcopacy: Insights for Ecclesiology." In *Episcopate: The Role of Bishops in A Shared Future,* edited by C. Andrew Doyle, 82–103. New York: Church Publishing, 2022.

Lauck, Jon K., Gleaves Whitney, Joseph Hogan, eds. *Finding A New Midwestern History.* Lincoln: University of Nebraska, 2018.

Legath, Jenny Wiley. *Sanctified Sisters. A History of Protestant Deaconesses.* New York: New York University, 2019.

Lewis, Herbert S., with L. Gordon McLester, III. *Oneida Lives. Long-Lost Voices of the Wisconsin Oneidas*. Foreword by Gerald L. Hill. Lincoln: University of Nebraska, 2005.

Lilly, May. *The Story of St. Clement's Church, Philadelphia*. Philadelphia" St Clement's Church, 1964.

Lindsay, John S. "Sisterhoods in the Episcopal Church." *Munsey's Magazine* 29 (1903) 329–33.

Lindsey, Donal F. *Indians at Hampton Institute, 1877–1923*. Urbana: University of Illinois, 1995.

Mammana, Richard J. "Charles Chapman Grafton: Second Bishop of Fond du Lac." *The Living Church*, August 22, 2010, 6-8.

Mary Hilary, Sister, CSM. *Ten Decades of Praise. The Story of the Community of Saint Mary During its First Century: 1865 to 1965*. Racine, WI: DeKoven Foundation, 1965.

Mary Theodore, Sister. "The Foundation of the Sisterhood of St. Mary." *Historical Magazine of the Protestant Episcopal Church*, 14 (1945) 38–52.

Mangion, Carmen M., "The 'Mixed Life': Challenging Understandings of Religious Life in Victorian England" In *Gender, Catholicism, and Spirituality*, edited by Carmen M. Mangion and Laurence Lux-Sterritt, 165–79. New York: Palgrave, 2010.

Mayer-Thurman, Crista C., *Raiment for the Lord's Service: A Thousand Years of Western Vestments*. Chicago: Art Institute of Chicago, 1975.

McCoy, Adam Dunbar. *Holy Cross. A Century of Anglican Monasticism*. Wilton, CT: Morehouse-Barlow, 1987.

McGuinness, Margaret M. *Called to Serve. A History of Nuns in America*. New York: New York University, 2013.

McIlhiney, David B. *A Gentleman in Every Slum. Church of England Missions in East London, 1837–1914*. Eugene, OR: Pickwick, 1988.

McLester, L. Gordon and Laurence M. Hauptman, eds. *A Nation within a Nation. Voices of the Oneidas in Wisconsin*. Madison; Wisconsin Historical Society Press, 2010.

McLester, L. Gordon and Laurence M. Hauptman, Judy Cornelius-Hawk, Kenneth Hoyan House, eds. *The Wisconsin Oneidas and the Episcopal Church. A Chain Linking Two Traditions*. Bloomington: Indiana University, 2019.

McNally, Michael D. "'Boss Women': Elders and Authority in Ojibwe Christianity." In *Deeper Joy: Lay Women and Vocation in the 20th Century Episcopal Church*, edited by Fredrica Harris Thompsett and Sheryl Kujawa-Holbrook, 41–54. New York: Church Publishing, 2005.

Melnyk, Julie. *Women's Theology in Nineteenth Century Britain. Transfiguring the Faith of Their Fathers*. Abingdon: Garland, 2019.

Merkle, Judith A. *Sensing the Spirit. Toward the Future of the Religious Life*. London: T & T Clark, 2023.

Morris, Betty Hughes. *A History of the Church of the Advent*. Boston: The Church of the Advent, 1995.

Muller, James Arthur. "Father Huntington and the Beginnings of Religious Orders for Men in the Episcopal Church." *Historical Magazine of the Protestant Episcopal Church*, 10 (1941) 312–29.

Mumm, Susan. *All Saints Sisters of the Poor. An Anglican Sisterhood in the 19th Century*. Woodbridge, Suffolk, UK: Boydell, 2001.

Mumm, Susan, *Stolen Daughters, Virgin Mothers: Anglican Sisterhoods in Victorian Britain*. London: Continuum, 1999.

Nadeau, Elaine. "Uncovering the Date of Twentieth-Century Benedictine Sisters," *Archival Outlook* (March/April 2022) 10–11, 20.

Nash, John F. *The Sacramental Church. The Story of Anglo-Catholicism*. Eugene, OR: Wipf & Stock, 2011.

Noyes, Daphne. "Adeline Blanchard Tyler," May 2022 www.episcopaldeacons.org, https://www.youtube.com/watch?v=L_JyvKDMQuU.

Oakes, Kaya. *The Defiant Middle. How Women Claim Life's In-Betweens to Remake the World*. Minneapolis: Broadleaf, 2021.

Order of St. Helena. *Early Days of the Order of St. Helena*. Newburgh, New York: Convent of St. Helena, ca. 1954.

Parker, Dorothy Mills. "Full Choral Services. Charles Winifred Douglas," *The Living Church*, 219.3 (July 18, 1999) 13.

Paulsen, David and Egan Millard, "Tribes repatriate remains of children who died at boarding school," *Episcopal Journal*, February 2022, 1, 6.

Peabody, Francis G. *Education for Life: The Story of the Hampton Institute*. New York: Doubleday, 1918.

Pendleton, Eldridge H, SSJE. *Press On, The Kingdom. The Life of Charles Chapman Grafton*. Cambridge: Society of Saint John the Evangelist, 2014.

Peters, Greg. *Reforming the Monastery. Protestant Theologies of the Religious Life*. Eugene, OR: Cascade, 2014.

Petersen, Kirk. "Council Focuses on Indigenous Boarding Schools," *The Living Church*, November 14, 2021, 5.

Placido, Nicholas. "A History of Charity and the Church," www.nacsw.org, n.d.

Platt, Warren C. "The Rise of Advanced Ritualism in New York City: The Rev. Thomas McKee Brown and the Founding of the Church of St. Mary the Virgin," *Anglican and Episcopal History* 85.3 (September 2016), 331–69.

Potter, Henry C. *Sisterhoods and Deaconesses at Home and Abroad*. New York. E.P. Dutton, 1873.

Power, Eileen. *Medieval English Nunneries, c. 1275–1535*. Cambridge: Biblio and Tanner, 1922.

Prelinger, Catherine M., ed. *Episcopal Women. Gender, Spirituality and Commitment in an American Mainline Denomination*. New York: Oxford, 1996.

———. "The Female Diaconate in the Anglican Church. What Kind of Ministry for Women? In *Religion in the Lives of English Women, 1760–1930*, edited by Gail Malmgren, 161–92. Bloomington: Indiana University, 1986.

Pettingell, Phoebe. "Bethlehem in Providence." In 150 Years on George Street. Essays on S. Stephen's, Providence, edited by John D. Alexander, 140–61. Foreword by Richard J. Mammana. New Haven: Project Canterbury, 2019.

———. "Bishop Grafton: An American Vision for Anglo-Catholicism." *The S. Stephen Parish Magazine of Saint Stephen's Church in Providence*. 10 (Pentecost 2011) 6–8.

———. "Saint Stephen's Witness: An Historical Note on the Influence of Our Parish in a Midwestern Diocese." *The S. Stephen*, Parish Magazine of Saint Stephen's Church in Providence. 11 (Michaelmas 2011) 4–5.

Pitt, Valerie, "The Oxford Movement: A case of cultural distortion." In *Essays Catholic and Radical. A Jubilee Group Symposium for the 150th Anniversary of the Beginning* of the Oxford Movement, 1833-1933, edited by Kenneth Leech and Rowan Williams, 230-40. Bowerdean, 1983.

Ramsey, Arthur Michael. "Charles C. Grafton, Bishop and Theologian, "Lecture at Nashotah House, September 26, 1967, printed in the *Nashotah Quarterly Review,* n.d. [1967] 5, 7.

Ranft, Patricia. *A Woman's Way. The Forgotten History of Women Spiritual Directors.* New York: Palgrave, 2000.

Rasmussen, Joel D.S., Judith Wolfe, Johannes Zachhuber. *The Oxford Handbook of Nineteenth Century Christian Thought.* Oxford: Oxford, 2017.

Reeves, Kathleen. "Sisters of the Holy Nativity, 1882-1982," *The Living Church* (October 31, 1982) 9-10.

Rich, Lawson Carter. "The Community of St. Mary." *The Churchman* 95 (1907) 171-179.

Rich, Lawson Carter. "The Society of St. Margaret." *The Churchman* 95 (1907) 319-327.

Ruth, The Reverend Mother, CHS. *In Wisdom Thou Hast Made Them.* New York: Adams, Bannister, Cox, 1986.

The S. Stephen, Parish Magazine of Saint Stephen's Church in Providence, 8 (August 1907); 7 (June 1910).

Scotti, Kiki. "Their Sacrifice Gives Strength: *Providence Evening Bulletin,* May 4, 1967, 14.

Schoeser, Mary. *The Watts Book of Embroidery. English Church Embroidery, 1833-1953.* London: Watts, 1998.

Sister Mariana, SHN, "Sisterhood of the Holy Nativity, *The Living Church,* n.d. [ca.1975-1976].

The Sisterhood of St. John the Divine. *A Journey Just Begun. The Story of an Anglican Sisterhood.* Toronto: Dundurn, 2015.

"Sisters Helping Sisters, *The Living Church,* December 16, 2007, 6.

Sisters of the Visitation Harrow. *The Life of Jeanne Charlotte de Brechard, 1580-1637.* London: Longmans Green & Co.

Skardon, Alvin W. *Church Leader in the Cities. William Augustus Muhlenberg.* Philadelphia: University of Pennsylvania Press, 1971.

Slocum, Robert Boak, and Travis Talmadge Du Priest. *To Hear Celestial Harmonies. Essays on the Witness of James Dekoven and The Dekoven Center.* Cincinnati: Forward Movement, 2002.

Smith, Dom Aloysius, trans. *The Rule of Saint Augustine.* Las Vegas: Chaucer House, 2021.

Smith, Robert Cheney. "Monasticism in Stained Glass: A Historical Survey." *Historical Society of the Episcopal Church* 19 (1950) 264-79.

Sockman, Ralph W. *The Revival of the Conventual Life in the Church of England in the Nineteenth Century.* New York: W.D. Gray, 1927.

Sparrow, Michael. *Nuns Across the Orange. A History of the Pioneering Anglican Community of*

St. Michael and All Angels, Bloemfontein. Bloemfontein, SA: Sun Media, 2021.

Strong, Rowan. "Origins of Anglo-Catholic Missions: Fr. Richard Benson and the Initial Missions of the Society of St. John the Evangelist, 1869-1882," *Journal of Ecclesiastical History* 66.1 (January 2015) 90-115.

Strong, Rowan, Carol Engelhardt Herringer, eds. *Edward Bouverie Pusey and the Oxford Movement.* New York: Wimbledon Press, 2012.

Stuart, Lisa. "Nuns on the Point," *The Green Light*. Summer and Fall 2020, 9.
Suenens, Kristien. *Humble Women, Powerful Nuns. A Female Struggle for Autonomy in a Men's Church*. Lueven, Belgium: Leuven, 2020.
Sumner, David. "Episcopal History From 1940-1980: A Brief Chronology," *Historical Magazine of the Episcopal Church* 54.1 (March 1985) 83–87.
Swamy, Muthuraj, Stephen Spencer. *Listening Together. Global Anglican Perspectives on Renewal of Prayer and the Religious Life*. London: Anglican Communion Office, 2020.
Thompsett, Fredrica Harris. "Introduction." In *Deeper Joy: Lay Women and Vocation in the 20th Century Episcopal Church*, edited by Fredrica Harris Thompsett and Sheryl Kujawa-Holbrook, 3–9. New York: Church Publishing, 2002.
Thompsett, Fredrica Harris and Sheryl Kujawa-Holbrook, eds., *Deeper Joy: Lay Women and Vocation in the 20th Century Episcopal Church*. New York: Church Publishing, 2005.
Thornton, Martin. *English Spirituality: An Outline of Ascetical Theology According to the English School*. London: SPCK, 1963.
Tribe, Shawn. "Revisiting the Liturgical Embroidery of the Sisters of Bethany," *Liturgical Arts Journal*, March 2, 2022.
Trounson, Rebecca, "Nuns facing eviction get help," *The Los Angeles Times*, November 15, 2007, SHNC.
Vasaethe, Veronica, "Sisters of the Church in the Solomon Islands," in *Listening Together, Global Anglican Perspectives on Renewal of Prayer and the Religious Life*, edited by Muthurai Swamy and Stephen Spencer, 140–51. London: Anglican Communion Office, 2020.
Wagner, Harold Ezra. *The Episcopal Church in Wisconsin, 1841-1947. A History of the Diocese of Milwaukee*. The Diocese of Milwaukee, 1947.
Welby, Justin, "Afterword: The Vowed Life." In *The Vowed Life. The Promise and Demand of Baptism*, edited by Sarah Coakley and Matthew Bullimore, 75–76. London: Canterbury, 2023.
Williams, Thomas J. "The Beginnings of Anglican Sisterhoods." *Historical Magazine of the Protestant Episcopal Church* 16 (1947) 350-73.
Williams, Thomas J. *Priscilla Lydia Sellon. The Restorer after Three Centuries of the Religious Life in the English Church*. London: SPCK, 1965.
Wittberg, Patricia, SC, Mary L. Gautier, Gemma Simmonds, CJ, Nathalie Becquart, XMCJ, *God's Call is Everywhere. A Global Analysis of Contemporary Religious Vocations for Women*. Collegeville: Liturgical Press, 2023.
Woods, Eric Taylor. *A Cultural Sociology of Anglican Mission and the Indian Residential Schools in Canada*. New York: Palgrave, 2016.
Yates, Nigel. *The Oxford Movement and Anglican Ritualism*. London: Historical Association, 1983.
Zimmerman, Jervis S. *An Embattled Priest. The Life of Father Oliver Sherman Prescott: 1824-1903*. Bloomington: Author House, 2012.

Unpublished Sources

Frith, Eleanor Joy. "Pseudonuns: Anglican Sisterhoods and the Politics of Victorian Identity."

PhD diss., Queen's University, Kingston, Ontario, Canada, 2004.

Huyck, Heather Ann. "To Celebrate A Whole Priesthood." PhD diss., University of Minnesota, Minneapolis, 1981.

Huntley, Gillian. "Stitching the Sacred: Marking Meaning and Female Presence in Twentieth Century British Ecclesiastical Embroidery." MA Thesis, University of Glasgow, 2020.

Leech, Kenneth, "The Radical Anglo-Catholic Vision," A lecture given at the Centre for Theology & Public Issues, University of Edinburgh, March 13, 1989.

Tyers, J.H. "Borrowed Silence: A History of the Practice of Retreat in the Church of England," PhD diss., University of Liverpool, United Kingdom, 2012.

Film and Visual Media

"Angelus: Sisters of the Holy Nativity," a film produced by Scott Schumate and Mike Flanagan, available in the Frances Donaldson Library, Nashotah House Seminary, ca. 1991.

"Owning Our Past: Christianity and Native Americans. Wisconsin Oneida and the Episcopal Church," Rodger Patience and Jennifer Webster, Grace Episcopal Church, Madison, Wisconsin, March 21, 2022.

"Saint Clement's Church Ordo Kalendar," St. Clement's Church, Philadelphia, 2021. Pencil drawings of the church by Sister Ruth Vera, SHN.

About the Author

SHERYL A. KUJAWA-HOLBROOK, EdD, PhD, FRHistS, is a priest of the Episcopal Diocese of Los Angeles, historian, editor, writer, religious educator, retreat leader, and pastoral/practical theologian. She is the current editor-in-chief of the academic journal *Anglican and Episcopal History*. Kujawa-Holbrook publishes widely, including books, articles, chapters, and reviews. Kujawa-Holbrook currently serves as professor of practical theology, religious education, and Christian histories at Claremont School of Theology, and professor of Anglican Studies emerita at Bloy House, the Episcopal Theological School at Los Angeles. An elected fellow of the Royal Historical Society, Kujawa-Holbrook is a board member for *Magistra* and the *Journal of Religious History*. A priest and theological educator for nearly forty years, Kujawa-Holbrook is the former vice president for academic affairs and dean of the faculty at Claremont School of Theology and the former academic dean and Suzanne Radley Hiatt professor of feminist pastoral theology and church history at the Episcopal Divinity School. She is on the board of Stillpoint, California. Active in interreligious engagement, Kujawa-Holbrook is a fellow of the Christian Leadership Institute (CLI) sponsored by the American Jewish Committee and the Shalom Hartman Institute in Jerusalem, Israel. She is also an associate of the Society of St. John the Evangelist (SSJE) in Cambridge, Massachusetts. An award-winning author, Kujawa Holbrook has published widely in Episcopal history, including books on Episcopal women's history, a historical biography of Presiding Bishop Edmond Lee Browning, and a social history of the Church of the Incarnation, Murray Hill, New York. In 2024, Kujawa-Holbrook was appointed the Historiographer of the Episcopal Church.